Pro JavaFX™ Platform

Script, Desktop and Mobile RIA with Java™ Technology / First Edition

James L. Weaver, Weiqi Gao, Ph.D., Stephen Chin, and Dean Iverson

Apress®

Distributed to the book trade worldwide by Springer-Verlag New York, Inc., 233 Spring Street, 6th Floor, New York, NY 10013. Phone 1-800-SPRINGER, fax 201-348-4505, e-mail orders-ny@springer-sbm.com, or visit http://www.springeronline.com.

For information on translations, please contact Apress directly at 2855 Telegraph Avenue, Suite 600, Berkeley, CA 94705. Phone 510-549-5930, fax 510-549-5939, e-mail info@apress.com, or visit http://www.apress.com.

Apress and friends of ED books may be purchased in bulk for academic, corporate, or promotional use. eBook versions and licenses are also available for most titles. For more information, reference our Special Bulk Sales–eBook Licensing web page at http://www.apress.com/info/bulksales.

The information in this book is distributed on an "as is" basis, without warranty. Although every precaution has been taken in the preparation of this work, neither the author(s) nor Apress shall have any liability to any person or entity with respect to any loss or damage caused or alleged to be caused directly or indirectly by the information contained in this work.

The source code for this book is available to readers at http://www.apress.com. You may need to answer questions pertaining to this book in order to successfully download the code.

Contents at a Glance

Contents

▪CHAPTER 6   Using the Media Classes 289

▪CHAPTER 7   Dynamically Laying Out Nodes in the User Interface 313

Foreword

JavaFX was born amid a particularly interesting confluence of upheavals in the technology industry and the way commerce was conducted in the developed world.

At the turn of the twenty-first century, companies were looking for ways to do business directly with their customers. Whether they had goods to sell, information to impart, or entertainment to offer, the immediacy and low overhead of the Internet compared with traditional in-person interactions were changing how business was done. Even the most traditional companies were seeking more compelling ways to conduct business with their customers through the devices they owned. And new businesses for search and retailing that relied on the Internet as the sole mode of interaction with their customers were gathering momentum.

During the same period, the number and variety of devices that connected to the Internet—cell phones, TV set-top boxes, or desktop computers—were rapidly increasing. Those devices were becoming more capable of processing information from the Internet in faster and increasingly sophisticated ways. Organizations of all kinds were given the potential to be mere inches from people's eyes. As early as the 1930s, the television set had been described by those in the nascent advertising industry as a "selling machine." By the 1990s selling machines were to be found not only in people's living rooms (where they had evolved interactive features), but in their offices, in their children's bedrooms, and in their pocket. The virtual doors of the retail world were being flung open. It was becoming less a matter of how to get people into your store, and more a matter of how to get a toehold on all their devices. The more intuitive, entertaining, and enriching the interaction those customers had through their various devices, the more likely that the business would be brisk.

The Internet had brought sweeping changes to how many user interfaces were designed. The tide had turned from the traditional rich-client GUIs. Web sites brought a new energy and simplicity to the limited palette of components supported in markup languages and its constrained interaction model. Thanks to the central update model of web applications, these applications employed a new and evolutionary development style. A web site could change its branding or functionality week to week, even day to day. This brought a radically less formal approach to presenting and gathering information to end users through the large new commerce web sites. These websites created venues for purchasing books, bidding on secondhand memorabilia, and searching for lost schoolmates, just to name a few. But in many ways, while the development process for the Web was lightweight and experimental, user interfaces still were constrained to a visual idiom that could be as boring as filling out the paper forms of yesteryear.

Ever searching for more compelling interactions via the Internet, a new wave of artistically savvy designers were starting to develop user interfaces that were fluid, playful, expressive, and entertaining. These designers often did not have the formal computer science background of a Lisp, C++, or even Java programmer, but they promised to enrich the experiences of people like you and me. We were starting to use their applications to interact online with one another and with the companies to whom we had given our most personal information. Activities like downloading music, playing games, sharing photos of embarrassing childhood experiences with friends, and even sharing viral videos of solitary music lipsyncers were replacing much of the time people had spent in front of the humble television: the original selling machine. And so a new generation of technologies such as Ajax and Adobe's Flex began to emerge to support the quest to create more of these rich applications. The Rich Internet Application (RIA) was born.

Java technology had established itself since its release in 1995 as one of the key languages and application development platforms in the computing industry. It had editions that spanned smart cards (JavaCard), cell phones and TV set-top boxes (Java Mobile Edition), PCs (Java Standard Edition), and the multinode distributed application servers that run some of the world's biggest and most complex web sites (Java Enterprise Edition). Yet despite Java technology's early fame as the intelligence that enriched the dull, static web pages of 1995, and despite having the most robust and scalable runtime architecture in the industry, Java was not being chosen to create RIAs by the newest generation of designers and developers.

My own involvement in the birth of JavaFX began when I led a series of internal meetings code-named Client.Next in early 2007 across the Java SE and Java ME engineering groups in order to define our technical direction for the next few years. We knew that we needed a much simpler way to attract the RIA developer-designer to the Java platform. We were aware that we had to make it easier for designers and developers to reach a variety of devices. In addition, we needed ways to create a new generation of media-rich, expressive user interfaces. It was obvious that we couldn't continue making incremental steps in each of the separate editions of Java. We knew where we wanted to go, but we didn't yet know how we would get there.

Meanwhile an engineer who had joined Sun as part of its storage product group was quietly working on a side project called F3. F3 was a new language for the Java runtime that was born out of this engineer's own frustration in trying to create rich web-based interfaces with Java and Swing. The engineer, Chris Oliver, was sure that F3 was a kite that could fly high but could not find the wind to lift it. So he built demos and blogged. His demos were impressive to see, but it was the simplicity of the code behind them was the clincher. The language was declarative and compact, meaning that looking at the code told you what the application would do when you ran it, not waste time telling you how it would do it.

It was clear when F3 met Client.Next that the seed of JavaFX had already germinated. At the annual JavaOne developer conference in 2007, we announced we were working on a new cross-device RIA environment built on Java called JavaFX. Inside Sun, we had begun the engineering work turning the F3 prototype language into what is now JavaFX Script, designing and building the first JavaFX APIs, and reshaping the underlying Java runtimes in anticipation of the first release.

And so JavaFX was released, after much hard work, in late 2008.

The central concepts of JavaFX are the JavaFX Script language and its scene graph. JavaFX Script is a declarative language with a Java-like syntax that is appealing to developers and designers with no more than a background in a scripting language. It uses object-oriented concepts like encapsulation, inheritance, and modules to organize code cleanly. It contains some highly appealing features, consciously designed to simplify GUI programming. Triggers simplify the tasks of associating the execution of a piece of code (for example, sending a multimedia message) with an event (the user clicks on a glowing face). The `bind` keyword makes it a trivial task to keep two pieces of data (for example, a slider and the zoom level in a map) synchronized by simply saying that it be so. The scene graph is a post-GUI toolkit approach to visual design, whereby visual objects are modeled simply as a hierarchy of nodes, expressed in a model to which it is easy to attach behaviors such as animation and transition effects, or to bind to an underlying data model. JavaFX contains fully integrated media capabilities, allowing media to break free of the display rectangle, and be fully integrated, layered, diffracted, mixed, and mashed into the application. And to connect the richness and power of a beautiful JavaFX application to interesting data on the Internet, the web services APIs supported in JavaFX provide a simple-to-use capability familiar to web developers. The beauty and appeal of JavaFX are in how simply it can express the moving characteristics of beautiful, immersive, fluid, and enticing applications—and do so consistently all the way from small cell phones to high-end PC desktops.

Pro JavaFX™ Platform: Script, Desktop and Mobile RIA with Java™ Technology is both a comprehensive grounding in the JavaFX Script language and APIs as well as a practical hands-on developer's guide to this exciting technology. You can read it chapter by chapter, starting with a must-read first chapter, "Getting a Jump Start in JavaFX," followed by a detailed language primer, "Taking a Close Look at the JavaFX Script Language." Subsequent chapters cover all aspects of the most up-to-date JavaFX APIs, including the latest additions to layout and UI components in JavaFX 1.2. You may choose to read these chapters either in sequence or focus on topic areas: from laying out interfaces, to mobile application development to media capabilities, to more advanced topics such as creating custom JavaFX components. By stepping through well-chosen example applications, hand in hand with clear and thorough explanations and end-of-chapter summaries, you will quickly acquire proficiency in exploiting all aspects of JavaFX technology.

This book brings together all the aspects of developing engaging, interactive, and beautiful RIAs that we envisioned when the seeds of JavaFX were first planted.

Danny Coward
Chief Architect, Client Software, Sun Microsystems

About the Authors

JAMES L. (JIM) WEAVER is the Senior VP of Technology at Veriana Networks, Inc. He writes books, speaks for groups and conferences, and provides training and consulting services on the subjects of Java and JavaFX. He also posts regularly to his blog at `http://JavaFXpert.com`, whose stated purpose is to help the reader learn JavaFX Script and other JavaFX technologies.

WEIQI GAO is a principal software engineer with Object Computing, Inc., in St. Louis, MO. He has more than 15 years of software development experience and has been using Java technology since 1998. He is interested in programming languages, object-oriented systems, distributed computing, and graphical user interfaces. He is a member of the steering committee of the St. Louis Java Users Group. Weiqi holds a Ph.D. in mathematics.

Open source developer and agile manager **STEPHEN CHIN** is founder of numerous open source projects, including WidgetFX and JFXtras, and is a senior manager at Inovis in Emeryville, CA. He has been working with Java desktop and enterprise technologies for over a decade, and has a passion for improving development technologies and process. Stephen's interest in Java technologies has led him to start a Java and JavaFX–focused blog that is targeted at early technology adopters (`http://steveonjava.com/`).

DEAN IVERSON has been developing software professionally for more than 15 years. He is currently employed by the Virginia Tech Transportation Institute, where he is a senior researcher and rich client application developer. He also has a small software consultancy, Pleasing Software Solutions, which he cofounded with his wife.

Acknowledgments

This book is dedicated to my wife Julie, daughters Lori and Kelli, son Marty, and grandchildren Kaleb and Jillian. Thanks to Merrill and Barbara Bishir, Marilyn Prater, and Walter Weaver for being such wonderful examples. Thanks also to Laura Lee and Steve Brown, Jill Weaver, Shari and Doug Beam, Wade Weaver, Jerry and Cheryl Bishir, my brother Daniel Wright, and pastor Steve Colter. Thanks to Casper Hamlet for creating the graphical assets for the "Browning's Books" example in Chapter 9, and to Chris Wright for helping me develop some code examples and graphics. A very special thanks to Weiqi Gao, Stephen Chin, and Dean Iverson, with whom I had the privilege of writing this book. Thanks also to the talented editors and project managers at Apress, and to the amazing JavaFX team at Sun. *Delight yourself in the LORD and he will give you the desires of your heart* (Psalm 37:4).

Jim Weaver

I would like to thank Jim Weaver for his leadership in pulling together the author team and my coauthors, Stephen Chin and Dean Iverson, for their enthusiasm and many months of hard work. I would like to thank my wife Youhong Gong for her support, understanding, and encouragement during the writing process. I would also like to thank my employer Object Computing, Inc., and my colleagues at OCI for creating a stimulating environment in which to learn and explore new technologies.

Weiqi Gao, Ph.D.

My thanks go out to my wife Justine and daughter Cassandra, who made great sacrifices to allow me to dedicate myself to this book. Also to Jim Weaver for inviting me to participate, and to my coauthors, Dean Iverson and Weiqi Gao, who were a pleasure to work with and there to help out at all junctures. I also appreciate the support given by my company, Inovis, and my coworkers, Adrian Yacub, Steve Bixby, and Keith Combs, who gave excellent feedback. One reviewer who deserves particular mention is Jonathan Giles, who made an extraordinary effort to review and provide detailed feedback on the entire book. Finally, my thanks to the JavaFX team at Sun, especially Amy Fowler and Richard Bair, who spent innumerable hours reviewing chapters, guiding us through the latest and greatest features, and responding to our voluminous feedback.

Stephen Chin

I would like to thank my wife Sondra and my sons Alex and Matt for their support and limitless patience throughout this long process. I would also like to thank our author team leader, Jim Weaver, and my coauthors, Stephen Chin and Weiqi Gao, for inviting me to the party and being remarkably tolerant of this first-time author. Their knowledge, professionalism, and enthusiasm for learning and teaching have been inspiring. Finally, a big thanks to all of the folks at Apress for their dedication to the book and their patient answers to question after question. The same goes for the fine folks at Sun Microsystems for their support and patient answers. You guys all rock!

Dean Iverson

Introduction

What an exciting time to be a software developer or designer! Opportunity is all around us. Never before have there been so many platforms capable of delivering compelling user experiences that utilize rich media and rich graphical interfaces. Whether you develop for the computer desktop, the Web, today's more powerful mobile devices, or even consumer electronics devices such as TVs, you are in the middle of a revolution in the way we think about designing the interactions between people and their devices. And these people! Now that they have tasted the forbidden fruit of rich interfaces, they have come to expect (no, demand!) compelling experiences from all of the software they use. An interface that is engaging, attractive, and (dare we say it?) even playful can be the difference between success and obscurity for an application or a mobile device. Your customers have seen the likes of the iPhone. If you can't give them an equally rich experience, your application, mobile device, or fancy new piece of electronic equipment is in very real danger of debuting to the resounding silence of indifference.

Unfortunately, opportunity and challenge often go together like 1s and 0s. To match the explosion of delivery platforms and devices we have an explosion of programming platforms and media standards. You may make the enormous investment to deliver a rich client application in a web browser, but what happens when you want to deliver it on a mobile device? It's not just the challenge of transferring your rich user experience to a smaller screen; you also need to learn a whole new platform, new tools, and new languages. Imagine, though: what if there were one technology platform that could be used to deliver rich client experiences to the desktop, the web browser, mobile devices, and consumer electronics? This is the vision driving the development of the JavaFX platform! At the heart of this audacious goal is a powerful new programming language that features a time-saving declarative syntax, built-in binding capabilities, and a sprinkling of functional programming—all running on top of the world's most mature and highest-performing virtual machine.

We are honored and excited that you have chosen us (Weiqi, Stephen, Dean, and Jim) as your tour guides in the amazingly cool new world of JavaFX technology. We collaborated daily in writing the pages of this book to ensure that it flows in a manner that will bring you up to speed quickly and completely in JavaFX. Each of us has different areas of expertise and passion that is reflected in the book:

- Jim's main interest in JavaFX is that it plays a key role in the long-awaited promise of ubiquitous rich-client Java, which will help restore sanity to Internet application development.

- Weiqi is a recognized expert in the JavaFX Script language. He is particularly interested in its object literal and sequence notations that create a declarative syntax for describing GUIs; its support for object-oriented and functional programming through classes, mixins, functions and closures; and its intuitive data binding syntax.

- Stephen is passionate about simplifying code with dynamic layouts, opening up mobile devices to new audiences with seamless mobile integration, and the JavaFX open source ecosystem.

- Dean is excited about the enhanced developer productivity that comes from the declarative syntax, powerful binding, functional programming, and a killer scene graph. To quote Dean: "What? I'm lazy! I just want to build awesome Internet-enabled applications as quickly as possible."

Along the way we will demonstrate how to effortlessly build rich graphics, animation, and media into your applications. We'll also show you how to distribute these applications to the desktop, web browser, and mobile devices. JavaFX even makes it easy for developers to collaborate with designers using plug-ins for the most popular design tools (but you're still on your own when trying to teach artists, bless their many-hued hearts, the value of revision control systems—not even JavaFX is all-powerful).

Let's get started!

Who This Book Is For

This book is targeted to software application developers and graphic artists who have some programming background.

How This Book Is Structured

This book is written in a tutorial-style, with lots of hands-on examples and instructions that walk you through using and understanding them.

Chapter 1, "Getting a Jump Start in JavaFX," helps you learn how to develop applications in the JavaFX language, brings you up-to-date on the brief history of JavaFX, and shows you how to get the JavaFX software development kit. It then walks you through the process of compiling and running JavaFX applications, and teaches you a lot about the JavaFX language and API while walking through example application code.

Chapter 2, "Taking a Closer Look at the JavaFX Script Language," covers the fundamentals of the JavaFX Script language, including concepts such as variables, primitive types, literal values, and basic operations. JavaFX sequences are introduced in this chapter, along with how to access their members and perform sequence comprehension.

Chapter 3, "Creating a User Interface in JavaFX," associates the metaphor of creating a theater play with JavaFX development, and discusses creating a stage, a scene, nodes, a model, and event handlers, and animating some of the nodes. It then delves into each of these concepts using JavaFX examples. We finish up with a Pong-like game that demonstrates how to detect when nodes in the scene have collided.

Chapter 4, "Using Functions, Classes, and Other Advanced Features," discusses how to define functions and classes of your own. It then covers function signatures and function types, and how to write anonymous functions. From there, this chapter explains how to define classes and class hierarchies, and covers details about class types. We also discuss what happens when an object is instantiated and how you can exert control over the process.

Chapter 5, "Creating Custom UI Components and Charts in JavaFX," explains how to define custom UI components of two fundamentally different types—custom nodes and UI controls. After showing you how to create custom nodes in the context of creating a couple of color selection components, we cover how to create UI controls in the context of a stoplight control that has multiple skins. The chapter finishes by showing you how to use the charting controls to simply and easily create charts in JavaFX.

Chapter 6, "Using the Media Classes," explores the capabilities of the JavaFX media classes that make it easy for developers to incorporate playback support for most of the popular formats out there. This chapter demonstrates how simple it is to include basic media playback support in your JavaFX applications and then shows you how to build more sophisticated playback applications.

Chapter 7, "Dynamically Laying Out Nodes in the User Interface," shows how you can leverage the dynamic layouts mechanisms of JavaFX to build complicated user interfaces with zero static positioning. These mechanisms include the bind statement, powerful custom layouts built on top of the Panel and Container classes, and the built-in layouts including HBox, VBox, Flow, Tile, and Stack.

Chapter 8, "Extending JavaFX with Third-Party Libraries," introduces several of the JavaFX third-party extensions that simplify the development of applications. All of the third-party extensions introduced in this chapter are available as free or open source libraries. This ensures that anyone can make use of these libraries, and also guarantees that you will not be locked into a specific vendor.

Chapter 9, "Building a Professional JavaFX Application," shows you some of the professional techniques we use to write real-world JavaFX applications. You will need them when working with a graphic designer, and you will find them useful when you are confronted with the memory usage and performance trade-offs that developers need to consider for real applications. This chapter also provides tips and techniques for enhancing the user's experience.

Chapter 10, "Developing JavaFX Mobile Applications," teaches you the basics of JavaFX Mobile development, which will enable you to write portable applications that work on both desktop and mobile devices. You'll gain an understanding of the Common Profile, learn how to take advantage of the Java ME capabilities beneath JavaFX Mobile, and adopt JavaFX Mobile best practices that will enable you to write high-performance applications.

CHAPTER 1

■ ■ ■

Getting a Jump Start in JavaFX

Don't ask what the world needs. Ask what makes you come alive, and go do it. Because what the world needs is people who have come alive.

—Howard Thurman

At the annual JavaOne conference in May 2007, Sun Microsystems announced a new product family named *JavaFX*. Its stated purpose includes enabling the development and deployment of content-rich applications on consumer devices such as cell phones, televisions, in-dash car systems, and browsers. According to Sun, the vision of the JavaFX product family is to deliver "the ability to create interactive content, applications and services from the desktop to mobile devices to the living room." More recently, Sun has articulated this vision as "Rich Internet Experiences for all screens of your life."

Stripping away the marketing-speak, our interest in JavaFX as software developers is to enable Java-based rich Internet applications (RIAs) on our computers, cell phones, and other devices that people frequently use. Josh Marinacci, a software engineer at Sun, made the following statement very appropriately in a recent Java Posse interview: "JavaFX is sort of a code word for reinventing client Java and fixing the sins of the past." Josh was referring to the fact that Java Swing and Java 2D have lots of capability, but are also very complex. JavaFX Script allows us to simply and elegantly express user interfaces (UIs) with a declarative programming style. It also leverages the full power of Java, because you can instantiate and use the millions of Java classes that exist today directly from JavaFX Script. Add features like binding the UI to attributes in a model and triggers that reduce the need for setter methods, and you have a language that will help restore Java to the client side of the RIA equation.

In this chapter, we're going to give you a jump start in developing applications in the JavaFX language. After bringing you up to date on the brief history of JavaFX, we'll show you how to get the JavaFX software development kit (SDK). We'll explore some great JavaFX resources and walk you through the process of compiling and running JavaFX applications. In the process you'll learn a lot about the JavaFX language and API as we walk through application code together. First, however, we're going to point out a related technology that is enabling the rise of rich-client Java.

JavaFX Can't Bring Rich-Client Java Back by Itself

When Java was first introduced in 1995, the hope was that the Java Runtime Environment (JRE) would become the common client platform on which the UI portion of client-server applications could be deployed. While the JRE became ubiquitous on the server side of the equation, factors such as the browser wars of the late 1990s delayed the prospect of achieving a consistent JRE on client machines. The result has been that web browser technologies such as HTML and JavaScript have stepped in to fill the gap, which we feel has proven suboptimal at best. The software development industry and the users we serve need to have the JRE on all client machines so that we can break free from browser technologies and enable graphically rich, fast-performing applications. Fortunately, the technology known as Java SE 6 Update 10 is solving that problem.

■**Note** What has come to be known as Java SE 6 Update 10 has actually had several names. It started life as the Consumer JRE, and then Java SE 6 Update N. Then it became known as Java SE 6 Update 10. As of this writing, Java SE 6 Update 14 has been released, but we're just going to refer this technology as Java SE 6 Update 10.

Java SE 6 Update 10 consists of several technologies that improve the user experience related to installing the JRE, and to deploying and running rich-client Java (and JavaFX) programs:

- *Java Kernel Online Installer*—The JRE is now divided into small bundles. If the user's machine doesn't have the JRE installed when a Java program is invoked, the online installer will ascertain which of the bundles are needed to run the program. Those bundles will be installed first and the program will begin executing as soon as this takes place.

- *Java Auto-Updater*: This provides a faster and more reliable process for updating the JRE by using a *patch-in-place* mechanism.

- *Java Quick Starter*: After a cold boot of the system, portions of the JRE are prefetched into memory. This enables a Java program to start more quickly.

- *Pack200 Format*: Pack200 is a highly compressed format that enables Java libraries and resources, for example, to download more quickly than traditional JAR files.

- *Java Deployment Toolkit*: This includes a simple JavaScript interface with which to deploy Java applets and applications. The JavaScript library is located at a well-known URL, and is engineered to make the right deployment decisions based on the detected JRE environment on the user's machine.

- *Next Generation Java Plug-in*: This Java plug-in is much more reliable and versatile than its predecessor. For example, you now have the ability to specify large heap sizes, and per-applet command-line arguments. Also, it has built-in Java Network Launching Protocol (JNLP) support as well as improved Java/JavaScript communications.

- *Hardware Acceleration Support*: In a media-rich environment, it is crucial to take advantage of the graphics capabilities on the underlying hardware. For example, Java SE 6 Update 10 currently has a hardware accelerated graphics pipeline based on the Microsoft Direct3D API.

The net result is that we are now at a point in software development history when two technologies (JavaFX and Java SE 6 Update 10) are working together to restore rich client Java. We feel that sanity is in the process of being restored to Internet software development, and we want you to join us in this RIA revolution. But first, a brief history lesson about JavaFX.

■**Note** JavaFX is the short name for the technology created by Sun called the JavaFX Rich Client platform. Components of this platform include a programming language named JavaFX Script, a runtime platform for various computers and devices, and tools for developing JavaFX applications. Because the main focus of this book is the JavaFX Script language, we'll often refer to JavaFX Script simply as JavaFX.

A Brief History of JavaFX

JavaFX started life as the brainchild of Chris Oliver when he worked for a company named SeeBeyond. They had the need for richer user interfaces, so Chris created a language that he dubbed F3 (Form Follows Function) for that purpose. In the article "Mind-Bendingly Cool Innovation" (cited in the Resources section at the end of this chapter), Chris is quoted as follows: "When it comes to integrating people into business processes, you need graphical user interfaces for them to interact with, so there was a use case for graphics in the enterprise application space, and there was an interest at SeeBeyond in having richer user interfaces."

SeeBeyond was acquired by Sun, who subsequently changed the name of F3 to JavaFX, and announced it at JavaOne 2007. Chris joined Sun during the acquisition and continued to lead the development of JavaFX.

The first version of JavaFX Script was an interpreted language, and was considered a prototype of the compiled JavaFX Script language that was to come later. Interpreted JavaFX Script was very robust, and there were two JavaFX books published in the latter part of 2007 based on that version. One was written in Japanese, and the other was written in English and published by Apress (*JavaFX Script: Dynamic Java Scripting for Rich Internet/Client-Side Applications*, Apress 2007).

While developers were experimenting with JavaFX and providing feedback for improvement, the JavaFX Script compiler team at Sun was busy creating a compiled version of the language. This included a new set of runtime API libraries. The JavaFX Script compiler project reached a tipping point in early December 2007, which was commemorated in a blog post entitled "Congratulations to the JavaFX Script Compiler Team—The Elephant Is Through the Door." That phrase came from the JavaFX Script compiler project leader Tom Ball in a blog post, which contained the following excerpt:

> *An elephant analogy came to me when I was recently grilled about exactly when the JavaFX Script compiler team will deliver our first milestone release. "I can't give you an accurate date," I said. "It's like pushing an elephant through a door; until a critical mass makes it past the threshold you just don't know when you'll be finished. Once you pass that threshold, though, the rest happens quickly and in a manner that can be more accurately predicted."*

A screenshot of the silly, compiled JavaFX application written by one of the authors, Jim Weaver, for that post is shown in Figure 1-1, demonstrating that the project had in fact reached the critical mass to which Tom Ball referred.

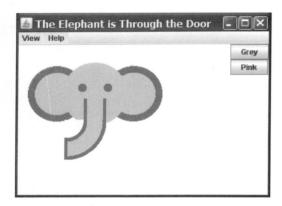

Figure 1-1. *Screenshot for the "Elephant Is Through the Door" program*

Much progress continued to be made on JavaFX in 2008:

- The NetBeans JavaFX plug-in became available for the compiled version in March 2008.

- Many of the JavaFX runtime libraries (mostly focusing on the UI aspects of JavaFX) were rewritten by a team that included some very talented developers from the Java Swing team.

- In July 2008, the JavaFX Preview SDK was released, and at JavaOne 2008 Sun announced that the JavaFX 1.0 SDK would be released in fall 2008.

- On December 4, 2008, the JavaFX 1.0 SDK was released. This event increased the adoption rate of JavaFX by developers and IT managers because it represented a stable codebase.

The JavaFX 1.2 SDK, released at JavaOne 2009, is significant because it is purportedly the version with which all future JavaFX APIs will be compatible.

Now that you've had the obligatory history lesson in JavaFX, let's get one step closer to writing code by showing you where some examples, tools, and other resources are.

Going to the Source: Sun's JavaFX Web Sites

When the JavaFX SDK was released, Sun's remodeled JavaFX.com site was unveiled as well. It is a great resource for seeing example JavaFX programs, downloading the JavaFX SDK and tools, taking tutorials on JavaFX, and linking to other resources. See Figure 1-2 for a screenshot of this web site.

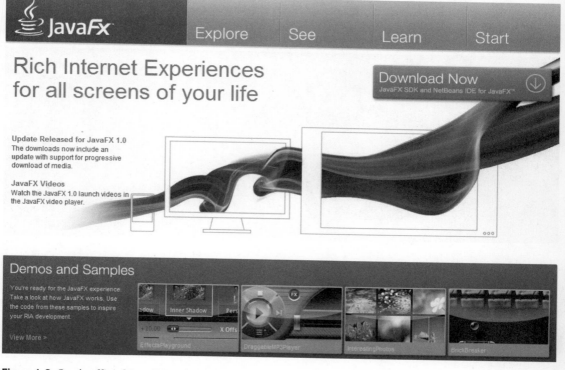

Figure 1-2. *Sun's official JavaFX web site*

In addition, Sun Developer Network (SDN) has a JavaFX Developer Home web site that has many useful developer resources, including links to JavaFX documentation such as the SDK API. The SDN JavaFX website is located at http://java.sun.com/javafx.

Take a few minutes to explore these sites. Next we'll point out some valuable resources you can take advantage of.

Accessing the JavaFX SDK API

A useful resource available from the JavaFX sites is the SDK API *JavaFXdoc* documentation. The SDK API JavaFXdoc is analogous to the SDK API *JavaDoc* in Java, but as you can see in Figure 1-3, its appearance has been updated.

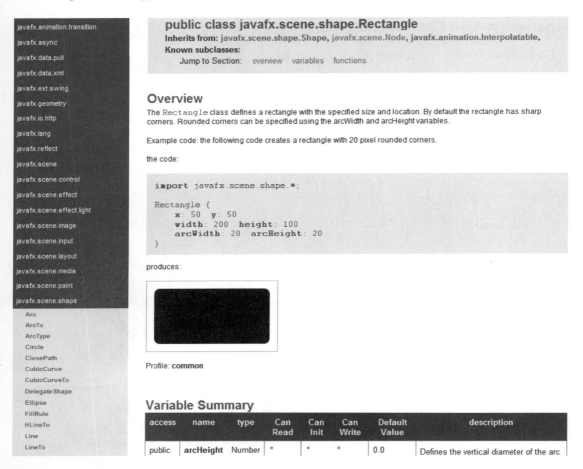

Figure 1-3. *JavaFX SDK API JavaFXdoc*

The API documentation in Figure 1-3, for example, shows how to use the Rectangle class, located in the javafx.scene.shape package, to draw a rectangle with rounded corners on the screen. Scrolling down this web page shows the variables in the Rectangle class, as well as functions and variables that it inherits from its super classes. By the way, this API documentation is available in the JavaFX SDK that you'll download shortly, but we wanted you to know how to find it online as well.

■**Note** If you are not familiar with concepts such as *inheritance* and *package*, don't be concerned. We'll cover such concepts soon in the context of the first program that you'll examine shortly.

Now that you've explored Sun's JavaFX web sites and available resources, it's time to obtain the JavaFX SDK and related tools so that you can begin developing JavaFX programs.

Obtaining the JavaFX SDK

You can get the JavaFX SDK from either of Sun's JavaFX web sites mentioned earlier, or you can use the URL listed in the Resources section at the end of this chapter. Currently you have the choice of downloading the JavaFX SDK bundled with the NetBeans integrated development environment (IDE), or by itself. We recommend that you choose the former, as it makes development much easier than compiling and running from the command line. This is due in part to the fact that it generates the deployment-related code contained in HTML and JNLP files and provides error annotations, formatting, import management, code completion, and syntax highlighting. The instructions for the examples in this first chapter will assume that you have NetBeans installed.

Go ahead and download the JavaFX SDK and follow the installation instructions. In addition, so that you can use the command-line tools (such as `javafxc` for compiling JavaFX files), add the directory that contains these commands to your system's `PATH` variable. As of this writing, the path to this directory is `javafx2/javafx-sdk/bin`, and is located subordinate to the NetBeans installation.

■**Note** Be sure to use the correct type of slashes (forward slash or backslash) in the path for your platform. This advice applies to anywhere in the book where a directory is specified. Also note that arguments to the JavaFX and Java command-line tools can take forward slashes in paths, regardless of platform.

JavaFX Production Suite

There is another download named the *JavaFX Production Suite* that has plug-ins for Adobe Photoshop and Adobe Illustrator. These plug-ins enable you to generate JavaFX data files from the graphics created in either of those applications. These data files have an `.fxd` extension, and when compressed have an `.fxz` extension. The JavaFX Production Suite also includes an *SVG Convertor* tool that converts scalable vector graphics (SVG) files to JavaFX data files. Download and install the JavaFX Production Suite so that you'll be ready to use it when we cover this topic.

Other Available Tools

There are other tools available for developing JavaFX applications. For example, there are JavaFX plug-ins for the Eclipse IDE, but at the time of this writing they aren't as mature as the NetBeans plug-in. There is also a preview release of a visual design tool from ReportMill named JFXBuilder that you might want to experiment with. The URLs for both of these tools are listed in the Resources section.

Now that you have the tools installed, we'll show you how to create a simple JavaFX program, and then we'll walk through it in detail. The first program that we've chosen for you is called "Hello Earthrise," which demonstrates more features than the typical beginning "Hello World" program.

Developing Your First JavaFX Program: "Hello Earthrise"

On Christmas Eve in 1968 the crew of Apollo 8 entered lunar orbit for the first time in history. They were the first humans to witness an "Earthrise," taking the magnificent picture shown in Figure 1-4. This image, and the accompanying audio MIDI file, is dynamically loaded from this book's web site when the program starts, so you'll need to be connected to the Internet to view and hear it.

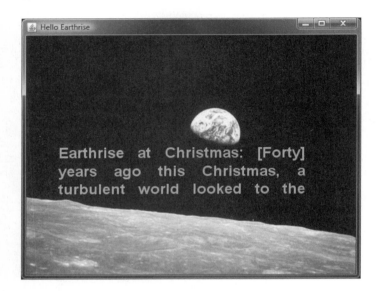

Figure 1-4. *The Hello Earthrise program*

In addition to demonstrating how to dynamically load images over the Internet and play audio media, this example shows you how to use animation in JavaFX. Now it's time for you to compile and run the program. We'll show you two ways to do this: from the command line, and using NetBeans with the JavaFX plug-in.

Compiling and Running from the Command Line

We usually use an IDE to build and run JavaFX programs, but to take all of the mystery out of the process we're going to use the command-line tools first.

■**Note** For this exercise, as with most others in the book, you'll need the source code. If you'd prefer not to type the source code into a text editor, you can obtain the source code for all of the examples in this book from the code download site. See the Resources section at the end of this chapter for the location of this site.

Assuming that you've downloaded and extracted the source code for this book into a directory, follow the directions in this exercise, performing all of the steps as instructed. We'll dissect the source code after the exercise.

COMPILING AND RUNNING THE HELLO EARTHRISE PROGRAM FROM THE COMMAND

You'll use the `javafxc` and `javafx` command-line tools to compile and run the program in this exercise. From the command-line prompt on your machine:

1. Navigate to the `Chapter01/Hello` directory.

2. Execute the following command to compile the `HelloEarthRiseMain.fx` file. Note that the `javafxc` command-line tool for JavaFX is analogous to the `javac` tool for Java programs.

   ```
   javafxc -d . HelloEarthRiseMain.fx
   ```

   Because the `-d` **option was used in this command, the class files generated are placed in directories matching the** `package` **statements in the source files.** The root of those directories are specified by the argument given for the `-d` option, in this case the current directory. We'll cover `package` statements in a bit.

3. To run the program, execute the following command. Note that the `javafx` command-line tool for JavaFX is analogous to the `java` tool for Java programs. Note as well that we use the fully qualified name of the script that will be executed, which entails specifying the nodes of the path name and the name of the script, all separated by periods. Unlike when compiling scripts, running and appending the FX extension will result in an error.

   ```
   javafx projavafx.helloearthrise.ui.HelloEarthRiseMain
   ```

The program should appear as shown in Figure 1-4 earlier, with the text scrolling slowly upward, reminiscent of the *Star Wars* opening crawls.

Congratulations on completing your first exercise as you explore JavaFX!

Understanding the Hello Earthrise Program

Now that you've run the application, let's walk through the program listing together. The code for the Hello Earthrise application is shown in Listing 1-1.

Listing 1-1. *The HelloEarthRiseMain.fx Program*

```
/*
 * HelloEarthRiseMain.fx - A JavaFX Script "Hello World" style example
 *
 * Developed 2009 by James L. Weaver jim.weaver [at] javafxpert.com
 * as a JavaFX Script SDK 1.2 example for the Pro JavaFX book.
 */
package projavafx.helloearthrise.ui;
```

```
import javafx.animation.transition.TranslateTransition;
import javafx.animation.*;
import javafx.stage.Stage;
import javafx.scene.*;
import javafx.scene.image.*;
import javafx.scene.media.*;
import javafx.scene.paint.Color;
import javafx.scene.shape.Rectangle;
import javafx.scene.text.*;

var textRef:Text;

// Provides the animated scrolling behavior for the text
var transTransition = TranslateTransition {
  duration: 75s
  node: bind textRef
  toY: -820
  interpolator: Interpolator.LINEAR
  repeatCount: Timeline.INDEFINITE
}

Stage {
  title: "Hello Earthrise"
  scene: Scene {
    height: 387
    width: 516
    content: [
      ImageView {
        image: Image {
          url: "http://projavafx.com/images/earthrise.jpg"
        }
      },
      Group {
        layoutX: 50
        layoutY: 180
        content: [
          textRef = Text {
            layoutY: 100
            textOrigin: TextOrigin.TOP
            textAlignment: TextAlignment.JUSTIFY
            wrappingWidth: 380
            // Note that this syntax creates one long string of text
            content:
              "Earthrise at Christmas: "
              "[Forty] years ago this Christmas, a turbulent world "
              "looked to the heavens for a unique view of our home "
              "planet. This photo of Earthrise over the lunar horizon "
              "was taken by the Apollo 8 crew in December 1968, showing "
```

```
                "Earth for the first time as it appears from deep space. "
                "Astronauts Frank Borman, Jim Lovell and William Anders "
                "had become the first humans to leave Earth orbit, "
                "entering lunar orbit on Christmas Eve. In a historic live "
                "broadcast that night, the crew took turns reading from "
                "the Book of Genesis, closing with a holiday wish from "
                "Commander Borman: \"We close with good night, good luck, "
                "a Merry Christmas, and God bless all of you -- all of "
                "you on the good Earth.\""
              // The approximate color used in the scrolling Star Wars intro
              fill: Color.rgb(187, 195, 107)
              font: Font.font("SansSerif", FontWeight.BOLD, 24);
            }
          ]
        clip: Rectangle {
          width: 430
          height: 85
        }
      }
    ]
  }
}
// Start playing an audio clip
MediaPlayer {
  autoPlay: true
  repeatCount: MediaPlayer.REPEAT_FOREVER
  media: Media {
    source: "http://projavafx.com/audio/zarathustra.mid"
  }
}// Start the text animation
transTransition.play();
```

Now that you've seen the code, let's take a look at its constructs and concepts in detail, beginning with one of the easiest: comments.

Comments

There are two types of comments in JavaFX: *multiline comments* and *single-line comments*. Multiline comments begin with the two characters /* and end with the same two characters in reverse order, */. JavaFX will ignore anything in between. The beginning of the listing shows an example of a multiline comment. Single-line comments begin with the two characters //. Anything that follows these two characters on a single line will be ignored. An example of a single-line comment is shown near the top of Listing 1-1.

The package Declaration

JavaFX packages are analogous to folders in a file system. They provide namespaces to logically organize the scripts and classes that comprise an application. Package names may consist of more than one node (for example, com.apress.projavafx). In fact, it is a common practice for a package name to begin with the domain name of the company or organization that developed the application (in reverse order, beginning with the top-level domain name, such as com or org).

The package declaration is optional, but it is good practice to use it in all but the most trivial programs. If used, the package statement must be at the top of the source code (excluding whitespace and comments).

import Statements

JavaFX programs typically use libraries that consist of JavaFX (and optionally Java) code. In this example, each import statement indicates the location (package) of the JavaFX classes that the code in the rest of this HelloEarthRiseMain.fx script depends on for rendering the user interface. An import statement can end with an asterisk (*), indicating that the program may use any of the classes in the package. An alternative form is to specifically name each class being used, as in the example near the top of Listing 1-1:

```
import javafx.stage.Stage;
```

All but the most trivial applications should organize their source code via package declarations. A source code file uses import statements to indicate its use of classes contained in source code files that have a different package statement.

Declarative Code That Defines the User Interface

One of the most exciting features of JavaFX is its ability to express a graphical user interface (GUI) using a simple, consistent, and powerful declarative syntax. Declarative code consists of a single expression (rather than multiple expressions that are executed sequentially).

■**Note** As you'll see a little later, JavaFX supports data binding, which is characterized by binding the value of a variable (such as the height of a rectangle) to an expression. Data binding is a major enabler of using declarative expressions.

In this example, most of the program is declarative in that it contains a large expression. This declarative expression begins by defining a Stage object followed by an open curly brace, and ends with the matching curly brace near the end of the program. Nested within that are instance variables of the Stage object, including the scene variable, which is assigned a Scene instance. A Scene has an instance variable named content that holds the graphical elements that are displayed on the Stage, in this case an ImageView instance (which displays an image) and a Group instance. Nested within the Group is a content instance variable that holds a Text instance (which is a graphical element, usually called a *graphical node*, or simply *node*) and so on.

■**Note** This declarative expression is an example of object literal syntax, in which instances of these classes are created when the expression is evaluated.

Declarative code automatically creates an instance (also known as an object) of each JavaFX class in the expression. It also assigns values to the variables of the new instance. For example, look at the portion of code that creates an instance of the Rectangle class:

```
Rectangle {
  width: 430
  height: 85
}
```

This code creates an instance of the JavaFX Rectangle class and assigns the value 430 to the width variable of the new Rectangle instance, and the value 85 to its height variable. Notice that the instance variable name is always followed by a colon (:), which in JavaFX declarative syntax means "assign the value of the expression on the right to the instance variable on the left." These same concepts are true for all of the classes (Stage, Scene, ImageView, Image, Group, Text, TranslateTransition, MediaPlayer and Media) in this script. Let's look at each of these classes individually.

Using the Stage Class

A Stage contains the user interface of a JavaFX app, whether it is deployed on the desktop, within a browser, or on a mobile device. On the desktop, for example, a Stage has its own top-level window, which typically includes a border and title bar. In the browser the Stage doesn't have a window, but is rendered as an applet within a rectangular area of the browser.

As with any class, the Stage class has a set of instance variables. Some of these variables, as shown in the following code snippet from the listing, are as follows:

- A title that appears in the title bar of the window (when deployed on the desktop)

- A scene that contains the graphical nodes in the user interface

```
Stage {
  title: "Hello Earthrise"
  scene: Scene {
    …some code omitted…
  }
}
```

Creating String Literals

One of the basic JavaFX data types is the String, which consists of zero or more characters strung together. As shown in the following title variable of the Stage instance, a String literal is defined by enclosing a set of characters in double quotes:

```
title: "Hello Earthrise"
```

For convenience, as shown in the content variable of the Text instance in Listing 1-1, a String literal may be defined with multiple sets of quoted characters. Alternatively, String literals may be enclosed in single quotes. Strings have more capabilities than described here, but we'll cover them as they occur in code examples.

Using the Scene Class

As mentioned previously, a Scene holds the graphical elements that are displayed on the Stage. Every element in a Scene is a graphical node, which is any class that extends the javafx.scene. Node class. Take another look at the declarative code that creates the Scene in our example program:

```
scene: Scene {
  content: [
    ImageView {
      …some code omitted…
    },
    Group {
      …some code omitted…
    }
  ]
}
```

Notice that the content variable of the Scene is followed by a left square bracket, [, which is the literal notation for a *sequence*. A sequence is a one-dimensional data structure that is native to JavaFX. Take a look at the JavaFX API documentation that we showed you how to access in the "Accessing the JavaFX SDK API" section earlier. You'll see that the content variable of the Scene class is of type Node[], which means that it can reference a sequence of Node instances.

While you're looking at the API docs, check out the Node class to see the variables and functions available to any graphical node. Also, take a look at the ImageView class in the javafx.scene.image package and the Group class in the javafx.scene package. In both cases, you'll see that they inherit from the Node class.

■**Tip** We can't emphasize enough the importance of having the JavaFX API documentation handy while reading this book. As classes, variables, and functions are mentioned, it's often a good idea to look at the documentation to get more information. In addition, this habit helps you become more familiar with what is available to you in the API.

Displaying Images

As shown in the following code, displaying an image entails using an ImageView instance in conjunction with an Image instance:

```
ImageView {
  image: Image {
    url: "http://projavafx.com/images/earthrise.jpg"
  }
},
```

The Image instance identifies the image resource and loads it from the URL assigned to its url variable. Both of these classes are located in the javafx.scene.image package.

Working with Graphical Nodes as a Group

One powerful graphical feature of JavaFX is the ability to create scene graphs, which consist of a tree of graphical nodes. You can then assign values to variables of a Group located in the hierarchy, and the nodes contained in the Group will be affected. In our current example from Listing 1-1, we're using a Group to contain a Text node and to *clip* a specific rectangular region within the Group so that the text doesn't appear on the moon or the Earth as it animates upward. Here's the relevant code snippet:

```
Group {
  layoutX: 50
  layoutY: 180
  content: [
    textRef = Text {
      layoutY: 100
      textOrigin: TextOrigin.TOP
      textAlignment: TextAlignment.JUSTIFY
      wrappingWidth: 380
      content:
        "Earthrise at Christmas: "
        ...some code omitted...
      fill: Color.rgb(187, 195, 107)
      font: Font.font("SansSerif", FontWeight.BOLD, 24);
    }
  ]
  clip:
    Rectangle {
      width: 430
      height: 85
    }
}
```

Notice that the Group is located 50 pixels to the right and 180 pixels down, from where it would have been located by default. This is due to the values assigned to the layoutX and layoutY variables of the Group instance. Because this Group is contained directly by the Scene, its upper-left corner's location is 50 pixels to the right and 180 pixels down from the upper-left corner of the Scene. Take a look at Figure 1-5 to see this example illustrated as you read the rest of the explanation.

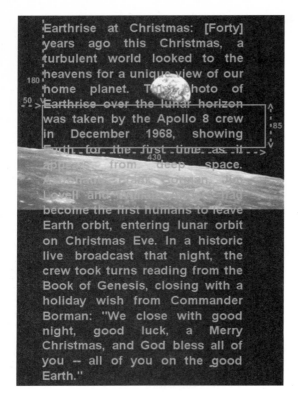

Figure 1-5. *The Scene, Group, Text, and clip illustrated*

Like a Scene, a Group instance contains instances of Node subclasses by assigning a sequence of them to the content variable. In the previous code snippet, the Group contains a Text instance that has a value assigned to its layoutY variable. Because this Text is contained by a Group, it assumes the two-dimensional space (also called the *coordinate space*) of the Group, with the origin of the Text node (0,0) coincident with the top-left corner of the Group. Assigning a value of 100 to the layoutY variable causes the Text to be located 100 pixels down from the top of the Group, which is just below the bottom of the clip region, thus causing it to be out of view until the animation begins. Because a value isn't assigned to the layoutX variable, its value is 0 (the default).

The layoutX and layoutY variables of the Group just described are examples of our earlier statement that nodes contained in a Group will be affected by values assigned to variables of the Group. Another example is setting the opacity variable of a Group instance to 0.5, which causes all of the nodes contained in that Group to become translucent. If the JavaFX API documentation is handy, look at the variables available in the javafx.scene.Group class. Then scroll down to see the variables inherited from the java.scene.Node class, which is where you'll find the layoutX, layoutY, and opacity variables.

Drawing Text

In the previous snippet, notice that several variables are available in the Text class. This particular example is a little more complicated than the normal use of the Text class. Let's first look at a typical case, shown in the following snippet, in which you simply want to draw a string of text characters somewhere in the scene:

```
Text {
  layoutX: 65
  layoutY: 12
  textOrigin: TextOrigin.TOP
  fill: Color.WHITE
  content: "Audio Configuration"
  font: Font.font("SansSerif", FontWeight.BOLD, 20)
},
```

This snippet, borrowed from the Audio Configuration example in Figure 1-7 and Listing 1-3 later in this chapter, draws the graphical Text string "Audio Configuration" in a bold, Sans Serif font. The font size is 20, and the color of the text is white.

Referring again to the JavaFX API documentation, you'll notice that the TextOrigin class (in the javafx.scene.text package) has three fields that serve as constants: BASELINE, BOTTOM, and TOP. These control the origin of the text with respect to vertical locations on the displayed Text:

- The TOP origin, as we're using it in the previous code snippet, places the top of the text (including ascenders) at the layoutY position, relative to the coordinate space in which the Text is located.

- The BOTTOM origin would place the bottom of the text, including descenders (located in a lowercase "g" for example) at the layoutY position.

- The BASELINE origin would place the baseline of the text (excluding descenders) at the layoutY position. This is the default value for the textOrigin variable of a Text instance.

While you're looking at the javafx.scene.text package in the API documentation, take a look at the font function of the Font class, which is used in the previous snippet to define the font family, weight, and size of the Text.

Turning back again to the Hello Earthrise example in Listing 1-1, we're using some additional variables of the Text class that enable it to flow from one line to the next:

- The wrappingWidth variable enables you to specify at what number of pixels the text will wrap.

- The textAlignment variable enables you to control how the text will be justified. In our example, TextAlignment.JUSTIFY aligns the text on both the left and right sides, expanding the space between words to achieve that.

The text that we're displaying is sufficiently long to wrap and be drawn on the Earth, so we need to define a rectangular region outside of which that text can't be seen.

Clipping Graphical Areas

To define a clipping area, we assign a Node subclass to the clip variable that defines the clipping shape, in this case a Rectangle that is 430 pixels wide and 85 pixels high. In addition to keeping the Text from covering the moon, when the Text scrolls up as a result of animation the clipping area keeps the Text from covering the earth.

Animating the Text to Make It Scroll Up

When the HelloEarthriseMain.fx script is invoked, the Text begins scrolling up slowly. To achieve this animation, we're using the TranslateTransition class located in the javafx. animation.transition package, as shown in the following snippet from Listing 1-1:

```
// Provides the animated scrolling behavior for the text
var transTransition = TranslateTransition {
  duration: 75s
  node: bind textRef
  toY: -820
  interpolator: Interpolator.LINEAR
  repeatCount: Timeline.INDEFINITE
}
...code omitted...
// Start the text animation
transTransition.play();
```

The javafx.animation.transition package contains convenience classes for animating nodes. This TranslateTransition instance translates the Text node from its original Y position of 100 pixels to a Y position of –820 pixels, over a duration of 75 seconds (the duration of the audio clip). Note that the Text node is referenced by the textRef variable, as we'll explain shortly, and that we're using the bind operator in the assignment to the node variable (we'll cover the bind operator later in this chapter). The Interpolator.LINEAR constant is assigned to the interpolator variable, which causes the animation to proceed in a linear fashion. A look at the API docs for the Interpolator class in the javafx.animation package will reveal that there are other forms of interpolation available, one of which is EASEOUT, which slows down the animation toward the end of the specified duration.

■**Note** *Interpolation* in this context is the process of calculating the value at any point in time, given a beginning value, an ending value, and a duration.

The last line in the previous snippet begins executing the play function of the TranslateTransition instance created earlier in the script. This makes the Text begin scrolling upward. Because of the value assigned to the repeatCount variable, this transition will repeat indefinitely.

Look again at the entire `HelloEarthRiseMain.fx` script in Listing 1-1 to get an overall picture of how it is processed when invoked:

1. The first statement declares a variable of type `Text`, named `textRef`, which is used to hold a reference to the `Text` instance that will have a transition applied to it (as we just finished discussing).

2. The second statement declares a variable named `transTransition` and creates an instance of the `TranslateTransition` class, assigning its reference to the `transTransition` variable.

3. Next, the declarative expression that comprises most of the rest of the script is evaluated, which creates an instance of the `Stage` class and the other classes in the UI scene graph.

4. The statement at the end of the script is executed, which plays the transition.

Finally, let's discuss how the audio media is played as the text is scrolling.

Playing Media

The following code snippet from Listing 1-1 demonstrates how to load and play audio media:

```
MediaPlayer {
  autoPlay: true
  repeatCount: MediaPlayer.REPEAT_FOREVER
  media: Media {
    source: "http://projavafx.com/audio/zarathustra.mid"
  }
}
```

As shown here, the audio clip automatically begins playing and repeats indefinitely (until the program exits). We'll have a lot more to say about playing audio and video media in Chapter 6, so stay tuned!

Now that you've compiled and run this example using the command-line tools and we've walked through the code together, it is time to begin using the NetBeans IDE with the JavaFX plug-in to make the development and deployment process faster and easier.

Building and Running the Program with NetBeans

Assuming that you've downloaded and extracted the source code for this book into a directory, follow the directions in this exercise to build and run the Hello Earthrise program in NetBeans with the JavaFX Plug-in. If you haven't yet downloaded the version of the JavaFX SDK that contains NetBeans, please do so from the JavaFX downloads page listed in the Resources section at the end of this chapter.

BUILDING AND RUNNING HELLO EARTHRISE WITH NETBEANS

To build and run the Hello Earthrise program, perform the following steps:

1. Start up the version of NetBeans that is available for download with the JavaFX SDK.

2. Choose File ➤ New Project from the menu bar. The first window of the New Project Wizard will appear:

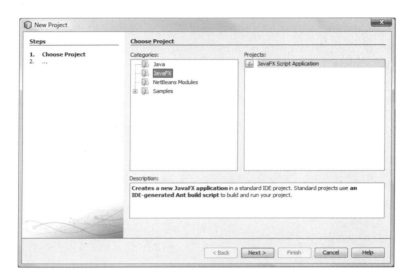

3. Choose JavaFX in the Categories pane and JavaFX Script Application in the Projects pane, and click the Next button. The next page in the New Project Wizard should appear:

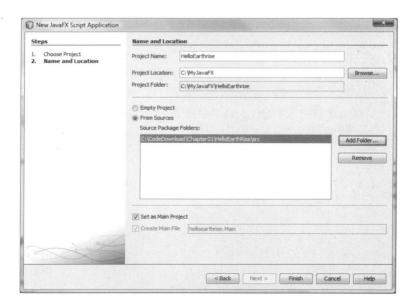

4. On this screen, type the project name (we used HelloEarthrise) and click the Browse button.

5. On the Select Project Location screen, navigate to the directory in which you'd like to create this project (we used C:\MyJavaFX), and click the Open button.

6. Select the From Sources radio button and click the Add Folder button.

7. On the Browse Source Packages Editor screen, navigate to the `Chapter01/HelloEarthrise/src` directory subordinate to where you expanded this book's code download bundle, and click the Open button.

■**Note** These instructions are for creating a new NetBeans project from JavaFX source code. Step 7 won't be successful if NetBeans finds a directory named `nbproject` and/or a `build.xml` file. This is because NetBeans assumes that the `src` directory is part of another project and refuses to add the source files to the new project. The build and run instructions in the Audio Configuration example later in this chapter demonstrate how to work with a NetBeans JavaFX project that already exists.

---

8. Click the Finish button. The HelloEarthrise project should now be created, and you're ready to run it.

9. Right-click on the HelloEarthrise project in the Projects pane and select Run Project from the context menu.

10. The Run Project dialog box, shown next, will appear the first time you run the project, asking for the main class. Choose the `projavafx.helloearthrise.ui.HelloEarthRiseMain` class (the only class in the list for this simple example), and click OK.

The `HelloEarthRise` program should begin executing, as you saw in Figure 1-4 earlier in the chapter.

At this point, you've built and run the "Hello Earthrise" program application—both from the command line and using NetBeans. Now we're going to show you how to deploy this program using Java Web Start, and then as an applet in a browser.

Deploying JavaFX Applications

As mentioned earlier in this chapter, the JavaFX and Java SE 6 update 10 technologies are working together to restore rich client Java. In this section you'll configure and deploy the Hello Earthrise application with Java Web Start and as a JavaFX applet. The underlying features of Java SE 6 Update 10 will be leveraged in this process.

Deploying JavaFX Applications with Java Web Start

To build the "Hello Earthrise" program with NetBeans to deploy as a Java Web Start application, you need to create a configuration for that purpose. The following exercise walks you through this process.

DEPLOYING THE HELLO EARTHRISE PROGRAM WITH JAVA WEB START

To create a configuration for deploying the Hello Earthrise program with Java Web Start, perform the following steps:

1. Right-click on the HelloEarthrise project in the Projects pane and select Set Configuration ➤ Customize from the context menu, as shown here:

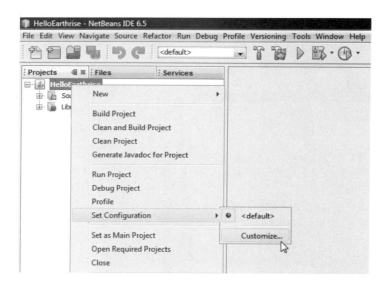

2. The Project Properties dialog box, shown next, will appear. Choose Run from the Categories pane, and click the Web Start Execution radio button in the Application Execution Model options.

3. While still in the Project Properties dialog box, choose Application from the Categories pane, as shown next. Select the Self Signed Jar and Pack200 Compression check boxes. The Applet Specific Properties section is not applicable for Web Start execution, so you can safely ignore these options for now. Click OK to close this dialog box.

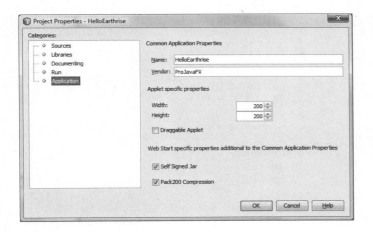

■**Caution** Selecting Self Signed Jar signs the Web Start application, but it doesn't use an authoritative certificate. A security dialog box will appear, but it will indicate that the signature can't be verified. For this reason, posting (or executing) JavaFX applications with self-signed JARs on the Internet is not a good practice. If the application doesn't require access outside the sandbox (for example, to the NASA web site as this one does), then there is no need to sign the code anyway. If the application needs access outside the sandbox and you want to put your application on the Internet, then we suggest that you get a code-signing certificate (from VeriSign or Thawte, for example).

Because of the configuration that you just performed, when you run the project as described previously it should be invoked via Java Web Start; see Figure 1-4 earlier.

Now that you've configured and run Hello Earthrise as a Java Web Start application, let's deploy it as an applet inside your web browser.

Deploying JavaFX Applets

To deploy the "Hello Earthrise" program as a Java Web Start application, you need to create a configuration in the NetBeans project for that purpose. The following exercise walks you through this process.

DEPLOYING THE HELLO EARTHRISE PROGRAM AS AN APPLET IN A WEB BROWSER

To create a configuration for deploying the Hello Earthrise program as an applet in a browser, perform the following steps:

1. Right-click on the HelloEarthrise project in the Projects pane and select Set Configuration ➤ Customize from the context menu.

2. The Project Properties dialog box, shown next, will appear. Choose Run from the Categories pane, and click the Run in Browser radio button from the Application Execution Model options.

3. While still in the Project Properties dialog box, choose Application from the Categories pane, as shown next. Select the Self Signed Jar and Pack 200 Compression check boxes. In Applet Specific Properties, enter 516 in the Width field and 387 in the Height field, and select the Draggable Applet check box. The reason for these particular width and height numbers is that these are the dimensions of the image that fills the scene. Choosing to make the applet draggable when run in a browser on which Java SE 6 Update 10 is installed allows that applet to be dragged from the browser onto the desktop. Click OK to close this dialog box.

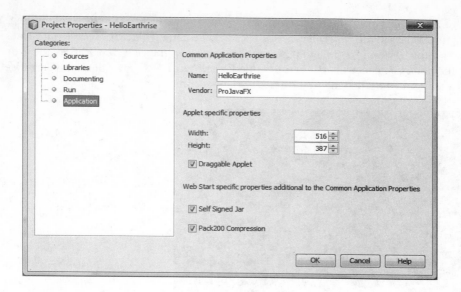

Because of the configuration that you just performed, when you run the project as described previously, it should be invoked in your default browser. If you have Java SE 6 Update 10 installed, then hold down the Alt key while clicking and dragging the applet onto the desktop, as shown here:

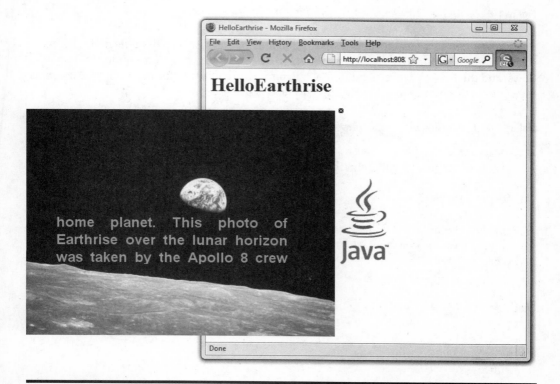

Before leaving this example, we'd like to show you another way to clip the scrolling Text node. There is a class in the `javafx.scene.layout` package named `ClipView` whose purpose is to provide a clipped view of a node that is typically larger than the view. In addition, the user can drag the node being viewed within the clipped area. Figure 1-6 shows the Hello Earthrise program after being modified to use the `ClipView` layout container.

Figure 1-6. *Using the ClipView layout container to clip the Text node*

Notice that the *move* cursor is visible, signifying that the user can drag the node around the clipped area. Note that the screenshot in Figure 1-6 is of the program running on Windows, and the *move* cursor has a different appearance on other platforms. Listing 1-2 contains the code for this example, named `HelloClipViewExample.fx`.

Listing 1-2. *The HelloClipViewExample.fx Program*

```
...code omitted...
import javafx.scene.layout.ClipView;

var textRef:Text;

// Provides the animated scrolling behavior for the text
var transTransition = TranslateTransition {
  ...code omitted...
}

Stage {
  title: "Hello ClipView"
  scene: Scene {
    height: 387
    width: 516
    content: [
```

```
    ImageView {
      image: Image {
        url: " http://projavafx.com/images/earthrise.jpg"
      }
    },
    ClipView {
      layoutX: 50
      layoutY: 180
      width: 430
      height: 85
      node:
        textRef = Text {
          layoutY: 100
          textOrigin: TextOrigin.TOP
          textAlignment: TextAlignment.JUSTIFY
          wrappingWidth: 380
          // Note that this syntax creates one long string of text
          content:
            "Earthrise at Christmas: "
            ...code omitted...
          // The approximate color used in the scrolling Star Wars intro
          fill: Color.rgb(187, 195, 107)
          font: Font.font("SansSerif", FontWeight.BOLD, 24);
        }
    }
  ]
 }
}
...code omitted...
```

Later chapters will cover other layout containers in the javafx.scene.layout package, such as HBox, VBox, Flow, Tile, and Stack. For now, let's examine another JavaFX example application to help you learn more JavaFX Script concepts and constructs.

Developing Your Second JavaFX Program: "More Cowbell!"

If you're familiar with the *Saturday Night Live* television show, you may have seen the More Cowbell sketch, in which Christopher Walken's character keeps asking for "more cowbell" during a Blue Oyster Cult recording session. The following JavaFX example program covers some of the simple but powerful concepts of JavaFX in the context of an imaginary application that lets you select a music genre and control the volume. Of course, "Cowbell Metal," shortened to "Cowbell," is one of the available genres. Figure 1-7 shows a screenshot of this application, which has a sort of iPhone application look.

Figure 1-7. *The Audio Configuration "More Cowbell" program*

Building and Running the Audio Configuration Program

Earlier in the chapter, we showed you how to create a new JavaFX project in NetBeans, and how to add a folder that contains source code files to the project.

For this example (and the rest of the examples in the book), we'll take advantage of the fact that the code download bundle for the book contains both NetBeans and Eclipse project files for each example. Follow the instructions in this exercise to build and run the Audio Configuration application.

BUILDING AND RUNNING THE AUDIO CONFIGURATION PROGRAM USING NETBEANS

To build and execute this program using NetBeans, perform the following steps:

1. From the File menu, select the Open Project menu item. In the Open Project dialog box, navigate to the Chapter01 directory where you extracted the book's code download bundle, as shown here:

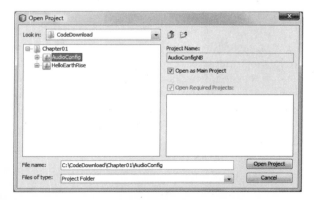

2. Select the AudioConfig project in the pane on the left, and click the Open Project button.

3. Run the project as discussed previously.

The application should appear as shown in Figure 1-7.

The Behavior of the Audio Configuration Program

When you run the application, notice that adjusting the volume slider changes the associated decibel (dB) level displayed. Also, selecting the Muting check box disables the slider, and selecting various genres changes the volume slider. This behavior is enabled by concepts that you'll see in the code that follows, such as

- Binding to a class that contains a model
- Using on replace triggers
- Creating sequences

Understanding the Audio Configuration Program

The Audio Configuration program contains two source code files, shown in Listing 1-3 and Listing 1-4 (which appears in the section "The Model Class for the Audio Configuration Example" in just a moment):

- The AudioConfigMain.fx file in Listing 1-3 contains the main script, and expresses the UI in a manner that you are familiar with from the Hello Earthrise example in Listing 1-1.
- The AudioConfigModel.fx file in Listing 1-4 contains a model for this program, which holds the state of the application, to which the UI is *bound*.

Take a look at the AudioConfigMain.fx source code in Listing 1-3, and then we'll examine it together, focusing on concepts not covered in the previous example.

Listing 1-3. *The AudioConfigMain.fx Program*

```
package projavafx.audioconfig.ui;

import javafx.ext.swing.SwingComboBox;
import javafx.ext.swing.SwingComboBoxItem;
import javafx.scene.*;
import javafx.scene.control.Slider;
import javafx.scene.control.CheckBox;
import javafx.scene.paint.*;
import javafx.scene.shape.*;
import javafx.scene.text.*;
import javafx.stage.Stage;
import projavafx.audioconfig.model.AudioConfigModel;
```

```
Stage {
  def acModel = AudioConfigModel {
    selectedDecibels: 35
  }
  title: "Audio Configuration"
  scene: Scene {
    content: [
      Rectangle {
        // No need to assign 0 to x and y, because 0 is the default
        width: 320
        height: 45
        fill: LinearGradient {
          // No need to assign 0 to startX and startY, because 0 is default
          endX: 0.0
          endY: 1.0
          stops: [
            Stop {
              color: Color.web("0xAEBBCC")
              offset: 0.0
            },
            Stop {
              color: Color.web("0x6D84A3")
              offset: 1.0
            }
          ]
        }
      },
      Text {
        layoutX: 65
        layoutY: 12
        textOrigin: TextOrigin.TOP
        fill: Color.WHITE
        content: "Audio Configuration"
        font: Font.font("SansSerif", FontWeight.BOLD, 20)
      },
      Rectangle {
        x: 0  // 0 is default, so assigning here just for clarity
        y: 43
        width: 320
        height: 300
        fill: Color.rgb(199, 206, 213)
      },
      Rectangle {
        x: 9
        y: 54
        width: 300
        height: 130
        arcWidth: 20
```

```
      arcHeight: 20
      fill: Color.WHITE
      stroke: Color.color(0.66, 0.67, 0.69)
    },
    Text {
      layoutX: 18
      layoutY: 69
      textOrigin: TextOrigin.TOP
      fill: Color.web("0x131021")
      content: bind "{%1.0f acModel.selectedDecibels} dB"
      font: Font.font("SansSerif", FontWeight.BOLD, 18)
    },
    Slider {
      layoutX: 135
      layoutY: 69
      width: 162
      disable: bind acModel.muting
      min: bind acModel.minDecibels
      max: bind acModel.maxDecibels
      value: bind acModel.selectedDecibels with inverse
    },
    Line {
      startX: 9
      startY: 97
      endX: 309
      endY: 97
      stroke: Color.color(0.66, 0.67, 0.69)
    },
    Text {
      layoutX: 18
      layoutY: 113
      textOrigin: TextOrigin.TOP
      fill: Color.web("0x131021")
      content: "Muting"
      font: Font.font("SansSerif", FontWeight.BOLD, 18)
    },
    CheckBox {
      layoutX: 280
      layoutY: 113
      selected: bind acModel.muting with inverse
    },
    Line {
      startX: 9
      startY: 141
      endX: 309
      endY: 141
      stroke: Color.color(0.66, 0.67, 0.69)
    },
```

```
    Text {
      layoutX: 18
      layoutY: 157
      textOrigin: TextOrigin.TOP
      fill: Color.web("0x131021")
      content: "Genre"
      font: Font.font("SansSerif", FontWeight.BOLD, 18)
    },
    SwingComboBox {
      layoutX: 204
      layoutY: 148
      width: 93
      items: bind for (genre in acModel.genres) {
        SwingComboBoxItem {
          text: genre
        }
      }
      selectedIndex: bind acModel.selectedGenreIndex with inverse
    }
  ]
  }
}
```

Now that you've seen the main script in this application, let's walk through the new concepts.

Creating an Instance of the Model, and the Magic of Binding

One of the powerful aspects of JavaFX is binding, which enables the application's UI to easily stay in sync with the state, or model, of the application. The model for a JavaFX application is typically held in one or more classes, in this case the AudioConfigModel class. To make an instance of this class, we use the same object literal syntax that we've used to create instances of UI classes. Look at the following snippet, taken from Listing 1-3:

```
def acModel = AudioConfigModel {
  selectedDecibels: 35
}
```

This instantiates the AudioConfigModel class, initializing its selectedDecibels instance variable to a value of 35. In addition, a reference to that instance is held by a variable named acModel.

■Note The def keyword in this snippet is similar to var, except that its value must be assigned and initialized when it is declared. Also, it cannot subsequently be assigned a value. The def keyword enables the compiler to perform related optimizations.

There are several graphical node instances in the scene of this UI (recall that a scene consists of a sequence of nodes). Skipping past several of them, we come to the graphical nodes shown in the following snippet that have an instance variable bound to the selectedDecibels variable in the model:

```
Text {
    layoutX: 18
    layoutY: 69
    textOrigin: TextOrigin.TOP
    fill: Color.web("0x131021")
    content: bind "{%1.0f acModel.selectedDecibels} dB"
    font: Font.font("SansSerif", FontWeight.BOLD, 18)
},
Slider {
    layoutX: 135
    layoutY: 69
    width: 162
    disable: bind acModel.muting
    min: bind acModel.minDecibels
    max: bind acModel.maxDecibels
    value: bind acModel.selectedDecibels with inverse
},
```

As shown in this snippet, the content variable of the Text object is bound to a String. The curly braces in this String contain an expression (that includes the selectedDecibels variable), which is evaluated and becomes part of the String. Look at Figure 1-7 (or check the running application) to see the content value of the Text node displayed to the left of the slider.

■**Note** The %1.0f *string formatting specification* causes the decimal portion of selectedDecibels to be suppressed. See Chapter 4 for details on string formatting and its use for internationalization.

Notice also in the snippet that the value instance variable of the Slider node is bound to the selectedDecibels variable in the model as well, but that it has the keywords with inverse at the end of the expression. This causes the bind to be bidirectional, so in this case when the slider is moved, the selectedDecibels value in the model changes. Conversely, when the selectedDecibels value changes (as a result of changing the genre), the slider moves.

Go ahead and move the slider to demonstrate the effects of the bind expressions in the snippet. The number of decibels displayed at the left of the slider should change as the slider is adjusted.

There are other bound instance variables in Listing 1-3 that we'll point out when we walk through the model class. Before leaving the UI, we'd like to point out some color-related concepts in this example.

Colors and Gradients

The following snippet from Listing 1-3 contains an example of defining a color gradient pattern, as well as defining colors:

```
Rectangle {
    // No need to assign 0 to x and y, because 0 is the default
    width: 320
    height: 45
    fill: LinearGradient {
        // No need to assign 0 to startX and startY, because 0 is default
        endX: 0.0
        endY: 1.0
        stops: [
          Stop {
            color: Color.web("0xAEBBCC")
            offset: 0.0
          },
          Stop {
            color: Color.web("0x6D84A3")
            offset: 1.0
          }
        ]
    }
},
```

If the JavaFX API docs are handy, first take a look at the javafx.scene.shape.Rectangle class and notice that it inherits an instance variable named fill that is of type javafx.scene.paint.Paint. Looking at the JavaFX API docs for the Paint class, you'll see that the Color, LinearGradient, and RadialGradient classes are subclasses of Paint. This means that the fill of any shape can be assigned a color or a gradient.

To create a LinearGradient, as shown in the snippet, you need to define at least two stops, which define the location and color at that location. In this example the offset value of the first stop is 0.0, and the offset value of the second stop is 1.0. These are the values at both extremes of the *unit square*, the result being that the gradient will span the entire node (in this case a Rectangle). The direction of the LinearGradient is controlled by its startX, startY, endX and endY values. In this case, the direction is only vertical because the startY value is 0.0 and the endY value is 1.0, while the startX and endX values are both 0.0.

Note that in the Hello Earthrise example in Listing 1-1, the constant named Color.WHITE was used to represent the color white. In the previous snippet, the web function of the Color class is used to define a color from a hexadecimal value.

The Model Class for the Audio Configuration Example

Take a look at the source code for the AudioConfigModel class in Listing 1-4.

Listing 1-4. *The Source Code for AudioConfigModel.fx*

```
package projavafx.audioconfig.model;

/**
 * The model class that the AudioConfigMain.fx script uses
 */
public class AudioConfigModel {
  /**
   * The minimum audio volume in decibels
   */
  public def minDecibels:Number = 0;

  /**
   * The maximum audio volume in decibels
   */
  public def maxDecibels:Number = 160;

  /**
   * The selected audio volume in decibels
   */
  public var selectedDecibels:Number;

  /**
   * Indicates whether audio is muted
   */
  public var muting:Boolean;  // false is default for Boolean

  /**
   * List of some musical genres
   */
  public def genres = [
    "Chamber",
    "Country",
    "Cowbell",
    "Metal",
    "Polka",
    "Rock"
  ];

  /**
   * Index of the selected genre
   */
  public var selectedGenreIndex:Integer on replace {
    if (genres[selectedGenreIndex] == "Chamber") {
      selectedDecibels = 80;
    }
```

```
      else if (genres[selectedGenreIndex] == "Country") {
        selectedDecibels = 100;
      }
      else if (genres[selectedGenreIndex] == "Cowbell") {
        selectedDecibels = 150;
      }
      else if (genres[selectedGenreIndex] == "Metal") {
        selectedDecibels = 140;
      }
      else if (genres[selectedGenreIndex] == "Polka") {
        selectedDecibels = 120;
      }
      else if (genres[selectedGenreIndex] == "Rock") {
        selectedDecibels = 130;
      }
    };
}
```

Structure of a Minimal JavaFX Class

JavaFX is fully object-oriented, and even supports *mixin inheritance* and *closures* (both of which will be discussed in Chapter 4). The minimum code that you need to create a class in JavaFX is the class declaration. The declaration of a class always includes the class keyword and, as shown in the preceding code snippet, has opening and closing curly braces. There are other JavaFX keywords, such as public and extends, that can modify the class keyword. We'll discuss these in detail in Chapter 4.

Another basic construct of a class declaration is the instance variable. The class in Listing 1-4 defines several instance variables. When an instance of this class is created, space is carved out in memory for each instance variable.

Defining Triggers in the Model Class

Triggers are a construct in JavaFX that helps enable declarative programming. For example, the on replace trigger shown in this snippet executes whenever the value of the selectedGenreIndex variable changes:

```
  public var selectedGenreIndex:Integer on replace {
    if (genres[selectedGenreIndex] == "Chamber") {
      selectedDecibels = 80;
    }
    else if (genres[selectedGenreIndex] == "Country") {
      selectedDecibels = 100;
    }
    else if (genres[selectedGenreIndex] == "Cowbell") {
      selectedDecibels = 150;
    }
    else if (genres[selectedGenreIndex] == "Metal") {
      selectedDecibels = 140;
    }
```

```
    else if (genres[selectedGenreIndex] == "Polka") {
      selectedDecibels = 120;
    }
    else if (genres[selectedGenreIndex] == "Rock") {
      selectedDecibels = 130;
    }
};
```

What causes selectedGenreIndex to change, though? To see the answer to this, we have to revisit the declarative UI script in Listing 1-3. Here's the relevant snippet:

```
SwingComboBox {
    layoutX: 204
    layoutY: 148
    width: 93
    items: bind for (genre in acModel.genres) {
      SwingComboBoxItem {
        text: genre
      }
    }
    selectedIndex: bind acModel.selectedGenreIndex with inverse
}
```

Notice that the selectedIndex variable of the SwingComboBox is bidirectionally bound (recall our with inverse discussion) to the selectedGenreIndex variable in the model. Because of this, whenever the user selects a different genre in the combo box, the on replace trigger is executed. Looking again at the code in the on replace trigger, you'll see that the value of the selectedDecibels variable changes, which as you may recall, is bidirectionally bound to the slider. This is why the slider moves when you select a genre in the combo box. Go ahead and test this out by running the Audio Config program.

We'll point out one more example of binding in this program, and then we'll let you study the code independently to find the rest. In the most recent code snippet, binding is used to populate the SwingComboBox with SwingComboBoxItem instances that each contains a genre. This snippet from the model code in Listing 1-4 contains the sequence to which the SwingComboBoxItem instances are bound:

```
/**
 * List of some musical genres
 */
public var genres = [
  "Chamber",
  "Country",
  "Cowbell",
  "Metal",
  "Polka",
  "Rock"
];
```

The means by which the genres sequence is bound to the SwingComboBox items variable (using the for keyword in the *explicit sequence expression*) will be covered in Chapter 2.

Surveying JavaFX Features

We'd like to close this chapter by surveying many of the features of JavaFX, some of which will be a review for you. We'll do this by describing several of the more commonly used packages and classes in the JavaFX SDK API.:

The javafx.stage package contains:

- The Stage class, which is the top level of the UI containment hierarchy for any JavaFX application, regardless of where it is deployed (such as the desktop, a browser, or a cell phone).

- The Alert class, which has functions that may be called to make alert dialog boxes (such as a confirmation dialog box) appear.

- The Screen class, which represents the displays on the machine in which a JavaFX program is running. This enables you to get information about the screens, such as size and resolution.

The javafx.scene package contains some classes that you'll use often:

- The Scene class is the second level of the UI containment hierarchy for JavaFX applications. It includes all of the UI elements contained in the application. These elements are called graphical nodes, or simply nodes.

- The Node class is the base class of all of the graphical nodes in JavaFX. As you'll see, UI elements such as text, images, media, shapes, and controls (such as text boxes and buttons) are all subclasses of Node. Take a moment to look at the variables and functions in the Node class to appreciate the capabilities provided to all of its subclasses, including bounds calculation and mouse and keyboard event handling.

- The CustomNode class enables you to create your own UI elements.

- The Group class is a subclass of the Node class whose purpose includes grouping nodes together into a single coordinate space and allowing transforms (such as rotate) to be applied to the whole group. Also, attributes of the group that are changed (such as opacity) apply to all of the nodes contained within the group.

Several packages begin with javafx.scene that contain subclasses of Node of various types. For example:

- The javafx.scene.image package contains the Image and ImageView classes, which enables images to be displayed in the Scene. The ImageView class is a subclass of Node.

- The javafx.scene.shape package contains several classes for drawing shapes such as Circle, Rectangle, Line, Polygon, and Arc. The base class of the shapes, named Shape, contains an attribute named fill that enables you to specify a color or gradient with which to fill the shape.

- The javafx.scene.text package contains the Text class for drawing text in the scene. The Font class enables you to specify the font name and size of the text.

- The `javafx.scene.media` package has classes that enable you to play media. The `MediaView` class is a subclass of `Node` that displays the media.

- The `javafx.scene.chart` package has classes that help you easily create *area, bar, bubble, line, pie,* and *scatter* charts. The corresponding UI classes in this package are `AreaChart`, `BarChart`, `BubbleChart`, `LineChart`, `PieChart`, and `ScatterChart`.

Although it doesn't begin with `javafx.scene`, the `javafx.ext.swing` package contains UI controls (such as `SwingCombobox`) that subclass `Node`. Many of the Swing "components" are available in this package, and because these components are actually nodes, any of the transforms and other capabilities of `Node` are available with these classes. Also, any Swing components that aren't in this package may be used in JavaFX by wrapping them with the `wrap` function of the `SwingComponent` class.

Here are the other packages in the JavaFX 1.2 API:

- The `javafx.scene.control` package contains several UI controls, each one having the ability to be skinned and styled via CSS. The `Control`, `Skin`, and `Behavior` classes in this package give you the ability to create your own skinned and CSS-styled controls.

- The `javafx.scene.transform` package enables you to transform nodes (scale, rotate, translate, shear, and affine).

- The `javafx.scene.input` package contains classes such as `MouseEvent` and `KeyEvent` that provide information about these events from within an event handler function such as the `Node` class's `onMouseClicked` event.

- The `javafx.scene.layout` package contains several layout containers, including `HBox`, `VBox`, `ClipView`, `Flow`, `Stack`, and `Tile`. The `Container` class in that package enables writing custom layout classes.

- The `javafx.scene.effect` and `javafx.scene.effect.light` packages contain easy-to-use effects such as `Reflection`, `Glow`, `Shadow`, `BoxBlur` and `Lighting`.

- The `javafx.animation` and `javafx.animation.transition` packages contain time-based interpolations typically used for animation, and convenience classes for common transitions, respectively.

- The `javafx.io.http`, `javafx.data.pull`, and `javafx.data.xml` packages provide a way to communicate with servers via HTTP, JSON, and XML from any JavaFX enabled device (such as the desktop and cell phones).

- The `javafx.data.feed.atom` and `javafx.data.feed.rss` packages contain classes that facilitate reading Atom and RSS feeds, respectively.

- The `javafx.async` package provides support for asynchronous processing. Classes in this package are extended by classes such as `HttpRequest` to provide asynchronous capability.

- The `javafx.io` package has classes that utilize local storage facilities of a machine without requiring that a JavaFX program be signed.

- The `javafx.util` package contains several utility classes such as `Math`, `Sequences`, and `Properties`.

Take a look at the JavaFX API docs again in the light of the information to get a deeper sense for how you can use its capabilities.

Summary

Congratulations, you learned a lot about JavaFX in this chapter, including:

- JavaFX is rich-client Java, and is needed by the software development industry.

- Java SE 6 Update 10 is a technology by Sun that solves the deployment problems that have prevented the Java Runtime Environment (JRE) from being ubiquitous on client machines. Java SE 6 Update 10 also addresses the ease and speed of deploying Java/JavaFX applications.

- Some of the high points of the history of JavaFX.

- Where to find JavaFX resources, including the JavaFX SDK with NetBeans and the API documentation.

- How to compile and run a JavaFX program from the command line, a skill that you'll practice a lot in Chapter 2.

- How to declaratively express a user interface in JavaFX, using object literal syntax.

- How to use several of the language features of JavaFX.

- How to build and run a JavaFX program using NetBeans.

- How to deploy a JavaFX application via Java Web Start.

- How to deploy a JavaFX applet in a browser, with the ability to drag it onto the desktop.

- How to use several of the classes in the JavaFX API.

- How to create a class in JavaFX and use it as a model contains the state of a JavaFX application.

- How to use the bind operator to easily keep the UI in sync with the model.

We also looked at many of the available API packages and classes, and you learned how you can leverage their capabilities.

Now that you have a jump start in JavaFX, you'll begin learning the details of the JavaFX language in Chapter 2. The examples in that chapter may be easily compiled and run using the `javafxc` and `javafx` command-line tools that you learned how to use earlier in this chapter.

Resources

For some background information on JavaFX, you can consult the following resources:

- *This book's code examples*: The Source Code/Download section at the Apress web site (`www.apress.com`)

- *Java Posse #163: Newscast for February 8, 2008*: This is a podcast of a Java Posse interview with Josh Marinacci and Richard Bair on the subject of JavaFX. The URL is `www.javaposse.com/index.php?post_id=305735`.

- *"Mind-Bendingly Cool Innovation"*: This article contains an interview with Chris Oliver, the founder of JavaFX. The URL is `http://research.sun.com/minds/2008-1202/`.

- *"Congratulations to the JavaFX Script Compiler Team—The Elephant Is Through the Door"*: A blog post by one of this book's authors, Jim Weaver, that congratulated the JavaFX compiler team for reaching a tipping point in the project. The URL is `http://learnjavafx.typepad.com/weblog/2007/12/congratulations.html`.

- *"Development and Deployment of Java Web Apps (Applets and Java Web Start Applications) for JavaSE 6u10"*: This set of web pages from Sun discusses the features of Java SE 6 Update 10 and how to use them. The URL is `http://java.sun.com/javase/6/docs/technotes/guides/jweb/index.html`.

- *Sun's JavaFX.com site*: This is a resource provided by Sun that provides examples of and downloadable tools for JavaFX. The URL is `www.javafx.com`.

- *Sun Developer Network's JavaFX Developer Home web site*: Contains JavaFX developer resources. The URL is `http://java.sun.com/javafx/`.

- *Jim Weaver's JavaFX Blog*: A blog, started in October 2007, whose stated purpose is to help the reader become a "JavaFXpert." The URL is `http://javafxpert.com`.

- *JavaFX Downloads page*: The Sun web page where you can download the JavaFX SDK and related tools. The URL is `http://javafx.com/downloads`.

- *JavaFX plug-in for Eclipse from Sun's Project Kenai*: The URL is `http://kenai.com/projects/eplugin`.

- *JavaFX plug-in for Eclipse from Exadel*: The URL for Exadel is `http://exadel.com`.

- *JFXBuilder*: A preview release of a visual designer tool for JavaFX. The URL is `www.reportmill.com/jfx/`.

CHAPTER 2

■ ■ ■

Taking a Closer Look at the JavaFX Script Language

A journey of a thousand leagues starts from where your feet stand.

—Lao Tzu

In Chapter 1, we introduced you to the JavaFX platform. You downloaded the JavaFX SDK or the JavaFX Plug-in for NetBeans or Eclipse. You wrote and ran your first JavaFX GUI script. You witnessed the simplicity and expressiveness of the JavaFX Script language and the power and versatility of the JavaFX APIs.

In the rest of this book, we will cover the JavaFX platform in more detail. We will split our coverage between the JavaFX Script programming language features and the JavaFX APIs that are built on top of the JavaFX Script programming language. Chapters 2 and 4 are dedicated to the JavaFX Script programming language. In the other chapters we teach you the various JavaFX APIs. This "split-and-intersperse" strategy allows us to keep the flow of the entire book at a fast pace to make it an engaging read while covering the lower-level language features at a slower pace.

■**Note** Although JavaFX Script is a programming language for the Java platform, our coverage does not require any prior Java programming experience. Because of the close relationship between JavaFX Script and Java, it is sometimes inevitable that we will use certain Java concepts to explain the corresponding JavaFX Script concepts. We will fully explain these Java concepts when the need arises.

An Overview of JavaFX Script

The JavaFX Script programming language is the foundation of the JavaFX platform. It has the following characteristics:

- It is an object-oriented language. It supports classes, instance variables, instance functions, and inheritance.

- It is a functional language. Functions are first-class entities that can be assigned to variables, passed in, and returned from functions.

- It is an expression language. All executable code in JavaFX consists of expressions.

- It supports a declarative style suitable for GUI programming. Its object literal syntax and sequence syntax make describing GUIs easy.

- It supports data binding. It allows for easy separation of GUI views and models, and gives rise to "the way of JavaFX."

- It is a statically typed, compiled language with basic type inference capabilities. It compiles source code into Java classes.

- It can leverage the vast number of Java libraries. JavaFX classes can extend Java classes and interfaces, and JavaFX code can instantiate Java objects and call Java methods.

We will use JavaFX Script data types as guideposts in our coverage of the programming language. There are four kinds of data types in JavaFX Script: primitive, sequence, class, and function types. We concentrate on primitive and sequence types in Chapter 2. We deal with function and class types in Chapter 4. Chapter 4 will also focus on advanced features like reflection and Java interoperability.

Understanding Variables, Values, and Their Types

The simplest construct in JavaFX Script is the *variable*. A variable can be assigned *values*. Values can be *literals* or *expressions*. Each variable has a *declared type*. Each value has a *runtime type*. An assignment is valid only if the runtime type of the value is compatible with the declared type of the variable.

As you can see in Listing 2-1, variable declarations are introduced by the var keyword, followed by the name of the variable, an optional type specifier, and an optional initializer, and are terminated by a semicolon (;).

Listing 2-1. *Variable Declarations*

```
var b: Boolean = true;
var i: Integer = 1024;
var n: Number = 3.14;
var str: String = "Hello, World";
var dur: Duration = 60s;
```

In Listing 2-1, we declare five variables:

- The variable b is of type Boolean and is initialized to the literal value true.

- The variable i is of type Integer and is initialized to the literal value 1024.

- The variable n is of type Number and is initialized to the literal value 3.14.

- The variable str is of type String and is initialized to the literal value "Hello, World".

- The variable dur is of type Duration and is initialized to the literal value 60s, meaning 60 seconds.

Understanding Variable Names

JavaFX Script variable names follow the JavaFX Script *identifier* syntax. A JavaFX Script identifier starts with a letter, followed by letters, digits, or both. For the purpose of forming JavaFX Script identifiers, letters include the uppercase and lowercase ASCII letters and other Unicode letters, the underscore (_), and the dollar character ($) and other currency characters. Digits include digits 0 through 9 and other Unicode digits.

The following are valid JavaFX Script identifiers:

```
i
x2
Builtins
toString
_tmp$getter
```

The following are invalid JavaFX Script identifiers:

```
2x
package-info
Hello, World
```

JavaFX Script identifiers are case sensitive. Therefore count, Count, and COUNT are considered three distinct identifiers.

Understanding Variable Types

JavaFX Script variables may be declared with an explicit type, as we did in Listing 2-1. The type of a variable follows the variable name and is separated from the name by a colon (:). The colon is not considered a part of the variable name or a part of the type name. The type of a variable dictates the kind of values that can be assigned to the variable. For example, it is illegal to assign a String value to an Integer variable.

JavaFX Script has a *type inference* facility that allows you to declare a variable without an explicit type. The JavaFX Script compiler will infer the variable's type from the initializer in the declaration or, if no initializer is given in the declaration, the first subsequent assignment.

Therefore, you can safely rewrite the variable declarations from Listing 2-1 as shown in Listing 2-2.

Listing 2-2. *Variable Declarations with Inferred Types*

```
var b = true;
var i = 1024;
var n = 3.14;
var str = "Hello, World";
var dur = 60s;
```

JavaFX Script's type system consists of various kinds of types. These include the primitive, sequence, function, and class types. You will learn about them in the next few sections and in Chapter 4.

Understanding the Primitive Types

JavaFX Script intrinsically understands a few data types. These are called the *primitive types*. You have already met some of them in the previous section: Boolean, Integer, Number, String, and Duration. These five types were present since JavaFX 1.0. JavaFX 1.1 introduced the primitive types Character, Byte, Short, Long, Float, and Double. These additional types allow JavaFX Script programs to integrate more smoothly with class libraries written in Java. You can also write programs that consume less memory by using the smaller-sized data types. However, for most JavaFX Script programs, the five primitive types from JavaFX 1.0 are sufficient.

The primitive types share some common characteristics:

- Each primitive type—except the three "small" types, Character, Byte, and Short—has its own literal syntax so that you can put values directly into a JavaFX Script program.

- Each primitive type has a default value that a variable of the type gets if it is declared without an initializer.

- Each primitive type supports a set of operations that are appropriate for the type.

- Each primitive type is backed by a class that provides more capabilities for working with variables of the type.

■**Caution** If you are familiar with the Java programming language, you should recognize that the concept of primitive types in JavaFX Script is different from that in Java. For example, String is a primitive type in JavaFX Script but is a reference type in Java, and Java primitive types are not backed by classes.

Understanding the Boolean Type

The Boolean type has two possible values: true and false. You can use a Boolean variable to denote a condition in a JavaFX Script program. Boolean values are used in conditional and looping expressions.

Boolean Literals and the Default Value

To specify an explicit Boolean value in JavaFX Script, you use the literals true and false. The default value of a Boolean variable is false.

Boolean Operators

JavaFX Script's Boolean operators allow you to build new Boolean values from existing ones.

The not operator is a unary operator. Its operand must evaluate to a Boolean value, and it negates its operand.

The and and or operators are binary infix operators. An infix operator is an operator that appears between its operands. Both operands must evaluate to Boolean values. The and operator produces true if both operands are true, and false otherwise; the or operator produces true if at least one operand is true, and false otherwise. Both operators perform their evaluation in a short-circuit fashion. If the first operand of an and expression is false, then the and expression's value will be false and the second operand is not evaluated. Similarly, if the first operand of an or expression is true, then the or expression's value will be true and the second operand is not evaluated.

The Backing Class of the Boolean Type

The Boolean type is backed by the Java class java.lang.Boolean. This means that you can call any Java methods, including static methods, in java.lang.Boolean on a JavaFX Script Boolean value.

Since java.lang.Boolean is a small class and most of its methods are geared toward supporting Java functionality, the fact that it is the backing class of the JavaFX Script Boolean type is rarely used.

In Listing 2-3, you can see JavaFX Script Boolean variables at work.

Listing 2-3. *Boolean Variables at Work*

```
var a = true;
var b = false;

println("a = {a}");
println("b = {b}");

println("not a = {not a}");
println("not b = {not b}");

println("a and a = {a and a}");
println("a and b = {a and b}");
println("b and a = {b and a}");
println("b and b = {b and b}");

println("a or a = {a or a}");
println("a or b = {a or b}");
println("b or a = {b or a}");
println("b or b = {b or b}");
```

In Listing 2-3, we used two features of JavaFX Script that we have not covered in detail so far. The `println()` function prints its argument to the console. It is a built-in function.

The curly braces embedded in a `String` allow us to put the `String` representation of an arbitrary JavaFX Script expression in a `String`. We will have more to say about them in the section "Understanding the String Type," later in this chapter.

Understanding the Integer Type

The `Integer` type represents 32-bit signed integral values, with valid values ranging from -2147483648 to 2147483647. You can use `Integer` values as counters and sequence indexes.

Integer Literals and the Default Value

JavaFX supports three forms of *integral type literals. Decimal literals* consist of a leading nonzero decimal digit (1 through 9) followed by a series of decimal digits (0 through 9). *Octal literals* consist of a leading digit zero (0) followed by a series of octal digits (0 through 7). *Hexadecimal literals* consist of a leading digit zero (0) followed by the character x or X, and then a series of hexadecimal digits (0 through 9, a through f, and A through F). The default value of an `Integer` variable is 0.

Here are some examples of integral type literals:

```
2009
03731
0x07d9
0X07D9
```

An integral type literal whose value falls within the range of the `Integer` type is an `Integer` literal. It has an inferred type of `Integer`. An integral type literal can also be a `Long` literal, as you'll see shortly.

■**Caution** When you're initializing or assigning to an `Integer` variable, the integral type literal that you use must be an `Integer` literal. Using an integral type literal outside the range of the `Integer` type will cause a compilation error. Catching errors early is one of the benefits of a compiled language.

Arithmetic Operators

JavaFX Script's arithmetic operators operate on `Character`, `Byte`, `Short`, `Integer`, and `Long` values as well as `Number`, `Float`, `Double`, and `Duration` values. These operators are the addition (+), subtraction (-), multiplication (*), division (/), and modulo (mod) operators. Notice that not all arithmetic operations are meaningful for `Duration` values. For example, you cannot multiply two `Duration` values.

When applied to `Integer` operands, these operators always produce `Integer` values. They associate from left to right. The *, /, and mod operators have higher precedence over the + and - operators. The +, -, and * operators are capable of overflowing the legal limits of the `Integer` type. In such cases JavaFX Script will silently produce an inaccurate result. Dividing an `Integer` value by 0 causes an exception to be thrown at runtime. You will learn more about exceptions in Chapter 4.

JavaFX Script supports the preincrement operator (++i), the post-increment operator (i++), the predecrement operator (--i), and the postdecrement operator (i--). JavaFX Script also supports the negation operator (-x).

The Backing Class of the Integer Type

The Integer type is backed by the Java class java.lang.Integer. This means that you can call any Java methods, including static methods in java.lang.Integer, on a JavaFX Script Integer value.

Again, since most methods of java.lang.Integer are geared toward supporting Java functionality, you will rarely call these methods on JavaFX Script Integer values.

Listing 2-4 shows JavaFX Script Integer variables at work.

Listing 2-4. *Integer Variables at Work*

```
var i = 1024;
var j = 2048;
var k = 15625;

println("i = {i}");
println("j = {j}");
println("k = {k}");

println("i + j = {i + j}");
println("i - j = {i - j}");
println("i * k = {i * k}");
println("k / i = {k / i}");
println("k mod j = {k mod j}");

var max = java.lang.Integer.MAX_VALUE;
var min = java.lang.Integer.MIN_VALUE;

println("max = {max}");
println("min = {min}");

println("max + 1 will overflow to {max + 1}");
println("min - 1 will overflow to {min - 1}");
println("max * min will overflow to {max * min}");

println("i = {i}, ++i = {++i}");
println("j = {j}, --j = {--j}");
println("k = {k}, k++ = {k++}");
println("k = {k}, k-- = {k--}");
```

In Listing 2-4, we used a JavaFX Script feature that allows us to access Java classes and their members directly. We accessed the static fields MAX_VALUE and MIN_VALUE of the Java class java.lang.Integer directly. You will learn how to access Java programming language features from JavaFX Script in Chapter 4.

Understanding the Character Type

The Character type represents 16-bit unsigned character values, with valid values in the range from 0 to 65535. You can use Character values to represent Unicode characters.

Sources of Character Values and the Default Value

JavaFX Script does not support Character literals. The main source of Character values is from Java code that contains fields and returns values of the Java char type or the java.lang. Character wrapper type. You can assign Integer literals that fall within the Character range to Character type variables. The default value of a Character variable is 0.

You can also assign values of other numeric types to variables of the Character type. However, doing so will result in a loss of precision and a compilation warning will be generated.

Here are some examples:

```
var ch: Character = 100;
println("ch={ch}.");
```

This will print ch=d to the console since 100 is the Unicode value, as well as the ASCII value, of the character d.

■**Caution** If you are familiar with Java, you might be tempted to try to assign 'd' to a variable of Character type. This will generate a compilation error because 'd' is a String value in JavaFX Script and cannot be assigned to a Character variable.

Arithmetic Operations

Character values may participate in arithmetic operations. The type of the result of an arithmetic operation involving a Character value depends on the type of the other operand:

- It is Integer if the other operand is a Character, Byte, Short, or Integer value.

- It is Long if the other operand is a Long value.

- It is Float if the other operand is a Float value.

- It is Double if the other operand is a Double value.

The Backing Class of the Character Type

The Character type is backed by the Java class java.lang.Character. This means that you can call any Java methods, including static methods in java.lang.Character, on a JavaFX Script Character value. Many of the methods are geared toward supporting Java functionality, and will rarely be called from JavaFX Script.

Understanding the Byte, Short, and Long Types

The Byte type represents 8-bit signed integer values, with valid values ranging from -128 to 127. The Short type represents 16-bit signed integer values, with valid values ranging from -32768 to 32767. The Long type represents 64-bit signed integer values, with valid values ranging from -2^{63} to 2^{63}-1.

Sources of Byte and Short Values, Long Literals, and the Default Values

JavaFX Script does not support Byte or Short literals. The main source of values of Byte and Short types is from Java code that contains fields and returns values of the corresponding Java primitive types, byte and short, and their wrapper types, java.lang.Byte and java.lang.Short. You can assign integral type literals that fall within their range to Byte or Short variables.

An integral type literal whose value falls outside the range of the Integer type but within the range of the Long type is a Long literal. It has an inferred type of Long. You can assign any Integer or Long literals to Long variables.

■**Caution** An integral type literal whose value falls outside the range of the Long type will generate a compilation error.

The default values of Byte, Short, or Long variables are 0.

You can also assign values of other numeric types to variables of Byte, Short, or Long types. A compilation warning is generated if you are assigning a wider typed value to a narrower typed variable, such as assigning an Integer value to a Short variable.

Arithmetic Operations

Values of Byte, Short, or Long types may participate in arithmetic operations with other numeric values. The general rules governing the type of the result of arithmetic operations of numeric values are the same as those in the Java programming language:

- If one of the operands is a Double value, the result is a Double value.

- Otherwise, if one of the operands is a Float value, the result is a Float value.

- Otherwise, if one of the operands is a Long value, the result is a long value.

- Otherwise, the result is an Integer value.

The Backing Classes of the Byte, Short, and Long Types

The Byte, Short, and Long types are backed by the Java classes java.lang.Byte, java.lang.Short, and java.lang.Long, respectively. This means that you can call any Java methods, including static methods in their backing classes on JavaFX Script Byte, Short, or Long values.

Understanding the Number Type

The Number type represents 32-bit floating-point numeric values, with valid absolute values between approximately 1.4×10^{-45} and 3.40×10^{38}. Not every real number can be represented by a floating-point number. Therefore, floating-point arithmetic is only an approximation.

■**Caution** If you are familiar with the Java programming language, notice that the JavaFX Script Number type is distinct from the `java.lang.Number` abstract class in Java. Note also that the meaning of the JavaFX Script Number type changed between JavaFX 1.0 and JavaFX 1.1. Whereas in JavaFX 1.0, Number represented 64-bit floating-point values backed by `java.lang.Double`, in JavaFX 1.1 it represents 32-bit floating-point values backed by `java.lang.Float`.

Number Literals and the Default Value

JavaFX Script supports two forms of *floating-point type literals*. In the *decimal notation*, you specify a floating-point type literal as an integral part followed by the decimal point (.) and then the fractional part. Either the integral part or the fractional part, but not both, may be omitted. In the *scientific notation*, you specify a floating-point type literal as a magnitude followed by the letter E or e and then an exponent. The magnitude may be an integral number or a decimal number. The exponent may be a positive or a negative integer. The default value for a Number variable is 0.0.

The following are some examples of floating-point type literals:

```
3.14
2.
.75
3e8
1.380E-23
```

A floating-point type literal whose value falls within the range of the Number type is a Number literal. It has an inferred type of Number. A floating-point type literal can also be a Double literal, as you will see shortly.

Arithmetic Operations

All the arithmetic operators you learned in the section "Understanding the Integer Type" apply to the Number type. Moreover, you can use the binary arithmetic operators on mixed Integer and Number values producing Number values. In such calculations, the Integer value is first promoted to a Number value before the arithmetic operation is performed.

Arithmetic operations on Number values may overflow the legal limits of the Number type and become positive infinity or negative infinity. Certain operations may produce results so small that they underflow the legal limits of the Number type and become zero (0.0). Certain invalid expressions, such as dividing infinity by infinity, produces a NaN value (Not a Number).

The Backing Class of the Number Type

The Number type is backed by the Java class java.lang.Float. This means that you can call any Java methods, including static methods, in java.lang.Float on a JavaFX Script Number value.

You can use the isInfinite() and isNaN() methods of java.lang.Float to test whether a Number value is infinity or a NaN.

Listing 2-5 shows JavaFX Script Number variables at work.

Listing 2-5. *Number Variables at Work*

```
var x = 3.14159;
var y = 2.71828;

println("x = {x}");
println("y = {y}");

println("x + y = {x + y}");
println("x - y = {x - y}");
println("x * y = {x * y}");
println("x / y = {x / y}");
println("x mod y = {x mod y}");

var max = java.lang.Float.MAX_VALUE;
var min = java.lang.Float.MIN_VALUE;

println("max = {max}");
println("min = {min}");

println("max * 2 will overflow to {max * 2}");
println("min / 2 will underflow to {min / 2}");

var inf = max * max;

println("inf = {inf}");
println("inf.isInfinite() = {inf.isInfinite()}");
println("inf / inf = {inf / inf}");

var nan = inf / inf;

println("nan = {nan}");
println("nan.isNaN() = {nan.isNaN()}");
```

Understanding the Float and Double Types

In JavaFX 1.1, the Float type is synonymous with the Number type. They have the same behavior under all circumstances. The Double type represents 64-bit floating-point numeric values, with valid absolute values between approximately 4.9×10^{-324} and 1.79×10^{308}.

Double Literals and the Default Value

A floating-point type literal whose value falls outside the range of the Float type but within the range of the Double type is a Double literal. It has an inferred type of Double. You can assign any Number (Float) or Double literals to Double variables.

The Backing Class of the Double Type

The Double type is backed by the Java class java.lang.Double. This means that you can call any Java methods, including static methods, in java.lang.Double on a JavaFX Script Double value.

Understanding the String Type

The String type represents a sequence of Unicode characters. You have seen JavaFX Script String values in use in previous examples.

String Literals and the Default Value

JavaFX Script supports String literals enclosed in double-quote (") or single-quote (') characters. The two notations are interchangeable with two exceptions:

- The double-quote character itself can appear unescaped in a single-quoted string but must be escaped by a backslash (\) prefix in a double-quoted string.

- The single-quote character itself can appear unescaped in a double-quoted string but must be escaped by a backslash prefix in a single-quoted string.

JavaFX Script does not support multi-line strings: String literals may not span multiple lines. The JavaFX Script compiler will automatically merge adjacent String literals and String expressions into one at compile time.

Unescaped open and close brace characters ({, }) have special meaning in String literals. They are used to form String expressions, which we will cover in the upcoming section.

The backslash character is an escape character. JavaFX Script understands the following escape sequences in its String literals:

- \udddd: A Unicode character, with each d a hexadecimal digit

- \ddd: An octal character, with each d an octal digit

- \b: Backspace (\u0008)

- \f: Form feed (\u000C)

- \n: Newline (\u000A)

- \r: Return (\u000D)

- \t: Tab (\u0009)

- \': Single quote
- \": Double quote
- \{: Open brace
- \}: Close brace

The default value of a String variable is "" (the empty string).
Here are some examples of String literals:

```
"Hello, World."
"It's raining."
'The string "abc" has three characters'
```

String Expressions

You can include a string representation of any JavaFX Script expression in a JavaFX Script string by forming *string expressions*. A string expression is formed by adding brace-delimited segments into a string literal, with each brace-delimited segment containing a JavaFX Script expression.

You have seen string expressions at work in Listings 2-3, 2-4, and 2-5.

The Backing Class of the String Type

The String type is backed by the Java class java.lang.String. This means that you can call any Java methods, including static methods, in java.lang.String on a JavaFX Script String value.

The java.lang.String class is a fairly extensive class, and you can take advantage of many of its methods in your JavaFX Script code. Here's a sampling of the methods that are of interest to JavaFX Script programmers:

- length()
- startsWith(prefix)
- startsWith(prefix, offset)
- endsWith(suffix)
- indexOf(str)
- indexOf(str, fromIndex)
- lastIndexOf(str)
- lastIndexOf(str, fromIndex)
- substring(beginIndex)
- substring(beginIndex, endIndex)
- matches(regex)
- contains(s)
- replaceFirst(regex, replacement)
- replaceAll(regex, replacement)

- replace(target, replacement)
- toLowerCase()
- toUpperCase()
- trim()

These methods do what their names suggest. Each character in a string has an index, which is zero based. Thus the first character has index 0, the second character has index 1, and so forth. JavaFX Script strings are immutable. None of the methods modify the string on which they are called. Some of the methods, such as trim(), return a new string. Therefore, if the variable str has the value " Hello ", calling str.trim() will not change what's stored in the str variable. To capture the trimmed string, you must assign the return value of the call to a variable.

In Listing 2-6, you can see JavaFX Script String variables at work.

Listing 2-6. *String Variables at Work*

```
var greeting = "Hello, World.";

println("greeting = {greeting}");
println("greeting.length() = {greeting.length()}");
println("greeting.startsWith(\"H\") = {greeting.startsWith("H")}");
println("greeting.endsWith(\".\") = {greeting.endsWith(".")}");
println("greeting.indexof(\",\") = {greeting.indexOf(",")}");
println("greeting.substring(3, 5) = {greeting.substring(3, 5)}");
println("greeting.toUpperCase() = {greeting.toUpperCase()}");
println("greeting.toLowerCase() = {greeting.toLowerCase()}");

var multiLine = "To construct a multi-line string in JavaFX Script,\n"
                "you can use its string litereal and string expression\n"
                "concatenation capabilities.";
println(multiLine);

var str = "abcabc";
println("str = {str}");
println("str.indexOf('b') = {str.indexOf('b')}");
println("str.lastIndexOf('b') = {str.lastIndexOf('b')}");
println("str.contains('cab') = {str.contains('cab')}");
println("str.replaceFirst('a', 'x') = {str.replaceFirst('a', 'x')}");
println("str.replaceAll('a', 'x') = {str.replaceAll('a', 'x')}");
```

One thing from Listing 2-6 that bears mentioning is that in the embedded expression region of a string expression, you do not need to escape the single-quote or double-quote characters even if they are the same ones used in the surrounding string expression.

Understanding the Duration Type

The Duration type represents an amount of time. Duration values are used in JavaFX's key-frame animation facilities. We will cover animation in Chapter 3.

Duration Literals and the Default Value

Duration literals are formed by appending a time unit to an integer or decimal literal. JavaFX Script understands four time units: hour (h), minute (m), second (s), and millisecond (ms). The default value of a Duration variable is 0.0ms.

The following are some examples of Duration literals:

```
0.1h
2m
30s
1000ms
```

Arithmetic Operations Involving Durations

By their nature, Duration values can enter into arithmetic operations. JavaFX Script supports adding two Duration values, subtracting one Duration value from another, multiplying a Duration value by a numeric value, and dividing a Duration value by a numeric value. The results of these operations are Duration values. JavaFX 1.1 added support for dividing one Duration value by another Duration value, resulting in a Number value. The negation operator also applies to Duration values.

The Backing Class of the Duration Type

Unlike the other four primitive types, which are backed by Java classes, the Duration type is backed by a JavaFX Script class javafx.lang.Duration. Here are instance functions of the javafx.lang.Duration class that should be of interest to you:

- toMillis()

- toSeconds()

- toMinutes()

- toHours()

- valueOf(ms)

Internally, JavaFX Script keeps track of Duration values in terms of numbers of milliseconds since midnight Greenwich Mean Time (GMT) January 1, 1970. The first four functions convert a Duration to the specified unit and return a Number.

The valueOf(ms) function is a factory function and should be called on the Duration class instead of on any Duration values. It returns a newly constructed Duration value that represents the supplied number of milliseconds.

■**Note** We will show you the usage of JavaFX Script classes in much more detail in the "Understanding Object Literals" section later in this chapter. We will teach you how to write JavaFX Script classes in Chapter 4.

Listing 2-7 shows the JavaFX Script Duration variables at work.

Listing 2-7. *Duration Variables at Work*

```
var oneHour = 1h;
var oneMinute = 1m;
var oneSecond = 1s;
var oneMillisecond = 1ms;

println("oneHour = {oneHour}");
println("oneMinute = {oneMinute}");
println("oneSecond = {oneSecond}");
println("oneMillisecond = {oneMillisecond}");

println("oneHour + 30 * oneMinute = {oneHour + 30 * oneMinute}");
println("oneMinute - 20 * oneSecond = {oneMinute - 20 * oneSecond}");
println("oneSecond / 2 = {oneSecond / 2}");
println("-oneMillisecond = {-oneMillisecond}");

println("oneHour.toHours() = {oneHour.toHours()}");
println("oneHour.toMinutes() = {oneHour.toMinutes()}");
println("oneMinute.toSeconds() = {oneMinute.toSeconds()}");
println("oneSecond.toMillis() = {oneSecond.toMillis()}");

var now = Duration.valueOf(1229923309734.0);
println("now = {now}");
```

Working with Sequences

In the previous section, you learned about JavaFX Script primitive types. Primitive types represent indivisible pieces of data. However, sometimes you need to aggregate individual data together and manipulate that data as a unit. JavaFX Script provides two mechanisms for data aggregation. First, you can group dissimilar data into classes, create objects of classes, and manipulate the objects in your code. Second, you can group similar data into a construct called a sequence, and manipulate the sequence and its values in your code.

You will learn how to create objects of existing classes in the "Understanding Object Literals" section later in this chapter. You will learn how to create classes in Chapter 4.

In this section, we will teach you the JavaFX Script sequence concept, how to create sequences, and how to manipulate sequences.

Understanding Sequence Types

A JavaFX Script *sequence* represents an ordered list of data of the same type. Each individual piece of data in a sequence is an *element* of the sequence. The type of elements of a sequence is called the sequence's *element type*. The type of a sequence is written as its element type followed by a pair of square brackets ([ ]).

Here are some examples of sequences of primitive types:

```
var booleans: Boolean[] = [true, false, true, true, false];
var integers: Integer[] = [1, 3, 5, 7, 9];
var numbers: Number[] = [3.14159, 2.71828];
var strings: String[] = ["hello", "hello again", "goodbye"];
var durations: Duration[] = [0.5m, 1.0m, 1.5m, 2.0m];
```

In these examples, the variables are of sequence types. With the help of JavaFX Script's type inference facility, you can omit the data types:

```
var booleans = [true, false, true, true, false];
var integers = [1, 3, 5, 7, 9];
var numbers = [3.14159, 2.71828];
var strings = ["hello", "hello again", "goodbye"];
var durations = [0.5m, 1.0m, 1.5m, 2.0m];
```

The element type of a sequence can be one of the primitive types, a class type, or a function type. We will cover class types and function types in detail in Chapter 4. In this section, we will use one small example of the class type to illustrate the interaction between sequence types and class types. We will use the class

```
class Point {
  var x: Number;
  var y: Number;
}
```

for the rest of this section. This defines a class type Point. You can declare a variable of type Point (called an object) and initialize it with an object literal as follows:

```
var p: Point = Point { x: 3.0, y: 4.0 };
```

Once again, you can omit the type specifier for the variable and let JavaFX Script's type inference facility deduce the type:

```
var p = Point { x: 5.0, y: 12.0 };
```

You can also declare a variable of a class type without giving it an initializer:

```
var p: Point;
```

In this case, the variable will get the default value for class types: null.

You are now ready to declare a variable of type Point[], a sequence of Point objects:

```
var points: Point[] = [Point {x: 3.0, y: 4.0}, Point {x: 5.0, y: 12.0}];
```

With the help of type inference, you can omit the type specifier:

```
var points = [Point {x: 3.0, y: 4.0}, Point {x: 5.0, y: 12.0}];
```

As is the case with primitive types, if a variable is declared to be of a sequence type but without an explicit initializer, then it gets the default value of the sequence type. The default value of a sequence type is a sequence with zero elements in it. This sequence is called the *empty sequence*.

Constructing Sequences Using Explicit Sequence Expressions

In the previous section, all variables of sequence types are initialized with explicit sequence expressions. An *explicit sequence expression* is constructed by enclosing its elements within a pair of brackets. The elements in an explicit sequence expression are separated by commas. The comma may be omitted after an element if it is an object literal or other expression that ends with a closing brace.

Thus, the declaration

```
var points = [Point {x: 3.0, y: 4.0}, Point {x: 5.0, y: 12.0}];
```

can be written as

```
var points = [
  Point {x: 3.0, y: 4.0}
  Point {x: 5.0, y: 12.0}
];
```

You cannot create a sequence with "holes" in it. In other words, every element in a sequence must be a non-null value of the element type. Since primitive values are always non-null, this rule applies only to sequences of nonprimitive types.

The empty sequence can be constructed with the [ ] expression.

Constructing Numeric Sequences Using Range Expressions

When creating numeric sequences—that is, sequences of Integer or Number values—you can use range expressions in addition to explicit sequence expressions. A JavaFX Script *range expression* allows you to create an arithmetic progression from a start value, an end value, and an optional step value. The step value defaults to 1 or 1.0, depending on whether the element type is Integer or Number. Here are a few examples:

```
var oneToTen = [1..10];
var oneToTenOdd = [1..10 step 2];
var ticks = [3.0 .. 5.0 step 0.5];
var decreasing = [10..1 step -1];
```

■**Tip** JavaFX Script represents range expressions internally in an efficient manner. When you use a range expression like [0..1000000], JavaFX Script will not actually build a sequence with a million elements and therefore will not take up megabytes of memory.

In the previous range expressions, the start value and the end value are separated with two dots (..), and the step value, if present, is separated from the end value with `step`. This notation produces sequences that may include the end value itself. To obtain a sequence that does not include the end value, two dots and a less-than sign (..<) may be places between the start value and the end value. Here is an example of this form of range expression:

```
var oneToNine = [1 ..< 10];
```

■**Caution** If the step value is negative while the end value is greater than the start value, or if the step value is positive while the end value is less than the start value, the range expression produces an empty sequence. This may happen when you try to construct a decreasing sequence, one in which the end value is less than the start value, but you fail to specify a negative step value. For example, the range expression [10..1] will produce an empty sequence. The JavaFX Script compiler will generate a warning for such expressions.

In Listing 2-8, you can see explicit sequence expressions and range expressions at work.

Listing 2-8. *Constructing Sequences with Explicit Sequence Expressions and Range Expressions*

```
var booleans = [true, false, true, true, false];
var integers = [1, 3, 5, 7, 9];
var numbers = [3.14159, 2.71828];
var strings = ["hello", "hello again", "goodbye"];
var durations = [0.5m, 1.0m, 1.5m, 2.0m];

print("booleans = "); println(booleans);
print("integers = "); println(integers);
print("numbers = "); println(numbers);
print("strings = "); println(strings);
print("durations = "); println(durations);

class Point {
  var x: Number;
  var y: Number;
}

var points = [Point {x: 3.0, y: 4.0}, Point {x: 5.0, y: 12.0}];

print("points = "); println(points);
```

```
integers = [1, 3, 5, 7, 9];
print("integers = "); println(integers);

var oneToTen = [1..10];
var oneToTenOdd = [1..10 step 2];
var ticks = [3.0 .. 5.0 step 0.5];
var decreasing = [10..1 step -1];
var oneToNine = [1 ..< 10];

print("oneToTen = "); println(oneToTen);
print("oneToTenOdd = "); println(oneToTenOdd);
print("ticks = "); println(ticks);
print("decreasing = "); println(decreasing);
print("oneToNine = "); println(oneToNine);

print("[10..1] = "); println([10..1]);
```

In Listing 2-8, we used another JavaFX Script built-in function, print(). The print() function differs from , println() in that it does not append a newline at the end of its output.

■**Note** In JavaFX 1.0, 1.1, and 1.2, converting a sequence to a string via "{seq}" will produce a string without the surrounding brackets and separators between elements. For example, println("{[1, 2, 3]}") prints 123, while println([1, 2, 3]) prints [1, 2, 3].

Manipulating Sequences

JavaFX Script provides a rich set of built-in facilities for you to easily manipulate sequences:

- You can access the size of a sequence, a single element of a sequence, a slice or a segment of consecutive elements of a sequence, or a subset of nonconsecutive elements that satisfy certain criteria.

- You can reverse a sequence.

- You can insert an element into a sequence.

- You can insert another sequence into a sequence.

- You can delete an element from a sequence.

- You can delete a slice from a sequence.

Each element in a sequence has an index and sequence indexes are zero-based. The first element has index 0, the second element has index 1, and so on.

Accessing the Size of a Sequence

You can use the `sizeof` operator to access the size of a sequence. The size of a sequence is the number of elements in the sequence. The size of an empty sequence is zero. In the following example:

```
var integers = [1, 3, 5, 7, 9];
var s = sizeof integers;
```

the value of s would be 5.

Note Although the `sizeof` operator is primarily used with sequences, you can use it with nonsequence variables and values. A primitive value always has size 1. A variable of class type has size 1 if it holds an object of the class, and it has size 0 if it is `null`.

Accessing an Element in a Sequence

To access a single element of a sequence, you use the *sequence indexing* expression. It consists of the sequence name or another expression that evaluates to a sequence followed by a pair of brackets that encloses the index of the element. Here are some examples:

```
var integers = [1, 3, 5, 7, 9];
var a = integers[0];
var b = integers[4];
var c = integers[-1];
var d = integers[5];
```

If the index is within the range between zero and one less than the size of the sequence, the appropriate element will be produced. If the index is outside of that range, the default value of the element type of the sequence will be produced. Thus in this example, a would be 1, b would be 9, and both c and d would be 0, the default value for the Integer type.

Note Although indexing a variable of sequence type is the most common use of sequence indexing expressions, the JavaFX Script syntax allows you to index any expression that evaluates to a sequence. For example, `[1, 3, 5, 7, 9][2]` is a valid sequence indexing expression. Its value is 5. This is also the case for the sequence slice expression and the sequence select expression that you will learn in the next two sections.

Accessing a Slice of a Sequence

To access a consecutive subset of elements of a sequence, you use the *sequence slice* expression. It consists of the sequence name or another expression that evaluates to a sequence, followed by a pair of brackets that encloses a starting index and an optional ending index separated by two dots (..) or two dots and a less-than sign (..<). If the ending index is not specified, it is understood to be the index of the last element of the sequence, namely, the size of the sequence minus one. This expression produces a *slice* of the original sequence. Here are some examples:

```
var integers = [1, 3, 5, 7, 9];
var seq1 = integers[0..2];
var seq2 = integers[0..<2];
var seq3 = integers[2..];
var seq4 = integers[-3..10];
var seq5 = integers[2..<2];
var seq6 = integers[2..0];
var seq7 = integers[-2..-1];
var seq8 = integers[5..6];
```

If the two dots notation is used, all elements of the original sequence whose index is greater than or equal to the starting index and less than or equal to the ending index are elements of the slice. If the two dots and a less-than sign notation is used, all elements of the original sequence whose index is greater than or equal to the starting index and less than the ending index are elements of the slice. The elements in the slice appear in the same order as they appear in the original sequence.

If no element of the original sequence satisfies the slice's condition, then the slice is an empty sequence. This is the case, for example, if the slice's ending index is less than the slice's starting index, if the slice's starting index is greater than or equal to the size of the sequence, or if the slice's ending index is less than zero. Notice that it is okay for the starting index to be less than zero or for the ending index to be greater than or equal to the size of the sequence.

Thus in the previous example, seq1 is [1, 3, 5], seq2 is [1, 3], seq3 is [5, 7, 9], and seq4 is [1, 3, 5, 7, 9]. And seq5, seq6, seq7, and seq8 are equal to the empty sequence [ ]. The conditions in seq5 and seq6 are not satisfied by any indexes. The condition in seq7 is satisfied only by -2 and -1, but integers does not contain elements with indexes -2 or -1. Similarly, the condition in seq8 is satisfied by 5 and 6, but integers does not contain elements with indexes 5 or 6.

Accessing a Subset of a Sequence through a Predicate

To access a not necessarily consecutive subset of elements of a sequence, you use the *sequence select* expression. It consists of

- The sequence name or another expression that evaluates to a sequence
- A pair of brackets that encloses a predicate in the form of a *selection variable*
- A vertical bar (|)
- A Boolean expression involving the selection variable

Here are some examples:

```
var integers = [1, 3, 5, 7, 9];
var seq1 = integers[x | x > 4];
var seq2 = integers[x | indexof x < 2];
var seq3 = integers[x | x > 10];
```

The resulting sequence will contain all elements of the original sequence whose value satisfy the predicate. A value satisfies a predicate if the Boolean expression in the predicate is true when the value is substituted for the selection variable. The indexof operator can be used inside the predicate to obtain the index of the selection variable x in the original sequence. If no elements of the original sequence satisfy the predicate, the resulting sequence is the empty sequence. The elements in the resulting sequence appear in the same order as they appear in the original sequence.

Thus, in the previous example seq1 is [5, 7, 9], seq2 is [1, 3], and seq3 is the empty sequence.

Reversing a Sequence

JavaFX Script provides the reverse operator that reverses a sequence. The reverse operator does not modify the original sequence but produces a new sequence that contains the same elements as the original sequence in the reverse order. Here is an example:

```
var integers = [1, 3, 5, 7, 9];
var seq1 = reverse integers;
```

In this example, seq1 is [9, 7, 5, 3, 1].

Inserting an Element into a Sequence

So far, you've learned four methods of accessing the elements of a sequence. One thing that these methods have in common is that they do not change the original sequence in any way. Coming up, we will show you methods for altering an existing sequence.

To add one element to a sequence, you use the insert expression. Only a value of a compatible type may be inserted into a sequence. The only time you are allowed to insert a value of one primitive type into a sequence of a different type is when you are inserting a numeric value into a sequence of a different numeric type. You may lose precision when the sequence's element type is narrower than the type of the value being inserted. For example, inserting a Number value into an Integer sequence will cause the Number value's fractional part to be dropped. For class types, you are allowed to insert an object of class type into a sequence of its super class type. You will learn about super classes in Chapter 4.

There are three forms of insert expressions: the insert into form, the insert before form, and the insert after form. Here are some examples:

```
var numbers = [3.14159, 2.71828];
insert 0.57722 into numbers;
insert 1.618 before numbers[0];
insert 1.4142 after numbers[2];
```

The insert into form takes two pieces of information as its input: the value to be inserted and the sequence variable to insert the value into. It then appends the value to the end of the sequence. Thus, after the first insert expression in the previous example, numbers will be [3.14159, 2.71828, 0.57722].

The insert before form takes three pieces of information as its input: the value to be inserted, the sequence variable to insert the value into, and an index. It then inserts the value into the sequence at a position just before the index. Thus, after the second insert expression, numbers will be [1.618, 3.14159, 2.71828, 0.57722].

The insert after form takes the same three pieces of information as the insert before form as its input, and inserts the value into the sequence at a position just after the index. Thus, after the third insert expression, numbers will be [1.618, 3.14159, 2.71828, 1.4142, 0.57722].

Attempting to insert an element after an invalid index will keep the sequence unchanged. Attempting to insert an element before an invalid index will also keep the sequence unchanged, except when the index is equal to the size of the sequence (in that case, the element is appended to the sequence).

■**Caution** The way you provide the requisite information to the three insert forms is somewhat unconventional. It is designed to make the whole expression easy to remember. You should keep in mind that although the last part of the insert before and the insert after forms looks identical to an element access expression, it is in fact not one.

Inserting Another Sequence into a Sequence

In addition to inserting a single element into a sequence, JavaFX Script supports inserting another sequence into a sequence. You can use the same three forms of insert expressions you just learned to do so. As with a single element insertion, the element type of the other sequence must be compatible with the target sequence.

Notice that after the insertion, the original sequence is still a flat sequence, only with more elements. JavaFX Script does not support nested sequences.

Attempting to insert an empty sequence will keep the original sequence unchanged. Attempting to insert null into a sequence will also keep the original sequence unchanged.

Here is an example:

```
var strings = ["hello", "hello again", "goodbye"];
insert ["how are you", "see you"] after strings[1];
```

After this insertion, the sequence strings will be ["hello", "hello again", "how are you", "see you", "goodbye"].

Deleting Elements from a Sequence

To delete elements from a sequence, you use the delete expression. There are four forms of delete expressions, as you can see here:

```
var strings = ["hello", "hello again", "how are you", "see you", "goodbye"];
delete "see you" from strings;
delete strings[2];
delete strings[0..1];
delete strings;
```

The delete from form takes two pieces of information as its input: the value to be deleted and the sequence variable to delete the value from. It then deletes all occurrences of the value from the sequence. The type of the value must be compatible with the element type of the sequence. If the value does not occur in the sequence, the sequence is unchanged. Thus, after the first delete expression in the previous example, strings will be ["hello", "hello again", "how are you", "goodbye"].

The other three forms are variants of the delete form. The first variant takes two pieces of information as its input: a sequence variable and an index. It then deletes the element at the index from the sequence. If the index is not a valid index, the sequence remains unchanged. Thus, after the second delete expression, strings will be ["hello", "hello again", "goodbye"].

The second variant takes three pieces of information as its input: a sequence variable, a starting index, and an optional ending index. It then deletes the slice from the sequence. The information is arranged in a form that reminds you of a sequence slice expression. Both the .. and the ..< forms are supported. If the ending index is not specified, it is understood to be the index of the last element of the sequence. Thus, after the third delete expression in the previous example, strings will be ["goodbye"].

The third variant takes only one piece of information, a sequence variable, and deletes all elements from the sequence. Thus, after the fourth delete expression, strings will be the empty sequence [].

■**Caution**   Although the last part of the first and the second variants of the delete form looks identical to a sequence indexing expression or a sequence slice expression, it is in fact not one.

A Sequence Manipulation Example

Listing 2-9 shows sequence manipulation constructs at work.

Listing 2-9. *Manipulating Sequences*

```
var integers = [1, 3, 5, 7, 9];

print("integers = "); println(integers);
print("sizeof integers = "); println(sizeof integers);
print("integers[0] = "); println(integers[0]);
print("integers[4] = "); println(integers[4]);
print("integers[-1] = "); println(integers[-1]);
print("integers[5] = "); println(integers[5]);

print("integers[0..2] = "); println(integers[0..2]);
print("integers[0..<2] = "); println(integers[0..<2]);
print("integers[2..] = "); println(integers[2..]);
print("integers[-3..10] = "); println(integers[-3..10]);
```

```
print("integers[2..<2] = "); println(integers[2..<2]);
print("integers[2..0] = "); println(integers[2..0]);
print("integers[-2..-1] = "); println(integers[-2..-1]);
print("integers[5..6] = "); println(integers[5..6]);

print("integers[x | x > 4] = "); println(integers[x | x > 4]);
print("integers[x | indexof x < 2] = "); println(integers[x | indexof x < 2]);
print("integers[x | x > 10] = "); println(integers[x | x > 10]);

print("reverse integers = "); println(reverse integers);

var numbers = [3.14159, 2.71828];
print("numbers = "); println(numbers);

insert 0.57722 into numbers;
print("numbers = "); println(numbers);

insert 1.618 before numbers[0];
print("numbers = "); println(numbers);

insert 1.4142 after numbers[2];
print("numbers = "); println(numbers);

var strings = ["hello", "hello again", "goodbye"];
print("strings = "); println(strings);

insert ["how are you", "see you"] after strings[1];
print("strings = "); println(strings);

delete "see you" from strings;
print("strings = "); println(strings);

delete strings[2];
print("strings = "); println(strings);

delete strings[0..1];
print("strings = "); println(strings);

delete strings;
print("strings = "); println(strings);
```

Understanding Sequence Comprehension

Sequences play an important role in JavaFX Script. They are a versatile container of application objects. The explicit sequence expression syntax, together with the object literal syntax, form the basis of the declarative GUI programming style that is a distinguishing characteristic of JavaFX applications.

In the previous section, you learned how to create sequences; how to access elements, slices, or subsets of sequences; and how to modify sequences with insert and delete expressions. JavaFX Script allows you to do more with sequences by using the *for expression*, which produces new sequences based on one or more existing sequences. Following the functional programming language tradition, syntaxes for generating new sequences from existing ones are called *sequence comprehension*.

The for expression starts with the for keyword. The for keyword is followed by one or more comma-separated in clauses enclosed in a pair of parentheses (()). Each in clause may have an optional where clause. The in clauses are followed by the body of the for expression. The following is a simple example of a for expression:

```
for (x in [1..4]) x*x
```

Its in clause has the form x in [1..4] and its body is the expression x*x. It produces the sequence [1, 4, 9, 16].

An in clause starts with a variable name followed by the in keyword and a sequence expression. The variable named in the in clause is called the *iteration variable*. The optional where clause, if present, follows the in clause with the where keyword and a Boolean expression involving the iteration variable of the in clause. The following example shows a for expression with a where clause:

```
for (x in [1..4] where x > 2) x*x
```

Its in clause has the form x in [1..4] where x > 2. The where clause serves to filter out some of the elements from the sequence in the in clause. This for expression produces the sequence [9, 16].

When a for expression has multiple in clauses, the iteration variable names of the in clauses must be distinct. The elements of the resulting sequence are ordered as if an iteration variable in a later in clause varies faster than iteration variables in earlier in clauses. Therefore in the following example:

```
var rows = ["A", "B"];
var columns = [1, 2];
var matrix = for (row in rows, column in columns) "{row}{column}";
```

the resulting sequence matrix will be ["A1", "A2", "B1", "B2"]. The sequences iterated by the different in clauses need not be different sequences, as shown here:

```
var digits = [1, 2, 3];
var seq = for (x in digits, y in digits) "{x}{y}";
```

The resulting sequence seq will be ["11", "12", "13", "21", "22", "23", "31", "32", "33"].

In a for expression with multiple in clauses, the where clause associated with a later in clause may refer to iteration variables of earlier in clauses. However, the where clause associated with an earlier in clause cannot refer to iteration variables of later in clauses. In other words, the *scope* of an iteration variable of an in clause is its own where clause, the where clause of later in clauses, and the body of the for expression. You will learn about more details of scopes of variables in JavaFX Script later in this chapter when we talk about JavaFX Script expressions. In the following example, the where clause of the second in clause refers to the iteration variable of both the first and the second in clauses:

```
var digits = [1, 2, 3];
var seq= for (x in digits where x > 1, y in digits where y >= x) {
  "{x}{y}"
}
```

The resulting sequence seq will be ["22", "23", "33"]. This example also illustrates the use of a block expression as the body of a for expression. You will learn more about block expressions in the "JavaFX Script Expressions" section later in this chapter.

In Listing 2-10, you can see sequence comprehension at work.

Listing 2-10. *Sequence Comprehension*

```
var seq = for (x in [1..4]) x*x;
print("seq = "); println(seq);

seq = for (x in [1..4] where x > 2) x*x;
print("seq = "); println(seq);

var rows = ["A", "B"];
var columns = [1, 2];
var matrix = for (row in rows, column in columns) "{row}{column}";
print("matrix = "); println(matrix);

var digits = [1, 2, 3];
var seq1 = for (x in digits, y in digits) "{x}{y}";
print("seq1 = "); println(seq1);

var seq2 = for (x in digits where x > 1, y in digits where y >= x) {
  "{x}{y}"
}
print("seq2 = "); println(seq2);
```

Using Utility Functions in javafx.util.Sequences

The JavaFX Script runtime includes a class javafx.util.Sequences that provides some useful sequence manipulation functions. It includes the following functions:

- binarySearch(seq, key)

- binarySearch(seq, key, comparator)

- indexByIdentity(seq, key)

- indexOf(seq, key)

- isEqualByContentIdentity(seq1, seq2)

- `max(seq)`

- `max(seq, comparator)`

- `min(seq)`

- `min(seq, comparator)`

- `nextIndexByIdentity(seq, key, pos)`

- `nextIndexOf(seq, key, pos)`

- `reverse(seq)`

- `shuffle(seq)`

- `sort(seq)`

- `sort(seq, comparator)`

All of the functions take at least one argument of the sequence type. A sequence that is passed in as a parameter is not modified by the functions. A new sequence is returned instead if necessary.

Some functions have a variant that takes an additional comparator argument. The variant that takes a comparator is necessary only if the element type of the sequence does not have its own natural ordering or if you want to override the natural ordering. All JavaFX Script primitive types have a natural ordering. A comparator is an object of a JavaFX Script or Java class that implements the `java.util.Comparator` Java interface. We will explain how to define JavaFX Script classes and how to use JavaFX Script's Java interoperability in Chapter 4.

A few of the methods deal with identities of elements in sequences. You will learn about identities of JavaFX Script objects in the "Understanding the Relational Operators" section later in this chapter. For now, suffice to say that every JavaFX Script object has an identity and a value, and object comparisons in JavaFX Script are usually carried out by comparing object values. However, under some special circumstances it is necessary to compare object identities. Values of primitive types have values but not identities.

The `binarySearch()` function takes a sorted sequence and a key (and an optional comparator) and uses a binary search algorithm to find the index of the key in the sequence. The result is a meaningless integer if the sequence is not sorted. The result is the index of the key in the sequence if the key appears in the sequence. If the key appears multiple times, then one of the indexes is returned, but we cannot tell which one. If the key does not appear in the sequence, then a negative integer is returned.

The `indexOf())` and `indexByIdentity()` functions take a sequence and a key and find the index of the first occurrence of the key in the sequence. If the key does not appear in the sequence, `-1` is returned.

The `nextIndexOf()` and `nextIndexByIdentity()` functions takes a sequence, a key, and a starting position and finds the index of the first occurrence of the key in the sequence on or after the specified position. If the key does not appear on or after the specified position, `-1` is returned.

The isEqualByContentIdentity() takes two sequences and determines if the sequences contain the same elements according to object identity.

The max(),min(), reverse(), shuffle(), and sort() functions work as their name suggests. A runtime exception will be thrown if an empty sequence is passed to the max() and min() functions.

Listing 2-11 uses some of the utility functions.

Listing 2-11. *Sequence Utility Functions*

```
import javafx.util.Sequences.*;

var seq = [1, 4, 2, 8, 5, 7];
print("seq = "); println(seq);

println("The index of 4 in seq = {indexOf(seq, 4)}");
println("The max value of seq = {max(seq)}");
println("The min value of seq = {min(seq)}");

print("reverse(seq) = "); println(reverse(seq));
print("shuffle(seq) = "); println(shuffle(seq));

var sorted = sort(seq);
print("sorted = "); println(sorted);

var index = binarySearch(sorted, 4);
println("Found 4 in sorted at index {index}");

var integers = [1, 3, 5, 3, 1];
print("integers = "); println(integers);
println("indexOf(integers, 3) = {indexOf(integers, 3)}");
println("nextIndexOf(integers, 3, 2) = {nextIndexOf(integers, 3, 2)}");
```

In Listing 2-11, the import statement import javafx.util.Sequences.*; allows you to call the functions of the class. We covered import statements briefly in Chapter 1 and will cover them in more detail in Chapter 4.

So far, you've learned about JavaFX Script variables and their declared types. We've explored JavaFX Script values and their runtime types, and you've learned about the primitive types, sequence types, and their literal representations. You also saw some simple expressions that are built out of primitive values and sequences.

JavaFX Script Expressions

In this section, we will explore JavaFX Script expressions. A JavaFX Script *expression* is a chunk of JavaFX Script code that the JavaFX Script compiler understands. The compiler will generate code that evaluates JavaFX Script expressions into JavaFX Script values. The values are fed into yet more expressions, which evaluate to more values, leading eventually to the solution of your problem.

Understanding Expressions and Their Types

JavaFX Script understands many kinds of expressions. The expressions that you have learned so far include `Boolean` expressions, arithmetic expressions, string expressions, explicit sequence expressions, range expressions, sequence indexing expressions, sequence slice expressions, sequence select expressions, insert expressions, delete expressions, and for expressions. You have also seen function invocation expressions, assignment expressions, and object literal expressions, which we have yet to cover in detail. Literals for the primitive types are also considered expressions.

All executable JavaFX Script code are expressions. In the rest of this chapter, you will see the majority of the remaining JavaFX Script expressions. But before going over the individual expressions, we'd like to point out some general characteristics of JavaFX Script expressions.

Every expression has some expectation for its constituent parts and makes certain guarantees for the value it produces. If these expectations are not met, the compiler will reject the program and report an error. For example, the expression `a and b` expects its operands to be values of type `Boolean`, and produces a `Boolean` value as a result. The compiler will flag the expression `3 and 4` as an error. As another example, consider the variant of the delete expression that deletes all elements from a sequence. This expression expects the operand following `delete` to be a variable of the sequence type, and produces no results. The compiler will flag the expression `delete 5;` as an error. The expression `delete [1, 3, 5, 7, 9];` is similarly in error because its operand, although a sequence, is not a variable of the sequence type but rather an explicit sequence expression. These checks are called *type checks*. And because the JavaFX Script compiler performs type checks at compile time, JavaFX Script falls into the category of *statically typed* programming languages. In JavaFX Script all variables have a static type: it is either explicitly specified or inferred. The type of a variable cannot be changed during the lifetime of the variable. This is another benefit of type checking.

Expressions such as the delete expression that produce no results are said to be of the *void type*. The void type is a special type. There could never be a value of the void type, and you cannot declare a variable to be of the void type. You can use `Void` as a function's return type to indicate that the function returns nothing. Expressions that are not of the void type are called *value expressions*.

■**Note** There is a difference between an expression being of the void type and having value `null`. An expression of the void type can never have a value, not even `null`. On the other hand, if an expression is capable of having a `null` value, then it is capable of having a non-`null` value.

Understanding the Block Expression

The block expression is formed by enclosing a number of other expressions within a pair of braces (`{}`). The type of the block expression is the type of the last expression it encloses. If the last expression is not of the void type, then the value of the last expression is the value of the block expression. Here is an example:

```
var x = {
  var a = 3;
  var b = 4;
  a*a + b*b
};
```

The block in the example contains three expressions: two variable declaration expressions and an arithmetic expression. After execution, the variable x will have the value 25.

Blocks introduce a new *scope*. Variables declared inside the block are not visible to code outside the block. You cannot declare a variable with the same name as another variable in the current block level or the surrounding level, up to the enclosing function or class.

In the next example, we use a block of the void type:

```
var a = 3;
var b = 4;
{
  var s = a*a + b*b;
  println("s = {s}");
}
```

Since the block is of the void type, we cannot assign it to a variable. The block only serves to confine the scope of the variable s.

Understanding Precedence and Groupings

When presented with a compound expression that involves multiple operators, JavaFX Script will carry out the operations in accordance with the precedence assigned to each operator. For operators of the same precedence, JavaFX Script will carry out the operations in accordance to the associativity assigned to the operators. For example, the well-known precedence rules for arithmetic operators are observed in JavaFX Script. Thus, the value of 1 + 2 * 3 is 7 rather than 9, and the value of 6 / 2 * 3 is 9 rather than 1.

A pair of parentheses can be used to force the operations to be done in a different order. Thus, the value of (1 + 2) * 3 is 9, and the value of 6 / (2 * 3) is 1.

Only value expressions can be surrounded by parentheses.

Understanding the Expression Separator

The semicolon (;)serves as an expression terminator. You have seen its use in all the example programs in this book so far. Some expressions have a natural termination point. For example, both the block expression you learned in this section and the for expression you learned in the previous section naturally terminate at the closing brace. For such expressions, the semicolon is optional; in other words, the compiler will not specifically look for a semicolon at these locations, but if a semicolon is present the compiler will not complain either. A few expressions that you will learn later in this chapter—such as the while expression, one form of the if expression, and the object literal expression—also fall into this category.

The semicolon is also optional after the last expression in a block. For all other expressions, a semicolon is required.

Understanding Variable and Constant Declarations

By now you have seen the basic form of a JavaFX Script variable declaration many times. In JavaFX Script, variable declarations are expressions. They are called *variable declaration expressions*. Here are examples of the basic forms of variable declaration expressions:

```
var a;
var b: Integer;
var c: Number = 3.14;
var d = "Hello, World.";
var e = bind c;
var f = d on replace { println("f changed.") };
```

Here we declared six variables:

- Variable a is declared with neither a type nor an initializer.

- Variable b is declared to be of type Integer but without an initializer.

- Variable c is declared to be of type Number and initialized to the value 3.14.

- Variable d is declared without a type specifier and initialized to the string "Hello, World.".

- Variable e is declared without a type but with a binding.

- Variable f is declared without a type but with an initializer and a trigger.

A variable declaration is introduced by the keyword var followed by a variable name and an optional type specifier, an optional value expression or bind expression, and an optional trigger. You have seen bindings and triggers at work in Chapter 1. We will provide an in-depth coverage of bind expressions in the section "Working with Data Bindings" later in this chapter. Chapter 4 covers triggers in more detail.

Notice that the colon that separates the variable name and the type is omitted if the type is omitted. If a type is not specified, then the type of the variable is determined by JavaFX Script's type inference facility. If an initializer is given in the variable declaration, the type of the initial value is taken as the type of the variable. Otherwise, the type of the variable is determined by the first subsequent assignment to the variable. If the variable is never assigned a value in the program, the variable is taken to be of type `Object`, which is a class type.

Once the compiler determines the type of a variable that is declared without a type, it will treat the variable as if it is declared with the inferred type.

If the type is specified, the type of the initializer value or the binding expression must be compatible with the specified type.

■**Caution** It is generally a good idea to either specify a type or an initializer in a variable declaration. If neither is specified, then only nonsequence values can be assigned to the variable.

Constants are named values that cannot be subsequently assigned. They are declared in *constant declaration expressions*. A constant declaration is introduced by the keyword `def` followed by a constant name and an optional type specifier, a required value expression or bind expression, and an optional trigger. Here are some examples:

```
def PI = 3.14159;
def GREETING = "Hello";
var x = 1024;
def y = bind x;
```

Although constants can never be assigned new values, their value may change if it is declared with a data binding and the expression it binds to changes.

Variable and constant names cannot be keywords and must be unique within the same function.

Understanding the Assignment Operator

The *assignment expression* assigns a new value to a previously declared variable. The second line in the following example is an assignment expression:

```
var x: Integer = 1024;
x = 2048;
```

The assignment expression consists of a variable name followed by the equal sign (=) and an expression. The value on the right-hand side must have a type that is compatible with the type of the variable. After the assignment expression, the value of the variable will be the value on the right-hand side.

As you have learned in the previous section, if the variable is declared without a type and without an initializer or binding, then the first subsequent assignment will determine the variable's type.

The assignment expression itself, considered as an expression, has a value that is the same as the value that is assigned to the variable. You can chain several assignments together, as shown in the following code:

```
var a;
var b;
a = b = 3;
```

The assignment operator is right associative. Thus, the third line in the previous code is equivalent to a = (b = 3). Therefore, b is assigned the value 3, and then a is assigned the value of the expression b = 3, which is also 3.

Understanding the Compound Assignment Operators

The *compound assignment expression* performs an arithmetic operation between the value of the left-hand side variable and the value of the right-hand side expression and assigns the result to the variable. The second to the fifth lines of the following example are compound assignment expressions:

```
var x: Integer = 1024;
x += 1;
x -= 2;
x *= 3;
x /= 4;
```

The compound assignment expression consists of a variable name followed by one of the compound assignment operators (+=, -=, *=, /=) and an expression. The value of the variable and the value of the expression must be numeric or duration values. The appropriate arithmetic operations indicated by the compound assignment operator is performed and the result assigned to the variable. Thus, x += 1 behaves the same as x = x + 1, and x will be 1025 after it. Similarly, x -= 2 behave the same as x = x - 2 and x will be 1023 after it. And x will be 3069 after x *= 3, and 767 after x /= 4.

Compound assignment operations play the same role as the regular assignment operation in inferring variable types.

The compound assignment expression itself has a value that is the same as the value that is assigned to the variable. The compound assignment operators are right associative and can be chained together, although such chaining is rarely used.

Understanding the Relational Operators

JavaFX Script supports six relational operators: the equals operator (==), the not-equals operator (!=), the less-than operator (<), the less-than or equal operator (<=), the greater-than
operator (>), and the greater-than or equal operator (>=).

The *relational expression* consists of a left-hand side expression followed by a relational
operator and a right-hand side expression. The equals and the not-equals operators can be
used to compare values of any types, whereas the other four operators can be used only to
compare values of numeric or duration type.

The JavaFX Script equals operator performs value comparisons. For primitive types this
gives you intuitive results. For example, the expressions true == true, 3 == 3, 4 == 4.0, 5.5
== 5.5, "hello" == "hello", and 1m == 60s all evaluate to true.

For class types, value comparison is done using the equals() instance function of the
class. You will learn more about classes in Chapter 4. For now it is enough to know that value
comparison for class types can be controlled by the programmer. The default behavior of the
equals() instance function is to perform object identity comparisons. In this comparison,
each newly created object is not equal to any previously created objects.

■**Caution** If you are familiar with the Java programming language, you should recognize that the seman-
tics of the == operator in JavaFX Script is different from that of the == operator in Java, where the former
performs value comparisons and the latter performs object identity comparisons.

Two sequences are equal if they have the same size and if for each valid index the corresponding elements are equal.

In Listing 2-12 you can see some of the expressions you have learned in this section at
work.

Listing 2-12. *Basic Expressions*

```
// block expressions
var x = {
  var a = 3;
  var b = 4;
  a*a + b*b
};
println("The value of x is {x}");

// precedence and groupings
println("1 + 2 * 3 = {1 + 2 * 3}");
println("(1 + 2) * 3 = {(1 + 2) * 3}");
println("6 / 2 * 3 = {6 / 2 * 3}");
println("6 / (2 * 3) = {6 / (2 * 3)}");
```

```
// var and def
var o;
var i: Integer;
var n: Number = 3.14;
var str = "Hello, World.";
var j = bind i;
var greeting = str on replace { println("greeting changed") };

def PI = 3.14159;
def k = bind i;

// assignment and type inference
var v1;
println("Before: v1 = {v1}");
v1 = 42;
println("After: v1 = {v1}");

class Point {
  var x: Number;
  var y: Number;
}
var v2;
println("Before: v2 = {v2}");
v2 = Point {x: 3, y: 4};
println("After: v2 ={v2}");

// compound assignment
x = 1024;
println("x = {x}");
x += 1;
println("x = {x}");
x -= 2;
println("x = {x}");
x *= 3;
println("x = {x}");
x /= 4;
println("x = {x}");

// relational operators
println("true == true is {true == true}");
println("3 == 3.0 is {3 == 3.0}");
println('"hello" == "hello" is {"hello" == "hello"}');

println("3.14159 > 2.71828 is {3.14159 > 2.71828}");
```

```
println("1h < 100m is {1h < 100m}");

var p1 = Point {x: 3, y: 4};
var p2 = Point {x: 3, y: 4};
println("p1 == p1 is {p1 == p1}");
println("p1 == p2 is {p1 == p2}");
```

Understanding the While Expression

A *while expression* is introduced by the while keyword, followed by a pair of parentheses that encloses a *condition*, which must be an expression of type Boolean, and a *body* expression after the closing parenthesis. Although the syntax allows any expression to be the body, a block is the most common body of while expressions. A semicolon is required to terminate the while expression if the body is not a block.

First the condition is checked. If it is true, the body of the while expression is evaluated and the condition is checked again. As long as the condition is true, the body is executed repeatedly. The while expression itself is of the void type, so you cannot assign a while expression to a variable as you can with blocks.

The following code prints the squares of the first ten natural numbers:

```
var i = 1;
while (i <= 10) {
  println("{i} squared: {i * i}");
  i += 1;
}
```

You can use the keyword break to break out of a while expression. The keyword continue can be used to skip the rest of the code in one iteration. If there are multiple nested loops in your code, these keywords only affect the innermost loop that encloses them. In the following code, the first loop prints natural numbers up to 7 and the second prints only the even ones:

```
var i = 1;
while (i <= 10) {
  if (i > 7) {
    break;
  } else {
    println(i);
  }
  i += 1;
}

var j = 1;
while (j <= 10) {
  if (j mod 2 != 0) {
    j += 1;
    continue;
  } else {
```

```
    println(j);
    j += 1;
  }
}
```

Revisiting the For Expression

Because of its close relationship with sequence comprehension, we covered the for expression in the "Working with Sequences" section earlier in this chapter. Recall that a *for expression* is introduced by the for keyword, followed by a pair of parentheses that enclose one or more comma-separated in clauses, and an expression after the closing parenthesis.

Strictly speaking, a for expression is sequence comprehension only if its body is a value expression. If the body of a for expression is of the void type, then the for expression is more like the while expression and exhibits a loop behavior. Here is an example that prints the first ten natural numbers:

```
for (x in [1..10]) {
  println(i);
}
```

As is the case for while loops, the keywords break and continue can be used in for loops. Again, you can use the break keyword to break out of a for loop and the continue keyword to skip the rest of the code in one iteration. In the following code, the first for loop prints natural numbers up to 7, and the second for loop prints only the even ones:

```
for (x in [1..10]) {
  if (x > 7) {
    break;
  } else {
    println(x);
  }
}

for (x in [1..10]) {
  if (x mod 2 != 0) {
    continue;
  } else {
    println(x);
  }
}
```

■**Caution** The syntax of the for expression allows the break and continue keywords to be used in any kind of for expression. However, with the JavaFX 1.0, 1.1, and 1.2 compiler, using these keywords in sequence comprehension will cause either a compiler crash or a runtime exception.

Understanding the If Expression

The *if expression* is introduced by the `if` keyword, followed by a pair of parentheses that enclose a *condition*, which must be an expression of type `Boolean`; a then clause after the closing parenthesis; and an optional `else` clause. The then clause has two forms: it can either be an expression or the then keyword followed by an expression. The `else` clause is the `else` keyword followed by an expression. The then keyword is customarily used in short if expressions where both the then clause and the `else` clause contain simple nonblock expressions. Here are some examples:

```
// short form if expression
var x = if (i == j) then 1 else 0;

// long form if expression
if (x < 0) {
  println("{x} < 0");
} else {
  println("{x} >= 0");
}
```

In the short-form if expression, the expressions for the then and the `else` clauses are simple `Integer` values. Thus, the entire if expression is of type `Integer`. In the long-form if expression, the expressions for the then and `else` clauses are both block expressions of the void type. Consequently, the entire if expression is of the void type and cannot be assigned to another variable.

In general, the type of an if expression is determined by the types of the two expressions in the then and `else` clauses. If both expressions are of the same type, then the entire if expression is of that type. If one of them is of the void type, the entire if expression is of the void type. If the `else` clause is omitted, the if expression is of the void type.

The situation becomes more complicated if the two expressions are of different types. In such situations JavaFX Script will attempt to find a type that will accommodate both expressions. Consider the following examples:

```
var x = if (true) then 3 else "4";
var y = if (true) then 5 else [6];
```

After the assignments, the variable x will have the type `Object` and value 3, and y will have the type `Integer[]` and value [5]. In practice, if expressions with dissimilar then clause and else clause expressions are rarely needed.

The `else` clause of one if expression can be another if expression. This joined if expression allows you to test for multiple conditions, as you can see here:

```
if (x < 0) {
  println("{x} < 0");
} else if (x == 0) {
  println("{x} = 0");
} else {
  println("{x} > 0");
}
```

Listing 2-13 shows the looping and conditional expressions at work.

Listing 2-13. *Looping and Conditional Expressions*

```
// while loop
var i = 1;
while (i <= 10) {
  println("{i} squared: {i * i}");
  i += 1;
}

// break from while loop
var j = 1;
while (j <= 10) {
  if (j mod 2 != 0) {
    j += 1;
    continue;
  } else {
    println(j);
    j += 1;
  }
}

// continue in for loop
for (x in [1..10]) {
  if (x > 7) {
    break;
  } else {
    println(x);
  }
}

// if expressions
var k = if (i == j) then 1 else 0;

if (k < 0) {
  println("{k} < 0");
} else {
  println("{k} >= 0");
}

for (x in [-1..1]) {
  if (x < 0) {
    println("{x} < 0");
  } else if (x == 0) {
    println("{x} = 0");
  } else {
    println("{x} > 0");
  }
}
```

```
// if expression with dissimilar then and else clauses
var a = if (true) then 3 else "4";
println("a = {a}");
// assign an Integer to a
a = 5;
println("a = {a}");
// assign a String to a
a = "hi";
println("a = {a}");

var b = if (true) then 7 else [8];
print("b = "); println(b);
```

In this section, we covered some of the most basic expressions in JavaFX Script. These expressions are building blocks for larger pieces of code. In the remaining sections of this chapter you'll learn about two more important expressions: object literals and data binding.

Understanding Object Literals

In this section, we continue our coverage of JavaFX Script expressions. So far we have illustrated basic language features using primitive values and sequences. Now let's concentrate on class types and their objects. We'll begin with using JavaFX Script classes since it is easier to use them than to write them, and there are plenty of classes already written for you in the JavaFX SDK. Writing your own classes is covered in Chapter 4.

Understanding Classes and Objects

The *class* is a unit of code that encapsulates a data model and functions that manipulates the data model. A class contains *instance variables*, *instance functions*, and *initialization blocks*. The instance variables represent the data modeled by the class, and the instance functions perform computations based on the values of the instance variables. The initialization blocks set up the initial values of the instance variables in a way that is meaningful to the class.

To use a class, you must instantiate it. When you instantiate a class, the JavaFX Script runtime system allocates memory to hold all the instance variables of the class and initialize the memory according to the initializers and initialization blocks. This properly initialized memory is called an *object* of the class. It is also called an *instance* of the class. The runtime system may also perform some other housekeeping chores before it hands you an *object reference*.

The object reference allows you to read from and write to its instance variables that are accessible to you as specified by the class. It also allows you to call its instance functions that are accessible to you as specified by the class.

When you are done with an object reference, you don't have to do anything special. You simply let it go out of scope. The runtime system will figure out that you will never use that object reference again and reclaim the memory that it occupies. This process is called *garbage collection*.

You can instantiate a class multiple times to create multiple objects of the class. Different objects of the same class may have the same set of instance variables, but each object's instance variable values are independent of every other object's instance variable values.

The Object Literal Expression

To instantiate a JavaFX Script class, you use an *object literal expression*. Unlike some of the expressions you encountered in the previous section, the object literal expression is quite involved and sometimes occupies numerous program lines.

To illustrate this point, we'll pick a class from the JavaFX SDK, whose fully qualified name is `javafx.scene.shape.Circle`, and try to instantiate it in various ways. We will refer to it by its simple name, `Circle`. Since this class represents an onscreen circle, when you compile and run the snippets of codes in this section, a window will pop up with a circle drawn in it. You will need to close the window manually when you are done examining its content.

To instantiate a class, you must know what the class offers. You get that information by reading the Javafxdoc of the class. Javafxdoc is the documentation that is generated directly from the source code using the `javafxdoc` tool.

Initializing Instance Variables

According to the API documentation, the `Circle` class defines three instance variables: `centerX`, `centerY`, and `radius`, all of type `Number` and all having a default value of `0.0`. We can read, write, and initialize all three instance variables. In the following example, we instantiate a circle of radius 100.0 centered at the point (100.0, 100.0):

```
import javafx.scene.shape.Circle;

var circle = Circle { centerX: 100.0, centerY: 100.0, radius: 100.0 }
```

An object literal expression starts with the name of the class, followed by a pair of braces that encloses the following parts:

- Instance variable initializers

- Variable declarations

- Instance variable overrides

- Instance function overrides

In the previous example, we supplied three instance variable initializers. An *instance variable initializer* consists of the instance variable name followed by a colon and a value or a bind expression. You will learn about bind expressions in the next section. The expression must be of a type that is compatible with the type of the instance variable. If multiple instance variable initializers are present, they can be separated by commas, semicolons, or spaces. Commas are typically used when the initializers all appear on the same line, and white spaces are typically used when the initializers contain complicated expressions and must be presented one per line. We could have written this example in a multi-line form:

```
import javafx.scene.shape.Circle;

var circle = Circle {
  centerX: 100.0
  centerY: 100.0
  radius: 100.0
};
```

Declaring Constants and Variables

You can declare constants and variables in an object literal expression to aid the initialization process. Constant and variable declarations in an object literal must be separated from other parts of the object literal by a semicolon. Constants and variables defined in an object literal expression are confined to the scope of the object literal expression. In Listing 2-14, we've introduced a variable r to help initialize the Circle instance.

Listing 2-14. *Declaring a Variable in an Object Literal Expression*

```
import javafx.scene.shape.Circle;

var circle = Circle {
  var r = 100.0;
  centerX: r
  centerY: r
  radius: r
};
```

Figure 2-1 shows the window that pops up when Listing 2-14 is compiled and run.

Figure 2-1. *A circle in a window*

Overriding Instance Functions and Instance Variables

You can override instance variables and instance functions in an object literal expression to change the behavior of the class just for the instance. Such overrides must be separated from other parts of the object literal by a semicolon if they do not end with a closing brace. You may want to override an instance variable to add a trigger. We will cover instance variable overrides and instance function overrides in more detail in Chapter 4. We will also discuss triggers in Chapter 4.

Listing 2-15 illustrates both instance variable and instance function overriding in object literal expressions. We overrode the instance variable x to add a replace trigger. We also overrode the toString() instance function to give our point p a nicer printed representation.

Listing 2-15. *Overriding Instance Variables and Functions in an Object Literal Expression*

```
class Point {
  var x: Number;
  var y: Number;
}

var p = Point {
  override var x on replace {
    println("x is now {x}");
  }
  override function toString(): String {
    "Point({x}, {y})"
  }
  x: 3.0
  y: 4.0
};

println(p);
```

The instance function toString() in Point is inherited from the java.lang.Object class. The println() function uses an object's toString() instance function to generate a string representation of the object. When the code in Listing 2-15 is run, the following output is printed to the console:

```
x is now 3.0
Point(3.0, 4.0)
```

Manipulating Objects

Once you obtain an object reference by instantiating a JavaFX Script class using an object literal notation, you can manipulate the object through the object reference. You can also assign the object reference to a variable and manipulate the object through the object variable. You can pass the object reference or the object variable as function parameters. In general, you can use object references and object variables the same way you use primitive values and variables or sequence values and variables.

To take advantage of the functionality the class provides, you need to access the instance variables and instance functions of the class.

Manipulating Object States

The values of all instance variables of an object are called the object's *state*. You access an object's instance variables using a *member access expression*. The member access expression consists of a left side, a dot (.), and a right side. The left side of the dot must be an expression that evaluates to an object reference. The right side of the dot must be the name of an instance variable or an instance function of the class. Assume p is a variable of type Point and is assigned a valid instance of Point; then p.x and p.y are member access expressions that refer to the state of the object.

It is the class writer's job to decide what kind of access rights you have regarding instance variables and instance functions of its instances. Access rights are granted based on whether your code is in the same script file, in the same package, or in a different package than the class you are accessing. You will learn how to use access modifiers to specify instance variable and instance function access rights in Chapter 4. For now, suffice to say that any code that is in the same file as the class has full access rights to all its instance variables and instance functions. Listing 2-16 shows code in the same file reading from and writing to instance variables x and y of the class Point.

Listing 2-16. *Accessing Instance Variables*

```
class Point {
  var x: Number;
  var y: Number;
  override function toString(): String {
    "Point({x}, {y})"
  }
}

// reading instance variables
var p = Point { x: 3.0, y: 4.0 };
println("p.x = {p.x}");
println("p.y = {p.y}");
println("p = {p}");

// writing to instance variables
p.x = 5.0;
p.y = 12.0;
println("p = {p}");
```

Invoking Instance Functions

The dot notation also allows you to access instance functions of a class. Functions play an important role in the JavaFX Script language. Not only can you define and call functions and instance functions, you can assign functions to variables, pass functions into other functions, and use functions as return values in another function. Variables that refer to functions have function types. Function types, along with primitive, sequence, and object types, are the only four kinds of types of JavaFX Script. We will fully explore this functional programming aspect of JavaFX Script in Chapter 4.

The *function invocation expression* consists of a function name or an expression of the function type followed by a pair of parentheses that encloses a comma-separated list of *arguments*. The number of arguments must agree with the number of arguments in the function's definition. The type of each argument must be compatible with the type that is specified for that argument in the function definition. The function invocation expression's type is the return type of the function it invokes. If that type is not the void type, the function invocation expression's value is the return value of the function.

You have seen function invocation expressions at work throughout this chapter. We have used the println() function in our examples.

As is the case for instance variables, it is the class writer's job to decide what kind of access rights you have regarding instance functions. Listing 2-17 shows several instance function invocations.

Listing 2-17. *Invoking Instance Functions*

```
import java.lang.Math.*;

class Point {
  var x: Number;
  var y: Number;
  function distanceFromOrigin(): Number {
    sqrt(x*x + y*y)
  }
  function translate(dx: Number, dy: Number) {
    x += dx;
    y += dy;
  }
  override function toString(): String {
    "Point({x}, {y})"
  }
}

var p = Point { x: 3.0, y: 4.0 };
println("p = {p}");
println("Distance between p and the origin = {p.distanceFromOrigin()}");

p.translate(2.0, 8.0);
println("p = {p}");
println("Distance between p and the origin = {p.distanceFromOrigin()}");

print("Distance between Point \{x: 8.0, y: 15.0\} and the origin = ");
println(Point {x: 8.0, y: 15.0}.distanceFromOrigin());
```

The first line in Listing 2-17 imports a number of methods, including `sqrt()`, from the Java class `java.lang.Math` into the program. We used `sqrt()` in the `distanceFromOrigin()` instance function to calculate the distance from the point to the origin. In the second line from the last, we escaped the brace characters in the string literal to turn off the special meaning of braces. The last line of the code demonstrates invoking an instance function directly on an object literal, without assigning the object reference to a variable.

Creating Java Objects with the new Operator

While we won't start our in-depth coverage of Java interoperability features until Chapter 4, we want to introduce you to the simplest form of Java interoperability now so that you can take advantage of them in your JavaFX Script programs.

The *new expression* consists of the keyword new, followed by the name of a Java class and an optional pair of parentheses that encloses a comma-separated list of constructor arguments. It calls the constructor of the Java class that matches the number and type of the arguments and results in an object reference. If the constructor without any arguments (also called the no-arg or default constructor) is intended, you can either use a pair of empty parentheses or omit the parentheses altogether.

In the following example, we instantiate the `java.util.Date` class and call its `getTime()` method:

```
import java.util.Date;

var date = new Date();
var time = date.getTime();
```

■**Note** JavaFX Script allows you to use a new expression to instantiate a JavaFX Script class. The effect of the new expression for a JavaFX Script class is the same as an object literal expression with an empty pair of braces. For consistency, you should always use object literal expressions to instantiate JavaFX Script classes.

The Making of a Declarative Syntax

One characteristic of object literal expressions is that they are self-explanatory. You can understand what is being instantiated by reading the object literal expression without having to refer to the class definition. If an instance variable in a class is itself of the class type or the sequence type, its instance variable initializer can be another nested object literal expression or an explicit sequence expression. This combination gives object literal expressions a hierarchical feel, which makes it ideal for describing graphical user interfaces (GUIs). You have seen some declarative GUIs in the two examples in Chapter 1, and you will see a lot more in the coming chapters.

Working with Data Bindings

JavaFX Script's data binding facility allows any variable to be bound to a value expression. When any constituent part of the bound expression is changed, the bound expression is recalculated and the variable's value is also changed. The data binding capability is at the center of the JavaFX approach for GUI development, in which onscreen UI controls' properties are bound to a model object and the GUI is controlled through state changes in the model object.

Understanding the Bind Expression

A *bind expression* is introduced by the bind keyword, followed by a value expression and optionally the with inverse keywords. Bind expressions are automatically reevaluated when their dependencies change. Unlike all the other expressions that you've learned so far, bind expressions are not true stand-alone expressions. A bind expression must appear on the right-hand side of constant declarations, variable declarations, or instance variable initializers in object literal expressions. It also puts restrictions on the value expression that appears on its right-hand side. The constant, variable, or instance variable is said to be *bound* to the expression.

Here are some examples of bind expressions:

```
var a = 3.14159;
def b = bind a;
var c = bind a;
var p = Point { x: bind a, y: bind a };
```

The constant b, variable c, and instance variables p.x and p.y are all bound to the bind expression bind a. Any value assigned to a after the binding will also become the new value of b, c, p.x, and p.y.

A bound variable or a bound instance variable (except for bindings with inverse, which we will explain shortly) cannot be assigned another value. The following lines will cause a compilation error:

```
var a = 1024;
var b = bind a;
b = 2048;
```

■**Caution** The compiler cannot effectively detect all assignments to bound variables at compile time. Assignments to bound variables will cause a runtime exception to be thrown.

What Does the Data Binding Remember?

With a regular (nonbinding) assignment or initialization, the right-hand side expression is evaluated and its value is assigned to the left-hand side variable. With a binding assignment or initialization, the JavaFX Script runtime system not only evaluates the expression and assigns the value to the variable, but also remembers the entire expression, figuring out which variables the expression depends on and keeping an eye on the *dependent variables*. When any one of them gets a new value, the saved expression is *updated in a bind context* and its value becomes the new value of the bound variable.

In the following example, the variable z becomes a bound variable in the third line. It gets the value 7. The JavaFX Script also remembers that z is bound to x + y, which depends on the variables x and y. When the value of x or y is changed, the expression x + y is updated, and its new value becomes the new value of z.

```
var x = 3;
var y = 4;
var z = bind x + y;
```

A bind expression cannot contain assignments, pre- or postincrement or decrement expressions, or while expressions.

Binding to If Expressions

When a variable is bound to an if expression, its dependencies are the union of the dependencies of the condition, the then clause, and the else clause. To update an if expression in a bind context, the if expression is simply reevaluated. Here is an example:

```
var b = true;
var x = 3;
var y = 4;
def z = bind if (b) then x else y;
```

In this example, z depends on b, x, and y. When any one of them changes, the value of z is updated by reevaluating the if expression.

Binding to For Expressions

Since for expressions of the void type are not value expressions, the only kind of for expressions that can appear in a bind expression are sequence comprehensions. When a variable is bound to a for expression, its dependencies are the union of the dependencies of the sequences specified in the in clauses and the dependencies of the where clauses, excluding the iteration variables. To update a for expression in the bind context, the body of the for expression is reevaluated for a minimal number of element tuples in the sequences.

In the example

```
var a = 1;
var b = 10;
var m = 4;
def c = bind for (x in [a..b] where x < m) { x * x };
```

the dependencies of c are the union of the dependencies of [a..b], which is a and b, and the dependencies of x < m, which is x and m. Excluding the iteration variable x, that gives us the dependencies a, b, and m. With the given values of a, b, and m, the qualified x values are 1, 2, 3. If m is changed to 7, then the qualified x values will also include 4, 5, and 6. The body of the for expression is only evaluated for the new x values of 4, 5, and 6.

Binding to a Block

JavaFX Script restricts the expressions that can appear in a block in a binding context. The block can only have a certain number of constant declarations and a final value expression. The constant declarations are treated as if they are binding declarations. When a variable is bound to a block, its dependencies are the dependencies of the last expression in the block, which may in turn depend on the constant declarations in the block or variables outside the block.

In the example

```
var a = 3;
var b = 4;
def c = bind {
  def d = a;
  def e = b;
  d * d
};
```

the dependencies of c are the same as the dependencies of d * d, which are the same as the dependencies of d, which is a. Therefore, the value of c is updated when the value of a is changed, but not when the value of b is changed.

The restrictions on the content of blocks under a binding context apply also to blocks in if and for expressions.

■**Note** The compiler allows you to include variable declarations in a block in the bind context. However, since no assignments can appear in the block, these variable declarations are effectively constant declarations. They are also treated as if they are binding declarations.

Binding to Function Invocation Expressions

JavaFX Script has two kinds of functions: functions and bound functions. Both kinds of functions behave the same way except when their invocation is under a binding context. You will learn how to define functions and bound functions in Chapter 4.

When a variable is bound to a (nonbound) function invocation expression, its dependencies are the union of the dependencies of the arguments. When a variable is bound to a bound function invocation expression, its dependencies are the dependencies of the bound function body treated like a block. The update rule for functions is that the function is re-invoked when the dependencies change. The update rule for bound functions is the same as the update rule for blocks.

In the example

```
function sumOfSquares(x, y) { x * x + y * y }
var a = 3;
def c = bind sumOfSquares(a + 5, a + 6);
```

the dependency of c is the union of that of a + 5 and a + 6, which is a. Therefore, the value of c is updated when the value of a is changed. The function is re-invoked with the new arguments.

Binding to Object Literal Expressions

When a variable is bound to an object literal expression, its dependencies are the union of the dependencies of the right-hand side expressions of those instance variable initializers whose right-hand side expression is not already a bound expression. When a dependency changes, a new object is instantiated.

In the example

```
var a = 3;
var b = 4;
def p = bind Point { x: a, y: b };
def q = bind Point { x: bind a, y: b };
def r = bind Point { x: bind a, y: bind b };
```

the dependencies of p are a and b, the dependency of q is b, and the dependency of r is empty. When a is changed, a new instance of Point is created for p, but not for q and r. However, since q.x and r.x are bound to a, their value will be updated. Similarly, when b is changed, a new instance of Point is created for p and q, but not for r. However r.y is updated. Since the dependencies of r are empty, the binding of r to the object literal expression is unnecessary.

■**Caution** There are two levels of binding at work in the above example: one at the object level, and one at the instance variable level. Changes in dependencies of bound instance variables will not cause a new instance of Point to be created; only the value of the instance variable is updated. Changes in dependencies of bound object literal will cause the creation of a new instance of Point. This subtle difference may not be readily differentiated when you print out the value of p, q, or r with println().

Understanding Bidirectional Bindings and Lazy Bindings

JavaFX Script supports bidirectional bindings. A bidirectional binding is specified by appending the with inverse keywords to the end of a bind expression. The only expression allowed is a variable name. The following trivial example illustrates this construct:

```
var a = 3;
var b = bind a with inverse;
```

A bidirectionally bound variable can be assigned to, and its new value will also become the new value of its peer. Bidirectional bindings are useful in GUI programs where several onscreen elements are used to edit the same underlying quantity, such as when you want the user to change the RGB settings of a color by using sliders and text fields.

JavaFX Script supports lazy bindings. A lazy binding is specified by adding the lazy keyword after bind. Both regular bindings and bidirectional bindings can be lazy bindings. Lazy bindings have the same meaning as regular bindings with the exception that the bound variable is not updated until its value is needed. This may reduce the number of recalculations to the minimum and therefore boost the performance of the code.

In Listing 2-18, you can see JavaFX Script bindings at work.

Listing 2-18. *Data Bindings*

```
class Point {
  var x: Number;
  var y: Number;
  override public function toString() {
    "Point({x}, {y})@{hashCode()}"
  }
}

// data bindings
var a = 3.14159;
def b = bind a;
var c = bind a;
var p = Point { x: bind a, y: bind a };
println("a = {a}, b = {b}, c = {c}, p.x = {p.x}, p.y = {p.y}");

a = 2.17828;
println("a = {a}, b = {b}, c = {c}, p.x = {p.x}, p.y = {p.y}");

// binding to arithmetic expressions
var x1 = 3;
var y1 = 4;
var z1 = bind x1 + y1;
println("x1 = {x1}, y1 = {y1}, z1 = {z1}");
x1 = 5;
println("x1 = {x1}, y1 = {y1}, z1 = {z1}");
y1 = 12;
println("x1 = {x1}, y1 = {y1}, z1 = {z1}");

// binding to if expression
var b2 = true;
var x2 = 3;
var y2 = 4;
def z2 = bind if (b2) then x2 else y2;
println("b2 = {b2}, x2 = {x2}, y2 = {y2}, z2 = {z2}");
b2 = false;
println("b2 = {b2}, x2 = {x2}, y2 = {y2}, z2 = {z2}");
x2 = 5;
println("b2 = {b2}, x2 = {x2}, y2 = {y2}, z2 = {z2}");
y2 = 12;
println("b2 = {b2}, x2 = {x2}, y2 = {y2}, z2 = {z2}");
```

```
// binding to for expression
var a3 = 1;
var b3 = 10;
var m3 = 4;
def c3 = bind for (x in [a3..b3] where x < m3) { x * x };
print("a3 = {a3}, b3 = {b3}, m3 = {m3}, c3 = "); println(c3);
m3 = 7;
print("a3 = {a3}, b3 = {b3}, m3 = {m3}, c3 = "); println(c3);
a3 = 2;
print("a3 = {a3}, b3 = {b3}, m3 = {m3}, c3 = "); println(c3);
b3 = 5;
print("a3 = {a3}, b3 = {b3}, m3 = {m3}, c3 = "); println(c3);

// binding to block
var a4 = 3;
var b4 = 4;
def c4 = bind {
  def d4 = a4;
  def e4 = b4;
  d4 * d4
};
println("a4 = {a4}, b4 = {b4}, c4 = {c4}");
a4 = 5;
println("a4 = {a4}, b4 = {b4}, c4 = {c4}");
b4 = 12;
println("a4 = {a4}, b4 = {b4}, c4 = {c4}");

// binding to function invocation expression
function sumOfSquares(x, y) { x * x + y * y }
var a5 = 3;
var b5 = 4;
def c5 = bind sumOfSquares(a5 + 5, a5 + 6);
println("a5 = {a5}, b5 = {b5}, c5 = {c5}");
a5 = 5;
println("a5 = {a5}, b5 = {b5}, c5 = {c5}");
b5 = 12;
println("a5 = {a5}, b5 = {b5}, c5 = {c5}");

// binding to object literals
var a6 = 3;
var b6 = 4;
def p6 = bind Point { x: a6, y: b6 };
def q6 = bind Point { x: bind a6, y: b6 };
def r6 = bind Point { x: bind a6, y: bind b6 };
println("a6 = {a6}, b6 = {b6}, p6 = {p6}, q6 = {q6}, r6 = {r6}");
a6 = 5;
println("a6 = {a6}, b6 = {b6}, p6 = {p6}, q6 = {q6}, r6 = {r6}");
b6 = 12;
println("a6 = {a6}, b6 = {b6}, p6 = {p6}, q6 = {q6}, r6 = {r6}");
```

```
// bidirectional binding
var a7 = 3;
var b7 = bind a7 with inverse;
println("a7 = {a7}, b7 = {b7}");
a7 = 4;
println("a7 = {a7}, b7 = {b7}");
b7 = 5;
println("a7 = {a7}, b7 = {b7}");
```

Summary

In this chapter, you learned the fundamentals of the JavaFX Script language, which include the following:

- Variables, values, and their types
- The primitive types that JavaFX Script supports, their literal representations, their backing classes, and their basic operations
- Sequences, sequence member accesses, and sequence comprehensions
- The basic expressions of JavaFX Script
- Object literals and data bindings

In the next chapter, you'll learn how to build a node-centric user interface using classes provided by the JavaFX SDK.

CHAPTER 3

Creating a User Interface in JavaFX

Life is the art of drawing without an eraser.

—John W. Gardner

Chapter 1 gave you a jump start using JavaFX by covering the basics in developing and executing JavaFX programs. Chapter 2 gave you an in-depth understanding of many of the JavaFX language constructs. Now we're going to cover many of the details about creating a user interface in JavaFX that were glossed over in the Chapter 1 jump start. First on the agenda is to get you acquainted with the *theater* metaphor used by JavaFX to express user interfaces and to cover the significance of what we call *a node-centric UI*.

Introduction to Node-Centric UIs

As you experienced in Chapter 1, creating a user interface in JavaFX is like creating a theater play in that it typically consists of these very simple steps:

1. *Create a* stage *on which your program will perform*: The realization of your stage will depend on the platform on which it is deployed (for example, a web page, the desktop, or a mobile device).

2. *Create a* scene *in which the actors and props (nodes) will visually interact with each other and the audience (the users of your program)*: JavaFX programs usually have just one Scene, but it is possible to create more than one and associate them one at a time to the Stage. Like any good set designer in the theater business, good JavaFX developers endeavor to make their scenes visually appealing. To this end, it is often a good idea to collaborate with a graphic designer on your "theater play."

3. *Create* nodes *in the scene using the declarative syntax that you experienced in Chapter 1*: These nodes are subclasses of the `javafx.scene.Node` class, which include UI controls, shapes, `Text` (a type of shape), images, media players, and *custom UI components* that you create. Nodes may also be containers for other nodes, often providing cross-platform layout capabilities. A scene has a *scene graph* that contains a directed graph of nodes. Individual nodes and groups of nodes can be manipulated in many ways (such as moving, scaling, and setting opacity) by changing the values of a very rich set of `Node` instance variables.

4. *Create variables and classes that represent the* model *for the nodes in the scene*: As mentioned in Chapter 1, one of the very powerful aspects of JavaFX is binding, which enables the application's UI to easily stay in sync with the state, or model, of the application.

■**Note** Most of the examples in this chapter are small programs intended to demonstrate UI concepts. For this reason, the model in many of these examples consists of variables appearing in the main script, rather than being contained by separate JavaFX classes (such as the `AudioConfigModel` class in Chapter 1). Later chapters in this book contain examples that have model classes that you can use for reference.

---

5. *Create* event handlers, *like* `onMousePressed`, *that allow the user to interact with your program*: Often these event handlers manipulate instance variables in the model.

6. *Create* timelines *and* transitions *that animate your scene*: For example, you may want the thumbnail images of a list of books to move smoothly across the scene or a page in the UI to fade into view. You'll see an example of these in the BookStoreFX application in Chapter 9. You may simply want a ping-pong ball to move across the scene, bouncing off of walls and paddles, which will be demonstrated later in this chapter in the section "The Zen of Node Collision Detection."

Let's get started with a closer look at step 1, in which we'll examine in a fair level of detail the capabilities of the stage.

Setting the Stage

The appearance and functionality of your stage will depend on the platform on which it is deployed. For example, if deployed in a web browser, your stage will be a rectangular area, called an *applet*, within a web page. The stage for a JavaFX program deployed via Java Web Start will be a window. When deployed on a mobile device such as a cell phone, the stage for your JavaFX program will live on that device's display.

Understanding the Stage Class

The Stage class is the top-level container for any JavaFX program that has a graphical UI. It has several instance variables that allow it, for example, to be positioned, sized, given a title, made invisible, or given some degree of opacity. The two best ways that we know of to learn the capabilities of a class are to study the JavaFX API documentation and to examine (and write) programs that use it. In this section, we'll ask you to do both, beginning with looking at the API docs.

Consulting the API Docs for the Stage Class

The JavaFX API docs may be found in the docs/api directory subordinate to where you installed the JavaFX SDK. Also, they are available online at the URL given in the Resources section at the end of this chapter. Open the index.html file in your browser, navigate to the javafx.stage package, and select the Stage class. That page should contain a table of variables as shown in the excerpt in Figure 3-1.

Variable Summary

access	name	type	Can Read	Can Init	Can Write	Default Value	description
public-read	**containsFocus**	Boolean	•				Whether or not this Stage has the keyboard or input focus.
public	**extensions**	StageExtension[]	•	•	•	empty	The extensions that a Stage may have depending on the target profile of the script. ▶
public	**fullScreen**	Boolean	•	•	•	false	Specifies whether this Stage should be a full-screen, undecorated window. ▶
public	**height**	Number	•	•	•		The height of this Stage. ▶

Figure 3-1. *A portion of the Stage class documentation in the JavaFX API*

This table lists the public variables in the Stage class, revealing information such as their access modifier (public, public-read, or public-init), type, default value, and description. Access modifiers will be covered in more detail in Chapter 4, but for now note that this table has three columns (Can Read, Can Init, and Can Write) that provide an easy reference for the access to each variable. For example, the containsFocus variable in the table shows that it may be read but not initialized when the Stage class is created, or subsequently written to.

Go ahead and explore the documentation for each of the variables and functions in the Stage class, remembering to click the right arrow button in the description column when available to expose more information. When you're finished, come back and we'll show you a program that demonstrates most of the variables and functions available in the Stage class.

Using the Stage Class: The StageCoach Example

A screenshot of the unassuming, purposely ill-fitting StageCoach example program is shown in Figure 3-2.

Figure 3-2. *A screenshot of the StageCoach example*

The StageCoach program was created to coach you through the finer points of using the Stage class and related classes such as StageStyle, Screen, and Alert. Also, we're going to use this program to show you how get arguments passed into the program, read system properties, and use local storage. Before walking through the behavior of the program, go ahead and open the project and execute it by following the instructions for building and executing the Audio-Config project in Chapter 1. The project file is located in the Chapter03 directory subordinate to where you extracted the book's code download bundle.

EXAMINING THE BEHAVIOR OF THE STAGECOACH PROGRAM

When the program starts, its appearance should be similar to the screenshot in Figure 3-2. To fully examine its behavior, perform the following steps. Note that for instructional purposes, the variable and function names on the UI correspond to the variables and functions in the Stage instance.

1. Notice that the StageCoach program's window is initially displayed near the top of the screen, with its horizontal position in the center of the screen. Drag the program's window and observe that the x and y values near the top of the UI are dynamically updated to reflect its position on the screen.

2. Resize the program's window and observe that the width and height values change to reflect the width and height of the Stage. Note that this size includes the decorations (title bar and borders) of the window.

3. Click the program (or cause it to be in focus some other way) and notice that the containsFocus value is true. Cause the window to lose focus, perhaps by clicking somewhere else on the screen, and notice that the containsFocus value becomes false.

4. Deselect the resizable check box and then notice that the resizable value becomes false. Then try to resize the window and note that it is not permitted. Select the resizable check box again to make the window resizable.

5. Select the fullScreen check box. Notice that the program occupies the full screen and that the window decorations are not visible. Also note that the fullScreen value is true. Deselect the fullScreen check box to restore the program to its former size, noticing that the fullScreen value changes back to false.

6. Edit the text in the text field below the title label and press the Enter key. Notice that the text in the window's title bar is changed to reflect the new value.

7. Drag the window to partially cover another window, and click the toBack() button. Notice that this places the program behind the other window, therefore causing the z-order to change.

8. With a portion of the program's window behind another window, but the toFront() button visible, press that button. Notice that the program's window is placed in front of the other window.

9. Make note of the location of the program on the screen. Click the close() button. Notice that the strings "properties written" and "Stage is closing" print to the console and that the window closes. Notice also that the program exits.

10. Execute the StageCoach program again, noticing that it appears in the same location on the screen as when you clicked the close() button.

11. Right-click somewhere on the blue area of the program's UI, and notice that an alert dialog containing some system properties appears, as shown in Figure 3-3.

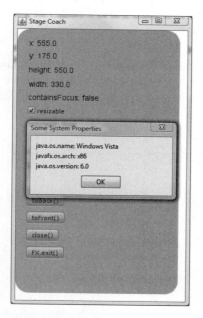

Figure 3-3. *Invoking an alert dialog that displays some system properties*

12. Click the OK button to close the dialog.

13. Drag the program to somewhere else on the screen. Click the FX.exit() button, noting that an alert dialog appears asking if you want to exit without saving the screen position. Click the No button. Click the FX.exit() button again, this time choosing the Yes button. Note that the program closes, but that the string "Stage is closing" does not print to the console.

14. Invoke the program again, passing in the string "undecorated". If invoking from NetBeans, use the Project Properties dialog to pass this argument as shown in Figure 3-4. See the Hello Earthrise example in Chapter 1 for instructions on accessing this dialog.

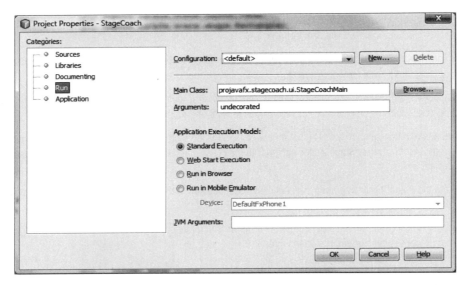

Figure 3-4. *Using NetBeans' Project Properties dialog to pass an argument into the program*

15. Notice that the program appears in a different location than it was in when you last exited. Also notice that this time the program appears without any window decorations, but that the white background of the program includes the background of the window. The black outline in the screenshot shown in Figure 3-5 is part of the desktop background.

16. Exit the program again by clicking either the close() or FX.exit() button, and then run the program again, passing in the string "transparent" as the argument. Notice that the program appears in the shape of a rounded rectangle, as shown in Figure 3-6.

Figure 3-5. *The StageCoach program after being invoked with the undecorated argument*

Figure 3-6. *The StageCoach program after being invoked with the transparent argument*

17. Click the application's UI and drag it around the screen, and click the close() or FX.exit() button when finished.

Congratulations on sticking with this 17-step exercise! Performing this exercise has prepared you to relate to the code behind it, which we'll now walk through together.

Understanding the StageCoach Program

Take a look at the code for the StageCoach program in Listing 3-1, and after that we'll point out new and relevant concepts.

Listing 3-1. *StageCoachMain.fx*

```
package projavafx.stagecoach.ui;

import java.io.InputStream;
import java.io.IOException;
import java.io.OutputStream;
import javafx.util.Properties;

import javafx.io.Storage;
import javafx.io.Resource;
import javafx.scene.Scene;
import javafx.scene.control.Button;
import javafx.scene.control.CheckBox;
import javafx.scene.control.Label;
import javafx.scene.control.TextBox;
import javafx.scene.input.MouseEvent;
import javafx.scene.layout.VBox;
import javafx.scene.shape.Rectangle;
import javafx.scene.paint.Color;
import javafx.scene.text.*;
import javafx.stage.Alert;
import javafx.stage.Screen;
import javafx.stage.Stage;
import javafx.stage.StageStyle;

var args = FX.getArguments();
var stageStyle = StageStyle.DECORATED;
if (sizeof args >= 1) {
  if (args[0].toLowerCase() == "transparent") {
    stageStyle = StageStyle.TRANSPARENT;
  }
  else if (args[0].toLowerCase() == "undecorated"){
    stageStyle = StageStyle.UNDECORATED;
  }
}
var resizable:Boolean = true;
var fullScreen:Boolean = false;
var title:String = "Stage Coach";
var stageRef:Stage;
var entry:Storage;
```

```
function saveProperties():Void {
  println("Storage.list():{Storage.list()}");
  entry = Storage {
    source: "stagecoach.properties"
  };
  var resource:Resource = entry.resource;
  var properties:Properties = new Properties();
  properties.put("xPos", "{stageRef.x}");
  properties.put("yPos", "{stageRef.y}");
  try {
    var outputStream:OutputStream = resource.openOutputStream(true);
    properties.store(outputStream);
    outputStream.close();
    println("properties written");
  }
  catch (ioe:IOException) {
    println("IOException in saveProperties:{ioe}");
  }
}

function loadProperties():Void {
  println("Storage.list():{Storage.list()}");
  entry = Storage {
    source: "stagecoach.properties"
  };
  var resource:Resource = entry.resource;
  var properties:Properties = new Properties();
  try {
    var inputStream:InputStream = resource.openInputStream();
    properties.load(inputStream);
    inputStream.close();
    if (properties.get("xPos") != null) {
      stageRef.x = Double.parseDouble(properties.get("xPos"));
      stageRef.y = Double.parseDouble(properties.get("yPos"));
    }
    println("properties read");
  }
  catch (ioe:IOException) {
    println("IOException in loadProperties:{ioe}");
  }
  stageRef.visible = true;
}
```

```
function showSystemProperties():Void {
  Alert.inform("Some System Properties",
                "java.os.name: {FX.getProperty("javafx.os.name")}\n"
                "javafx.os.arch: {FX.getProperty("javafx.os.arch")}\n"
                "java.os.version: {FX.getProperty("javafx.os.version")}");
}

stageRef = Stage {
  visible: false
  title: bind title
  width: 330
  height: 550
  style: stageStyle
  resizable: bind resizable
  fullScreen: bind fullScreen
  onClose: function():Void {
    println("Stage is closing");
  }
  scene:Scene {
    fill: Color.TRANSPARENT
    content: [
      Rectangle {
        width: 300
        height: 500
        arcWidth: 50
        arcHeight: 50
        fill: Color.SKYBLUE
        onMouseDragged: function(me:MouseEvent):Void {
          stageRef.x += me.dragX;
          stageRef.y += me.dragY;
        }
        onMousePressed: function(me:MouseEvent):Void {
          if (me.popupTrigger) showSystemProperties();
        }
        onMouseReleased: function(me:MouseEvent):Void {
          if (me.popupTrigger) showSystemProperties();
        }
      },
      VBox {
        layoutX: 20
        layoutY: 20
        spacing: 10
```

```
content: [
  Text {
    textOrigin: TextOrigin.TOP
    font: Font.font("Sans Serif", 14)
    content: bind "x: {stageRef.x}"
  },
  Text {
    textOrigin: TextOrigin.TOP
    font: Font.font("Sans Serif", 14)
    content: bind "y: {stageRef.y}"
  },
  Text {
    textOrigin: TextOrigin.TOP
    font: Font.font("Sans Serif", 14)
    content: bind "height: {stageRef.height}"
  },
  Text {
    textOrigin: TextOrigin.TOP
    font: Font.font("Sans Serif", 14)
    content: bind "width: {stageRef.width}"
  },
  Text {
    textOrigin: TextOrigin.TOP
    font: Font.font("Sans Serif", 14)
    content: bind "containsFocus: {stageRef.containsFocus}"
  },
  CheckBox {
    blocksMouse: true
    text: "resizable"
    selected: bind resizable with inverse
  },
  Text {
    textOrigin: TextOrigin.TOP
    font: Font.font("Sans Serif", 14)
    content: bind "resizable: {stageRef.resizable}"
  },
  CheckBox {
    blocksMouse: true
    text: "fullScreen"
    selected: bind fullScreen with inverse
  },
  Text {
    textOrigin: TextOrigin.TOP
    font: Font.font("Sans Serif", 14)
    content: bind "fullScreen: {stageRef.fullScreen}"
  },
```

```
            Label {
              font: Font.font("Sans Serif", 14)
              text: "title:"
            },
            TextBox {
              blocksMouse: true
              text: bind title with inverse
              columns: 15
            },
            Button {
              text: "toBack()"
              action: function():Void {
                stageRef.toBack();
              }
            },
            Button {
              text: "toFront()"
              action: function():Void {
                stageRef.toFront();
              }
            },
            Button {
              text: "close()"
              action: function():Void {
                saveProperties();
                stageRef.close();
              }
            },
            Button {
              text: "FX.exit()"
              action: function():Void {
                if (Alert.question("Are You Sure?",
                                "Exit without saving screen position?")) {
                  FX.exit();
                }
              }
            }
          ]
        }
      ]
    }
  }
}
stageRef.x = (Screen.primary.visualBounds.width - stageRef.width) / 2;
stageRef.y = (Screen.primary.visualBounds.height - stageRef.height) / 4;
loadProperties();
```

Obtaining Program Arguments

The first new concept introduced by this program is the ability to read the arguments passed into a JavaFX program. The javafx.lang package includes a class named FX that has utility functions such as println(), which you used in Chapter 2. Another function in the FX class is getArguments(), which returns a sequence of strings containing the arguments passed into the program. Here's the relevant code snippet from Listing 3-1 for your convenience:

```
var args = FX.getArguments();
var stageStyle = StageStyle.DECORATED;
if (sizeof args >= 1) {
  if (args[0].toLowerCase() == "transparent") {
    stageStyle = StageStyle.TRANSPARENT;
  }
  else if (args[0].toLowerCase() == "undecorated"){
    stageStyle = StageStyle.UNDECORATED;
  }
}
```

■Tip It is not necessary to import the javafx.lang package to use its classes (such as the FX class in the preceding code snippet). Also, any functions in the javafx.lang.Builtins class are automatically imported and may be used without qualifying them with a class name. This is why the FX.println() function may be expressed as simply println().

Setting the Style of the Stage

We're using the getArguments() function described previously to get an argument that tells us whether the stageStyle variable of the Stage instance should be its default (StageStyle.DECORATED), StageStyle.UNDECORATED, or StageStyle.TRANSPARENT. You saw the effects of each in the preceding exercise, specifically in Figures 3-2, 3-5, and 3-6.

Controlling Whether a Stage Is Resizable

As shown in Listing 3-1, to make this application's window resizable, we're setting the resizable variable of the Stage instance to true. To make it nonresizable, we set it to false. To accomplish this, the resizable check box is bidirectionally bound to a variable in our model, arbitrarily named resizable. The resizable variable of the Stage instance is then bound to the resizable variable in the model. As mentioned earlier in the chapter, the model in this chapter's example programs is typically a set of variables declared at the top of the script.

Making a Stage Full Screen

Making the Stage show in full-screen mode is done by setting the fullScreen variable of the Stage instance to true. This is accomplished in the same manner as manipulating the resizable value.

Working with the Bounds of the Stage

The bounds of the Stage are represented by its x, y, width, and height instance variables. Because these variables are public (and not public-init or public-read), their values can be changed at will. This is demonstrated in the following snippet from Listing 3-1 where the Stage is placed near the top and centered horizontally on the primary screen after the Stage has been instantiated:

```
stageRef.x = (Screen.primary.visualBounds.width - stageRef.width) / 2;
stageRef.y = (Screen.primary.visualBounds.height - stageRef.height) / 4;
```

We're using the Screen class of the javafx.stage package to get the dimensions of the primary screen so that the desired position may be calculated.

■**Note** We intentionally made the Stage in Figure 3-2 larger than the Scene contained within to make the following point: the width and height of a Stage includes its decorations (title bar and border), which vary on different platforms. It is therefore usually better to control the width and height of the Scene (we'll show you how in a bit), and let the Stage conform to that size.

Drawing Rounded Rectangles

As pointed out in Chapter 1, you can put rounded corners on a Rectangle by specifying the arcWidth and arcHeight for the corners. The following snippet from Listing 3-1 draws the sky-blue rounded rectangle that becomes the background for the transparent window example in Figure 3-6:

```
Rectangle {
  width: 300
  height: 500
  arcWidth: 50
  arcHeight: 50
  fill: Color.SKYBLUE
  onMouseDragged: function(me:MouseEvent):Void {
    stageRef.x += me.dragX;
    stageRef.y += me.dragY;
  },
  ...code omitted...
},
```

Dragging the Stage on the Desktop When a Title Bar Isn't Available

The Stage may be dragged on the desktop using its title bar, but in the case where its stageStyle is UNDECORATED or TRANSPARENT, the title bar isn't available. To allow dragging in this circumstance, we added the code shown at the end of the preceding code snippet.

Event handlers will be covered a little later in the chapter, but as a preview, the anony-mous function that is assigned to the onMouseDragged variable is called when the mouse is dragged. As a result, the values of the x and y instance variables are altered by the number of pixels that the mouse was dragged, which moves the Stage as the mouse is dragged.

Note By changing the stage's position in the onMouseDragged handler, we are effectively changing the behavior of the dragX/dragY variables. Instead of being relative to the pressed event (as we'll cover in the "Handling a Pop-up Trigger Event" section), they become relative to the last drag (due to the change in Stage position).

Using UI Layout Containers

When developing applications that will be deployed in a cross-platform environment or are internationalized, it is good to use *layout containers*. One advantage of using layout containers is that when the node sizes change, their visual relationships with each other are predictable. Another advantage is that you don't have to calculate the location of each node that you place in the UI.

The following snippet from Listing 3-1 shows how the VBox layout class, located in the javafx.scene.layout package, is used to arrange the Text, CheckBox, Label, TextBox, and Button nodes in a column:

```
...code omitted...
stageRef = Stage {
  ...code omitted...
  scene:Scene {
    fill: Color.TRANSPARENT
    content: [
      Rectangle {
        ...code omitted...
      },
      VBox {
        layoutX: 20
        layoutY: 20
        spacing: 10
        content: [
          Text {
            textOrigin: TextOrigin.TOP
            font: Font.font("Sans Serif", 14)
            content: bind "x: {stageRef.x}"
          },
          ...code omitted...
```

```
        CheckBox {
          blocksMouse: true
          text: "resizable"
          checked: bind resizable with inverse
        },
        ...code omitted...
        Label {
          font: Font.font("Sans Serif", 14)
          text: "title:"
        },
        TextBox {
          blocksMouse: true
          text: bind title with inverse
          columns: 15
        },
        ...code omitted...
        Button {
          text: "toFront()"
          action: function():Void {
            stageRef.toFront();
          }
        }
      ]
    }
  ]
}
}
```

The VBox layout class is similar to the Group class discussed in the Hello Earthrise example in Chapter 1, in that it contains a sequence of nodes within it. Like the Group class, this sequence is referred to by the content instance variable. Unlike the Group class, the VBox class arranges its contained nodes vertically, spacing them apart from each other by the number of pixels specified in the spacing variable.

Also in the javafx.scene.layout package is a class named HBox, which arranges nodes contained within the HBox node just like VBox does, only in a horizontal orientation. See Chapter 7 for information about HBox and how to use other layout containers in the javafx.scene.layout package.

On the subject of layout containers, the MigLayout manager, popular in the Java development world, is one of several layout containers available for JavaFX in the open source JFXtras project. See the Resources section at the end of this chapter for a URL to that project. Also, see Chapter 8, which contains information on the growing functionality available through third-party JavaFX libraries.

Ascertaining Whether the Stage Is in Focus

To know whether your JavaFX application is the one that currently is in focus (e.g., keys pressed are delivered to the application), simply consult the containsFocus instance variable of the Stage instance. The following snippet from Listing 3-1 demonstrates this:

```
Text {
  textOrigin: TextOrigin.TOP
  font: Font.font("Sans Serif", 14)
  content: bind "containsFocus: {stageRef.containsFocus}"
},
```

Here's a pop-quiz: can you set the containsFocused variable in order to make your application gain or lose focus? Hint: consult the JavaFX API docs to see whether the Can Write column of the containsFocused variable is checked.

Note The answer to the containsFocus question will be revealed when we cover the requestFocus() function of the Node class in the "Giving Keyboard Input Focus to a Node" section.

Controlling the Z-Order of the Stage

In the event that you want your JavaFX application to appear on top of other windows or behind other windows onscreen, you can use the toFront() and toBack() functions, respectively. The following snippet from Listing 3-1 shows how this is accomplished:

```
Button {
  text: "toBack()"
  action: function():Void {
    stageRef.toBack();
  }
},
Button {
  text: "toFront()"
  action: function():Void {
    stageRef.toFront();
  }
},
```

Closing the Stage and Detecting When It Is Closed

As shown in the following code snippet from Listing 3-1, you can programmatically close the Stage with its close() function. This is important when the stageStyle is undecorated or transparent, because the close button supplied by the windowing system is not present.

```
Button {
  text: "close()"
  action: function():Void {
    saveProperties();
    stageRef.close();
  }
},
```

Note In the preceding snippet, before closing the Stage, we save its screen position in the user's local storage area. Looking at the saveProperties() function defined earlier in this program, you'll see that we use the Storage and Resource classes in the javafx.io package to save Properties that contain the screen position. Conversely, the loadProperties() function uses the Storage and Resource classes to load the Properties that contain the screen position.

By the way, you can detect when the Stage has been closed by using the onClose event handler as shown in the following code snippet from Listing 3-1:

```
onClose: function():Void {
  println("Stage is closing");
}
```

Exiting the Application

A JavaFX application that has a Stage will end when the last Stage is closed. Normally there is just one Stage in an application, but nothing prevents you from creating other Stage instances. If you would like to end the application more abruptly, you can use the FX.exit() function as shown in the following snippet from Listing 3-1:

```
Button {
  text: "FX.exit()"
  action: function():Void {
    if (Alert.question("Are You Sure?",
                       "Exit without saving screen position?")) {
      FX.exit();
    }
  }
}
```

As you noticed when using the StageCoach program earlier, the program ends immediately without calling the onClose event handler that we previously discussed.

Tip If you want to specify actions to be executed when FX.exit() is encountered, you can use the addShutdownAction function of the javafx.lang.FX class. Here's an example:

FX.addShutdownAction(function():Void {println("shutdown action called")});

Displaying Alert Dialogs

As shown in the previous snippet, you can display an alert dialog that presents the user with some information and requires that the dialog be dismissed.

Three types of alert dialogs are available: confirm, inform, and question. Each type of dialog may be displayed by calling the corresponding function of the javafx.stage.Alert class.

Handling a Pop-up Trigger Event

Recall that when you right-clicked the blue rectangular area in the StageCoach program, an alert dialog appeared that contained some system properties such as your operating system type. The following snippet from Listing 3-1 shows how to determine when a mouse event is a "pop-up trigger" gesture (e.g., right-click on a Windows system, Ctrl-click on a Mac). It also demonstrates how to obtain system properties.

```
function showSystemProperties():Void {
  Alert.inform("Some System Properties",
               "java.os.name: {FX.getProperty("javafx.os.name")}\n"
               "javafx.os.arch: {FX.getProperty("javafx.os.arch")}\n"
               "java.os.version: {FX.getProperty("javafx.os.version")}");
}

stageRef = Stage {
  ...code omitted...
  scene:Scene {
    fill: Color.TRANSPARENT
    content: [
      Rectangle {
        width: 300
        height: 500
        arcWidth: 50
        arcHeight: 50
        fill: Color.SKYBLUE
        onMouseDragged: function(me:MouseEvent):Void {
          stageRef.x += me.dragX;
          stageRef.y += me.dragY;
        }
        onMousePressed: function(me:MouseEvent):Void {
          if (me.popupTrigger) showSystemProperties();
        }
        onMouseReleased: function(me:MouseEvent):Void {
          if (me.popupTrigger) showSystemProperties();
        }
      },
      ...code omitted...
    ]
  }
}
```

To make the alert dialog appear when the mouse is right-clicked, the onMousePressed and onMouseRelease event handlers shown in this snippet check to see whether the mouse event was a "pop-up trigger" gesture. If it was, our showSystemProperties() function is invoked.

■**Note** In the interest of keeping this example as simple and clear as possible, we didn't factor out the common code in the `onMousePressed` and `onMouseReleased` handlers. Of course, a nonexample application should always adhere to the *DRY* (don't repeat yourself) practice.

Obtaining System Properties

Also shown in the previous snippet is `getProperty()`, a function in the `FX` class that you can use to obtain some system properties. Here we're using it to get the OS name, version number, and architecture. Several other properties are available by calling the `getProperty()` function, such as the user's home directory (`javafx.user.home`) and the user's time zone (`javafx.timezone`). To see a list of these, take a look at the JavaFX API docs for that function in the FX class.

Making a Scene

Continuing on with our theater metaphor for creating JavaFX applications, we're going to now discuss putting a `Scene` on the `Stage`. The `Scene`, as you recall, is the place in which the actors and props (nodes) will visually interact with each other and the audience (the users of your program).

Using the Scene Class: The OnTheScene Example

As with the `Stage` class, we're going to use a contrived example application whose purpose is to demonstrate and teach the details of the available capabilities in the `Scene` class. See Figure 3-7 for a screenshot of the OnTheScene program.

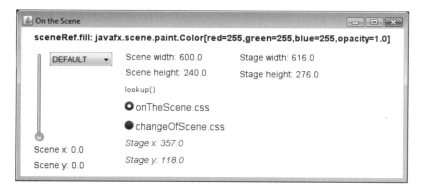

Figure 3-7. *The OnTheScene program when first invoked*

Go ahead and run the OnTheScene program, putting it through its paces as instructed in the following exercise. We'll follow up with a walkthrough of the code so that you can associate the behavior with the code behind it.

EXAMINING THE BEHAVIOR OF THE ONTHESCENE PROGRAM

When the OnTheScene program starts, its appearance should be similar to the screenshot in Figure 3-7. To fully examine its behavior, perform the following steps. Note that the variable and function names on the UI correspond to the variables and functions in the Scene, Stage, and Cursor classes, as well as CSS (Cascading Style Sheets) file names.

1. Drag the application around, noticing that although the Stage x and y values are relative to the screen, the Scene's x and y values are relative to the upper-left corner of the exterior of the Stage (including decorations). Similarly, the width and height of the Scene are the dimensions of the interior of the Stage (which doesn't include decorations). As noted earlier, it is best to set the Scene width and height explicitly (or let it be set implicitly by assuming the size of the contained nodes), rather than setting the width and height of a decorated Stage.

2. Resize the program's window and observe that the width and height values change to reflect the width and height of the Scene. Also notice that the position of much of the content in the scene changes as you change the height of the window.

3. Click the lookup() hyperlink and notice that the string "Scene height: XXX.X" prints in the console, where XXX.X is the Scene's height.

4. Hover the mouse over the combo box and notice that its text becomes blue. Click the combo box and choose a cursor style in the list, noticing that the cursor changes to that style. Be careful with choosing NONE, as the cursor may disappear, and you'll need to use the keyboard (or psychic powers while moving the mouse) to make it visible.

5. Drag the slider on the left, noticing that the fill color of the Scene changes and that the string at the top of the Scene reflects the red-green-blue (RGB) and opacity values of the current fill color.

6. Notice the appearance and content of the text on the Scene. Then click the changeOfScene.css button, noticing that the color and font and content characteristics for some of the text on the Scene changes as shown in the screenshot in Figure 3-8.

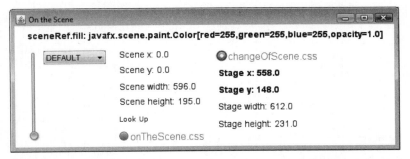

Figure 3-8. *The OnTheScene program with the changeOfScene CSS style sheet applied*

7. Click the onTheScene.css button, noticing that the color and font characteristics return to their previous state.

Now that you've explored this example program that demonstrates features of the Scene, let's walk through the code!

Understanding the OnTheScene Program

Take a look at the code for the OnTheScene program in Listing 3-2, and after that we'll point out new and relevant concepts.

Listing 3-2. *OnTheSceneMain.fx*

```
package projavafx.onthescene.ui;

import javafx.ext.swing.SwingComboBox;
import javafx.ext.swing.SwingComboBoxItem;
import javafx.geometry.HPos;
import javafx.scene.control.Hyperlink;
import javafx.scene.control.Slider;
import javafx.scene.control.RadioButton;
import javafx.scene.control.ToggleGroup;
import javafx.scene.Cursor;
import javafx.scene.Scene;
import javafx.scene.layout.Flow;
import javafx.scene.layout.HBox;
import javafx.scene.paint.Color;
import javafx.scene.text.*;
import javafx.stage.Stage;

var sceneRef: Scene;
var cursorNames = [
  "DEFAULT",
  "CROSSHAIR",
  "WAIT",
  "TEXT",
  "HAND",
  "MOVE",
  "N_RESIZE",
  "NE_RESIZE",
  "E_RESIZE",
  "SE_RESIZE",
  "S_RESIZE",
  "SW_RESIZE",
  "W_RESIZE",
  "NW_RESIZE",
  "NONE"
];

var cursors = [
  Cursor.DEFAULT,
  Cursor.CROSSHAIR,
  Cursor.WAIT,
  Cursor.TEXT,
```

```
        Cursor.HAND,
        Cursor.MOVE,
        Cursor.N_RESIZE,
        Cursor.NE_RESIZE,
        Cursor.E_RESIZE,
        Cursor.SE_RESIZE,
        Cursor.S_RESIZE,
        Cursor.SW_RESIZE,
        Cursor.W_RESIZE,
        Cursor.NW_RESIZE,
        Cursor.NONE
];

var selectedCursorIndex: Integer;
var fillVals:Number = 255;

var onTheSceneSelected:Boolean = true on replace {
    if (onTheSceneSelected) {
        sceneRef.stylesheets = "{__DIR__}onTheScene.css";
    }
};

var changeOfSceneSelected:Boolean on replace {
    if (changeOfSceneSelected) {
        sceneRef.stylesheets = "{__DIR__}changeOfScene.css";
    }
};

Stage {
    title: "On the Scene"
    scene: sceneRef = Scene {
        width: 600
        height: 240
        cursor: bind cursors[selectedCursorIndex]
        fill: bind Color.rgb(fillVals, fillVals, fillVals)
        content: [
            Flow {
                var toggleGrp:ToggleGroup = ToggleGroup {}
                layoutX: 20
                layoutY: 40
                width: bind sceneRef.width - 20
                height: bind sceneRef.height - 40
                vertical: true
                vgap: 10
                hgap: 20
                nodeHPos: HPos.LEFT
```

```
        content: [
          HBox {
            spacing: 10
            content: [
              Slider {
                min: 0
                max: 255
                vertical: true
                value: bind fillVals with inverse
              },
              SwingComboBox {
                items: bind for (cursorName in cursorNames) {
                  SwingComboBoxItem {
                    text: cursorName
                  }
                }
                selectedIndex: bind selectedCursorIndex with inverse
                id: "combo"
              }
            ]
          },
          Text {
            font: Font.font("Sans Serif", 14)
            content: bind "Scene x: {sceneRef.x}"
          },
          Text {
            font: Font.font("Sans Serif", 14)
            content: bind "Scene y: {sceneRef.y}"
          },
          Text {
            font: Font.font("Sans Serif", 14)
            content: bind "Scene width: {sceneRef.width}"
          },
          Text {
            font: Font.font("Sans Serif", 14)
            content: bind "Scene height: {sceneRef.height}"
            id: "sceneHeightText"
          },
          Hyperlink {
            text: "lookup()"
            id: "lookup"
            action: function():Void {
              var textRef = sceneRef.lookup("sceneHeightText") as Text;
              println(textRef.content);
            }
          },
```

```
            RadioButton {
              text: "onTheScene.css"
              toggleGroup: toggleGrp
              selected: bind onTheSceneSelected with inverse
              id: "radio1"
              styleClass: "radios"
            },
            RadioButton {
              text: "changeOfScene.css"
              toggleGroup: toggleGrp
              selected: bind changeOfSceneSelected with inverse
              id: "radio2"
              styleClass: "radios"
            },
            Text {
              id: "stageX"
              font: Font.font("Sans Serif", 14)
              content: bind "Stage x: {sceneRef.stage.x}"
            },
            Text {
              id: "stageY"
              font: Font.font("Sans Serif", 14)
              content: bind "Stage y: {sceneRef.stage.y}"
            },
            Text {
              font: Font.font("Sans Serif", 14)
              content: bind "Stage width: {sceneRef.stage.width}"
            },
            Text {
              font: Font.font("Sans Serif", 14)
              content: bind "Stage height: {sceneRef.stage.height}"
            }
          ]
        }
      ]
    stylesheets: "{__DIR__}onTheScene.css";
  }
}


// Demonstrate adding an element to the content sequence of the Scene
def textRef = Text {
  layoutX: 20
  layoutY: 10
  textOrigin: TextOrigin.TOP
  fill: Color.BLUE
  font: Font.font("Sans Serif", FontWeight.BOLD, 14)
  content: bind "sceneRef.fill: {sceneRef.fill}"
};
insert textRef into sceneRef.content;
```

Setting the Cursor for the Scene

The cursor can be set for a given node and/or for the entire scene. To do the latter, set the cursor variable of the Scene instance to one of the constant values in the Cursor class, as shown in the following snippet from Listing 3-2:

```
cursor: bind cursors[selectedCursorIndex]
```

These cursor values can be seen by looking at the javafx.scene.Cursor class in the JavaFX API docs; we've created a sequence of these constants in Listing 3-2. We've also created a corresponding sequence of strings that appear as items in the combo box.

Painting the Scene's Background

The Scene class has a fill variable whose type is javafx.scene.paint.Paint. Looking at the JavaFX API will reveal that the known subclasses of Paint are Color, LinearGradient, and RadialGradient. Therefore, a Scene's background may be filled with solid colors and gradients. If you don't set the fill variable of the Scene, the default color (white) will be used.

■Tip One of the Color constants is Color.TRANSPARENT, so you may make the Scene's background completely transparent if desired. In fact, the reason that the Scene behind the rounded-cornered rectangle in the StageCoach screenshot in Figure 3-6 isn't white is that its fill variable is set to Color.TRANSPARENT (see Listing 3-1 again).

To set the fill variable in the OnTheScene example, instead of using one of the constants in the Color class (such as Color.BLUE), we're using an RGB formula to create the color. Take a look at the javafx.scene.paint.Color class in the JavaFX API docs and scroll down past the variables such as ALICEBLUE and WHITESMOKE to see the functions. We're using the color function of the Color class, binding the fill variable to it, as shown in the following snippet from Listing 3-2:

```
fill: bind Color.rgb(fillVals, fillVals, fillVals)
```

As you move the Slider, which is bidirectionally bound to the fillVals variable, each of the arguments to the Color.rgb() function are set to a value from 0 to 255, as indicated in the following code snippet from Listing 3-2:

```
Slider {
  min: 0
  max: 255
  vertical: true
  value: bind fillVals with inverse
},
```

■**Note** Most of the binding discussed in the book so far has been to variables. Here we're binding the `fill` variable to a function. Chapter 4 explains the concept of *bound functions* in a good bit of detail.

Populating the Scene with Nodes

As covered in Chapter 1, the way to populate a `Scene` with nodes is to instantiate them in the content sequence, typically using the object literal syntax that you've become familiar with. We've also discussed that some nodes (such as `Group` and `VBox`) can contain other nodes. These capabilities enable you to construct complex *scene graphs* containing nodes. In the current example, the content sequence contains a `Flow` layout container, which causes its contents to flow either vertically or horizontally, wrapping as necessary. The `Flow` container in our example contains an `HBox` (which contains a `Slider` and a `SwingComboBox`) and several other nodes (instances of `Text`, `Hyperlink`, and `RadioButton` classes).

Finding a Scene Node by ID

Each node in a `Scene` can be assigned an ID in the `id` variable of the node. For example, in the following snippet from Listing 3-2, the `id` variable of a `Text` node is assigned the `String` "sceneHeightText". When the `action` event handler in the `Hyperlink` control is called, the `lookup()` function of the `Scene` instance is used to obtain a reference to the node whose `id` is "sceneHeightText". The event handler then prints the `content` of the `Text` node to the console.

■**Note** The `Hyperlink` control is essentially a button that has the appearance of hyperlink text. It has an `action` event handler in which you could place code that opens a browser page, or any other desired functionality.

```
Text {
  font: Font.font("Sans Serif", 14)
  content: bind "Scene height: {sceneRef.height}"
  id: "sceneHeightText"
},
Hyperlink {
  text: "lookup()"
  id: "lookup"
  action: function():Void {
    var textRef = sceneRef.lookup("sceneHeightText") as Text;
    println(textRef.content);
  }
},
```

A close examination of the action event handler reveals a construct that we haven't covered yet: casting in JavaFX. It is used here because the lookup() function returns a Node, but the actual type of object returned in this snippet is a Text object. Because we need to access an instance variable of the Text class (content) that isn't in the Node class, it is necessary to coerce the compiler into trusting that at runtime the object will be an instance of the Text class. To do this, we use the syntax as Text. Concepts related to subclassing and casting are covered in Chapter 4.

Accessing the Stage from the Scene

To obtain a reference to the Stage instance from the Scene, we use an instance variable in the Scene class named stage. This variable appears in the following snippet from Listing 3-2 to get the x and y coordinates of the Stage on the screen:

```
var sceneRef:Scene;
  ...code omitted...
  scene: sceneRef = Scene {
            ...code omitted...
          Text {
            id: "stageX"
            font: Font.font("Sans Serif", 14)
            content: bind "Stage x: {sceneRef.stage.x}"
          },
          Text {
            id: "stageY"
            font: Font.font("Sans Serif", 14)
            content: bind "Stage y: {sceneRef.stage.y}"
          },
```

Inserting a Node into the Scene's Content Sequence

Sometimes it is useful to dynamically add a node to the content sequence of the Scene instance. For example, in the drawing exercise that we'll challenge you to do in Chapter 5, the user can choose shapes from a toolbox and make them appear dynamically on the Scene. Likewise, the user can delete shapes that have been drawn on the Scene. To accomplish this, the example solution uses the technique demonstrated in the following snippet from Listing 3-2:

```
def textRef = Text {
  layoutX: 20
  layoutY: 10
  textOrigin: TextOrigin.TOP
  fill: Color.BLUE
  font: Font.font("Sans Serif", FontWeight.BOLD, 14)
  content: bind "sceneRef.fill: {sceneRef.fill}"
};
insert textRef into sceneRef.content;
```

This technique uses the `insert into` syntax that you learned in Chapter 2 to add a Text node to the Scene. This particular Text node is the one at the top of the Scene shown in Figures 3-7 and 3-8, in which the value of the Scene's `fill` variable is displayed. Any of the sequence manipulation constructs may be used to directly affect what nodes are displayed on the Scene.

CSS Styling the Nodes in a Scene

A very powerful aspect of JavaFX is the ability to use CSS to dynamically style the nodes in a Scene. You used this capability in step 6 of the previous exercise when you clicked the changeOfScene.css button to change the appearance of the UI from what you saw in Figure 3-7 to what was shown in Figure 3-8. Also, in step 7 of the exercise, the appearance of the UI changed back to what was shown in Figure 3-7 when you clicked the onTheScene.css radio button. The relevant code snippet from Listing 3-2 is shown here:

```
var onTheSceneSelected:Boolean = true on replace {
  if (onTheSceneSelected) {
    sceneRef.stylesheets = "{__DIR__}onTheScene.css";
  }
};

var changeOfSceneSelected:Boolean on replace {
  if (changeOfSceneSelected) {
    sceneRef.stylesheets = "{__DIR__}changeOfScene.css";
  }
};
Stage {
  title: "On the Scene"
  scene: sceneRef = Scene {
          ...code omitted...
          RadioButton {
            text: "onTheScene.css"
            toggleGroup: toggleGrp
            selected: bind onTheSceneSelected with inverse
            id: "radio1"
            styleClass: "radios"
          },
          RadioButton {
            text: "changeOfScene.css"
            toggleGroup: toggleGrp
            selected: bind changeOfSceneSelected with inverse
            id: "radio2"
            styleClass: "radios"
          },
          ...code omitted...
      stylesheets: "{__DIR__}onTheScene.css"
  }
}
```

In this snippet, the stylesheets variable of the Scene is initialized to the location of the onTheScene.css file. __DIR__ is a predefined variable definition, known as a *pseudo-variable*, that is a string representation of the same directory as the class file that references it. Because this script is in the projavafx.onthescene.ui package, when compiled, the CLASS files will be located in a directory named projavafx/onthescene/ui, which is where it will look for the changeOfScene.css file. We enclose __DIR__ in curly braces so that this pseudo-variable is evaluated and placed in front of "changeOfScene.css" in the resultant string. The value of the __DIR__ pseudo-variable includes a trailing slash, which is why we don't have to include one in the string.

Also shown in the snippet is the assignment of the CSS files to the stylesheets instance variable as the appropriate buttons are clicked. Take a look at Listing 3-3 to see the style sheet that corresponds to the screenshot in Figure 3-7. The CSS *selectors* in this style sheet represent the nodes whose id variable value is either "lookup", stageX", "stageY", "radio1", "radio2", or "combo". There is also a selector in this style sheet that represents nodes whose styleClass variable is "radios". The *properties* in this style sheet correspond to instance variables of their respective nodes (such as fill) or, in the case of UI control styles, the instance variables of their skins (such as base or dotFill). You can also use some standard CSS properties such as font, font-style, font-weight, and font-size. The *values* in this style sheet (such as red, italic, and 16pt) are expressed as standard CSS values.

Listing 3-3. *onTheScene.css*

```css
#lookup {
  text: "lookup()";
}

#stageX, #stageY {
  font-style: italic;
  font-weight: bold;
  fill: red;
}

.radios {
  font-size: 16pt;
}

#radio1 {
  base: blue;
  textFill: darkblue;
  size: 14;
}

#radio2 {
  base: blue;
  textFill: darkblue;
  dotFill: lightblue;
  size: 14;
}
```

```
#combo:hover {
  foreground: blue
}
```

Listing 3-4 is the style sheet that corresponds to the screenshot in Figure 3-8. For more information on CSS style sheets, see the Resources section at the end of this chapter.

Listing 3-4. *changeOfScene.css*

```
#lookup {
  text: "Look Up";
}

#stageX, #stageY {
  font-weight: bold;
  fill: blue;
}

.radios {
  font-size: 16pt;
}

#radio1 {
  base: orange;
  textFill: darkorange;
  size: 14;
}

#radio2 {
  base: orange;
  textFill: darkorange;
  dotFill: lightcyan;
  size: 14;
}
```

Understanding the JavaFX Node Class Hierarchy

JavaFX has a rich, ever-increasing set of UI nodes, each of which extend the Node class. Figure 3-9 shows a high-level view of this hierarchy. We've included package names in this diagram for ease of locating them in the JavaFX API documentation.

Figure 3-9. *JavaFX API node class hierarchy with some intermediary classes removed*

You've seen many of these node types in use so far in this book. Some notable exceptions are as follows:

- MediaView, which displays media and is covered in Chapter 6
- CustomNode and Control, which enable the creation of custom UI elements and are covered in Chapter 5

■**Note**   Many of the object-oriented concepts in JavaFX, including class hierarchy and inheritance, will be covered in Chapter 4.

Now that you've had some experience with using the Stage and Scene classes, several of the Node subclasses, and CSS styling, we'll show you how to handling events that can occur when your JavaFX program is running.

Handling Input Events

So far we've shown you a couple examples of event handling. For example, we used the onClose event handler of the Stage class to execute code when the Stage is closing. We also used the action event handler to execute code when a button is clicked. In this section, we'll explore more of the event handlers available in JavaFX.

Surveying Mouse and Keyboard Events and Handlers

Most of the events that occur in JavaFX programs are related to the user manipulating input devices such as a mouse and keyboard. To see the available event handlers and their associated event objects, we'll take yet another look at the JavaFX API documentation. First, navigate to the javafx.scene.Node class and look for the variables that begin with the letters "on". These variables represent the event handlers common to all nodes in JavaFX. Here is a list of these event handlers in the JavaFX 1.2 API:

- *Key event handlers*: onKeyPressed, onKeyReleased, onKeyTyped

- *Mouse event handlers*: onMouseClicked, onMouseDragged, onMouseEntered, onMouseExited, onMouseMoved, onMousePressed, onMouseReleased, onMouseWheelMoved

Each of these is a variable whose value is a function. In the case of the key event handlers, as shown in the JavaFX API docs, the function's parameter is a javafx.scene.input.KeyEvent instance. The function's parameter for the mouse event handlers is a javafx.scene.input. MouseEvent. The return type for both functions is Void.

Understanding the KeyEvent Class

Take a look at the JavaFX API docs for the KeyEvent class, and you'll see that it contains several variables, a commonly used one being code. The code variable contains a KeyCode instance representing the key that caused the event when pressed. Looking at the javafx.scene.input. KeyCode class in the JavaFX API docs reveals that a multitude of constants exist that represent keys on an international set of keyboards. Another way to find out what key was pressed is to check the char variable, which contains a string that represents the character associated with the key pressed.

The KeyEvent class also enables you to see whether the Alt, Ctrl, Meta, and/or Shift keys were down at the time of the event by checking the altDown, controlDown, metaDown, or shiftDown variables, respectively.

Another useful variable is node, which is a reference to the node in which the event originated. Consider carefully, however, between accessing the node directly and getting/setting model variables to which instance variables of the node are bound. The latter is sometimes the preferred approach.

Understanding the MouseEvent Class

Take a look at the MouseEvent class in the JavaFX API docs, and you'll see that significantly more instance variables are available than in KeyEvent. Like KeyEvent, MouseEvent has the altDown, controlDown, metaDown, shiftDown, and node variables. In addition, it has several variables that pinpoint various coordinate spaces where the mouse event occurred, all expressed in pixels:

- x and y contain the horizontal and vertical position of the mouse event, relative to the origin of the node in which the mouse event occurred.

- sceneX and sceneY contain the horizontal and vertical position of the mouse event, relative to the Scene.

- screenX and screenY contain the horizontal and vertical position of the mouse event, relative to the screen.

Here are a few other commonly useful variables:

- `dragAnchorX` and `dragAnchorY` contain the horizontal and vertical *position* of the most recent mouse pressed event, if the user is performing a mouse press-and-drag gesture.

- `dragX` and `dragY` contain the horizontal and vertical *distance from* the most recent mouse pressed event, if the user is performing a mouse press-and-drag gesture.

- `button`, `primaryButtonDown`, `secondaryButtonDown`, `middleButtonDown`, `clickCount`, `popupTrigger`, and `wheelRotation` contain information about what button was clicked, how many times it was clicked, whether the button has the semantic meaning of "show a pop-up menu," and how many *clicks* the mouse wheel was rotated.

Using Mouse and Key Events: The MobileEqualizer Example

In February, 2009 Sun released JavaFX Mobile so that JavaFX programs can run on mobile devices such as cell phones. The following MobileEqualizer example not only demonstrates how to respond to key and mouse events, but also runs on the JavaFX Mobile platform.

The screenshot in Figure 3-10 shows the MobileEqualizer program running in the JavaFX Mobile Emulator, but you can also run it as a JavaFX application via Web Start or as an applet on a web page. Before we dig into the code, go ahead and try the program by doing the following exercise.

Figure 3-10. *The MobileEqualizer program running in the JavaFX Mobile Emulator*

EXAMINING THE BEHAVIOR OF THE MOBILEEQUALIZER PROGRAM

When the MobileEqualizer program starts, its appearance should be similar to the phone's display in Figure 3-10. To fully examine its behavior, perform the following steps:

1. Press the down arrow key a few times. Notice that each time you press the key, the blue bar below the highlighted one becomes highlighted. When the bottom bar is highlighted and you press the down arrow key once more, the top bar should become highlighted.

2. Perform step 1 as instructed, using the up arrow key instead, noticing that the bar above the currently highlighted bar becomes highlighted each time.

3. While a bar is highlighted, press the right arrow key a few times, noticing that the length of the bar grows and that the Level value at the bottom of the Stage increases in value. Do the same with the left arrow key, noticing the opposite results.

4. Click one of the bars and notice that it becomes highlighted, dragging the end of the bar to the right and left. Notice that the length of the bar changes to correspond with the position of the mouse and that the Level value at the bottom of the Stage changes appropriately.

5. If your platform supports the JavaFX Mobile Emulator, click the right, left, up, and down buttons on the phone keypad to observe the behavior in steps 1, 2, and 3.

Now let's take a look at the code behind the behavior that you observed while performing the preceding steps.

Understanding the MobileEqualizer Program

Take a look at the code for the MobileEqualizer program in Listing 3-5, and after that we'll elaborate on event handling and other relevant concepts that occur in this program.

Listing 3-5. *MobileEqualizerMain.fx*

```
package projavafx.mobilebinding.ui;

import javafx.stage.Stage;
import javafx.scene.Group;
import javafx.scene.Scene;
import javafx.scene.input.KeyCode;
import javafx.scene.input.KeyEvent;
import javafx.scene.input.MouseEvent;
import javafx.scene.paint.Color;
import javafx.scene.paint.LinearGradient;
import javafx.scene.paint.Stop;
import javafx.scene.shape.Rectangle;
import javafx.scene.text.*;
```

```
var levels: Number[] = [30, 40, 50, 45, 35];
var selectedBarIndex: Integer = 0;
def MAX_LEVEL: Number = 230;
def MIN_LEVEL:Number = 10;
var groupRef: Group;

Stage {
  title: "Binding Example"
  scene: Scene {
    fill: Color.BLACK
    width: 240
    height: 320
    content: [
      Text {
        layoutX: 25
        layoutY: 20
        textOrigin: TextOrigin.TOP
        font: Font {
          name: "Sans serif"
          size: 18
        }
        content: "Binding / KeyEvent 2"
        fill: Color.WHITE
      },
      groupRef = Group {
        focusTraversable: true
        content: bind for (level in levels)
          Rectangle {
            x: 0
            y: 60 + (indexof level * 30)
            width: level
            height: 20
            fill: LinearGradient {
              startX: 0.0, startY: 0.0, endX: 0.0, endY: 1.0
              stops: [ Stop { offset: 0.0 color: Color.LIGHTBLUE },
                   Stop { offset: 1.0 color: Color.DARKBLUE } ]
            }
            opacity: if (indexof level == selectedBarIndex) 1 else 0.7
            onMousePressed: function(me:MouseEvent):Void {
              selectedBarIndex = indexof level;
            }
            onMouseDragged: function(me:MouseEvent):Void {
              if (me.x >= MIN_LEVEL and me.x <= MAX_LEVEL) {
                levels[indexof level] = me.x;
              }
            }
          }
```

```
        onKeyPressed: function(ke:KeyEvent):Void {
          if (ke.code == KeyCode.VK_RIGHT and levels[selectedBarIndex] <=
              MAX_LEVEL - 10) {
            levels[selectedBarIndex] += 10;
          }
          else if (ke.code == KeyCode.VK_LEFT and levels[selectedBarIndex] >
                    MIN_LEVEL + 10) {
            levels[selectedBarIndex] -= 10;
          }
          else if (ke.code == KeyCode.VK_DOWN) {
            selectedBarIndex = (selectedBarIndex + 1) mod sizeof levels;
          }
          else if (ke.code == KeyCode.VK_UP) {
            selectedBarIndex = (sizeof levels + selectedBarIndex - 1) mod
                              sizeof levels;
          }
        }
      },
      Text {
        layoutX: 25
        layoutY: 220
        textOrigin: TextOrigin.TOP
        font: Font {
          name: "Sans serif"
          size: 18
        }
        content: bind
            "Bar:{selectedBarIndex + 1}, Level: {levels[selectedBarIndex]}"
        fill: Color.WHITE
      }
    ]
  }
}
groupRef.requestFocus();
```

Understanding the Model Used in This Program

The model for this simple program consists of two variables and two constants near the top of the script in Listing 3-5. The levels variable is a sequence that represents the number of bars and length of each bar. The selectedBarIndex variable is the index in the levels sequence of the currently selected bar. The two constants, MAX_LEVEL and MIN_LEVEL, are the maximum and minimum allowable lengths for the bars.

Now we'll elaborate on the event handling used in the program, beginning with mouse events.

Using the onMousePressed Event Handler

As shown in the following snippet from Listing 3-5, the for expression causes several Rectangle nodes to be drawn on the UI, one for each element in the levels sequence. Recall from Chapter 2 that the iteration variable, in this case level, contains the value held in the element of the levels sequence corresponding to a given iteration.

When the user presses a mouse button while on one of the Rectangle nodes, the anonymous function assigned to the onMousePressed variable of the rectangle is invoked. This function, shown in the following snippet, causes the selectedBarIndex variable to be assigned the value of indexof level. Because the opacity of the Rectangle is bound to an if expression whose value is determined by the equality of indexof level and selectedBarIndex, the opacity of the Rectangle is immediately affected. In this case, the opacity value of the rectangle is 1.0 (fully opaque) when selected and 0.7 (70% opaque) when not selected. Check the opacity variable of the Node class in the JavaFX API docs for details.

```
groupRef = Group {
  focusTraversable: true
  content: bind for (level in levels)
    Rectangle {
      x: 0
      y: 60 + (indexof level * 30)
      width: level
      height: 20
      ...code omitted...
      opacity: if (indexof level == selectedBarIndex) 1 else 0.7
      onMousePressed: function(me:MouseEvent):Void {
        selectedBarIndex = indexof level;
      }
      onMouseDragged: function(me:MouseEvent):Void {
        if (me.x >= MIN_LEVEL and me.x <= MAX_LEVEL) {
          levels[indexof level] = me.x;
        }
      }
    }
  ...code omitted...
},
```

Using the onMouseDragged Event Handler

When the user presses a mouse button and begins dragging the mouse, the anonymous function assigned to the onMouseDragged variable is invoked, passing a MouseEvent instance that contains information about the event. As shown in the preceding snippet from Listing 3-5, if the horizontal location of the mouse cursor (me.x) is within the minimum and maximum levels, the appropriate element in the levels sequence is assigned that value.

As a result, the width of the rectangle is altered, because it is bound to the level variable.

■**Note** As pointed out in the "Understanding the MouseEvent Class" section previously, the `dragX` and `dragY` instance variables of the `MouseEvent` object are available within an `onMouseDragged` event handler. We were able to use the `x` variable of the `MouseEvent` object for simplicity in this particular case. You'll see an example of using the `dragY` variable of the `MouseEvent` object in the ZenPong example later in this chapter.

Now we'll show you how the program responds when the user presses keys on the keyboard.

Giving Keyboard Input Focus to a Node

In order for a node to receive key events, it has to have keyboard focus. This is accomplished in the MobileEqualizer example by doing these two things, as shown in the snippet that follows from Listing 3-5:

1. Assigning `true` to the `focusTraversable` instance variable of the `Group` node. This allows the node to accept keyboard focus.

2. Calling the `requestFocus()` function of the `Group` node (referred to by the `groupRef` variable). This requests that the node obtains focus.

■**Tip** The answer to the pop quiz earlier in the chapter, as you probably gleaned from the hint given, is that you cannot directly set the value of the `focused` variable of a `Stage`. Consulting the API docs will also reveal that neither can you set the value of the `focused` variable of a `Node` (e.g., the `Group` that we're discussing now). However, as discussed in point 2, you can call `requestFocus()` on the node, which if granted (and `focusTraversable` is true) sets the `focused` variable to `true`. By the way, `Stage` doesn't have a `requestFocus()` function, but it does have a `toFront()` function, which should give it keyboard focus.

```
...code omitted...
Stage {
     groupRef = Group {
        focusTraversable: true
        content: bind for (level in levels)
         Rectangle {
           x: 0
           y: 60 + (indexof level * 30)
           width: level
           height: 20
           ...code omitted...
           opacity: if (indexof level == selectedBarIndex) 1 else 0.7
           ...code omitted...
         }
```

```
    onKeyPressed: function(ke:KeyEvent):Void {
      if (ke.code == KeyCode.VK_RIGHT and levels[selectedBarIndex] <=
          MAX_LEVEL - 10) {
        levels[selectedBarIndex] += 10;
      }
      else if (ke.code == KeyCode.VK_LEFT and levels[selectedBarIndex] >
                MIN_LEVEL + 10) {
        levels[selectedBarIndex] -= 10;
      }
      else if (ke.code == KeyCode.VK_DOWN) {
        selectedBarIndex = (selectedBarIndex + 1) mod sizeof levels;
      }
      else if (ke.code == KeyCode.VK_UP) {
        selectedBarIndex = (sizeof levels + selectedBarIndex - 1) mod
                            sizeof levels;
      }
    }
  },
  ...code omitted...
}
groupRef.requestFocus();
```

Now that the node has focus, when the user interacts with the keyboard, the appropriate event handlers will be invoked. In this example, we're interested in whenever certain keys are pressed, as discussed next.

Using the onKeyPressed Event Handler

When the user presses a key, the anonymous function assigned to the onKeyPressed variable is invoked, passing a KeyEvent instance that contains information about the event. This function, shown in the preceding snippet from Listing 3-5, compares the code variable of the KeyEvent instance to the KeyCode constants that represent the arrow keys.

If the up or down arrow keys are pressed, this function causes the previous or next bar, respectively, to be selected, cycling around by using the mod operator (the modulus operator was covered in Chapter 2).

If the left and right arrow keys are pressed, this function decreases or increases, respectively, the value of the selected element in the levels sequence.

■**Note** You may have noticed that we used the onMousePressed and onMouseDragged event handlers of the rectangles, but used the onKeyPressed event handler of the Group that contains the rectangles. The Group is the node for which we requested keyboard focus, because the user needs to be able to navigate from one rectangle to another with the keyboard. Putting the onKeyPressed event handler in the Group allows it to have logic that controls all of the rectangles contained by the Group. In contrast, the user is controlling individual Rectangle nodes when clicking and dragging on them with the mouse.

Now that you've had some experience with creating key and mouse event handlers, we'll give you a look at how you can animate the nodes that you put in your scene.

Animating Nodes in the Scene

One of the strengths of JavaFX is the ease in which you can create graphically rich user interfaces. Part of that richness is the ability to animate nodes that live in the Scene. At its core, animating a node involves changing the value of its attributes over a period of time. Examples of animating a node include the following:

- Gradually increasing the size of a node when the mouse enters its bounds, and gradually decreasing the size when the mouse exits its bounds. Note that this requires scaling the node, which is referred to as a *transform*. (We cover transforms in Chapter 5.)

- Gradually increasing or decreasing the opacity of a node to provide a fade-in or fade-out effect, respectively.

- Gradually altering values of variables in a node that change its location, causing it to move from one location to another. This is useful, for example, when creating a game such as Pong. A related capability is detecting when a node has collided another node.

Animating a node involves the use of the Timeline class, located in the javafx.animation package. Depending on the requirements of an animation and personal preference, you'll use one of two general techniques:

1. Create an instance of the Timeline class directly and supply *key frames* that specify values and actions at specific points in time.

2. Use the javafx.animation.transition.Transition subclasses to define and associate specific transitions to a node. Examples of transitions include causing a node to move along a defined path over a period of time and rotating a node over a period of time. Each of these transition classes extends the Timeline class.

We'll cover these techniques, showing examples of each, beginning with the first one listed.

Using a Timeline for Animation

Take a look at the javafx.animation package in the JavaFX API docs, and you'll see three of the classes that are used when directly creating a timeline: Timeline, KeyFrame, and Interpolator. Peruse the docs for these classes, and then come back so we can show you some examples of using them.

■**Note** Hopefully it is now second nature to consult the JavaFX API docs for any new packages, classes, variables, and functions that you encounter. If you agree to do that, we'll try not to remind you so frequently.

The Metronome1 Example

We're going to use a simple metronome example to demonstrate how to create a timeline.

As the screenshot in Figure 3-11 shows, the Metronome1 program has a pendulum as well as four buttons that start, pause, resume, and stop the animation. The pendulum in this example is a Line node, and we're going to animate that node by *interpolating* its startX variable over the period of 1 second. Go ahead and take this example for a spin by doing the following exercise.

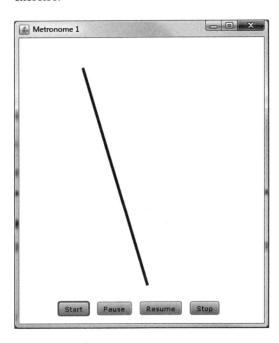

Figure 3-11. *The Metronome1 program*

EXAMINING THE BEHAVIOR OF THE METRONOME1 PROGRAM

When the Metronome1 program starts, its appearance should be similar to the screenshot in Figure 3-11. To fully examine its behavior, perform the following steps:

1. Observe that of the four buttons on the scene, only the Start button is enabled.

2. Click the Start button. Notice that the top of the line moves back and forth, taking 1 second to travel each direction. Also, observe that the Start and Resume buttons are disabled and that the Pause and Stop buttons are enabled.

3. Click the Pause button, noticing that the animation pauses. Also, observe that the Start and Pause buttons are disabled and that the Resume and Stop buttons are disabled.

4. Click the Resume button, noticing that the animation resumes from where it was paused.

5. Click the Stop button, noticing that the animation stops and that the button states are the same as they were when the program was first started (see step 1).

6. Click the Start button again, noticing that the line jumps back to its starting point before beginning the animation (rather than simply resuming as it did in step 4).

7. Click the Stop button.

Now that you've experienced the behavior of the Metronome1 program, we'll walk through the code behind it.

Understanding the Metronome1 Program

Take a look at the code for the Metronome1 program in Listing 3-6, and then we'll point out relevant concepts.

Listing 3-6. *Metronome1Main.fx*

```
package projavafx.metronome1.ui;

import javafx.animation.KeyFrame;
import javafx.animation.Interpolator;
import javafx.animation.Timeline;
import javafx.scene.Scene;
import javafx.scene.control.Button;
import javafx.scene.shape.Line;
import javafx.scene.layout.HBox;
import javafx.scene.paint.Color;
import javafx.stage.Stage;

var startXVal:Number = 100;
var anim = Timeline {
  autoReverse: true
  keyFrames: [
    KeyFrame {
      time: 0s
      values: startXVal => 100
    },
    KeyFrame {
      time: 1s
      values: startXVal => 300 tween Interpolator.LINEAR
    }
  ]
  repeatCount: Timeline.INDEFINITE
};
```

```
Stage {
  title: "Metronome 1"
  width: 400
  height: 500
  visible: true
  scene: Scene {
    content: [
      Line {
        startX: bind startXVal
        startY: 50
        endX: 200
        endY: 400
        strokeWidth: 4
        stroke: Color.BLUE
      },
      HBox {
        layoutX: 60
        layoutY: 420
        spacing: 10
        content: [
          Button {
            text: "Start"
            disable: bind anim.running
            action: function():Void {
              anim.playFromStart();
            }
          },
          Button {
            text: "Pause"
            disable: bind anim.paused or not anim.running
            action: function():Void {
              anim.pause();
            }
          },
          Button {
            text: "Resume"
            disable: bind not anim.paused
            action: function():Void {
              anim.play();
            }
          },
          Button {
            text: "Stop"
            disable: bind not anim.running
            action: function():Void {
              anim.stop();
```

```
            }
          }
        ]
      }
    ]
  }
}
```

Understanding the Timeline Class

The main purpose for the `Timeline` class is to provide the ability to change the values of variables in a gradual fashion over given periods of time. Take a look at the following snippet from Listing 3-6 to see the timeline being created, along with some of its commonly used instance variables:

```
var startXVal:Number = 100;
var anim = Timeline {
  autoReverse: true
  keyFrames: [
    KeyFrame {
      time: 0s
      values: startXVal => 100
    },
    KeyFrame {
      time: 1s
      values: startXVal => 300 tween Interpolator.LINEAR
    }
  ]
  repeatCount: Timeline.INDEFINITE
};

Stage {
  ...code omitted...
  scene: Scene {
    content: [
      Line {
        startX: bind startXVal
        startY: 50
        endX: 200
        endY: 400
        strokeWidth: 4
        stroke: Color.BLUE
      },
      ...code omitted...
    ]
  }
}
```

Inserting Key Frames into the Timeline

Our timeline contains a sequence of two KeyFrame instances. One of these instances assigns 100 to the startXVal variable at the beginning of the timeline, and the other assigns 300 to the startXVal variable when the timeline has been running for 1 second. Because the startX variable of the Line is bound to the value of the startXVal variable, the net result is that the top of the line moves 200 pixels horizontally over the course of 1 second. Recall from Chapter 2 that 0s and 1s are examples of Duration literals.

In the second KeyFrame of the timeline, the values variable is assigned a value that specifies that the interpolation from 100 to 300 will occur in a linear fashion over the 1-second duration. Other Interpolation constants include EASEIN, EASEOUT, and EASEBOTH. These cause the interpolation in a KeyFrame to be slower in the beginning, ending, or both, respectively.

■**Tip** The time variable in the KeyFrame instances of a Timeline indicates the accumulated duration over the entire timeline. For example, if we inserted another KeyFrame whose time value is 2s at the end of the sequence, that KeyFrame would be reached at 2 seconds from the beginning of the timeline, not at 3 seconds. Also, even though it is not a requirement, declaring key frames in ascending order (by time) is certainly a good practice.

The KeyFrame instance created previously is assigned to the keyFrame variable of the timeline. Following are the other timeline variables used in this example:

- autoReverse, which we're initializing to true. This causes the timeline to automatically reverse when it reaches the last KeyFrame. When reversed, the interpolation goes from 300 to 100 over the course of 1 second.

- repeatCount, which we're initializing to Timeline.INDEFINITE. This causes the timeline to repeat indefinitely until stopped by the stop() function of the Timeline class.

Speaking of the functions of the Timeline class, now is a good time to show you how to control the timeline and monitor its state.

Controlling and Monitoring the Timeline

As you observed when using the Metronome1 program, clicking the buttons causes the animation to start, pause, resume, and stop. This in turn has an effect on the states of the animation (running and/or paused). Those states are reflected in the buttons in the form of being enabled/disabled. The following snippet from Listing 3-6 shows how to start, pause, resume, and stop the timeline, as well as how to tell whether the timeline is running and/or paused.

```
var anim = Timeline {
    ...code omitted...
};
            ...code omitted...
        Button {
          text: "Start"
          disable: bind anim.running
          action: function():Void {
            anim.playFromStart();
          }
        },
        Button {
          text: "Pause"
          disable: bind anim.paused or not anim.running
          action: function():Void {
            anim.pause();
          }
        },
        Button {
          text: "Resume"
          disable: bind not anim.paused
          action: function():Void {
            anim.play();
          }
        },
        Button {
          text: "Stop"
          disable: bind not anim.running
          action: function():Void {
            anim.stop();
          }
        }
      }
```

As shown here in the action event handler of the Start button, the playFromStart() function of the Timeline instance is called, which begins playing the timeline from the beginning. In addition, the disable variable of that Button is bound to the running variable of the timeline, which causes the button to be disabled when the timeline is running. By the way, the running state of a timeline is true from when it has been started until it has stopped, regardless of whether it is currently paused.

When the user clicks the Pause button, the action event handler calls the timeline's pause() function, which pauses the animation. The expression bound to the Pause button's disable variable evaluates to true when the timeline is paused or the timeline is not running.

The Resume button is only disabled when the timeline is not paused. To resume the timeline from where it was paused, the action event handler calls the play() function of the timeline.

Finally, the Stop button is disabled when the timeline is not running. To stop the timeline, the action event handler calls the stop() function of the timeline.

Shorthand Syntax for Key Frames

An abbreviated syntax, shown in Listing 3-7, exists for creating KeyFrame instances. This is the preferred syntax for cases in which you don't need to handle an action event on the key frame.

■**Note** The ZenPong example in the section "The Zen of Node Collision Detection" later in the chapter demonstrates the use of an action event on a key frame.

Listing 3-7. *Shorthand Syntax for Key Frames from Metronome2Main.fx*

```
var anim = Timeline {
  autoReverse: true
  keyFrames: [
    at(0.0s) { startXVal => 100 },
    at(1.0s) { startXVal => 300 tween Interpolator.LINEAR}
  ]
  repeatCount: Timeline.INDEFINITE
};
```

Now that you know how to animate nodes by creating a Timeline class and creating KeyFrame instances, it's time to learn how to use the transition classes to animate nodes.

Using the Transition Classes for Animation

The javafx.animation.transition package contains several classes whose purpose is to provide convenient ways to do commonly used animation tasks. For example, Table 3-1 contains a list of transition classes in that package.

Table 3-1. *Transition Classes in the javafx.animation.transition Package for Animating Nodes*

Transition Class Name	Description
TranslateTransition	Translates (moves) a node from one location to another over a given period of time. This was employed in the Hello Earthrise example program in Chapter 1.
RotateTransition	Rotates a node over a given period of time.
ScaleTransition	Scales (increases or decreases the size of) a node over a given period of time.
FadeTransition	Fades (increases or decreases the opacity of) a node over a given period of time.
PathTransition	Moves a node along a geometric path over a given period of time.
PauseTransition	Executes an action at the end of its duration. Designed mainly to be used in a SequentialTransition as a means to wait for a period of time.
SequentialTransition	Allows you to define a series of transitions that execute sequentially.
ParallelTransition	Allows you to define a series of transitions that execute in parallel.

Let's take a look at a variation on the metronome theme in which we'll create a metronome using TranslateTransition for the animation.

The MetronomeTransition Example

When using the transition classes, we take a different approach toward animation than when using the Timeline class directly:

- In the timeline-based Metronome1 program, we bound an instance variable of a node (specifically startX) to a variable in the model (startXVal), and then used the timeline to interpolate the value of the variable in the model.

- When using a transition class, however, we assign values to the instance variables of the Transition subclass, one of which is node. The net result is that the node itself is affected, rather than just a bound attribute of the node being affected.

The distinction between these two approaches will become clear as we walk through the MetronomeTransition example. Figure 3-12 shows a screenshot of this program when it is first invoked.

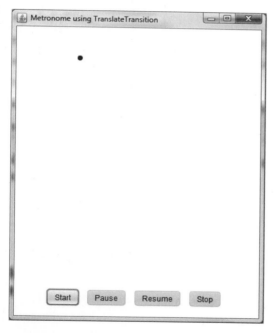

Figure 3-12. *The MetronomeTransition program*

The first noticeable difference between this example and the previous (Metronome1) example is that instead of one end of a line moving back and forth, we're going to make a Circle node move back and forth.

The Behavior of the MetronomeTransition Program

Go ahead and run the program, and perform the same steps that you did in the previous "Examining the Behavior of the Metronome1 Program" exercise. Everything should function the same, except for the visual difference pointed out previously.

Understanding the MetronomeTransition Program

Take a look at the code for the MetronomeTransition program in Listing 3-8, and then we'll point out relevant concepts.

Listing 3-8. *MetronomeTransitionMain.fx*

```
package projavafx.metronometransition.ui;

import javafx.animation.Interpolator;
import javafx.animation.Timeline;
import javafx.animation.transition.TranslateTransition;
import javafx.scene.Scene;
import javafx.scene.control.Button;
import javafx.scene.shape.Circle;
import javafx.scene.layout.HBox;
import javafx.scene.paint.Color;
import javafx.stage.Stage;

var circle:Circle;

var anim = TranslateTransition {
  duration: 1s
  node: bind circle
  fromX: 0
  toX: 200
  interpolator: Interpolator.LINEAR
  autoReverse: true
  repeatCount: Timeline.INDEFINITE
};

Stage {
  title: "Metronome using TranslateTransition"
  width: 400
  height: 500
  visible: true
  scene: Scene {
    content: [
      circle = Circle {
        centerX: 100
        centerY: 50
        radius: 4
        fill: Color.BLUE
      },
```

```
HBox {
    layoutX: 60
    layoutY: 420
    spacing: 10
    content: [
      Button {
        text: "Start"
        disable: bind anim.running
        action: function():Void {
          anim.playFromStart();
        }
      },
      Button {
        text: "Pause"
        disable: bind anim.paused or not anim.running
        action: function():Void {
          anim.pause();
        }
      },
      Button {
        text: "Resume"
        disable: bind not anim.paused
        action: function():Void {
          anim.play();
        }
      },
      Button {
        text: "Stop"
        disable: bind not anim.running
        action: function():Void {
          anim.stop();
        }
      }
    ]
  }
 ]
 }
}
```

Using the TranslateTransition Class

As shown in the following snippet from Listing 3-8, to create a TranslateTransition we're
supplying values that are reminiscent of the values that we used when creating a timeline
in the previous example. For example, we're setting autoReverse to true and repeatCount to
Timeline.INDEFINITE. Also, just as when creating a KeyFrame for a timeline, we're supplying a
duration and an interpolation type here as well.

In addition, we're supplying some values to variables that are specific to a TranslateTransition, namely fromX and toX. These values are interpolated over the requested duration and assigned to the layoutX variable of the node controlled by the transition (in this case, the circle). If we also wanted to cause vertical movement, assigning values to fromY and toY would cause interpolated values between them to be assigned to the ayoutY variable.

An alternative to supplying toX and toY values is to provide values to the byX and byY variables, which enables you to specify the distance in each direction to travel rather than start and end points. Also, if you don't supply a value for fromX, the interpolation will begin with the current value of the node's layoutX variable. The same holds true for fromY (if not supplied, the interpolation will begin with the value of layoutY).

```
var circle:Circle;

var anim = TranslateTransition {
  duration: 1s
  node: bind circle
  fromX: 0
  toX: 200
  interpolate: Interpolator.LINEAR
  autoReverse: true
  repeatCount: Timeline.INDEFINITE
};
```

Controlling and Monitoring the Transition

The TranslateTransition class, like all of the classes in Table 3-1 earlier, extend the javafx. animation.transition.Transition class, which in turn extends the Timeline class. As a result, as you can see by comparing Listings 3-6 and 3-8, all of the code for the buttons in this example is identical to that in the previous example.

The MetronomePathTransition Example

As shown in Table 3-1 earlier, PathTransition is a transition class that enables you to move a node along a defined geometric path. Figure 3-13 shows a screenshot of a version of the metronome example, named MetronomePathTransition, that demonstrates how to use the PathTransition class.

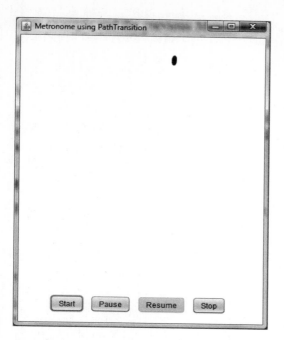

Figure 3-13. *The MetronomePathTransition program*

The Behavior of the MetronomePathTransition Program

Go ahead and run the program, performing once again the same steps that you did in the
"Examining the Behavior of the Metronome1 Program" exercise. Everything should function
the same as it did in the MetronomeTransition example, except that the node is an ellipse
instead of a circle, and the node moves along the path of an arc.

Understanding the MetronomePathTransition Program

Listing 3-9 contains code snippets from the MetronomePathTransition program that highlight
the differences from the preceding (MetronomeTransition) program. Take a look at the code,
and we'll point out relevant concepts.

Listing 3-9. *Portions of MetronomePathTransitionMain.fx*

```
package projavafx.metronometransition.ui;
...imports omitted...
var ellipse:Ellipse;
var path:Path = Path {
  elements: [
    MoveTo {
      x: 100
      y: 50
    },
```

```
    ArcTo {
      x: 300
      y: 50
      radiusX: 350
      radiusY: 350
      sweepFlag: true
    }
  ]
}

var anim = PathTransition {
  duration: 1s
  node: bind ellipse
  path: AnimationPath.createFromPath(path)
  orientation: OrientationType.ORTHOGONAL_TO_TANGENT
  interpolator: Interpolator.LINEAR
  autoReverse: true
  repeatCount: Timeline.INDEFINITE
};

Stage {
  title: "Metronome using PathTransition"
  width: 400
  height: 500
  visible: true
  scene: Scene {
    content: [
      ellipse = Ellipse {
        centerX: 100
        centerY: 50
        radiusX: 4
        radiusY: 8
        fill: Color.BLUE
      },
      ...HBox and Button instances omitted...
    ]
  }
}
```

Using the PathTransition Class

As shown in Listing 3-9, defining a PathTransition includes supplying a value to the path variable that represents the geometric path that the node is to travel. This variable is of type AnimationPath, which is located in the javafx.animation.transition package and has helper functions that create an AnimationPath from a Path, an SVGPath, or a Shape. Each of the three classes just mentioned, by the way, reside in the javafx.scene.shape package.

In Listing 3-9, we're creating a Path instance that defines an arc beginning at 100 pixels on the x axis and 50 pixels on the y axis, ending at 300 pixels on the x axis and 50 pixels on the y axis, with 350 pixel horizontal and vertical radii. This is accomplished by assigning a sequence to the elements variable that contains the MoveTo and ArcTo path elements shown previously. Take a look at the javafx.scene.shapes package in the JavaFX API docs for more information on the PathElement class and its subclasses, which are used for creating a path.

■**Tip** The variables in the ArcTo class are fairly intuitive except for sweepFlag. If sweepFlag is true, the line joining the center of the arc to the arc itself sweeps through increasing angles. Otherwise, it sweeps through decreasing angles.

Another instance variable in the PathTransition class is orientation, which controls whether the node's orientation remains unchanged or stays perpendicular to the path's tangent as it moves along the path. Listing 3-9 uses the OrientationType.ORTHOGONAL_TO_TANGENT constant to accomplish the latter, as the former is the default.

Drawing an Ellipse

As shown in Listing 3-9, drawing an Ellipse is similar to drawing a Circle, the difference being that an additional radius is required (radiusX and radiusY instead of just radius).

Now that you've learned how to animate nodes by creating a timeline and by creating transitions, we're going to create a very simple Pong-style game that requires animating a ping-pong ball. In the process, you'll learn how to detect when the ball has hit a paddle or wall in the game.

The Zen of Node Collision Detection

When animating a node, you sometimes need to know when the node has collided with another node. To demonstrate this capability, our colleague Chris Wright developed a simple version of the Pong-style game that we call ZenPong. Originally we asked him to build the game with only one paddle, which brought the famous Zen koan (philosophical riddle) "What is the sound of one hand clapping" to mind. Chris had so much fun developing the game that he snuck a second paddle in, but we're still calling this example ZenPong. Figure 3-14 shows this very simple form of the game when first invoked.

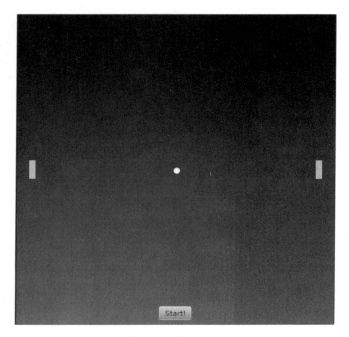

Figure 3-14. *The initial state of the ZenPong game*

Try out the game by following the instructions in the upcoming exercise, remembering that you control both paddles (unless you can get a colleague to share your keyboard and play).

EXAMINING THE BEHAVIOR OF THE ZENPONG GAME

When the program starts, its appearance should be similar to the screenshot in Figure 3-14. To fully examine its behavior, perform the following steps:

1. Even before clicking the Start button, drag each of the paddles vertically to other positions. One game cheat is to drag the left paddle up and the right paddle down, which will put them in good positions to respond to the ball after being served.

2. Practice using the A key to move the left paddle up, the Z key to move the left paddle down, the up arrow key to move the right paddle up, and the down arrow key to move the right paddle down.

3. Click the Start button to begin playing the game. Notice that the Start button disappears and the ball begins moving at a 45 degree angle, bouncing off of paddles and the top and bottom walls. The screen should look similar to Figure 3-15.

Figure 3-15. *The ZenPong game in action*

4. If the ball hits the left or right wall, one of your hands has lost the game. Notice that the game resets, looking again like the screenshot in Figure 3-14.

Now that you've experienced the behavior of the ZenPong program, we'll walk through the code behind it.

Understanding the ZenPong Program

Examine the code for the ZenPong program in Listing 3-10, and then we'll highlight some concepts demonstrated within.

Listing 3-10. *ZenPongMain.fx*

```
package projavafx.zenpong.ui;
...imports omitted...
/**
 * The center points of the moving ball
 */
var centerX: Number;
var centerY: Number;
```

```
/**
 * The y coordinate of the left paddle
 */
var leftPaddleY: Number;

/**
 * The y coordinate of the right paddle
 */
var rightPaddleY: Number;

/**
 * The moving ball
 */
var ball: Circle;

/**
 * The Group containing all of the walls, paddles, and ball.  This also
 * allows us to requestFocus for KeyEvents on the Group
 */
var pongComponents: Group;

/**
 * The left and right paddles
 */
var leftPaddle: Rectangle;
var rightPaddle: Rectangle;

/**
 * The walls
 */
var topWall: Rectangle;
var rightWall: Rectangle;
var leftWall: Rectangle;
var bottomWall: Rectangle;

/**
 * Controls whether the startButton is visible
 */
var startVisible: Boolean = true;

/**
 * The animation of the ball
 */
var pongAnimation: Timeline;
```

```
/**
 * Controls whether the ball is moving right
 */
var movingRight: Boolean = true;

/**
 * Controls whether the ball is moving down
 */
var movingDown: Boolean = true;

/**
 * The action calls the "checkForCollision" function to control the
 * direction of the ball.
 */
pongAnimation = Timeline {
  keyFrames: KeyFrame {
    time: 10ms
    action: function():Void {
      checkForCollision();
      centerX += if (movingRight) 1 else -1;
      centerY += if (movingDown) 1 else -1;
    }
  }
  repeatCount: Timeline.INDEFINITE
};

/**
 * Sets the inital starting positions of the ball and paddles
 */
function initialize():Void {
  centerX = 250;
  centerY = 250;
  leftPaddleY = 235;
  rightPaddleY = 235;
  startVisible = true;
  pongComponents.requestFocus();
}

/**
 * Checks whether or not the ball has collided with either the paddles,
 * topWall, or bottomWall.  If the ball hits the wall behind the paddles,
 * the game is over.
 */
```

```
function checkForCollision() {
  if (ball.intersects(rightWall.boundsInLocal) or
      ball.intersects(leftWall.boundsInLocal)) {
    pongAnimation.stop();
    initialize();
  }
  else if (ball.intersects(bottomWall.boundsInLocal) or
           ball.intersects(topWall.boundsInLocal)) {
    movingDown = not movingDown;
  }
  else if (ball.intersects(leftPaddle.boundsInLocal) and not movingRight) {
    movingRight = not movingRight;
  }
  else if (ball.intersects(rightPaddle.boundsInLocal) and movingRight) {
    movingRight = not movingRight;
  }
}

Stage {
  title: "ZenPong Example"
  scene: Scene {
    width: 500
    height: 500
    fill: LinearGradient {
      startX: 0.0,
      startY: 0.0,
      endX: 0.0,
      endY: 1.0
      stops: [
        Stop {
          offset: 0.0
          color: Color.BLACK
        },
        Stop {
          offset: 1.0
          color: Color.GRAY
        }
      ]
    }
    content: [
      /*
       * Note that each wall must have a height and width of at least one
       * pixel for the Node intersects function to work.
       */
      pongComponents = Group {
        focusTraversable: true
```

```
content: [
  ball = Circle {
    centerX: bind centerX
    centerY: bind centerY
    radius: 5
    fill: Color.WHITE
  },
  topWall = Rectangle {
    x: 0
    y: 0
    width: 500
    height: 1
  },
  leftWall = Rectangle {
    x: 0
    y: 0
    width: 1
    height: 500
  },
  rightWall = Rectangle {
    x: 500
    y: 0
    width: 1
    height: 500
  },
  bottomWall = Rectangle {
    x: 0
    y: 500
    width: 500
    height: 1
  },
  leftPaddle = Rectangle {
    var dragStartY: Number = 0;
    x: 20
    y: bind leftPaddleY
    width: 10
    height: 30
    fill: Color.LIGHTBLUE
    onMousePressed: function(me:MouseEvent):Void {
      dragStartY = leftPaddle.y;
    }
    onMouseDragged: function(me:MouseEvent):Void {
      leftPaddleY = dragStartY + me.dragY;
    }
  },
```

```
        rightPaddle = Rectangle {
          var dragStartY: Number = 0;
          x: 470
          y: bind rightPaddleY
          width: 10
          height: 30
          fill: Color.LIGHTBLUE
          onMousePressed: function(me:MouseEvent):Void {
            dragStartY = rightPaddle.y;
          }
          onMouseDragged: function(me:MouseEvent):Void {
            rightPaddleY = dragStartY + me.dragY;
          }
        }
      ]
      /**
       * Controls the movement of the left and right paddles
       * Left paddle: A(up), Z(down)
       * Right paddle: Up Arrow(up), Down Arrow(down)
       */
      onKeyPressed: function(k:KeyEvent):Void {
        if (k.code == KeyCode.VK_UP and
            not rightPaddle.intersects(topWall.boundsInLocal)) {
          rightPaddleY -= 6;
        }
        else if (k.code == KeyCode.VK_DOWN and
            not rightPaddle.intersects(bottomWall.boundsInLocal)) {
          rightPaddleY += 6;
        }
        else if (k.code == KeyCode.VK_A and
            not leftPaddle.intersects(topWall.boundsInLocal)) {
          leftPaddleY -= 6;
        }
        else if (k.code == KeyCode.VK_Z and
            not leftPaddle.intersects(bottomWall.boundsInLocal)) {
          leftPaddleY += 6;
        }
      }
    },
    Group {
      var startButton: Button;
      layoutX: 225
      layoutY: 470
```

```
      content: startButton = Button {
        text: "Start!"
        visible: bind startVisible
        action: function():Void {
          startVisible = false;
          pongAnimation.playFromStart();
        }
      }
    }
  ]
 }
}
// Initialize the game
initialize();
```

Using the KeyFrame Action Event Handler

We're using a different technique in the timeline than demonstrated in the Metronome1 program earlier in the chapter (see Figure 3-11 and Listing 3-6). Instead of interpolating two values over a period of time, we're using the action event handler of the KeyFrame instance in our timeline. Take a look at the following snippet from Listing 3-10 to see this technique in use:

```
pongAnimation = Timeline {
  keyFrames: KeyFrame {
    time: 10ms
    action: function():Void {
      checkForCollision();
      centerX += if (movingRight) 1 else -1;
      centerY += if (movingDown) 1 else -1;
    }
  }
  repeatCount: Timeline.INDEFINITE
};
```

As shown in the snippet, we use only one KeyFrame, and it has a very short time (10 milliseconds). When a KeyFrame has an action event handler, the code in that handler is executed when the time for that KeyFrame is reached. Because the repeatCount of this timeline is indefinite, the action event handler will be executed every 10 milliseconds. The code in this event handler does two things:

1. Calls a function named checkForCollision() which is defined in this program, whose purpose is to see whether the ball has collided with either paddle or any of the walls

2. Updates the variables in the model to which the position of the ball is bound, taking into account the direction that the ball is already moving

Using the Node intersects() Function to Detect Collisions

Take a look inside the checkForCollision() function in the following snippet from Listing 3-10 to see how we check for collisions by detecting when two nodes intersect (share any of the same pixels):

```
function checkForCollision() {
  if (ball.intersects(rightWall.boundsInLocal) or
      ball.intersects(leftWall.boundsInLocal)) {
    pongAnimation.stop();
    initialize();
  }
  else if (ball.intersects(bottomWall.boundsInLocal) or
           ball.intersects(topWall.boundsInLocal)) {
    movingDown = not movingDown;
  }
  else if (ball.intersects(leftPaddle.boundsInLocal) and not movingRight) {
    movingRight = not movingRight;
  }
  else if (ball.intersects(rightPaddle.boundsInLocal) and movingRight) {
    movingRight = not movingRight;
  }
}
```

The intersects() function of the Node class shown here takes an argument of type Bounds, located in the javafx.geometry package. It represents the rectangular bounds of a node, for example, the leftPaddle node shown in the preceding code snippet. Notice that we're using the boundsInLocal instance variable that the leftPaddle (a Rectangle) inherited from the Node class. The boundsInLocal instance variable is of type Rectangle2D, and its value is the bounds of the leftPaddle node.

The net results of the intersect function invocations in the preceding snippet is as follows:

- If the ball intersects with the bounds of the rightWall or leftWall, the pongAnimation Timeline is stopped and the game is initialized for the next play. Note that the rightWall and leftWall nodes are 1-pixel-wide rectangles on the left and right sides of the Scene. Take a peek at Listing 3-10 to see where these are defined.

- If the ball intersects with the bounds of the bottomWall or topWall, the vertical direction of the ball will be changed by negating the program's Boolean movingDown variable.

- If the ball intersects with the bounds of the leftPaddle or rightPaddle, the horizontal direction of the ball will be changed by negating the program's Boolean movingRight variable.

Tip For more information on `boundsInLocal` and its related variables, `layoutBounds` and `boundsInParent`, see the "Bounding Rectangles" discussion at the beginning of the `javafx.scene.` `Node` class in the JavaFX API docs. For example, it is a common practice to find out the width or height of a node by using the expression *myNode*`.layoutBounds.width` or *myNode*`.layoutBounds.height`. Also see Chapter 7, which includes a detailed discussion of this topic.

Dragging a Node

The MobileEqualizer example earlier in this chapter demonstrated a simplistic technique for dragging the mouse and affecting the width of a rectangle node in the process. The ZenPong example shows a technique which employs the `dragX` and `dragY` variables of the `MouseEvent` class to drag a node. See the following snippet from Listing 3-10 for an example of this technique:

```
var rightPaddleY: Number;
...code omitted...
function initialize():Void {
  centerX = 250;
  centerY = 250;
  leftPaddleY = 235;
  rightPaddleY = 235;
  startVisible = true;
  pongComponents.requestFocus();
}
...code omitted...
Stage {
        ...code omitted...
        rightPaddle = Rectangle {
          var dragStartY: Number = 0;
          x: 470
          y: bind rightPaddleY
          width: 10
          height: 30
          fill: Color.LIGHTBLUE
          onMousePressed: function(me:MouseEvent):Void {
            dragStartY = rightPaddle.y;
          }
          onMouseDragged: function(me:MouseEvent):Void {
            rightPaddleY = dragStartY + me.dragY;
          }
        }
        ...code omitted...
}
```

Note that in this ZenPong example, we're dragging the paddles only vertically, not horizontally. Therefore, the code snippet only deals with dragging on the y axis. The elements of this technique when applied to both x and y axes are as follows:

- Variables are declared in the model to which the x and y locations of the node are bound. The x and y locations are relative to the node's local coordinate space (plus any transforms, which will be discussed in Chapter 5). The node's local coordinate space could be the Scene or a Group in which the node is a member (which is the case in this example). Note that in this example, the rightPaddle node is only allowed to be dragged vertically, so we're only declaring one variable, named rightPaddleY.

- Variables are declared that store the x and y locations of where the mouse was pressed prior to being dragged. The dragStartY variable in the preceding snippet is declared for this purpose.

- In the onMousePressed event handler, assign the x and y locations of the MouseEvent to the variables declared for this purpose.

- In the onMouseDragged event handler, update the model variables that represent the node's location (in this example, just rightPaddleY) with the location in which the drag started (dragStartY) plus the number of pixels in each dimension that the mouse was dragged (me.dragY).

Note that we bound the y value of the rightPaddle Rectangle to the rightPaddleY variable. While this is convenient, a more generalized approach for dragging nodes is to bind the layoutX and layoutY instance variables to model variables.

Summary

Congratulations, you have learned a lot in this chapter about creating UIs in JavaFX, including the following:

- Creating a user interface in JavaFX, which we loosely based on the metaphor of creating a theater play and typically consists of creating a stage, a scene, nodes, a model, and event handlers, and animating some of the nodes

- The details about using most of the variables and functions of the Stage class, including how to create a Stage that is transparent with no window decorations

- How to use the HBox and VBox layout containers to organize nodes horizontally and vertically, respectively

- The details about using most of the variables and functions of the Scene class

- How to create and apply CSS styles to nodes in your program by associating one or more style sheets to the Scene

- The UI nodes that are available when creating a UI and what packages the nodes are contained in

- How to handle keyboard and mouse input events

- How to animate nodes in the scene, both with the `Timeline` class and the `transition` classes

- How to detect when nodes in the scene have collided

Now that you have learned more about JavaFX user interface development, it is time to move on to Chapter 4 to learn how to define functions and classes in JavaFX.

Resources

For some additional information on creating JavaFX user interfaces, you can consult the following resources:

- *JavaFX 1.2 SDK documentation online*: `http://java.sun.com/javafx/1.2/docs/api/`.

- *The JFXtras project*: `http://code.google.com/p/jfxtras/`. This is an open source project whose purpose is to fill in the gaps during early releases of JavaFX.

- *The w3schools.com CSS Tutorial*: `http://www.w3schools.com/css/`.

CHAPTER 4
■ ■ ■

Using Functions, Classes, and Other Advanced Features

Learning without thought is labor lost; thought without learning is perilous.

—Confucius

In Chapter 3, you began the journey of learning the rich JavaFX APIs. You saw how JavaFX organizes its functionality into packages, classes, and functions. You encountered the classes that are at the center of any JavaFX application, such as `javafx.stage.Stage` and `javafx.scene.Scene`. You learned about the `Rectangle` and the `Circle` classes and how, in addition to having their own instance variables, they *inherit* instance variables from their super classes. You also learned how to create an anonymous function to initialize the `onMouseClicked` instance variable in object literal expressions of various subclasses of `javafx.scene.Node`.

In this chapter, you will discover how to define functions and classes of your own. You will learn about function signatures and function types, and how to write anonymous functions. From there, you will see how to define classes and class hierarchies, and come to understand all about class types. You will also learn what happens when an object is instantiated and how you can exert control over the process.

Together with the primitive types and sequence types that you read about in Chapter 2, function types and class types round out the JavaFX Script type system. The JavaFX Script compiler performs *static type checking* during compile time to make sure your program does not violate any of the rules of the type system.

As the JavaFX Script code you write grows in size, you must organize it in a sensible way so that it is easy to work with. JavaFX Script provides mechanisms to split your code into separate files and organize it into packages. We will teach you how to use JavaFX Script's code organization facilities, including packages, modules, access modifiers that allow entities defined in one module to be used in other modules, and `import` statements that bring entities defined in other modules into the current module.

Working with Functions

In JavaFX Script, functions serve to break long and complicated code into manageable pieces. Once written, functions can be invoked multiple times with different arguments, so they also provide a code reuse mechanism. Additionally, functions are one of the ingredients of the two programming paradigms: functional programming and object-oriented programming.

Functions come into being in two ways: as function definitions or as anonymous function expressions. The following sections explore how to create functions each way.

Understanding Function Definitions

A *function definition* is introduced by the function keyword, followed by the name of the function, a pair of parentheses that encloses zero or more argument specifications (if more than one, the arguments will appear in a comma-separated list), an optional return type specifier, and a *body* block.

In Listing 4-1, we define a function that calculates the nth value of the recursively defined Fibonacci series. The first two numbers in the series are 0 and 1, and any subsequent number in the series is the sum of the two preceding numbers.

Listing 4-1. *The Fibonacci Series*

```
function fib(n:Integer):Integer {
  if (n <= 0) then 0 else
  if (n == 1) then 1 else
  fib(n - 1) + fib(n - 2)
}

println("fib(6) = {fib(6)}");
```

When you run the program in Listing 4-1, the following output is printed to the console:

```
fib(6) = 8
```

In the preceding definition, we defined a function named fib. It takes one argument of type Integer named n. It returns an Integer value. And its body is a block that contains a single if expression. Both the parameter type and the return type are explicitly specified.

Function definitions are not expressions. They can appear in only two places: either at the top level of a JavaFX Script source file or within the scope of a JavaFX Script class. Function definitions that appear at the top level of a JavaFX Script source file are called *script functions*. Those that appear within the scope of a class are called *instance functions*. They cannot appear inside other expressions, such as in a block. You will learn about classes and instance functions in the "Working with Classes" section later in this chapter.

In JavaFX Script, function names introduced by function definitions live in their own space, which is different from the space where variable and constant names introduced by variable or constant declarations live. As a result, in a JavaFX Script file you can define both a function foo and a variable foo, and the compiler will happily compile your source file.

Understanding Return Types

In JavaFX Script, the return type of a function is specified after the closing parenthesis of the argument list, separated from the argument list by a colon (:). Any JavaFX Script types, including primitive types, sequence types, function types, and class types, can serve as the return type of a function. A special type specifier, Void, can also be used as the return type of functions. As a matter of fact, the only legitimate use of Void is as the return type of a function.

Listing 4-2 shows some examples of function definitions.

Listing 4-2. *Function Definitions with Explicit Return Types*

```
function primes(n:Integer):Integer[] {
  [2..n][k | sizeof [2..<k][d | k mod d == 0] == 0];
}

function midpoint(p1:Point, p2:Point):Point {
  Point { x: (p1.x + p2.x) / 2, y: (p1.y + p2.y) / 2 }
}

function printSquaresTable(n:Integer):Void {
  for (x in [1..n]) {
    println("{x} squared = {x*x}");
  }
}
```

The function primes returns a sequence of integers consisting of all prime numbers less than or equal to the parameter value n. Its body is a block that contains a sequence comprehension consisting of all ks in the range from 2 to n for which a condition is true. The condition involves another sequence comprehension that contains all factors of k, between 2 and k-1, and the condition is true only if the size of the factor sequence is zero.

The midpoint function calculates the midpoint between its two arguments.

The printSquaresTable function prints a table of squares of integers between 1 and the function parameter n. It has a return type of Void, which means that this function does not return any values.

■**Note** One subtlety of the Void return type is that it does not prevent the body of the function from implicitly returning a value as the last expression of its body. The value will simply be ignored, and any function invocation expressions cannot be used in contexts where a value expression is expected. For example, var x = printSquareTables() will generate a compilation error.

As is the case for variable declarations, under certain restrictions, JavaFX Script's type inference facility can infer the return type of a function if an explicit type specifier is not given. Three of the four functions that you have seen earlier can also be defined without explicit return types, as demonstrated in Listing 4-3.

Listing 4-3. *Function Definitions with Implicit Return Types*

```
function primes(n:Integer) {
  [2..n][k | sizeof [2..<k][d | k mod d == 0] == 0];
}

function midpoint(p1:Point, p2:Point) {
  Point { x: (p1.x + p2.x) / 2, y: (p1.y + p2.y) / 2 }
}

function printSquaresTable(n:Integer) {
  for (x in [1..n]) {
    println("{x} squared = {x*x}");
  }
}
```

A restriction on inferring the return types of functions is that the function definition cannot have cycles. The fib function cannot be defined with implicit return types because it is recursively defined. This restriction also applies to two or more functions that reference each other in their bodies in such a way as to cause a cycle. For example, if function f calls function g, function g calls function h, and function h calls back to function f, all three functions need to have explicit return types.

Understanding Parameters and Their Types

A JavaFX Script function can have zero or more parameters. In function definitions, the function parameters appear after the function name as a comma-separated list enclosed in a pair of parentheses. In the four examples from the last section, the functions fib, primes, and printSquaresTable have one parameter, and the midpoint function has two parameters.

Each parameter is specified as a parameter name followed by an optional type specifier. If more than one parameter is specified, they all must have distinct names.

When a parameter's type is not explicitly specified, the type inference facility will infer the type of the parameter. However, the power of JavaFX Script's type inference facility for implicitly typed function parameters is weaker than that for either variables or return types. The inferred type will be either Object or Double depending on whether the parameter participates in arithmetic operations inside the function body.

None of the four functions from the last section is a good candidate for type inference on parameter types. Because the parameter n in the function fib participates in arithmetic operations, its inferred type is Double, not Integer as we intended. Because the function bodies of primes, midpoint, and printSquaresTable do not contain any arithmetic operations on their parameters, the inferred types of the parameters will be Object, which is not specific enough for these functions to compile successfully.

Naturally, function definitions that are candidates for type inference on parameter types are ones that perform numerical calculations. Listing 4-4 gives an example.

Listing 4-4. *Function Definitions with Implicit Parameter Types*

```
import java.lang.Math.*;

function hypot(x, y) {
   sqrt(x*x + y*y)
}

println("hypot(3, 4) = {hypot(3, 4)}");
```

This function calculates the hypotenuse of a right triangle given the other two sides. When you run the program in Listing 4-4, the following output is printed to the console:

```
hypot(3, 4) = 5.0
```

Note that we used the `import java.lang.Math.*;` statement to bring all the functions in the Java class `java.lang.Math` into our program. We used the `sqrt()` function in our calculations. We will cover `import` statements in the "Understanding Import Directives" section later in this chapter.

Understanding Function Bodies and the Return Expression

The body of a function is a block. Recall from Chapter 2 that a block is a pair of braces that encloses a number of other expressions. Everything that you learned about blocks also applies to function bodies. Additionally, function bodies may contain *return expressions*. When a function is invoked, its function body is executed until the end of the body or a return expression is reached. The execution of a function body may also end because of exceptions. We will cover exceptions in the "Understanding Exceptions" section.

A return expression is introduced by the `return` keyword, followed optionally by an expression. If the `return` keyword is not followed by an expression, the return expression is a stand-alone return expression. A stand-alone return expression is of the void type and has no value. If the `return` keyword is followed by an expression, the return expression is of the same type as the following expression, and its value is the value of the following expression.

Here is a stand-alone return expression:

```
return;
```

And here is a return expression that returns an integer value of 1024:

```
return 1024;
```

Return expressions may appear only inside a function body. If the function definition has an explicit return type that is not `Void`, all the return expressions inside the function body as well as the last expression of the function body must be compatible with the specified return type. If the function definition has an explicit return type of `Void`, all return expressions inside the function body must be stand-alone return expressions. If the function definition has no explicit return type, the return type of the function is inferred from the last expression of the function body and all the return expressions. The inferred return type will be a type that can accommodate all the return expressions.

Listing 4-5 presents some examples of function definitions whose bodies contain return expressions.

Listing 4-5. *Function Definitions with Return Expressions*

```
function gcd(a:Integer, b:Integer):Integer {
  if (b == 0) {
    return a;
  } else {
    return gcd(b, a mod b);
  }
}

function ampm(hour:Integer, minute:Integer):Void {
  if (hour == 0 and minute == 0) {
    println("midnight");
    return;
  }
  if (hour < 12) {
    println("a.m.");
    return;
  }
  if (hour == 12 and minute == 0) {
    println("noon");
    return;
  }
  println("p.m.");
}

function onClick(n:Integer) {
  if (n == 0) {
    return "No click";
  }
  if (n == 1) {
    return "Single click";
  }
  if (n == 2) {
    return "Double click";
  }
  return "Multiple click";
}
```

```
println("gcd(24, 18) = {gcd(24, 18)}");
ampm(0, 0);
ampm(6, 0);
ampm(12, 0);
ampm(18, 0);
println(onClick(0));
println(onClick(1));
println(onClick(2));
println(onClick(3));
```

The function gcd() calculates the greatest common divisor of parameters a and b using the Euclidean algorithm. It has an explicit return type of Integer, and both return expressions in the function body are of type Integer. The function ampm() prints out midnight, a.m., noon, or p.m. depending on the hour and minute parameters. It has an explicit return type of Void, and all three return expressions in the function body are stand-alone return expressions. The function onClick() attempts to return a string that describes the type of click based on the parameter n. It does not have an explicit return type, and since all return expressions in the function body are of type String, the return type of the function is inferred to be String.

When you run the program in Listing 4-5, the following output is printed to the console:

```
gcd(24, 18) = 6
midnight
a.m.
noon
p.m.
No click
Single click
Double click
Multiple click
```

What Can a Function Body See?

Within the body of a script function, you can access three kinds of variables:

- *Script variables and constants* declared in the same JavaFX Script source file

- *Function parameters* that are passed into the function invocation expression

- *Local variables and constants* that are declared in the function body

You also have access to other script functions in the same JavaFX Script source file. This list of accessible entities to script functions will grow when you learn how to organize your JavaFX Script code into multiple files and how to make entities from one file accessible from other files in the "Organizing JavaFX Script Code" section later in this chapter.

Listing 4-6 illustrates the accessibility of script variables from script functions.

Listing 4-6. *Accessing Script Variables from Function Definitions*

```
var q:Integer[];

function enqueue(i:Integer):Void {
  insert i into q;
  println("Enqueued {i}.  Size of q is {sizeof q} now.");
}

function dequeue():Integer {
  if (sizeof q == 0) {
    println("Size of q is {sizeof q} now. Returning -1.");
    return -1;
  } else {
    var i = q[0];
    delete q[0];
    println("Dequeued {i}.  Size of q is {sizeof q} now.");
    return i;
  }
}

enqueue(1);
enqueue(2);
enqueue(3);
println(dequeue());
println(dequeue());
enqueue(4);
println(dequeue());
println(dequeue());
println(dequeue());
```

The script variable q is a sequence of Integers. The two script functions enqueue() and dequeue() manipulate q in their bodies. The enqueue() function uses the insert statement to add the parameter i at the end of the sequence q and prints a message to the console. The dequeue() function first checks whether q is empty. If q is empty, the function prints a message and returns -1. Otherwise, it saves q[0] into a local variable i, uses the delete statement to remove the first element from q, prints a message, and returns the local variable i.

When you run the program in Listing 4-6, the following output is printed to the console:

```
Enqueued 1.  Size of q is 1 now.
Enqueued 2.  Size of q is 2 now.
Enqueued 3.  Size of q is 3 now.
Dequeued 1.  Size of q is 2 now.
1
Dequeued 2.  Size of q is 1 now.
2
```

```
Enqueued 4.  Size of q is 2 now.
Dequeued 3.  Size of q is 1 now.
3
Dequeued 4.  Size of q is 0 now.
4
Size of q is 0 now. Returning -1.
-1
```

Function parameters and local variables and constants can be seen only in the body of the function where they are defined. One function cannot see the parameters and local variables of another function. Function parameters are read-only. You cannot change the values of a function's parameters in the body of that function.

The following function will generate the compilation error message "You cannot change the value(s) of 'x' because it is a parameter":

```
// Won't compile
function f(x:Number):Void {
  x = 1024;
}
```

Understanding Overloaded Functions

In JavaFX Script, you can have several function definitions with the same name, as long as they can be distinguished by differences in either the number of parameters or the types of parameters. Multiple functions with the same name but different parameters are called *overloaded functions.*

The definitions of overloaded functions are no different from the definitions of nonoverloaded functions. You simply use the same function name in two or more function definitions.

Listing 4-7 shows an example of some overloaded functions.

Listing 4-7. *Overloaded Function Definitions*

```
function f(i:Integer):Void {
  println("Integer version of f is called with i = {i}.");
}

function f(n:Number):Void {
  println("Number version of f is called with n = {n}.");
}

function f(str:String):Void {
  println("String version of f is called with str = {str}.");
}

f(1024);
f(3.14);
f("Hello, World");
```

When these functions are invoked, the function invocation expression will all look like f(*exp*), where *exp* is some expression. The JavaFX Script compiler determines which of the overloaded functions is called by examining the type of the expression *exp* and selects the most appropriate function to call. In the three function invocation expressions in Listing 4-7, because 1024 is of type Integer, 3.14 is of type Number, and "Hello, World" is of type String, f(1024) invokes the version of f that takes a single Integer parameter, f(3.14) invokes the version of f that takes a single Number parameter, and f("Hello, World") invokes the version of f that takes a single String parameter.

When you run the program in Listing 4-7, the following output is printed to the console:

```
Integer version of f is called with i = 1024.
Number version of f is called with n = 3.14.
String version of f is called with str = Hello, World.
```

Without adding a version of f for a single Boolean parameter, the function invocation expression f(false) would cause a compilation error because the compiler cannot find an appropriate version of f to call.

■Caution To cut down the confusion of the program that calls overloaded functions, you should overload a function name only with functions that logically perform the same task, with slight differences in the parameters passed in.

Understanding Implicit Type Conversions

Up to this point, we have used the term *compatible* when we referred to the ability to assign a value to a variable or to pass a value into a function invocation expression as a parameter.

JavaFX Script will allow a value of one type to be assigned to a variable of a different type in three situations:

- Numeric conversions
- Sequence conversions
- Class hierarchies

Numeric conversions happen when a value of one numeric type is assigned to a variable of a different numeric type. Here is an example:

```
var n:Number = 1024;
```

This code looks normal, and you probably wouldn't think twice about it. Yet it does involve an implicit numeric conversion. The literal value 1024, which is of type Integer, is assigned to the variable n, which is of type Number. This assignment succeeds because JavaFX Script allows Integer values to be converted to Number values.

Sequence conversions happen when a value of a nonsequence type is assigned to a variable of the corresponding sequence type. JavaFX Script allows this conversion to simplify sequence manipulation code because in many cases a sequence variable contains only one element. Therefore, the two assignments in the following snippet of code are equivalent:

```
var strs:String[];

strs = ["Hello, World"];
strs = "Hello, World";
```

As this conversion demonstrates, if a sequence contains only one element, the brackets are optional.

Note that there is no implicit conversion from a sequence type to its element type. The following code will cause a compilation error:

```
// Won't compile
var str:String = ["Hello, World"];
```

We will show you how to define class hierarchies in the "Creating Class Hierarchies" section later in this chapter; for now, you just need to understand the rule for assignability regarding such hierarchies: if class Bar extends class Foo, an instance of Bar can be assigned to a variable of type Foo. Here is a simple example:

```
class Foo {}
class Bar extends Foo {}
var foo:Foo = Bar {};
```

In the third line, we created a new instance of Bar with an object literal expression and assigned the resulting instance of Bar to the variable foo, which is declared with type Foo. Notice that no conversion on the instance is performed nor is it needed. An instance of a subclass is naturally also an instance of its super classes. This is different from numeric conversions or sequence conversions.

For the purposes of assignment and function parameter passing, the primitive types and function types (which you will learn shortly in the "Understanding Function Types and Anonymous Functions" section) are considered assignable to the Object type. Sequence types are not considered assignable to the Object type.

Rules for Overloaded Function Resolution

With a deeper understanding of compatibilities between values and variables, we can state the rules the JavaFX Script compiler uses to find the function to invoke for a function invocation expression:

- Find all functions with the given name, with the same number of parameters as in the function invocation expression, and with compatible types for each parameter. If only one function matches, invoke that function.

- If more than one function remains, and if one function in the set has parameter types that are more specific than another function in the set, eliminate the less-specific function. Repeat this process until no more eliminations can be made.

- If exactly one function remains, invoke that function. If more than one function remains, the function invocation expression cannot be resolved, and a compilation error results.

Listing 4-8 presents an example of an ambiguous invocation of overloaded functions.

Listing 4-8. *Resolving Overloaded Function Definitions*

```
function f(i:Integer, n:Number):Void {
  println("Integer, Number version of f is called with ({i}, {n}).");
}

function f(n:Number, i:Integer):Void {
  println("Number, Integer version of f is called with ({n}, {i}).");
}

f(1024, 3.14);
f(6.28, 2048);
// f(1024, 2048); // Won't compile
```

Both overloaded functions match the third (commented out) invocation. However, because the first function definition is more specific in the first parameter and the second function definition is more specific in the second parameter, neither function can be eliminated in the second step of the resolution rules.

When you run the program in Listing 4-8, the following output is printed to the console:

```
Integer, Number version of f called with (1024, 3.14).
Number, Integer version of f called with (6.28, 2048).
```

Understanding Function Types and Anonymous Functions

Although JavaFX Script's function definition facility allows you to define functions at the script and class level, JavaFX Script's *anonymous function expression* allows you to create functions anywhere an expression can appear.

Because an anonymous function expression is an expression, you may naturally ask two questions of any JavaFX Script expressions: What is the type of the expression? And what is the value of the expression? The answers are straightforward. JavaFX Script anonymous function expressions have *function types*, and they evaluate to *closures*.

The concepts of anonymous function expressions, closures, and function types are intricately related, so we will first present a simple example, shown in Listing 4-9, that involves all of these concepts. We will then point to portions of the example when we explain the relevant concepts.

Listing 4-9. *Anonymous Function Example*

```
import java.lang.Math.*;

{
  var hypot: function(:Number, :Number):Number;
```

```
hypot = function(x, y) {
  sqrt(x*x + y*y);
};

println("hypot(3, 4) = {hypot(3, 4)}");
}
```

We deliberately put all the code inside a block, where a function definition is not allowed but anonymous function expressions are allowed.

We first declare a variable, hypot, with the type specifier function(:Number, :Number):Number. This specifies a function type representing all functions that takes two Number parameters and returns a Number value. We then assign an anonymous function expression to the variable hypot. The anonymous function expression, which is shown in bold type, resembles an ordinary function definition without the function name. After the assignment, the variable hypot has as its value a closure that is the result of evaluating the anonymous function expression. We finally invoke the closure, which performs the calculation specified in the anonymous function expression, in this case calculating the hypotenuse of a right triangle.

More Details on Function Type Specifiers

The format of a function type specifier is simple. It starts with the function keyword, followed by a pair of parentheses enclosing a comma-separated list of parameter type specifiers, and then the return type specifier. You define the parameter type specifier by including a colon (:) followed by the type name or by including a parameter name followed by a colon and then the type name. You provide the return type specifier by using a colon followed by the type name.

Because no function body is associated with a function type specifier, all parameter types must be provided. You can omit the return type specifier. However, if you do so, the return type is assumed to be Void.

The following is a list of function type specifiers that are found in the JavaFX SDK documentation:

```
function(:Duration):Void
function(:Event):Void
function(:Exception):Void
function(:InputStream):Void
function(:KeyEvent):Void
function(:MediaError):Void
function(:MediaTimer):Void
function(:MouseEvent):Void
function(:MouseEvent):Boolean
function(:OutputStream):Void
function(:Sequence):Void
function(:String):Void
function(:String):Boolean
function(:Boolean):Void
function(:Integer):Void
```

These are the data types of various event handlers in JavaFX API classes. The function(:MouseEvent):Void type, for example, is the type of instance variables named onMousePressed, onMouseReleased, and onMouseMoved in the javafx.scene.CustomNode class. You've seen them at work in Chapter 3.

You can build more complicated function types. Here is an example:

```
function(:Integer):function(:Integer):Integer
```

This is the type of a function that takes an Integer parameter and returns a function. The function it returns takes an Integer parameter and returns an Integer.

More Details on Anonymous Function Expressions

As you saw in Listing 4-9, an anonymous function expression is almost identical with a function definition in form. In that program, we used a form of anonymous function expression that relied on JavaFX Script's type inference facility to determine the function type of the resulting closure.

You can also use the form of anonymous function expression that explicitly specifies the parameter and return types, as you see in Listing 4-10.

Listing 4-10. *Anonymous Function with Explicit Types*

```
{
  var primes = function(n:Integer):Integer[] {
    [2..n][k | sizeof [2..<k][d | k mod d == 0] == 0]
  };
  println(primes(64));
}
```

In this example, we redefine our earlier primes function as an anonymous function expression with explicitly specified types. Because we do not explicitly specify the type of primes, it gets the type of the first value that is assigned to it. In this case, the value is the closure resulting from evaluating the anonymous function expression.

If you attempt to assign a closure to an explicit function type variable and the type of the closure is different from the type of the variable, a compilation error will be generated.

More Details on Closures

One of the benefits of supporting function types in a language is that functions can be assigned to variables, passed into functions, and returned from functions. Programming languages that support such features are usually said to support *first-class functions*. And you can use a style of programming that relies heavily on first-class functions called *functional programming*.

Listing 4-11 shows a typical first example of functional programming.

Listing 4-11. *Functional Programming*

```
{
  var addN: function(:Integer):function(:Integer):Integer;
  addN = function(n) {
    function(i:Integer) {
      i + n
    }
  };

  var addTen = addN(10);
  println("addTen(4) = {addTen(4)}.");
}
```

We declare addN as a function type variable that takes an Integer parameter and returns a function, which in turn takes an Integer parameter and returns an Integer. We then assign a closure to it: any Integer parameter will return a function that adds the Integer to its parameter. We then assign addN(10) to the variable addTen. The variable addTen is therefore of the function type function(:Integer):Integer, which is the return type addN, and the closure that is assigned to addTen will simply add 10 to its parameter. Finally, we invoke addTen with a parameter of 4, which should produce the result 14.

When we run the program in Listing 4-11, the following output is printed to the console:

```
addTen(4) = 14.
```

In the "What Can a Function Body See" section earlier in the chapter, we showed that the function definition's body can access all script variables and constants and all script functions. In much the same way, the body of an anonymous function expression can also access all the functions, variables, and constants that are in scope when the anonymous function expression is evaluated. The resulting closure will capture these functions, variables, and constants.

Much of the power of closure comes from the fact that the environment that it captures remains available even after the original environment is gone. In Listing 4-11, for example, by the time addTen(4) is invoked, the earlier invocation addN(10) has already returned, yet addTen can still access the parameter 10 that is passed into the invocation of addN(10).

Understanding Bound Functions

In the "Working with Data Bindings" section of Chapter 2, we mentioned bound functions but deferred the discussion to this chapter. Now that you are up to speed with function definitions, it's time to teach you about bound functions.

A *bound function* is a function definition decorated with the bound modifier whose body is restricted to a number of variable and constant declarations followed by one final expression.

When a variable is bound to a function invocation expression which includes a bound function, its dependency is the dependency of the last expression of the bound function, traced transitively to either a parameter of the function or a script variable. Listing 4-12 shows an example of a bound function.

Listing 4-12. *Binding to a Bound Function*

```
var x = 3;

bound function f(y:Number, z:Number):Number {
   var u = y;
   var v = z;
   x + u
}

var a = 4;
var b = 5;
var c = bind f(a, b) on replace {
   println("x = {x}, a = {a}, b = {b}, c = {c}.");
};

println("About to change x...");
x = 5;
println("About to change a...");
a = 6;
println("About to change b...");
b = 7;
```

In Listing 4-12, the dependency of c is the dependency of x + u, the last expression of the bound function f. Because x is a script variable, and u depends on the first parameter y, the dependency of c is the script variable x and the first parameter of the function invocation expression, a. We add an on replace trigger to monitor the update of c. We will cover triggers in the "Understanding Triggers" section later in this chapter.

When we run the program in Listing 4-12, the following output is printed to the console:

```
x = 3, a = 4, b = 5, c = 7.0.
About to change x...
x = 5, a = 4, b = 5, c = 9.0.
About to change a...
x = 5, a = 6, b = 5, c = 11.0.
About to change b...
```

As you can see, the value of c is indeed updated when x and a changed, but not when b changed.

When a bound function is invoked in a bind expression, its function body is also evaluated in a bound context, which causes each assignment in the body to behave as if it were a binding assignment.

This allows complicated expressions to be bound to a variable through a series of simpler bound functions. You will see this trick at work in Chapter 7.

Understanding Exceptions

As your JavaFX Script code base grows, the need for handling errors in a systematic way becomes more important. The exception facility is JavaFX Script's way of dealing with exceptional conditions.

Understanding the Call Stack

As your program runs, the code will call into and exit from functions. Every time the code calls into a function, the JavaFX Script runtime creates a *stack frame*. The stack frame for each function call contains the parameters that are passed into the function as well as local variables and constants declared within the function. The *call stack* is the accumulation of stack frames of all active function calls. As the code makes deeper and deeper function calls, the call stack grows. As the code exits the called functions, the call stack shrinks.

As you saw earlier, reaching a return expression inside a function body and reaching the end of the function body are two ways to return from function calls. These are called *normal exits* from function calls.

If your code encounters an exceptional condition or an error condition and cannot complete the calculation the function is designed to do, you can use JavaFX Script's exception facility to throw an exception. If your code calls functions that may throw exceptions, you can use a try-catch-finally expression to install handlers for the exceptions that it is prepared to handle. When an exception is thrown, the JavaFX Script runtime will look for a handler for the exception. If one cannot be found in the current function, it will exit the function and continue looking for one in the calling function. The runtime may exit several levels of function calls before a handler is found. These are called *abnormal exits* from function calls. The process of exiting functions abnormally in search of an exception handler is called *unwinding of the call stack*.

Throwing Exceptions

You throw an exception using a *throw expression*. A throw expression is introduced by the throw keyword, followed by an instance of a class that extends the Java class java.lang. Throwable. When a throw expression is evaluated, the JavaFX Script exception handling facility is started.

The class java.lang.Throwable is the root of the exception class hierarchy for Java, which include many exception classes that can be used directly in JavaFX Script. You can also define your own exception classes for use in your code. However, for the majority of JavaFX Script programs, the Java exceptions are adequate.

Listing 4-13 shows an example of a function that throws an exception.

Listing 4-13. *Throwing an Exception*

```
import java.lang.IllegalArgumentException;

function weekday(i:Integer):String {
  if (i == 0) then "Sunday" else
  if (i == 1) then "Monday" else
  if (i == 2) then "Tuesday" else
```

```
    if (i == 3) then "Wendesday" else
    if (i == 4) then "Thursday" else
    if (i == 5) then "Friday" else
    if (i == 6) then "Saturday" else
    throw new IllegalArgumentException("Invalid weekday: {i}.");
}

for (i in [0..7]) {
  println("weekday({i}) = {weekday(i)}.");
}
```

In Listing 4-13, we define a simple function that translates numeric representations of weekdays into their corresponding string representations. When the parameter is not in the correct range, we throw a newly constructed instance of java.lang.IllegalArgumentException. We then called the function eight times in a for loop, the last time with an illegal argument. Because java.lang.IllegalArgumentException is a Java class, we use the new keyword to create an instance of it for use in our thrown exception. You will find out more about instantiating Java classes in the "Leveraging Java from JavaFX Script" section later in this chapter.

When we run the program in Listing 4-13, the following output is printed to the console:

```
weekday(0) = Sunday.
weekday(1) = Monday.
weekday(2) = Tuesday.
weekday(3) = Wendesday.
weekday(4) = Thursday.
weekday(5) = Friday.
weekday(6) = Saturday.
java.lang.Exception: Invalid weekday: 7.
        at ThrowingException.weekday(ThrowingException.fx:11)
        at ThrowingException.javafx$run$(ThrowingException.fx:15)
```

We call the function without a custom exception handler, so when JavaFX Script unwinds the stack, it exits not only the weekday() function, but also the calling code into the default exception handler, which simply prints the stack trace to the console.

The following are general-purpose exception classes that can be used when appropriate in your JavaFX Script code:

```
java.lang.Exception
java.lang.IllegalArgumentexception
java.lang.IllegalStateException
java.lang.RuntimeException
java.lang.UnsupportedOperationException
```

Handling Exceptions

To handle potential exceptions that may be thrown from a piece of code, use a try-catch-finally expression.

A *try-catch-finally expression* starts with a *try block*, which is introduced by the try key-word and encloses the code that may throw exceptions. This in turn is followed by zero or more catch clauses and an optional finally block. A *catch clause* is introduced by the *catch* key-word, followed by a pair of parentheses that encloses an exception specification in the same format as an explicitly or implicitly typed function parameter, and a block that is the *handler* for the specified exception. Only subclasses of java.lang.Throwable are allowed in exception specifications of catch clauses. If a type is not specified, the inferred type of an exception spec-ification is java.lang.Throwable. A *finally block* is introduced by the finally keyword followed by a block.

At least one catch clause or finally block must be present in a try-catch-finally expression.

When a try-catch-finally expression is evaluated, the try block is executed. If no exception is thrown, the finally block, if present, is executed, and execution continues past the try-catch-finally expression. If an exception is thrown, the catch blocks are checked one by one for compatibility with the thrown exception. If a compatible catch clause is found, the exception is said to be handled by the try-catch-finally expression. If the exception is handled, its handler and the finally block, if present, are executed, and execution continues past the try-catch-finally expression. If the exception is not handled, the finally block, if present, is executed, and the exception is propagated outside the try-catch-finally expression.

In Listing 4-14, we define a wheelOfException() function that throws the five general-purpose exceptions you learned in the last section, and then call the function through several levels of function calls in a try-catch-finally expression.

Listing 4-14. *Handling Exceptions*

```
import java.lang.*;

function wheelOfException(i:Integer):Void {
  if (i == 0) throw new Exception("Zero");
  if (i == 1) throw new IllegalArgumentException("One");
  if (i == 2) throw new IllegalStateException("Two");
  if (i == 3) throw new RuntimeException("Three");
  if (i == 4) throw new UnsupportedOperationException("Four");
  println("Out of exceptions for i = {i}");
}

function catchExceptions(i:Integer):Void {
  try {
    wheelOfException(i);
  } catch (iae:IllegalArgumentException) {
    println("Caught IllegalArgumentException with message: "
            "{iae.getMessage()}.");
  } catch (ise:IllegalStateException) {
    println("Caught IllegalStateException with message: "
            "{ise.getMessage()}.");
  } catch (uoe:UnsupportedOperationException) {
    println("Caught UnsupportedOperationException with message: "
            "{uoe.getMessage()}.");
```

```
  } catch (re:RuntimeException) {
    println("Caught RuntimeException with message: "
            "{re.getMessage()}.");
  } catch (e:Exception) {
    println("Caught Exception with message: "
            "{e.getMessage()}.");
  } finally {
    println("Reached finally block.");
  }
}

function callWheelOfException() {
  for (i in [0..5]) {
    catchExceptions(i);
  }
}

callWheelOfException ();
```

When we run the program in Listing 4-14, the following output is printed to the console:

```
Caught Exception with message: Zero.
Reached finally block.
Caught IllegalArgumentException with message: One.
Reached finally block.
Caught IllegalStateException with message: Two.
Reached finally block.
Caught RuntimeException with message: Three.
Reached finally block.
Caught UnsupportedOperationException with message: Four.
Reached finally block.
Out of exceptions for i = 5
Reached finally block.
```

Two points from the preceding example are worth noting. First, the catch clauses in the try-catch-finally expression are ordered from the most specific to the least specific. Because RuntimeException extends Exception, and the other three exceptions extend RuntimeException, we have to put the catch clauses for the other three exceptions before that of RuntimeException, and we also have to put the catch clause for RuntimeException before that of Exception. Had the order been reversed, the catch clause for Exception would have caught all the exceptions because all five exceptions are compatible with Exception.

The second point to note is that the finally block is always executed regardless of whether an exception is thrown.

Working with Classes

Now that you have a solid understanding of functions, its time to move on to the fourth and final major type in JavaFX Script, the class type. You create class types by defining classes. JavaFX Script's class facility supports instance variables and instance functions, member access control, and inheritance. Classes can be instantiated at runtime to create objects. Objects are linked together to form a network of objects that communicate by calling each other's instance functions. Such systems of well-behaved communicating objects are called *object-oriented software systems.* JavaFX Script's class facilities make it an object-oriented programming language, just like its function facilities make it a functional programming language.

The software industry has many years of experience with object-oriented systems. Most of the design principles, patterns, and methodologies are readily applicable to JavaFX Script programming.

Understanding Class Definitions

A *class definition* is introduced by the class keyword, followed by the name of the class, an optional super class and mixin list, and a pair of braces that encloses zero or more class members. The super class and mixin list, if present, starts with the keyword extends, followed by a comma-separated list of names of classes that serve as the super classes and mixins of the class being defined. Four kinds of members may be included in a class definition: instance variables and constants, instance functions, the init block, and the postinit block. *Instance variable and constant* declarations have the same form as script variable and constant declarations. *Instance function* definitions have the same form as script function definitions but may use two more kinds of expressions in their function bodies, the expressions this and super. The *init block* is introduced by the init keyword, followed by a block. The *postinit block* is introduced by the postinit keyword, followed by a block. A class definition may include zero or more instance variables and constants, zero or more instance functions, an optional init block, and an optional postinit block.

You saw some class definitions in Chapters 2 and 3. In this section and the next, we teach you class definitions in more detail. You will learn how each part of a class definition works.

In the example in Listing 4-15, we define a class that keeps track of coins in a piggy bank. For simplicity, we consider only pennies (1 cent) and nickels (5 cents). The class has tree instance variables and two instance functions. After the class definition, we create two instances of the class using object literal expressions and invoke instance functions on the object references.

Listing 4-15. *A PiggyBank Class*

```
import java.lang.*;

class PiggyBank {
  var name: String;
  var pennies: Integer;
  var nickels: Integer;
```

```
  function putInPennies(count: Integer):Void {
    if (count <= 0) {
      throw new IllegalArgumentException("count must be positive.");
    } else {
      pennies += count;
      println("You put {count} pennies into {name}.");
    }
  }

  function putInNickels(count: Integer):Void {
    if (count <= 0) {
      throw new IllegalArgumentException("count must be positive.");
    } else {
      nickels += count;
      println("You put {count} nickels into {name}.");
    }
  }

  function total():Integer {
    pennies + nickels * 5
  }
}

var myPiggyBank = PiggyBank { name: "My Piggy Bank" };
myPiggyBank.putInPennies(7);
myPiggyBank.putInNickels(3);
myPiggyBank.putInNickels(1);
println("{myPiggyBank.name} has {myPiggyBank.total()} cents:  "
  "{myPiggyBank.pennies} pennies and {myPiggyBank.nickels} nickels.");

var yourPiggyBank = PiggyBank { name: "Your Piggy Bank" };
yourPiggyBank.putInPennies(4);
yourPiggyBank.putInNickels(6);
yourPiggyBank.putInPennies(9);
println("{yourPiggyBank.name} has {yourPiggyBank.total()} cents:  "
  "{yourPiggyBank.pennies} pennies and {yourPiggyBank.nickels} nickels.");
```

When we run the program from Listing 4-15, the following output is printed to the console:

```
You put 7 pennies into My Piggy Bank.
You put 3 nickels into My Piggy Bank.
You put 1 nickels into My Piggy Bank.
My Piggy Bank has 27 cents:  7 pennies and 4 nickels.
You put 4 pennies into Your Piggy Bank.
You put 6 nickels into Your Piggy Bank.
You put 9 pennies into Your Piggy Bank.
Your Piggy Bank has 43 cents:  13 pennies and 6 nickels.
```

One thing to note in this example is that we instantiated the class twice to get two distinct instances of the same class. Even though the two instances are created from the same class, they are independent of each other. You can contrast this with the queue example in Listing 4-6, where we use a script variable to represent the queue, and consequently only one queue exists in the program. You can think of classes as molds out of which we make instances.

Class definitions are not expressions. They can appear only at the top level of a JavaFX Script source file. As of JavaFX 1.2, the language does not support anonymous class expressions, which would be analogous to anonymous function expressions. A class definition does, however, introduce a new type, called a *class type*, which you can use in your programs. The class name is also the name of the class type introduced by the class. Object references created by object literal expressions have class types. In Listing 4-15, the variables myPiggyBank and yourPiggyBank are both of type PiggyBank.

In JavaFX Script, class names introduced by class definitions live in their own space, which is different from the space where names of variables and constants live, as well as the space where function names live. As a result, in a JavaFX Script source file, you can define a class foo, a function foo, and a variable foo, and the compiler will happily compile your source file. However, by convention (not enforced by the compiler), JavaFX Script class names start with an uppercase letter, whereas variable names and function names start with lowercase letters.

Understanding Instance Variables

In Listing 4-15, we defined the class PiggyBank with three instance variables. Here is how they are declared:

```
var name: String;
var pennies: Integer;
var nickels: Integer;
```

Although these instance variables look like ordinary script-level variable declarations and local variable declarations in a function body or a block, they mean quite different things. For one thing, script-level and local variable declarations are expressions that when executed create the variable right there and then. Instance variable declarations in a class are not expressions and therefore are not executed immediately. The effects of instance variable declarations are felt when an instance of the class is created with an object literal expression.

Recall from Chapter 2 that an object literal expression may itself include initializers for instance variables of the class. Both the instance variable declaration in the class definition and the instance variable initializer in the object literal expression have influence on the instance variable.

Like ordinary variable declarations, instance variable declarations may include information about the variable's name, type, default initializer, and trigger. Here is an example of a class with a fuller-featured instance variable declaration:

```
class A {
  var i: Integer = 1024 on replace {
    println("Trigger in class definition: i = {i}.");
  }
}
```

This class declares an instance variable i of type Integer, with a default initializer of 1024 and a trigger that fires when the instance variable's value changes.

In object literal expressions, you can override instance variables and you can provide initializers for instance variables. Instance variable overrides must include the override modifier before the var keyword and can override the default initializer or the trigger. Here are some examples of object literal expressions that create instances of class A:

```
var a1 = A {};
var a2 = A { i: 2048 };
var a3 = A {
  override var i = 3072 on replace {
    println("Trigger in object literal override: i = {i}.");
  }
};
var a4 = A {
  override var i = 4096 on replace {
    println("Trigger in object literal override: i = {i}.");
  }
  i: 5120
};
```

Now let's examine the meaning of the instance variable declaration in the class and the instance variable overrides and initializers in the object literals.

The type of the instance variable is dictated by the instance variable declaration in the class. You cannot change the type of the instance variable in an object literal. So naturally a1.i, a2.i, a3.i, and a4.i are Integer variables, just as the class definition indicates.

The value of the instance variable may come from three sources: the instance variable initializer in the object literal expression, the default initializer of the instance variable override in the object literal expression, and the default initializer of the instance variable declaration in the class definition. These sources are searched in this order until a value is found. In the case of a1, neither an instance variable initializer nor an instance variable override is found in the object literal expression, so the value of a1.i comes from the instance variable declaration in the class definition, which gives a1.i a value of 1024. For a2, the instance variable initializer in the object literal gives a2.i the value of 2048. For a3, no instance variable initializer exists, but it does have an instance variable override, so a3.i gets its value 3072 from the override. And finally, a4.i gets its value 5120 from the instance variable initializer.

Triggers will be covered in the "Understanding Triggers" section later in this chapter. For now, just understand that triggers are blocks of code that can be attached to a variable so that they are executed every time the variable changes its value. The on replace triggers that we use in the preceding example are the simplest triggers. When you override an instance variable in an object literal, the trigger you provide does not replace the trigger in the instance variable declaration in the class definition. Instead, both triggers are added to the instance variable, and both will fire when the instance variable's value changes. Therefore, a1.i and a2.i each has one trigger attached, whereas a3.i and a4.i each has two triggers attached.

■**Note** The reason that triggers are cumulative with instance variable overrides is that one of the uses for triggers is to maintain some invariants on a variable. For example, instance variables that represent the red, green, and blue values of a color may have triggers that keep their values within the legal range. These triggers will remain in effect even if the instance variable is overridden.

In the program presented in Listing 4-16, you can see the forces that influence the instance variables at work.

Listing 4-16. *Instance Variable Initializations*

```
class A {
  var i: Integer = 1024 on replace {
    println("Trigger in class definition: i = {i}.");
  }
}

var a1 = A {};
var a2 = A { i: 2048 };
var a3 = A {
  override var i = 3072 on replace {
    println("Trigger in object literal override: i = {i}.");
  }
};
var a4 = A {
  override var i = 4096 on replace {
    println("Trigger in object literal override: i = {i}.");
  }
  i: 5120
};

println("a1.i = {a1.i}");
println("a2.i = {a2.i}");
println("a3.i = {a3.i}");
println("a4.i = {a4.i}");
```

When we run the program in Listing 4-16, the following output is printed to the console:

```
Trigger in class definition: i = 1024.
Trigger in class definition: i = 2048.
Trigger in class definition: i = 3072.
Trigger in object literal override: i = 3072.
Trigger in class definition: i = 5120.
Trigger in object literal override: i = 5120.
a1.i = 1024
a2.i = 2048
a3.i = 3072
a4.i = 5120
```

Notice that the triggers are fired because when the initial values of the instance variables took effect, they all changed their values from 0 to the new value.

Understanding Instance Functions

Instance function definitions are function definitions that appear inside a class definition. Aside from the top level of a JavaFX Script source file, this is the only other place where function definitions may appear. You saw examples of instance functions in the `PiggyBank` class in Listing 4-15.

Instance function definitions have the same form as script function definitions, and two more keywords may be used in instance function bodies: the `this` keyword and the `super` keyword. We will teach you the meaning of `this` presently, and the meaning of `super` will become clear when we cover it in the "Creating Class Hierarchies" section.

A natural question to ask is, "What can instance function bodies see?" The body of an instance function definition has access to four kinds of variables:

- Script variables and constants declared in the same JavaFX Script source file
- Instance variables declared in the same class as the instance function
- Function parameters that are passed into the function invocation expression
- Local variables and constants that are defined in the instance function body

The instance function body also has access to other instance functions in the same class, and script functions and other classes in the same source file. This list of accessible entities to instance functions will grow when you learn how to organize your JavaFX Script code into multiple files and how to make entities from one file accessible from other files in the "Organizing JavaFX Script Code" section later in this chapter.

Listing 4-17 illustrates the accessibility of the aforementioned variables.

Listing 4-17. *Instance Functions Example*

```
var total: Integer = 0;

function displayTotal() {
  println("The total in all piggy banks is {total} cents now.");
}

class PiggyBank {
  var name: String;
  var pennies: Integer = 0;

  function putInPennies(n: Integer) {
    println("Putting {n} pennies into {name}.");
    pennies += n;
    total += n;
    displayTotal();
  }
}

var myPiggyBank = PiggyBank { name: "My Piggy Bank" };
var yourPiggyBank = PiggyBank { name: "Your Piggy Bank" };
```

```
myPiggyBank.putInPennies(15);
yourPiggyBank.putInPennies(22);
myPiggyBank.putInPennies(6);

println("{myPiggyBank.name} has {myPiggyBank.pennies} cents.");
println("{yourPiggyBank.name} has {yourPiggyBank.pennies} cents.");
```

Listing 4-17 contains a script variable, total; a script function, displayTotal(); a class, PiggyBank, that has two instance variables, name and pennies; and an instance function, putInPennies(). The instance function putInPennies() uses the script variable total, the instance variable pennies, and the parameter n, and calls the script function displayTotal(). This program allows you to maintain any number of piggy banks, and it knows the total amount in all the piggy banks created in the program.

When we run the program in Listing 4-17, the following output is printed to the console:

```
Putting 15 pennies into My Piggy Bank.
The total in all piggy banks is 15 cents now.
Putting 22 pennies into Your Piggy Bank.
The total in all piggy banks is 37 cents now.
Putting 6 pennies into My Piggy Bank.
The total in all piggy banks is 43 cents now.
My Piggy Bank has 21 cents.
Your Piggy Bank has 22 cents.
```

In the last section, you learned that instance variables live only within instances of the class. Because instance functions make use of instance variables, the invocation of instance functions must also be done through instances of the class. In Listing 4-17, we invoke the instance function putInPennies() as follows:

```
myPiggyBank.putInPennies(15);
```

In this instance function invocation expression, the myPiggyBank instance of the PiggyBank class supplies the instance variables used in the putInPennies() function. The object through which an instance function is invoked is also called the *target* of the invocation.

■**Note** You can override instance functions in object literal expressions. Examples of instance function overrides can be found in the "Understanding Object Literals" section of Chapter 2.

Understanding the this Expression

The target of an instance function invocation is available to the instance function body as the *this expression*. It is perhaps the simplest JavaFX Script expression, consisting of the this keyword only. Its type is the type of the class, and it evaluates to the target of the invocation. The this expression can be used just like any other expression in the instance function body. It can be passed to other functions as parameters, and it can be used as the return value of the instance function. You can also use the this expression to access the instance variables and functions of the target object, although you already have a simpler way of accessing them by using their names directly. The putInPennies() instance function from Listing 4-17 can be rewritten as follows:

```
function putInPennies(n: Integer) {
  println("Putting {n} pennies into {this.name}.");
  this.pennies += n;
  total += n;
  displayTotal();
}
```

As you will see in the next section, where we cover extending classes and building class hierarchies, the target of an instance function invocation is not necessarily of the same class where the instance function is defined. An instance function can be invoked on objects of derived classes.

The this expression can also appear in other parts of the class definition, including in instance variable declarations, init blocks, and postinit blocks.

Understanding Init Blocks

Class definitions can also include an init block and a postinit block. An *init block* is introduced by the init keyword, followed by a block. A postinit block is introduced by the postinit keyword, followed by a block. The init block and the postinit block of a class are executed as an object is being created.

Both the init block and the postinit block of a class are executed during the evaluation of object literal expressions. They are guaranteed to execute after all the instance variable initializers are evaluated.

The postinit block is further guaranteed to execute after the instance initializers of the most derived class are evaluated. This is a useful feature when designing object hierarchies.

You will learn how to extend classes in the next section. In the meantime, we will use a simple example, shown in Listing 4-18, to illustrate the relative order in which the various parts of an object literal expression are executed. We will also use some nonconventional expressions as instance variable initializers. Most JavaFX Script classes do not have to be written this way.

Listing 4-18. *Init Blocks*

```
var counter = 0;

class Base {
  var i: Integer;
  init {
    println("Step {counter}: Base init block.  i = {i}.");
    counter++;
  }
  postinit {
    println("Step {counter}: Base postinit block.  i = {i}.");
    counter++;
  }
}
```

```
class Derived extends Base {
  var str: String;
  init {
    println("Step {counter}: Derived init block.  i = {i}, str = {str}.");
    counter++;
  }
  postinit {
    println("Step {counter}: Derived postinit block.  i = {i}, str = {str}.");
    counter++;
  }
}

var o = Derived {
         i: { println("Step {counter}: i initialized to 1024.");
              counter++;
              1024 },
         str: { println('Step {counter}: str initialized to "Hello, World".');
                counter++;
                "Hello, World" }
       };
```

The initializers in the object literal expression might look a little bit strange, but rest assured that they are legitimate JavaFX Script expressions.

When we run the program in Listing 4-18, the following output is printed to the console:

```
Step 0: i initialized to 1024.
Step 1: str initialized to "Hello, World".
Step 2: Base init block.  i = 1024.
Step 3: Derived init block.  i = 1024, str = Hello, World.
Step 4: Base postinit block.  i = 1024.
Step 5: Derived postinit block.  i = 1024, str = Hello, World.
```

Notice that the init blocks and postinit blocks are executed after the instance variable initializers. Notice also that the postinit block of Base is executed after the init block of Derived.

Creating Class Hierarchies

JavaFX Script supports object-oriented programming through its class facilities. It supports such concepts as data abstraction, encapsulation, polymorphism, and inheritance. In this section, we teach you how to extend JavaFX Script classes and point out the important features of the language such as dynamic dispatch that make object-oriented programming possible.

To become fluent with object-oriented design and programming requires a lot of learning and experience. In the rest of the book, you will see many examples of good object-oriented design and programming.

Understanding Mixin Classes

JavaFX Script supports a form of inheritance called *mixin inheritance*. A JavaFX Script class can optionally extend one JavaFX Script class and any number of JavaFX Script mixin classes. We will cover the syntax for extending classes and mixin classes in the next section. In this section, we teach you what a mixin class is.

A *mixin class* is a class whose primary purpose is to be extended by other classes and cannot be instantiated directly. Such a class is defined by using the mixin modifier before the class keyword. Like regular classes, mixin classes may contain instance variable and constant declarations, instance function definitions, init blocks, and postinit blocks. Here is an example:

```
mixin class Locatable {
  var x: Number;
  var y: Number;

  function moveToOrigin() {
    x = 0.0;
    y = 0.0;
  }

  function setLocation(x: Number, y: Number) {
    this.x = x;
    this.y = y;
  }
}
```

The mixin class Locatable will cause classes that extend it to have instance variables x and y and instance functions moveToOrigin()and setLocation().

Extending Classes

You extend JavaFX Script classes by including a super class and mixin list in a class definition. The super class and mixin list appear after the class name and consist of the extends keyword followed by a comma-separated list of class names. The list may contain an optional regular (non-mixin) class and any number of mixin classes. The regular class in the super class and mixin list is called a *super class* of the class. The mixin classes in the super class and mixin list are called *parent mixins* of the class. A class is called a *subclass* of its super class and a *mixee* of its parent mixins.

A class inherits its super class's instance variables, instance constants, and instance functions to which the writer of the super class has allowed access. The smallest unit of access rights in JavaFX Script is the JavaFX Script source file. Therefore, if a subclass is in the same file as the super class, it inherits all of its instance variables, instance constants, and instance functions.

A mixee will inherit its parent mixin's instance variables, instance constants, and instance functions to which the writer of the parent mixin has allowed access.

In Chapter 2 and up to this point in Chapter 4, we have used single-source-file programs to demonstrate language features. As you might imagine, this approach will soon become inadequate because restricted access rights can only be demonstrated with multi-file programs. And most real-world applications consist of more than one file; some may have hundreds of files. We will cover code organization in the "Organizing JavaFX Script Code" section, which discusses the details of access modifiers and access control. For the remainder of this section, we will operate under the single-source-file model, where everything is accessible by everything else.

In Listing 4-19, class C extends classes A and mixin class B. It inherits instance variables and instance functions from both A and B.

Listing 4-19. *Inheritance*

```
class A {
  var b: Boolean;
  function f() {
    println("A.f() called: b is {b}.");
  }
}

mixin class B {
  var i: Integer;
  function g() {
    println("B.g() called: i is {i}");
  }
}

class C extends A, B {
  var n: Number;
  function h() {
    println("C.h() called: b = {b}, i = {i}, n = {n}.");
  }
}

var c = C { b: true, i: 1024, n: 3.14 };
c.f();
c.g();
c.h();
```

When we run the program in Listing 4-19, the following output is printed to the console:

```
A.f() called: b is true.
B.g() called: i is 1024
C.h() called: b = true, i = 1024, n = 3.14.
```

Notice that in the object literal expression we initialize three instance variables, b, i, and n. The resulting object reference is assigned to the variable c, which the code will infer is type C. And we invoke three instance functions, f(), g(), h(), through c. Regarding the code that uses class C, the instance variables and instance functions C inherited from A and B can be used the same way as those defined directly in C.

■**Note** A mixin class itself can extend other mixin classes, but a mixin class cannot extend a regular class. If you are familiar with Java programming, the distinction between JavaFX Script classes and mixin classes is analogous to that between Java classes and interfaces.

Overriding Instance Variables

When you extend a class, you can override the super class or parent mixin's instance variables. You saw examples of overriding instance variables in Chapter 2 when you learned about object literal expressions and in the last section when you learned about instance variables.

An *instance variable override* is an instance variable declaration that has the same name as an instance variable of one of its direct or indirect super classes. It must include override as one of its modifiers and can have other access modifiers, as well as a default initializer and/or a trigger. It must not include the type specifier.

The overriding default initializer will be used instead of the super class default initializer as the initializer for the instance variable if an initializer is not provided in an object literal expression. The overriding trigger will be added to the set of triggers of the instance variable so that both the super class triggers and the overriding triggers will fire when the value of the instance variable is changed. Listing 4-20 shows a simple example of an instance variable override.

Listing 4-20. *Instance Variable Override*

```
class A {
  var i: Integer = 1024;
}

class B extends A {
  override var i = 2048;
}

var a = A {};
var b = B {};

println("a.i = {a.i}.");
println("b.i = {b.i}.");
```

When we run the program in Listing 4-20, the following output is printed to the console:

```
a.i = 1024.
b.i = 2048.
```

Because we do not provide an initializer in the object literal expressions, the instance variable a.i is initialized by the default initializer of i in the class A, which is 1024, and the instance variable b.i is initialized by the default initializer of i in the class B, which is 2048.

Overriding Instance Functions

When you extend a class, you can also override the super class or parent mixin's instance functions.

An *instance function override* is an instance function definition that has the same name, number, and type of variables as an instance function in the super class or the parent mixin. It must include override as one of its modifiers and may have other access modifiers. The overriding instance function must have the same return type as the overridden instance function.

When an overridden instance function is invoked through an object of the subclass type, the overriding instance function's body is executed. If the instance function is invoked through an object of the super class type, the body of the original version of the instance function is executed. Listing 4-21 shows an example of an instance function override.

Listing 4-21. *Instance Function Override*

```
class A {
  function f(i:Integer):Integer {
    println("A.f() is invoked with parameter i = {i}.");
    i + 3
  }
}

class B extends A {
  override function f(i:Integer):Integer {
    println("B.f() is invoked with parameter i = {i}.");
    i * 5;
  }
}

var a = A {};
var b = B {};
var ra = a.f(4);
var rb = b.f(7);
println("a.f(4) = {ra}.");
println("b.f(7) = {rb}.");
```

When we run the program in Listing 4-21, the following output is printed to the console:

```
A.f() is invoked with parameter i = 4.
B.f() is invoked with parameter i = 7.
a.f(4) = 7.
b.f(7) = 35.
```

Because a is an instance of A and not an instance of B, a.f(4) invokes the version of f() defined in class A. Similarly, because b is an instance of B, b.f(7) invokes the version of f() defined in class B.

If you accidentally leave out the override modifier when overriding an instance function, the JavaFX Script compiler will issue an error message telling you so.

Notice that when the JavaFX Script compiler tries to figure out whether an instance function is an override of a super class or parent mixin instance function, it checks the name, the number of the parameters, and the type of each parameter. The names of the parameters are not considered. Having determined that an instance function definition is an override of a super class instance function, the compiler will further check whether they have the same return type and reports an error if the overriding instance function has a different return type.

Understanding the super Keyword

When one class extends another class or mixin class, you can use the super keyword in the subclass or mixee's instance function bodies, but only as the target of instance function invocations. The super keyword will find a matching instance function from the instance functions of the super classes or parent mixins. Although it can be used for any instance functions of any super class or parent mixin, its use is necessary only if the instance function in the super class or parent mixin is overridden in the subclass or mixee. Nonoverridden instance functions of the super class and parent mixins may be invoked directly without using the super target.

The technique of invoking an overridden instance function is useful in certain programming tasks. Listing 4-22 presents a fun example that illustrates the use of the super keyword.

Listing 4-22. *Using the super Keyword*

```
class Hamburger {
  function whatsInIt() {
    "Beef patties"
  }
}

class HamburgerWithCheese extends Hamburger {
  override function whatsInIt() {
    "{super.whatsInIt()} and cheese"
  }
}

var Hamburger = Hamburger {};
var cheeseburger = HamburgerWithCheese {};
println("Hamburger.whatsInIt() = {Hamburger.whatsInIt()}.");
println("cheeseburger.whatsInit() = {cheeseburger.whatsInIt()}.");
```

Simple as this example is, it illustrates one principle of object-oriented programming: information ought to be stored in one place. By calling super.whatsInIt(), the HamburgerWithCheese class can avoid its listing of what's in it ever going out of sync with that of Hamburger.

When we run the program in Listing 4-22, the following output is printed to the console:

```
Hamburger.whatsInIt() = Beef patties.
cheeseburger.whatsInit() = Beef patties and cheese.
```

Using Abstract and Mixin Classes

One style of object-oriented programming calls for the separation of the interfaces of an object from the implementation details. Under this context, an *interface* of a class consists of the function types of its important instance functions, and *implementation details* of a class consists of the bodies of these instance functions.

JavaFX Script supports the concept of interfaces through its abstract instance function, abstract class, and mixin facilities.

An *abstract instance function* in a class or a mixin class is an instance function definition without a body, prefaced with the keyword abstract. A class that includes an abstract instance function is automatically an abstract class and must be marked by the abstract keyword. A class that does not include any abstract instance functions can also be made abstract by marking it with this keyword. A mixin class is implicitly abstract. In the following discussion, we focus on abstract classes. However, the principles discussed also apply to mixin classes.

You cannot create instances of abstract classes with object literal expressions. So how are abstract classes useful? The answer is twofold. Obviously, you have to extend the abstract classes to fill in the missing function bodies by overriding the abstract instance functions. This is sometimes called *implementing the interface*. On the other hand, you can hide the implementation details from the code that uses the class by using only the abstract class. The calling code will not create instances of the implementing classes directly using object literal expressions because that will defeat the purpose of hiding the implementation detail from the calling code. A client will get its instance using some other means.

Listing 4-23 illustrates this separation of interface from the implementation detail by using abstract classes.

Listing 4-23. *Separating an Interface from Implementation Details with an Abstract Class*

```
// The interface
abstract class Food {
  abstract function getName():String;
  abstract function whatsInIt():String;
}

// The implementation
class Hamburger extends Food {
  override function getName() {
    "Hamburger"
  }
  override function whatsInIt() {
    "beef patties"
  }
}

// A function that gives the calling code an instance of Food
function getTodaysSpecial():Food {
  Hamburger {}
}
```

```
// The calling code, no direct mentioning of Hamburger is made here
var food = getTodaysSpecial();
println("Today's special is {food.getName()}.  "
        "It has {food.whatsInIt()} in it.");
```

In practice, one group develops the interface, the implementation, and the function that hands out the instance, and another group develops the calling code. The calling code never directly uses the name of the implementation detail class.

When we run the program in Listing 4-23, the following output is printed to the console:

```
Today's special is Hamburger.  It has beef patties in it.
```

Another important detail to learn from Listing 4-23 has to do with the type of the variable food. Because it does not have an explicit type, it gets its type from its initializer. In our case, the initializer is a function invocation expression, which would have a type that is the same as its return type. So food is a variable of type Food. However, when the compiler sees the instance function invocation expressions food.getName() and food.whatsInIt(), it does not merely determine that the instance functions are abstract, and therefore the calls are invalid. It will instead wait until runtime to choose which version of these instance functions to execute based on the type of the value of the variable. When we run the program, the food variable will contain an instance of the Hamburger subclass, and the instance function overrides in that class are executed.

This way of choosing which instance function to execute based on the type of the value at runtime is called *dynamic dispatch*. (You may be familiar with the same concept being referred to as dynamic binding or late binding in other languages. However, because the term *binding* means something quite different in JavaFX Script, we will stick to the term *dynamic dispatch* here.)

Conflict Resolution in Mixin Inheritance

Early versions of JavaFX up to 1.1 supported multiple inheritance. The mixin inheritance, introduced in JavaFX 1.2, is designed to support the common use cases of multiple inheritance while reducing the complexity and error-prone nature of full-blown multiple inheritance.

The key to the simplification of mixin inheritance lies in the way conflicts are resolved when a mixee extends multiple parent mixins that have competing instance variable names. In mixin inheritance, a parent mixin will cause the mixee to have the parent mixin's instance variables, if the mixee does not already have them. This process is applied for all the parent mixins in the order that they appear in the super class and mixins list of the mixee. As a consequence, if two parent mixins have the same instance variable with the same type, the mixee only gets one copy of the variable, not two.

This can be illustrated with the following example:

```
mixin class A {
  var i:Integer;
  function f() {
    println("f() called: i = {i}.");
    i++;
  }
}
```

```
mixin class B {
  var i: Integer;
  function g() {
    println("g() called: i = {i}.");
    i++;
  }
}

class C extends A, B {
}

var o = C { i: 1024 };
o.f();
o.g();
o.f();
```

Since both parent mixin A and parent mixin B have an instance variable i of Integer type, the mixee C gains the instance variable i as mixin inheritance processes A. By the time the parent mixin B is processed, C already has instance variable i, so parent mixin B's requirement that its mixee have instance variable i is met, and C does not gain an additional copy of i.

When this program is run, you should see the following result:

```
f() called: i = 1024.
g() called: i = 1025.
f() called: i = 1026.
```

Understanding that all parent mixins share the same set of instance variables is something that is not very intuitive. However, once you understand it, this fact should steer you clear of designing mixins that contain instance variables with the same name.

■**Caution** The mixin inheritance implementation in JavaFX 1.2 does not yet handle the example in this section as we described. However, this behavior is the eventual goal of the JavaFX Script compiler team and should be functional in a future version of JavaFX.

A compilation error results if two parent mixins have instance variables of the same name but different types. A compilation error also results if the mixee has, or inherits from its super class, an instance variable with the same name as an instance variable of a parent mixin but with different types. Similarly, if an instance function is declared in multiple parent mixins, or a parent mixin and a mixee, or a parent mixin and a super class with the same name but with non-override-compatible function types, a compilation error results.

Understanding Casting and the instanceof and as Operators

The ability to assign an instance of a subclass or a mixee to a variable of a super class or a parent mixin type is a fundamental feature of the JavaFX Script language. It is what makes dynamic dispatching possible.

Sometimes a situation may arise that necessitates your code to test whether a value in a super class or a parent mixin type variable is indeed an instance of a subclass or a mixee type. This is done with the instanceof operator. The *instanceof expression* consists of a value expression, the instanceof keyword, and a type name.

Here are some examples:

```
class A {};
class B extends A {}
var a:A;
a = A {};
println(a instanceof B);
a = B {};
println(a instanceof B);
```

The variable a is of static type A. We first assign an instance of A to it and print out the value of a instanceof B, which should be false. We then assign an instance of B to a and print out the value of the same expression, which this time should be true.

Once you have ascertained that a super class or parent mixin variable is holding an instance of a subclass or a mixee type, you can *cast* it to the subclass or mixee type. The *cast expression* consists of a value expression, the as keyword, and a type name. You may want to cast an expression to a subclass or a mixee type so that you can assign it to a variable of the subclass or mixee type or use it to access instance variables and instance functions that are defined in the subclass or mixee but not in the super class or the parent mixin. The compiler will not allow you to do these things without a cast, because the compiler has no knowledge of the dynamic type of values. Listing 4-24 shows some examples of casting.

Listing 4-24. *Casting Examples*

```
class A {
  function f() {
    println("A.f() called.");
  }
}

class B extends A {
  function g() {
    println("B.g() called.");
  }
}

var a: A;
a = B {};
a.f();
(a as B).g();
```

We assign an instance of subclass B to the variable a of super class type A. We can call instance function f() of A directly, but we have to cast a into B in order to call the instance function g() of B.

If you try to cast a value to a wrong type, a java.lang.ClassCastException will be thrown.

This concludes our coverage of class types. You now know the four kinds of data types in JavaFX Script, primitive types, sequence types, function types, and class types, and can implement expressions involving these data types.

In the next section, we will show you how to organize larger JavaFX Script programs into multiple files so that your projects will be easier to maintain.

Organizing JavaFX Script Code

The single-file programs you have been writing and experimenting with in Chapter 2 and up to this point in Chapter 4 so far do not represent an efficient way to develop larger JavaFX Script applications. Fortunately, JavaFX Script has some code organization features that help you to split your code into multiple files and create a hierarchical structure:

- *Scripts*: A script is a single JavaFX Script source file that can be run as a program.

- *Modules*: A module is a single JavaFX Script source file whose main purpose is to be used by other JavaFX Script source files.

- *Packages*: A JavaFX Script source file can be declared to belong to a named package. Packages make it much easier to avoid name conflicts when you use libraries of different origins together.

- *Access modifiers*: Access modifiers can be applied to classes, functions, class members, and so forth to make them visible to the outside world. Some access modifiers also control what can be done to a variable from the outside world.

The concepts here takes the single JavaFX Script file model you've seen thus far and opens it up for access from other JavaFX Script files.

What Is a Script?

All the programs that you saw in Chapter 2 and up to this point in Chapter 4 are examples of scripts in JavaFX Script. A *script* is a JavaFX Script source file that can be compiled and then run, and may contain class definitions, function definitions, variable and constant declarations, and loose expressions. *Loose expressions* are expressions that appear at the top level of a script.

Scripts are saved in files on a file system. JavaFX Script files use the .fx file name extension, which the JavaFX Script compiler javafxc requires. The file name without the .fx extension will become the script's name. A script is run with the javafx command followed by the script name.

Since we opened the book with a somewhat elaborate Hello Earthrise example, we still owe you a traditional Hello World example. Here it is, presented as a script named HelloWorld that is saved in the HelloWorld.fx file; as you can see, it contains a comment line and a loose function invocation expression:

```
// HelloWorld.fx
println("Hello, World")
```

We compile and run the script with the following command lines:

```
$ javafxc HelloWorld.fx
$ javafx HelloWorld
```

Here the $ character represents the operating system command prompt. This prompt may be something different on your operating system. The compilation step will compile the script file into a Java class files: HelloWorld.class.

Of course, the traditional greeting appears when we run the script:

```
Hello, World
```

An alternative way of organizing a script is to define a function named run that takes either no arguments or a sequence of Strings as arguments and move all the loose expressions into it. The run function is the entry point to the script. And if you use a run() function that takes a sequence of Strings as arguments, the arguments sequence will contain any command-line arguments that you specify on the JavaFX command line after the name of the script. The JavaFX Script compiler actually transforms a script with loose expressions into a script with a run() function automatically. As far as the JavaFX Script runtime system knows, all scripts are of the neater form containing class definitions, function definitions, and variable and constant definitions, and one of the function definitions just happens to have the name run().

Here is an example script that prints out the command-line arguments, one per line:

```
function run(args: String[]) {
  for (arg in args) {
    println(arg);
  }
}
```

Understanding Modules

Now that you understand scripts, grasping the concept of modules will come easy. A *module* is a JavaFX Script source file that contains class definitions, function definitions, and variable and constant declarations that are intended for use in other JavaFX Script source files.

You make a class, a function, a variable, or a constant usable by other JavaFX Script source files by prefacing its definition or declaration with an access modifier. Without an access modifier, such items can be used only by the source file in which they appear. This level of access is called the *script-level of access*. Two access modifiers are available that widen the scope of these entities. The public modifier enables any JavaFX Script source file anywhere to use these entities. This level of access is called *public access*. The package modifier allows any JavaFX Script source file that is tagged to be in the same package as the module itself to use the functions, classes, variables, and constants within that module. This level of access is called the *package level of access*. We will teach you about packages in the "Understanding Packages" section in just a little bit. For now, we concentrate on the public modifier.

A module is said to *export* the entities it contains that have either package-level access or public access. The JavaFX Script compiler does not allow source files that export their entities to also contain loose expressions. So the only way that a module can also be a script is to have a run() function. And in most cases, your modules will not also be scripts.

A module's name is its file name without the `.fx` extension. An exported entity from a module is known to the outside world by a *qualified name*, which is the module name followed by a dot (`.`) and the entity name.

Listing 4-25 shows an example of a module, and Listing 4-26 presents a script that makes use of the module.

Listing 4-25. *A Queue Module*

```
// Queue.fx
var q:Integer[];

public function enqueue(i:Integer):Void {
  insert i into q;
  println("Enqueued {i}.  Size of q is {sizeof q} now.");
}

public function dequeue():Integer {
  if (sizeof q == 0) {
    println("Size of q is {sizeof q} now. Returning -1.");
    return -1;
  } else {
    var i = q[0];
    delete q[0];
    println("Dequeued {i}.  Size of q is {sizeof q} now.");
    return i;
  }
}
```

Listing 4-26. *A Program That Uses the Queue Module*

```
// QueueDemonstration.fx
Queue.enqueue(1);
Queue.enqueue(2);
Queue.enqueue(3);
println(Queue.dequeue());
println(Queue.dequeue());
Queue.enqueue(4);
println(Queue.dequeue());
println(Queue.dequeue());
println(Queue.dequeue());
```

You may recognize that this is the same queue implementation that we showed you in the "What Can a Function Body See?" section earlier in this chapter in Listing 4-6. Here we simply pull the queue implementation into its own module, export the functions by giving them public access, and modify the demo part by qualifying the function calls with the module name. Notice that the variable that holds the content of the queue is kept at the script level of access. This prevents it from being accidentally modified by foreign code.

■**Tip** Although you can create modules with unconventional characters in its names, doing so may render the module unusable within JavaFX Script programs. We recommend using module names that are valid JavaFX Script identifiers.

A Special Provision for Classes

Because of its Java heritage, JavaFX Script supports a special arrangement for classes that are defined in JavaFX Script source files that also bear the name of the class. This is by far the most popular code organization for Java projects.

If a class is defined in a source file bearing its name, the class is referred to by using the class name just once, not twice. Other entities defined in the source file, such as other classes, functions, and variables and constants, are still referred to as before. Listings 4-27 and 4-28 illustrate this.

Listing 4-27. *A Class Defined in a File with the Same Name*

```
// Car.fx
public class Car {
  public var make: String;
  public var model: String;
}
public function getACar() {
  Car { make: "BMW", model: "Z5" }
}
```

Listing 4-28. *A Class Defined in a File with a Different Name*

```
// Parts.fx
public class Wheel {
  public var diameter: Number;
}
```

Because the Car class is defined in a file named Car.fx, the outside world can refer to it just by the name Car. The getACar() function in Car.fx is still referred to as Car.getACar(). The Wheel class is not defined in a file with the same name, so Parts is considered to be a regular module, and Wheel must be referred to by the outside world as Parts.Wheel. Listing 4-29 shows the different treatment for these classes.

Listing 4-29. *Usage of Classes*

```
// UseCarAndWheel.fx
var car = Car { make: "Ford", model: "Taurus" };
var anotherCar = Car.getACar();
var wheel = Parts.Wheel { diameter: 16 };
```

■**Caution** Because of the special treatment of classes defined in a file with the same name, some conflicts may result. For example, in such a file, you cannot define a script function that has the same name as
an instance function of the class.

Understanding Packages

JavaFX Script's package facility is a mechanism for separating source files into logical name
spaces. Source files belonging to the same package are considered to be more closely related
than source files in different packages. Access can be granted to source files in the same package with the package modifier.

   To tag a source file as belonging to a package, you put a *package directive* at the beginning
of the source file. A package directive consists of the package keyword followed by one or more
identifiers connected by dots (.) and terminated by a semicolon. The package directive must
be the first noncomment, nonwhitespace line in the source file. Source files that do not contain a package directive are said to belong to the *unnamed package*. That's the package all of
our example code in Chapters 2 and 4 belong to so far.

■**Caution** The unnamed package is provided as a place to experiment with your code and is not meant to
be the permanent home of your code. In JavaFX Script, as in Java, code in named packages cannot access
code in unnamed packages.

   Following the recommendation of the Java platform, if your JavaFX Script code will have
worldwide exposure, you should use the Internet domain name of your organization in reverse
order as the starting portions of package names for your code. For smaller-scale projects, a
simpler package name is sufficient.

   The package name becomes the leading portion of an entity's fully qualified name.

   Listings 4-30 and 4-31 demonstrate the use of packages.

Listing 4-30. *Drinks Module in a Food Package*

```
// Drinks.fx
package food;

public class Coffee {
  public var brand: String;
}

public class Tea {
  public var kind: String;
}
package var drinksOffered:Integer;
```

```
public function getCoffee():Coffee {
  drinksOffered++;
  Coffee { brand: "Folgers" }
}
public function getTea():Tea {
  drinksOffered++;
  Tea { kind: "Iced" }
}
public function numberOfDrinksOffered() {
  drinksOffered
}
```

Listing 4-31. *Consuming Drinks from the Food Package*

```
// ConsumeDrinks.fx
package consumer;

var coffee = food.Drinks.getCoffee();
println("Good coffee.  It's {coffee.brand}.");
var tea = food.Drinks.getTea();
println("Good tea.  It's {tea.kind} tea.");
println("Number of drinks offered = {food.Drinks.numberOfDrinksOffered()}.");
```

In Listing 4-31, we invoke public functions getCoffee(), getTea(), and numberOfDrinksOffered() in the Drinks module of the food package through their fully qualified names, shown in bold. The drinksOffered variable in the Drinks module has package level of access and cannot be used from the calling code because it is in a different package.

The recommended way of organizing JavaFX Script source files is to use a directory hierarchy that mirrors the package hierarchy. Thus to store the code shown in Listings 4-29 and 4-30 into source files, we need to create two directories, food and consumer, and put Drinks.fx in the food directory and ConsumeDrinks.fx in the consumer directory. From the directory where we have created the food and consumer directories, we can compile and run the program with the following command line:

```
$ javafxc food/Drinks.fx consumer/ConsumerDrinks.fx
$ javafx consumer.ConsumeDrinks
```

When we invoke the javafxc compiler without an explicit -d command-line argument, it will leave the compiled class files in the same directory where the source file is found. Because we start with a source directory hierarchy that mirrors the package hierarchy, this will leave the class files in the same hierarchy, which is exactly where the JavaFX Script runtime expects them. Notice also that when we finally run the program, we have to use the fully qualified module name on the javafx command line.

■**Caution** The package keyword is used in two contexts in JavaFX Script. It is used at the beginning of a source file to tag the file as belonging to a package. It is also used as a modifier on an entity in a module to make it visible to other modules and scripts in the package.

Understanding Import Directives

Modules and packages are great ways of organizing JavaFX Script code into a structure that's easier to maintain. However, they involve names that are longer and with more parts. JavaFX Script's import facility will help you regain the ability to use simple names in your code, even for entities from foreign modules, classes, and packages.

The *import directive* consists of the import keyword, an indication of what is to be imported, and a semicolon. Four variants exist for the import directive:

- A package name followed by .*, which imports all module names of the package

- A package name followed by a dot (.) and a module name, which imports just that one module name from the package

- A package name followed by a dot, a module name, and .*, which imports all the entities defined in that module

- A package name followed by a dot, a module name, a dot, and an entity name, which imports just that entity name from the module

When modules from the same package import each other's names, the package name may be omitted from the import directives.

Listings 4-32 through 4-35 show the four versions of the program in Listing 4-31 we get when we applying the four import variants to it.

Listing 4-32. *Importing All Modules in a Package*

```
// ConsumeDrinksImportPackageStar.fx
package consumer;

import food.*;

var coffee = Drinks.getCoffee();
println("Good coffee.  It's {coffee.brand}.");
var tea = Drinks.getTea();
println("Good tea.  It's {tea.kind} tea.");
println("Number of drinks offered = {Drinks.numberOfDrinksOffered()}.");
```

Listing 4-33. *Importing One Module in a Package*

```
// ConsumeDrinksImportPackageModule.fx
package consumer;

import food.Drinks;

var coffee = Drinks.getCoffee();
println("Good coffee.  It's {coffee.brand}.");
var tea = Drinks.getTea();
println("Good tea.  It's {tea.kind} tea.");
println("Number of drinks offered = {Drinks.numberOfDrinksOffered()}.");
```

Listing 4-34. *Importing All Entities from a Module*

```
// ConsumeDrinksImportModuleStar.fx
package consumer;

import food.Drinks.*;

var coffee = getCoffee();
println("Good coffee.  It's {coffee.brand}.");
var tea = getTea();
println("Good tea.  It's {tea.kind} tea.");
println("Number of drinks offered = {numberOfDrinksOffered()}.");
```

Listing 4-35. *Importing Specific Entities from a Module*

```
// ConsumeDrinksImportModuleEntities.fx
package consumer;

import food.Drinks.getCoffee;
import food.Drinks.getTea;
import food.Drinks.numberOfDrinksOffered;

var coffee = getCoffee();
println("Good coffee.  It's {coffee.brand}.");
var tea = getTea();
println("Good tea.  It's {tea.kind} tea.");
println("Number of drinks offered = {numberOfDrinksOffered()}.");
```

Which style of import directive is used depends mostly on taste. You should pick a style that makes the development and maintenance of your JavaFX Script project easy and hassle free.

■**Caution** The JavaFX Script compiler actually allows import directives to appear anywhere below the package directive. Because the effect of import directives is for the entire file and not merely the source lines below the directive, there is no good reason to put the import directives anywhere but just below the package directive.

Understanding Access Modifiers

In the last few sections, you learned about the `public` and the `package` access modifiers and their effects on script-level entities (i.e., class definitions, script function definitions, and script variable and script constant declarations) in JavaFX Script source files.

In this section, we will teach you the access modifiers for class-level entities (i.e., instance variable and constant declarations and instance function definitions. The usage scenarios of class-level entities are more complex than script-level entities, so the access modifiers for them are naturally more complex.

You can apply the public and package modifiers to instance variables and instance functions, and they mean the same thing as when they are applied to script-level entities. A public instance variable can be read from or written to from anywhere in the application. A public instance function can be invoked from anywhere in the application. An instance variable with a package modifier can be read from and written to from any code in the same package. An instance function with a package modifier can be invoked from any code in the same package.

Understanding the protected Modifier

You can apply the protected modifier to both instance variables and instance functions. A protected instance variable can be read from and written to by code in the same package or in subclasses or mixees. A protected instance function can be invoked by code in the same package or in subclasses or mixees. The protected level of access implies package level of access.

One subtlety of protected level of access is that a subclass or a mixee that is not in the same package as the super class or parent mixin may access a protected instance variable or an instance function in that super class or parent mixin only through an object of the subclass type.

Protected instance variables and instance functions are often used to delegate implementation detail decisions to subclasses.

The simple examples in Listings 4-36 and 4-37 show what is and is not permitted when a subclass accesses a protected instance variable or instance function in the super class.

Listing 4-36. *A Class with a Protected Variable*

```
// a/A.fx
package a;

public class A {
  protected var i: Integer;
  public function getI() {
    i
  }
}
```

Listing 4-37. *Accessing a Protected Instance Variable*

```
// b/B.fx
package b;

import a.A;

public class B extends A {
  public function adjustI(adj: Integer) {
    i += adj;   // OK.
  }
  public function adjustI(a: A, adj: Integer) {
    // a.i += adj; // Not allowed
  }
}
```

We define class A in package a with a protected instance variable i. We then define a subclass B of a.A that resides in a different package b. In the first adjustI() instance function in B, we modify a simple variable reference i, which refers to the i in the target of the invocation. This access is allowed because the target of the invocation is the class B. In the second adjustI() instance function in B, we try to modify the instance variable i of an instance a of A that is passed in as a function parameter. Because a is not of the subclass type, access is not allowed.

Understanding the public-init and public-read Modifiers

You can apply the public-init and public-read modifiers to instance variables. A public-init variable can be initialized in object literal expressions from anywhere in the application. A public-read variable can be read from anywhere in the application.

Listings 4-38 and 4-39 illustrate public-init and public-read instance variables.

Listing 4-38. *Instance Variables with public-init and public-read Access*

```
// Sandwiches.fx
package food;

public class Club {
  public-init var kind: String;
  public-read var price: Number;
}

public function calculatePrice(club: Club) {
  if (club.kind == "Roast Beef") {
    club.price = 7.99;
  } else if (club.kind == "Chicken") {
    club.price = 6.99;
  }
}
```

Listing 4-39. *Uses of public-init and public-read Instance Variables*

```
package consumer;

import food.Sandwiches.*;

var club = Club { kind: "Roast Beef" };
calculatePrice(club);
println("The price of the {club.kind} club sandwich is {club.price}.");
```

The public-init modifier for the kind instance variable in Club allows us to provide an initializer to the kind instance variable in the object literal expression for Club. The public-read modifier for the price instance variable in Club allows us to read the value of the price variable out of the club object.

When used in conjunction with the package or protected modifiers, the public-init and public-read modifiers open the scope of write access.

Understanding Triggers

Triggers are an integral part of the JavaFX Script variable and constant declaration expression syntax. We introduced this syntax in Chapter 2 and have used the simplest form of triggers in the preceding chapters. In this section, we examine the JavaFX Script trigger syntax in detail.

The trigger is the optional last part of variable declaration expressions and constant declaration expressions. A trigger is introduced by the `on replace` keywords, followed by a (possibly empty) *variable modification specification* and a block called the *trigger block*. The variable or constant to which the trigger is attached is called the *observed variable* or *observed constant*.

The trigger block is executed once after every change to the variable or constant being declared. A variable is considered changed when a different value is assigned to it, or, if it is initialized to a bound expression, when its bound expression is reevaluated and the new value is different from the old value. A variable of sequence type is considered changed also when elements are inserted into or deleted from the sequence or when elements of the sequence change. Because it is impossible to assign to constants, only a constant initialized to a bind expression can change, and this occurs when its bind expression is reevaluated.

The variable modification specification provides information to the trigger block. Six forms of variable modification specification exist, and these provide zero, one, two, three, or four pieces of information to the trigger block. Two of the six forms apply to sequence-type and nonsequence-type variables and constants. The other four forms make sense only for sequence-type variables and constants.

Accessing the Old and New Values in Trigger Blocks

The first form is the *empty form*. This is the form presented in examples of previous chapters. In this form, the trigger block has access to the variables in the surrounding scope, including the variable or constant itself, as shown in Listing 4-40.

Listing 4-40. *A Trigger with an Empty Variable Modification Specification*

```
var i = 1024 on replace {
  println("Variable i changed to {i}.");
};
i = 2048;
i = 2048;
```

The trigger in this example will be executed twice: once when the variable i is initialized, which counts as a change from the default value of 0 to the initializer value of 1024, and once when the variable i is assigned the value 2048 for the first time. The second assignment is not considered a change because the new value is the same as the old value. Within the trigger block, the variable i has the newly changed value.

When we run the program in Listing 4-40, the following output is printed to the console:

```
Variable i changed to 1024.
Variable i changed to 2048.
```

JavaFX Script allows you to further modify the observed variable in a trigger. This is useful when some invariants must be maintained for the observed variable, as shown in Listing 4-41.

Listing 4-41. *A Trigger That Further Modifies the Observed Variable to Maintain Invariants*

```
// Using a trigger to keep the value of i to be between 0 and 9999.
var i = 1024 on replace {
  println("Variable i changed to {i}.");
  if (i < 0) {
    println("Since {i} < 0, setting i to 0.");
    i = 0;
  } else if (i > 9999) {
    println("Since {i} > 9999, setting i to 9999.");
    i = 9999;
  }
};

i = -100;
i = 20000;
```

The trigger in this example will be executed five times: when i is initialized to 1024, when i is assigned the value -100, when i is modified to 0 inside the trigger because -100 is less than 0, when i is assigned the value 20000, and when i is modified to 9999 inside the trigger because 20000 is greater than 9999.

When we run the program in Listing 4-41, the following output is printed to the console:

```
Variable i changed to 1024.
Variable i changed to -100.
Since -100 < 0, setting i to 0.
Variable i changed to 0.
Variable i changed to 20000.
Since 20000 > 9999, setting i to 9999.
Variable i changed to 9999.
```

■**Caution** It is your responsibility to make sure that triggers are not executed in an infinitely recursive fashion. Programs that contain such triggers will cause a `java.lang.StackOverflowError`. The simplest such erroneous program is `var x = 0 on replace { x++; };`. However, with more complicated models and data bindings, the error may not be so obvious.

The second form of variable modification specification in a trigger consists of just a variable name. A variable so named can be accessed from within the trigger block in a read-only fashion, and it would contain the value of the observed variable just prior to the change. Listing 4-42 presents an example.

Listing 4-42. *Accessing the Old Value from a Trigger*

```
var i = 1024 on replace oldValue {
  println("Variable i changed from {oldValue} to {i}.");
};
```

```
i = 2048;
```

When we run the program in Listing 4-42, the following output is printed to the console:

```
Variable i changed from 0 to 1024.
Variable i changed from 1024 to 2048.
```

The meaning of the variable name in this form of variable modification specification is not apparent from the syntax alone, so we recommend you use a name that reminds you of its role of providing the old value of the observed variable to the trigger block, such as `oldValue`, as we have done in the example.

For nonsequence-type variables, the old values and the new values of the variables are all we are interested in, and the first two forms of the variable modification specification suffice for all their triggers.

Accessing Sequence Modification Information in Trigger Blocks

For sequence-type variables, the modification scenarios are more complicated, and the other four forms of the modification specification are designed to provide the relevant information to their trigger blocks.

The third form of variable modification specification consists of a variable name, a pair of brackets ([ ]) enclosing a pair of variable names separated by two dots (..), an equal sign (=), and another variable name. The four variable names so designated can be accessed from within the trigger block in a read-only fashion. The first variable, the one before the brackets, contains the old value of the observed variable. The two variables between the brackets contain the low index and the high index of the portion of the sequence that has changed. The last variable, the one after the equal sign, is a sequence that contains any newly inserted elements to the observed variable. See Listing 4-43 for an example.

Listing 4-43. *A Trigger for a Sequence Variable with Access to the Complete Set of Modification Information*

```
println("Initializing seq...");
var seq = [1, 3, 5, 7, 9] on replace oldValue[lo..hi] = newSlice {
  print("  Variable seq changed from ");
  print(oldValue);
  print(" to ");
  println(seq);
  println("  The change occurred at low indexe {lo} and high index {hi}.");
  print("  The new slice is ");
  println(newSlice);
};
```

```
println('Executing "insert [2, 4, 6] before seq[3]"...');
insert [2, 4, 6] before seq[3];

println('Executing "delete seq [1..2]"...');
delete seq [1..2];

println('Executing "seq[4..5] = [8, 10]"...');
seq[4..5] = [8, 10];
```

This form of the variable modification specification is designed to resemble an assignment to a slice of a sequence in order to remind you of the meaning of the four variable names inside the trigger block. However, because the meaning of these variable names is still not apparent, we recommend that you use descriptive names such as the ones we used in the example: oldValue, lo, hi, and newSlice.

In Listing 4-43, we attach a trigger with the third form of variable modification specification to a sequence of Integer variable seq. The trigger will be executed four times: when the variable is initialized, when a sequence is inserted, when a slice is deleted, and when a slice is replaced with another slice.

When we run the program in Listing 4-43, the following output is printed to the console:

```
Initializing seq...
  Variable seq changed from [ ] to [ 1, 3, 5, 7, 9 ]
  The change occurred at low indexe 0 and high index -1.
  The new slice is [ 1, 3, 5, 7, 9 ]
Executing "insert [2, 4, 6] before seq[3]"...
  Variable seq changed from [ 1, 3, 5, 7, 9 ] to [ 1, 3, 5, 2, 4, 6, 7, 9 ]
  The change occurred at low indexe 3 and high index 2.
  The new slice is [ 2, 4, 6 ]
Executing "delete seq [1..2]"...
  Variable seq changed from [ 1, 3, 5, 2, 4, 6, 7, 9 ] to [ 1, 2, 4, 6, 7, 9 ]
  The change occurred at low indexe 1 and high index 2.
  The new slice is [ ]
Executing "seq[4..5] = [8, 10]"...
  Variable seq changed from [ 1, 2, 4, 6, 7, 9 ] to [ 1, 2, 4, 6, 8, 10 ]
  The change occurred at low indexe 4 and high index 5.
  The new slice is [ 8, 10 ]
```

This output should pretty much match your intuitive ideas of what the four variables should contain under each of the triggering conditions. The only thing that we would like to point out is that the values of the high index are one less than the values of the low index under insertions.

The remaining forms of the variable modification specification are shortened versions of the third form, which is also known as the *full form*.

The fourth form omits the old value portion from the third form, offering only the low and high indexes and the new slice, as is shown in the following example:

```
var seq = [1, 3, 5, 7, 9] on replace [lo..hi] = newSlice {
  // ...
}
```

The fifth form omits the low and high indexes portion from the third form, offering only the old value and the new slice, as is shown in the following example:

```
var seq = [1, 3, 5, 7, 9] on replace oldValue = newSlice {
  // ...
}
```

The sixth form omits the old value and the low and high indexes portion from the third form, offering only the new slice, as is shown in the following example:

```
var seq = [1, 3, 5, 7, 9] on replace = newSlice {
  // ...
}
```

By far the most popular forms of variable modification specifications are the empty form and the full form.

Debugging with Triggers

Aside from their uses in production code, triggers are surprisingly useful tools for tracing the values of variables throughout the life of a program. Although the JavaFX Script debugger in the NetBeans plug-in is quite powerful, in certain situations, you need a little bit of `println` debugging to help you understand the behavior of your JavaFX Script program.

When used in conjunction with data binding, you don't even have to attach triggers to the module variables or instance variables that you want to monitor. You can simply declare a variable that binds to the module variable or instance variable you want to monitor and attach a trigger to your variable. Listing 4-44 presents a simple example of this.

Listing 4-44. *Using Triggers to Monitor States of Another Object*

```
class Gcd {
  var a: Integer;
  var b: Integer;
  function gcd(): Integer {
    if (b == 0) {
      return a;
    } else {
      var tmp = a mod b;
      a = b;
      b = tmp;
      return gcd();
    }
  }
}

var o = Gcd { a: 165, b: 105 };

var x = bind o.b on replace {
  println("Iterating: o.a={o.a}, o.b = {x}.");
}
```

```
var result = o.gcd();
println("The gcd of 165 and 105 is {result}.");
```

The class Gcd uses the Euclidean algorithm to calculate the greatest common divisor of its two instance variables, a and b. We are able to hook into the internal states of instance o of class Gcd without making any changes to the class itself. All we have to do is to declare a variable, x, that binds to o.b so that whenever o.b changes x is updated accordingly; and then we attach a trigger to x that prints out the value of o.a, which we know is updated before o.b is updated, and prints out the value of x, which we know reflects the value of o.b.

When we run the program in Listing 4-44, the following output is printed to the console:

```
Iterating: o.a=165, o.b = 105.
Iterating: o.a=105, o.b = 60.
Iterating: o.a=60, o.b = 45.
Iterating: o.a=45, o.b = 15.
Iterating: o.a=15, o.b = 0.
The gcd of 165 and 105 is 15.
```

Understanding String Formatting and Internationalization

By now you should be familiar with the practice of embedding a value of a JavaFX Script expression into a string using the braces notation, as demonstrated countless number of times in our examples. However, what you have learned so far is not the complete story of JavaFX Script strings. We want to teach you about two more features of strings: the fine-grained formatting of numerical, date/time, and other types of values using format specifiers, and the internationalization and localization of JavaFX Script applications.

Using String Format Specifications

Chapter 2 introduced you to one form of string expression: string literals with added brace-delimited segments, each segment containing a JavaFX Script expression. JavaFX Script actually supports a more versatile form of string expression in which each brace-delimited segment may contain a string format specification and a JavaFX Script expression. Listing 4-45 shows some examples of this form of string expression.

Listing 4-45. *Format Specifiers in String Expressions*

```
var b = true;
var i = 1024;
var n = 3.14;
var str = "Hello, World";

println("Display b in a 15 character field    [{%15b b}].");
println("Display i in a 15 character field    [{%15d i}].");
println("Display n in a 15 character field    [{%15f n}].");
println("Display str in a 15 character field [{%15s str}].");
```

A *string format specification* starts with a percent character (%), followed by an optional set of *flags*, an optional *field width specifier*, an optional *precision specifier*, and a mandatory *conversion character*. The conversion character determines how the accompanying JavaFX Script expression is to be formatted into a resulting string. The optional flags, field width, and precision specifier control some detailed aspects of the conversion.

In Listing 4-45, we use four string format specifications, %15b, %15d, %15f, and %15s, with conversion characters b (Boolean), d (integer), f (floating), and s (string). They all have a field width of 15. We surrounded the braces with brackets to illustrate the field into which the expressions are rendered.

When we run the program in Listing 4-45, the following output is printed to the console:

```
Display b in a 15 character field   [           true].
Display i in a 15 character field   [           1024].
Display n in a 15 character field   [       3.140000].
Display str in a 15 character field [   Hello, World].
```

JavaFX Script relies on the Java class java.util.Formatter to perform the conversions. This class draws its inspirations from the C programming language printf() format specifications. Table 4-1 summarizes some of the most useful conversion characters and their flags. Note that the double-character conversion specifications, starting from tH in the table, convert java.util.Date values.

Table 4-1. *JavaFX Script String Format Specifications*

Conversion Character	Effect
s	Format as string. Its use is necessary only with nontrivial flags and field width and precision specifiers. The - flag causes the string to be flush left in the field. The precision specifier limits the number of characters in the output.
d	Format as decimal integer. The - flag causes the number to be flush left in the field. The + flag causes the sign to be included. The 0 flag causes the number to be zero padded. The , (comma) flag causes locale-specific grouping separators to be included. The ((open parenthesis) flag causes negative numbers to be surrounded with parentheses.
o	Format as octal integer. The - and 0 flags work the same way as with decimal integers.
x, X	Format as hexadecimal integer. The - and 0 flags work the same way as with decimal integers.
f	Format as floating-point number. The -, +, 0, ,, and (flags work the same way as with decimal integers.
e, E	Format as scientific notation. The -, +, 0, and (flags work the same way as with decimal integers.
g, G	Format as either floating-point number or scientific notation depending on the value of the expression. The -, +, 0, and (flags work the same way as with decimal numbers.
tH	Format a java.util.Date value to hour of the day (24-hour clock). Valid values: 00–23.

Continued

Table 4-1. *Continued*

Conversion Character	Effect
tI	Format as hour (12-hour clock). Valid values: 01–12.
tk	Format as hour (24-hour clock). Valid values: 0–23.
tl	Format as hour (12-hour clock). Valid values: 1–12.
tM	Format as minutes. Valid values: 00–59.
tS	Format as seconds. Valid values: 00–59.
tL	Format as milliseconds within seconds. Valid values: 000–999.
tN	Format as nanoseconds within seconds. Valid values: 000000000–999999999.
tp, Tp	Format as am, AM or pm, PM.
tz	Format as time zone offset from GMT (e.g., -0600).
tZ	Format as time zone abbreviation (e.g., CST).
tB	Format as full month name (e.g., March).
tb	Format as abbreviated month name (e.g., Mar).
tA	Format as full day of the week (e.g., Monday).
ta	Format as abbreviated day of the week, (e.g., Mon).
tC	Format as century number. Valid values: 00–99.
tY	Format as four-digit year (e.g., 2009).
ty	Format as two-digit year (e.g., 09).
tj	Format as day of the year. Valid values: 001–366.
tm	Format as month. Valid values: 01–12.
td	Format as day of the month. Valid values: 01–31.
te	Format as day of the month. Valid values: 1–31.
tR	Format as HH:MM time (24-hour clock, e.g., 20:42).
tT	Format as HH:MM:SS time (24-hour clock, e.g., 20:42:51).
tr	Format as HH:MM:SS AM/PM time (12-hour clock, e.g., 08:42:51 PM).
td	Format as mm/dd/yy date (e.g., 03/02/09).
tF	Format as yyyy-mm-dd date (e.g., 2009-03-02).
tc	Format as full date/time (e.g., Mon Mar 02 20:42:51 CST 2009).

The string and number conversions are similar but not identical to the conversions found in C programming language. The date/time conversions can be somewhat overwhelming because of the many components making up a date/time value. However, the last six composite conversions should cover many use cases. Some of the conversions, for example, the character used as the decimal point and the month and weekday names, are locale-sensitive.

Internationalizing JavaFX Script Programs

Internationalization is the process of extracting user-visible strings out of a program written in one language or culture to be translated into other languages and cultures. *Localization* is the process of translating an internationalized program into one or several specific languages or cultures.

JavaFX Script provides an internationalization and localization mechanism that is easy to use. To internationalize a program, you go through the string literals and string expressions of the program and prepend a double-hash mark (##) before the ones that you wish to be translated. The double-hash mark may optionally be followed by a pair of brackets ([ ]) that encloses a *key* to the string literal or string expression.

Listing 4-46 shows a simple JavaFX Script program that contains several string literals and string expressions that are marked for translation.

Listing 4-46. *A JavaFX Script Program with Strings Marked for Translations*

```
// GreetingTrivia.fx
var name = "Weiqi";
var i = 1024;
var j = 9765625.0;
println(##[greeting]"Hello, {name}.");
println(##[trivia]"Do you know that "
  "{i} * {j} = {%,.1f i * j}?");
println(##"1024 is the 10th power of 2, "
  "and 9765625 is the 10th power of 5.");
```

The program in Listing 4-46 contains two string expressions and a string literal that are marked for internationalization. The first string expression is given the key greeting. The second string expression is given the key trivia. The string literal is not given a key. If a string literal is marked for internationalization without a key, JavaFX Script will take the entire string literal as the key. Notice also that adjacent string literals and string expressions merged into one string literal or string expression are treated as one for the purposes of internationalization. Therefore, you need to put a double-hash mark in front of only the first component.

If a string expression is marked for internationalization without a key, JavaFX Script will use a transformed version of the string expression as the key. This transformation replaces each embedded, brace-enclosed expression with its string format specification augmented with its position in the string. An embedded expression that does not have a string format specification is considered to have an implicit %s specification. The position numbers, which start with 1, are inserted after the % character and separated from the rest of the string format specification with an inserted $ character.

These transformed versions of the strings are also candidates for translation. For the program in Listing 4-46, the strings to translate are as follows:

```
Hello, %1$s.
Do you know that %1$s * %2$s = %3$,.1f?
1024 is the 10th power of 2, and 9765625 is the 10th power of 5.
```

To localize a program for a particular language or a language and culture combination, you create a set of translation files, one for each JavaFX Script source file that contains strings marked for translation. The translation files must have the .fxproperties file name extension. The names of these files are derived from the JavaFX Script source file names by appending a language suffix or a language and culture suffix.

Listing 4-47 shows a translation file in Simplified Chinese for the program in Listing 4-46.

Listing 4-47. *Translation File for GreetingTrivia.fx*

```
// GreetingTrivia_zh_CN.fxproperties
"greeting" = "%1$s你好."
"trivia" = "你知道%1$s*%2$s=%3$,.1f吗?"
"1024 is the 10th power of 2, and 9765625 is the 10th power of 5." = ➥
  "1024是2的10次方,9765625是5的10次方."
```

When we run the program in Listing 4-46 in a non-Chinese locale, the following output is printed to the console:

```
Hello, Weiqi.
Do you know that 1024 * 9765625.0 = 10,000,000,000.0?
1024 is the 10th power of 2, and 9765625 is the 10th power of 5.
```

When we run this program in a Simplified Chinese locale or with command-line options that set the user.language property to zh (Chinese) and user.country to CN (China), as in the following command line (the .fxproperties file is saved in UTF-8, so we also need to set the file.encoding property to utf-8):

```
javafx -Dfile.encoding=utf-8 -Duser.language=zh -Duser.country=CN GreetingTrivia
```

we get this output:

```
Weiqi你好.
你知道1024*9765625.0=10,000,000,000.0吗?
1024是2的10次方,9765625是5的10次方.
```

The translation files must be in the class path when the program is run. If the JavaFX Script source file belongs to a package, the translation files must also be in a directory structure that reflects the package.

There is far more to internationalization and localization than merely having strings translated, but JavaFX Script's translation mechanism gets you started very quickly.

Leveraging Java from JavaFX Script

In Chapter 2 and so far in Chapter 4, we have focused on explaining JavaFX Script language features without assuming that you have any Java experience. However, JavaFX Script is built on top of the Java platform, so it can leverage the vast number of available Java libraries.

In the following sections, we assume that you are familiar with the Java programming language and show you how to take advantage of Java libraries in JavaFX Script.

Instantiating Java Classes

Concrete Java classes can be instantiated in JavaFX Script using *new expressions*. A new expression is introduced by the new keyword, followed by a Java class name and a pair of parentheses that encloses a comma-separated list of zero or more expressions. The Java class must have a constructor with the same number of parameters, and each expression in the expression list must be convertible to the corresponding type of the Java constructor. Here are some examples of instantiating Java objects:

```
var now = new java.util.Date();
var fw = new java.io.FileWriter("output.txt");
```

The JavaFX Script string that we pass to the `FileWriter` constructor will be converted to a Java string when the Java constructor is called.

Note The JavaFX Script syntax allows you to use an object literal expression to create objects of Java reference types that have a default constructor (i.e., a constructor that takes no arguments). Thus you can also use `var now = java.util.date {};` to create a new `java.lang.Date` object. Similarly, the new expression without any arguments allows you to create objects of JavaFX Script class types with the same effect as an object literal expression without any initializers. To keep your life simple, we recommend using new expressions for creating Java objects and using object literal expressions for creating JavaFX Script objects.

Accessing Java Object Fields

Accessing fields of a Java object is achieved using the same member access expression (the dot notation) for accessing instance variables of JavaFX Script objects. Exposing public fields is not a common practice in Java API design, so this feature is not used as often as some of the other features.

Calling Java Methods

Once you create a Java object, you can call its methods using function invocation expressions. The parameters are converted from JavaFX Script types to Java types on the invocation, and the return values, if any, are converted back to JavaFX Script types.

JavaFX Script `Boolean` and numerical primitive types are converted to the corresponding Java primitive types. The JavaFX Script `String` type is converted to `java.lang.String`. The JavaFX Script `Duration` type is converted to `javafx.lang.Duration`. JavaFX Script class types are not converted but are checked for assignability to Java class types. JavaFX Script sequence types are converted to Java arrays.

In the following example, we create a `java.util.HashMap` and insert several key value pairs into it:

```
var map = new java.util.HashMap();

map.put("b", true);
map.put("i", 1024);
map.put("n", 3.14159);
map.put("str", "Hello, World");
```

Because JavaFX Script does not yet contain a map-like data structure, the `java.util.HashMap` is a very handy class to have at your disposal.

■Note JavaFX 1.0, 1.1, and 1.2 do not yet support Java generics. Therefore, when you use a Java generic class or method, you have to use it in the raw type form.

Accessing Static Fields and Methods

Static fields in a Java class are shared across all instances of the Java class. Static methods in a Java class do not receive an implicit `this` parameter when invoked. JavaFX Script does not support static variables and static functions in its classes. However, static fields and static methods in Java are very similar to JavaFX Script's script variables and script functions in a module. You can use the same syntax for accessing script-level entities in a module to access static members of a Java class.

In the following example, we access some static members of the `java.lang.Math` class:

```
var pi = java.lang.Math.PI;
var x = java.lang.Math.sin(pi/6);
```

After the calculation, the variable x has value `sin(pi/6)`, which is 0.5.

You can also use the following import directive to access all static members of a Java class:

```
import java.lang.Math.*;
var pi = PI;
var x = sin(pi/6);
```

This JavaFX Script import directive has the same power as Java's static import directive.

Quoting JavaFX Script Keywords

JavaFX Script does not come with its own input/output facilities aside from the `println()` function that you have seen in our examples. Therefore, it is natural to use Java's input/output facilities. For example, instead of printing something to the console, you might want to read some user input from the console. The `java.lang.System` class contains a static field called `in` that represents the standard input.

However, if you try to compile the following line of code:

```
java.lang.System.in.read();
```

you will get a compilation error because `in` is a JavaFX Script keyword. JavaFX Script allows you to *quote* such keywords by surrounding them with << and >>. Thus the preceding line of code could be rewritten as

```
java.lang.System.<<in>>.read();
```

Other JavaFX Script keywords that are often quoted include `insert`, `delete`, and `reverse`, which are legitimate method names in Java.

Accessing Nested Classes

In Java a class may contain other classes as members. A *static nested class* is a class that is declared inside another class with a `static` modifier. Static nested classes can be accessed from JavaFX Script using the same strategy for accessing static fields and static methods. Here is an example of how to access a Java class with a static nested class from JavaFX Script:

```
// Outer.java
package food;

public class Outer {
  public static class Nested {
  }
}

// Main.fx
import food.Outer.*;

var o = new Nested();
```

An *inner class* is a class that is declared inside another class without the `static` modifier. Instances of inner classes must have access to an instance of the containing class. JavaFX 1.0, 1.1, and 1.2 do not provide a way to access an inner class. The best advice we can give you is to write such code in Java.

Accessing Java Enums

Java enums can be accessed from JavaFX Script the same way as in Java. Here is an example:

```
// Suit.java
public enum Suit {
  CLUBS, DIAMONDS, HEARTS, SPADES
}

// Main.fx
var a = Suit.CLUBS;
var c = Suit.DIAMONDS;
var b = Suit.HEARTS;
var d = Suit.SPADES;
```

You can also access methods that you define in Java enums.

Extending Java Classes and Interfaces

A JavaFX Script class can extend Java classes and interfaces. JavaFX Script does not have an `implements` keyword, as Java does. And the extends keyword is used for both Java classes and interfaces. As far as extending Java classes and interfaces is concerned, JavaFX Script counts Java classes (including abstract classes) as regular classes and Java interfaces as mixin classes. Therefore, the rule for JavaFX Script inheritance, which you learned in the "Extending Classes" section earlier in this chapter, can be restated as follows: JavaFX Script classes can extend zero or one Java or JavaFX Script class, any number of Java interfaces, and any number of JavaFX Script mixin classes.

In Listing 4-48, we define a Java interface, Sum, with two methods: addInts, which takes two ints and returns an int; and addDoubles, which takes two doubles and returns a double. We implement addInts and addDoubles in the JavaFX Script class FXSum, which extends Sum. The SumClient Java class holds an instance of Sum and contains methods that exercise Sum's methods.

Listing 4-48. *Extending Java Classes*

```java
// Sum.java
public interface Sum {
  int addInts(int a, int b);
  double adddoubles(double x, double y);
}
```

```
// FXSum.fx
public class FXSum extends Sum {
  public override function addInts(a:Integer, b:Integer):Integer {
    a + b
  }
  public override function addDoubles(x:Double, y:Double):Double {
    x + y
  }
}
```

```java
// SumClient.java
public class SumClient {
  private Sum sum;
  public SumClient(Sum sum) {
    this.sum = sum;
  }
  public int addUpInts(int[] ints) {
    int result = 0;
    for (int i = 0; i < ints.length; i++) {
      result = sum.addInts(result, ints[i]);
    }
    return result;
  }
  public double addUpDoubles(double[] doubles) {
    double result = 0.0;
    for (int i = 0; i < doubles.length; i++) {
      result = sum.addDoubles(result, doubles[i]);
    }
    return result;
  }
}
```

```
// ExercisingSum.fx
var fxSum = FXSum {};
var sumClient = new SumClient(fxSum);
var sumOfInts = sumClient.addUpInts([1, 3, 5, 7, 9]);
var sumOfDoubles = sumClient.addUpDoubles([3.14159, 2.71828]);
println("sumOfInts={sumOfInts}.");
println("sumOfDoubles={sumOfDoubles}.");
```

When we run the program in Listing 4-48, the following output is printed to the console:

```
sumOfInts=25.
sumOfDoubles=5.859870195388794.
```

Even though Java classes can be extended by JavaFX Script classes, some differences between Java classes and JavaFX Script classes remain. One important difference is between Java fields and JavaFX Script instance variables. Some of the most powerful things that you can do with JavaFX Script instance variables, such as using them on the right-hand side of bind expressions or attaching a trigger using an instance variable override, cannot be done to fields in Java objects because Java lacks the facilities to track the changes made to fields.

Dealing with Java Arrays

JavaFX 1.2 introduced a native array type that allows JavaFX Script to efficiently handle Java APIs that either require a Java array parameter or return a Java array.

A *native array type* is declared as the keywords nativearray of followed by a Java class type or a JavaFX Script class type or primitive type. To illustrate its usage, we use the java.lang.Package.getPackages() API. This method returns an array of java.lang.Package objects that represent all the Java packages that are already loaded into the JVM.

```
import java.lang.Package;
import java.lang.Package.*;

var b = getPackages();

for (i in [0..b.length - 1]) {
  println(b[i]);
}
```

The getPackages() call is a static method call on the java.lang.Package class. It returns a Java array of type Package[]. Instead of converting it to a JavaFX Script sequence, as JavaFX 1.0 and 1.1 did, JavaFX 1.2 will use nativearray of Package to represent this return type. Since the return value is used as an initializer for the variable b, the type of variable b is also nativearray of Package. Just like with Java arrays, you can access its length field, and you can access the array elements using bracket notation: b[i].

It is possible to declare native array types for multidimensional Java arrays. For example, the Java type int[][] corresponds to the JavaFX Script native array type nativearray of nativearray of Integer.

Iterating Through Java Collections

Objects of Java classes that implement the `java.lang.Iterable` interface can be iterated over using the JavaFX Script for expression. Because the Java collection interfaces `java.util.List`, `java.util.Set`, and `java.util.Queue` all implement `java.lang.Iterable`, objects of any concrete Java collection classes that implement these interfaces (e.g., `java.util.ArrayList`, `java.util.HashSet`, and `java.util.ArrayDeque`) can be iterated over using for expressions, as demonstrated in Listing 4-49.

Listing 4-49. *Iterating Through Java Collections*

```
import java.util.*;

var list = new java.util.ArrayList();
list.add("One");
list.add("Two");
list.add("Three");

for (elem in list) {
  println("index: {indexof elem}, element: {elem}.");
}
```

When we run the program in Listing 4-49, the following output is printed to the console:

```
index: 0, element: One.
index: 1, element: Two.
index: 2, element: Three.
```

Understanding JavaFX Script Reflection

JavaFX Script includes a reflection API that allows you to perform certain metaprogramming tasks. *Metaprogramming* is the act of manipulating a programming facility using a language rather than using the programming facility itself.

The JavaFX Script provides its reflection API as a set of Java classes in the JavaFX Script runtime library. The fact that the JavaFX Script reflection API is written in Java rather than in JavaFX Script means that you can use it in either JavaFX Script code or Java code. We will show you its usage mostly in JavaFX Script.

Because the reflection API is written in Java, we will use Java's terminology to describe its parts. Therefore, in the upcoming text we will talk about fields and methods instead of instance functions and instance variables.

Understanding Mirror-Based Reflection

JavaFX Script's reflection facility follows a design principle called *mirrors*, which seek to separate conventional programming facilities from metaprogramming facilities and at the same time achieve symmetry between the conventional and metaprogramming facilities.

■Note The Java reflection facility does not follow the mirrors principle. This is mostly manifested through code like `employee.getClass();` where `employee` is an object of an `Employee` class. Although methods like `getEmployeeId()` or `getName()` have a legitimate place in an `Employee` class, one can argue that `getClass()` does not.

The interfaces and abstract classes in the `javafx.reflect` package presented in Table 5-2 provide the fundamental abstractions of the reflection facilities of the JavaFX Script programming language.

Table 5-2. *Interfaces and Abstract Classes of the JavaFX Script Reflection API*

Name	JavaFX Script Concept
FXType	A JavaFX Script type
FXValue	A JavaFX Script value
FXMember	A member of a class or a module
FXLocation	The location of a variable, used in data binding
FXContext	A reflection context, the entryway into reflection

Concrete subclasses of the `FXType` abstract class include `FXPrimitiveType`, `FXSequenceType`, `FXFunctionType`, `FXClassType`, and `FXJavaArrayType`. This reflects the four kinds of JavaFX Script types plus the native array types that we covered in Chapter 2 and Chapter 4.

Implementations of the `FXValue` interface include `FXPrimitiveValue`, `FXSequenceValue`, `FXFunctionValue`, and `FXObjectValue`. `FXPrimitiveValue` has additional subclasses: `FXBooleanValue`, `FXIntegerValue`, `FXLongValue`, `FXFloatValue`, `FXDoubleValue`.

Implementations of the `FXMember` interface include `FXFunctionMember` and `FXVarMember`. They reflect instance functions and instance variables as well as script functions and script variables. Script functions and script variables are considered members of the script or module to which they belong.

Concrete subclasses of the `FXLocation` abstract class include `FXVarMemberLocation`.

Entering the Reflection World

By design, the JavaFX Script reflection API can support reflections in a local Java virtual machine as well as remote Java virtual machines. JavaFX 1.0, 1.1, and 1.2 SDKs ship with a concrete implementation for local Java virtual machine reflections called `FXLocal`. Its `getContext()` method returns a `FXLocal.Context` object, which is an implementation of `FXContext`.

The `FXLocal.Context` class has a family of overloaded `mirrorOf()` methods that bridges the conventional programming and metaprogramming world. To get an `FXPrimitiveValue` or an `FXObjectValue` from a primitive value or an object, you use a version of `mirrorOf()` that takes one parameter. To get an `FXSequenceValue` or an `FXFunctionValue` from a sequence or a function, you use a version of `mirrorOf()` that takes two parameters, the second parameter being the type of the sequence or the function.

The FXValue objects are where further reflection tasks are performed. Its getType() method returns an appropriate FXType subclass. Its asObject() method returns the original JavaFX Script value.

Listing 4-50 shows an example of obtaining and examining the mirror reflections of the four kinds of JavaFX Script values.

Listing 4-50. *Examining the Mirrors of Conventional JavaFX Script Types*

```
// MirrorsOfValues.fx
import java.lang.Math.*;
import javafx.reflect.*;

public class Point {
  public var x: Number;
  public var y: Number;

  public function dist() {
    sqrt(x * x + y * y);
  }

  public override function toString() {
    "Point \{ x: {x}, y: {y} \}"
  }
}

public function run() {
  var i = 1024;
  var o = Point { x: 3, y: 4 };
  var seq = [3.14159, 2.71828];
  var func = o.dist;

  var context: FXLocal.Context = FXLocal.getContext();

  println("Examining...");
  var mirrorOfI = context.mirrorOf(i);
  print("  original: "); println({i});
  print("  mirror: "); println(mirrorOfI);
  print("  type: "); println({mirrorOfI.getType()});
  print("  back from mirror: "); println({mirrorOfI.asObject()});

  println("Examining...");
  var mirrorOfO = context.mirrorOf(o);
  print("  original: "); println({o});
  print("  mirror: "); println(mirrorOfO);
  print("  type: "); println({mirrorOfO.getType()});
  print("  back from mirror: "); println({mirrorOfO.asObject()});
```

```
      println("Exemining...");
      var seqType = context.getNumberType().getSequenceType();
      var mirrorOfSeq = context.mirrorOf(seq, seqType);
      print("  original: "); println({seq});
      print("  mirror: "); println(mirrorOfSeq);
      print("  type: "); println({mirrorOfSeq.getType()});
      print("  back from mirror: "); println({mirrorOfSeq.asObject()});

      println("Exemining...");
      var classType = context.findClass("MirrorsOfValues.Point");
      var funcMember = classType.getFunction("dist");
      var funcType = funcMember.getType();
      var mirrorOfFunc = context.mirrorOf(func, funcType);
      print("  original: "); println({func});
      print("  mirror: "); println(mirrorOfFunc);
      print("  type: "); println({mirrorOfFunc.getType()});
      print("  back from mirror: "); println({mirrorOfFunc.asObject()});
}
```

Notice that in order to obtain the mirrors of the sequence and function values, we have to construct their types beforehand and pass them into the mirrorOf() method as the second parameter. To obtain the type of a Number sequence, we call getNumberType() on context and then getSequenceType() on the result. The FXLocal.Context class has methods that return the FXPrimitiveType object of every primitive type. To obtain the function type, we call findClass() on context to get the FXClassType, getFunction() on classType to get the FXFunctionMember, and finally getType() on funcMember to get the FXFunctionType.

When we run the program in Listing 4-50, the following output is printed to the console:

```
Examining...
  original: 1024
  mirror: IntegerValue(1024)
  type: Integer
  back from mirror: 1024
Examining...
  original: Point { x: 3.0, y: 4.0 }
  mirror: javafx.reflect.FXLocal$ObjectValue@1e97f9f
  type: class MirrorsOfValues.Point
  back from mirror: Point { x: 3.0, y: 4.0 }
Exemining...
  original: [ 3.14159, 2.71828 ]
  mirror: javafx.reflect.FXLocal$SequenceValue@ee7a14
  type: Float[]
  back from mirror: [ 3.14159, 2.71828 ]
Exemining...
  original: MirrorsOfValues$1@126f75b
  mirror: javafx.reflect.FXLocal$FunctionValue@139b78e
  type: function():Double
  back from mirror: MirrorsOfValues$1@126f75b
```

Notice that the type of the Number sequence is reported as Float[]. This is a consequence of the primitive type enhancements of JavaFX 1.1, which makes java.lang.Float the backing class of the JavaFX Script Number type.

Programming Through Reflection

In this section, we show you a series of small code snippets that can be used to perform some common programming tasks using reflection. Reflection code is always considerably longer than nonreflection code. However, its length depends on the classes and functions being programmed.

Creating a New Instance of a Class

The idiomatic way of creating a new instance of a JavaFX Script class is as follows:

```
// CreatingInstance.fx
import javafx.reflect.*;

public class Point {
  public var x: Number;
  public var y: Number;
  public override function toString() {
    "Point \{ x: {x}, y: {y} \}"
  }
}

public function run() {
  var context = FXLocal.getContext();
  var classType = context.findClass("CreatingInstance.Point");
  var objectValue = classType.allocate();
  objectValue.initVar("x", context.mirrorOf(3.0));
  objectValue.initVar("y", context.mirrorOf(4.0));
  objectValue.initialize();
  var p = (objectValue as FXLocal.ObjectValue).asObject();
  println(p);
}
```

Here classType is of type FXLocal.ClassType, a subclass of FXClassType, and objectValue is of type FXLocal.ObjectValue, a subclass of FXObjectValue. The allocate() call allocates the memory for an instance of the class. The initVar() call supplies the initial values of instance variables of the object. Another version of initVar() takes an FXVarMember object as the first parameter instead of a string. The initialize() call performs the actual setting of the instance variables to their initial values and the running of the init and postinit blocks that the class may have.

Getting and Setting Values of Instance and Script Variables

The following code works with instance variables of JavaFX Script classes and script variables of JavaFX Script modules:

```
// GettingSettingVariables.fx
import javafx.reflect.*;

public class Point {
  public var x: Number;
  public var y: Number;
}

public var a:String;

public function run() {
  var p = Point { x: 3, y: 4 };

  // Working with instance variable x
  var context = FXLocal.getContext();
  var classType = context.findClass("GettingSettingVariables.Point");
  var xVar = classType.getVariable("x");
  xVar.setValue(context.mirrorOf(p), context.mirrorOf(7.0));
  println("p.x={p.x}.");

  // Working with script variable a
  var moduleClassType = context.findClass("GettingSettingVariables");
  var aVar = moduleClassType.getVariable("a");
  aVar.setValue(null, context.mirrorOf("Hello, World"));
  println("a={a}.");
}
```

Here we obtain the mirror of an instance variable in a class using the getVariable()
call on classType, passing in the variable name. Two other methods exist for getting instance
variables. One version of the overloaded getVariables() call takes a Boolean parameter and
returns a java.util.List<FXVarMember>. If the parameter is false, only instance variables
declared in the class are included in the list. If the parameter is true, all instance variables,
including those declared in the super classes, are included. Another version of the
getVariables() call takes an extra first parameter of type FXMemberFilter, which allows you
to get only those instance variables that pass the filter.

The type of xVar is FXVarMember. It represents the instance variable x of class Point. The
setValue() call on xVar takes two parameters: the first is a mirror of p and the second is a
mirror of the new value of x. FXVarMember has a corresponding getValue() call, which takes
one parameter, the mirror of an instance of the class, and returns a mirror of the value of the
instance variable.

■**Note** The JavaFX Script compiler compiles JavaFX Script modules into Java classes and JavaFX Script
classes in a module into nested Java classes. Therefore the reflection facility represents both classes and modules as FXLocal.ClassType. The getVariable() and getVariables() calls on a module class type will
return information related to script variables in the module. The setValue() and getValue() calls on instances
of FXVarMember that represent script variables will ignore the first parameter, and we usually pass in null.

Invoking Instance and Script Functions

The reflection code for invoking instance functions and script functions is very similar to the
code for accessing instance variables and script variables, as you can see here:

```
// InvokingFunctions.fx
import javafx.reflect.*;

public class A {
  public function f(i:Integer):Integer {
    i * i
  }
}

public function g(str:String):String {
  "{str} {str}"
}

public function run() {
  var o = A {};

  var context = FXLocal.getContext();

  // Working with instance function f() of A
  var classType = context.findClass("InvokingFunctions.A");
  var fFunc = classType.getFunction("f", context.getIntegerType());
  var fVal = fFunc.invoke(context.mirrorOf(o), context.mirrorOf(4));
  println("o.f(4)={(fVal as FXPrimitiveValue).asObject()}.");

  // Working with script function g()
  var moduleClassType = context.findClass("InvokingFunctions");
  var gFunc = moduleClassType.getFunction("g", context.getStringType());
  var gVal = gFunc.invoke(null, context.mirrorOf("Hello"));
  println('g("Hello")={(gVal as FXLocal.ObjectValue).asObject()}.');
}
```

Here we call the getFunction() method on classType to obtain a mirror of an instance function. This method can take a variable number of parameters. The first parameter is the name
of the function. The rest of the parameters are mirrors of the types of the instance function.
Two other methods are available for getting instance functions. One version of the overloaded
getFunctions() call takes a Boolean parameter and returns a java.util.List<FXVarFunction>.
If the parameter is false, only instance functions defined in the class are included in the list. If
the parameter is true, all instance functions, including those defined in the super classes, are
included. Another version of a getFunctions() call takes an extra first parameter of type
FXMemberFilter, which allows you to get only those instance functions that pass the filter.

The type of fFunc is FXFunctionMember. It represents the instance function f of class A. The
invoke() call on fFunc takes a variable number of parameters, in this case two: the first parameter is a mirror of o, an instance of A, and the second parameter is the mirror of the instance
function parameter. It returns an instance fVal of type FXValue that represents a mirror of the
value of the function invocation expression.

The situation with the script function g is analogous to the situation for instance functions, except that we search for the script function in the module class type, and that we pass a null as the first parameter to the invoke() call.

Other Reflection Capabilities

The reflection API also provides the following capabilities:

- The FXLocal.ClassType class has getMember(String, FXType), getMembers(boolean), and getMembers(FXMemberFilter, boolean) methods to get at member functions and member variables through the same API.

- The FXLocal.ClassType class has a getSuperClasses(boolean) method to get a list of direct or indirect super classes.

- The FXLocal.ObjectValue class has overloaded bindVar(String, FXLocation) and bindVar(FXVarMember, FXLocation) methods to bind member variables to FXLocations associated to other FXVarMembers.

- The FXVarMember class has a getLocation(FXObjectvalue) method that gets the location of member variables for use in bindVar() calls.

Summary

Now that you have finished this chapter, you have a basic understanding of the JavaFX Script language features, include the following:

- All about functions, including function definitions, anonymous function expressions, closures and function types, overloaded functions, and bound functions

- How the exception facility allows your code to signal an exceptional condition

- Working with classes, which covered the object system of the JavaFX Script language, instance variables and instance functions, the init and postinit blocks in class definitions, extending classes, and abstract classes and abstract functions

- Organizing your JavaFX Script code for better development and maintenance, which involves scripts, modules, and packages

- How to export entities from modules

- How the import facility makes using entities from faraway packages and modules the same as using locally created ones

- Using access modifiers for script-level entities as well as for instance variables and instance functions.

- Understanding triggers, string formatting, and internationalization of JavaFX Script programs

- Using the Java integration features of the JavaFX Script language that allow you to leverage the vast number of existing Java libraries in your JavaFX Script program

- Using the JavaFX Script reflection API

We believe you are well on your way to mastering the JavaFX Script programming language and are ready to tackle some of the more interesting JavaFX APIs. In the next chapter, we will show you how to create custom UI components in JavaFX.

Resources

Following are some useful online resources for the JavaFX Script language:

- *The openjfx-compiler home page*: https://openjfx-compiler.dev.java.net/
- *The JavaFX Script tutorial on JavaFX.com*: http://java.sun.com/javafx/1/tutorials/core/w

CHAPTER 5

■ ■ ■

Creating Custom UI Components and Charts in JavaFX

Miracles are a retelling in small letters of the very same story which is written across the whole world in letters too large for some of us to see.

—C. S. Lewis

In Chapter 3 you learned how to create user interfaces (UIs) in JavaFX by creating a stage, putting a scene on the stage, and putting nodes in the scene. You also learned how to handle mouse and keyboard events, as well as how to animate nodes in the scene. In Chapter 4 you dove into the details of creating JavaFX classes and functions.

In this chapter we're going to pick up the UI discussion from Chapter 3 by showing you how to create custom UI components and charts. The knowledge you've gained about the JavaFX language in Chapter 4 will serve you well in this chapter, as it leans heavily on concepts such as creating and extending classes.

Creating Custom UI Components

As shown in Chapter 3, the JavaFX SDK has several UI components available for use in programs, but the need for developers to create new types of UI components will always exist.

There are two types of custom UI components in JavaFX:

- *UI controls*: These are skinnable and highly user-interactive UI components. An example of a UI control that exists in the JavaFX SDK is the TextBox, located in the `javafx.scene.control` package. A UI control consists of a model class, which you create by extending `javafx.scene.control.Control`, a behavior class that extends `javafx.scene.control.Behavior`, and one or more skins that extend `javafx.scene.control.Skin`.

- *Custom nodes*: These are UI components that aren't skinnable and that don't have a built-in model class. You can create a custom node by extending the `javafx.scene.CustomNode` class.

Let's take the latter (and simpler) case first.

Creating a Custom Node

Take a look in the JavaFX API docs in the `CustomNode` class in the `javafx.scene` package. You'll see that this class extends the `javafx.scene.Node` class and introduces a function named `create()`. To define a custom node, you extend the `CustomNode` class and override the `create()` function, returning the root of the scene graph that expresses the custom node. To see this more clearly, we'll look at an example of a custom node.

The ColorPickerNode Example

At the end of this chapter, we'll challenge you to create a drawing program in JavaFX (glance ahead at Figure 5-14 if you're curious). One of the requirements is for the user to be able to choose a color with which to fill and outline a shape. To give you some help with this requirement, we created a custom node that presents the user with swatches that contain each of the 216 so-called web-safe colors. The `ColorPickerSnowFlakeNode` that you'll see later in the chapter is the finished product, and the `ColorPickerNode` (Figure 5-1) is a step in that direction that will serve as a starter example.

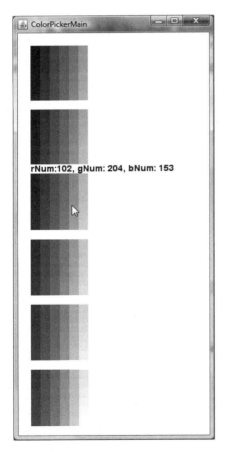

Figure 5-1. *The ColorPickerNode example*

In the following exercise, you'll run the ColorPickerNode project; the main program file is ColorPickerMain.fx.

EXAMINING THE BEHAVIOR OF THE COLORPICKERNODE EXAMPLE

When the program starts, its appearance should be similar to the screenshot in Figure 5-1. To fully examine its behavior, perform these steps:

1. Notice that the ColorPickerNode custom node consists of six blocks, arranged vertically, consisting of 36 colored squares each, with each of the 216 colors in the custom node unique.

2. Notice that the upper-left corner of the ColorPickerNode custom node is located at an x/y pixel location of 20/20.

3. Hover over various colored squares in various blocks. The RGB color values are displayed directly above the block of colors in which the mouse cursor is located.

Now that you've checked out the appearance and behavior of the ColorPickerNode, let's walk through the code together.

Understanding the ColorPickerNode Custom Node

Take a look at the code for the ColorPickerNode custom node in Listing 5-1, and after that we'll point out new and relevant concepts.

Listing 5-1. *ColorPickerNode.fx*

```
package projavafx.colorpicker.ui;

import javafx.scene.CustomNode;
import javafx.scene.Node;
import javafx.scene.Group;
import javafx.scene.text.*;
import javafx.scene.paint.Color;
import javafx.scene.shape.Rectangle;

/**
 * A graphical node that shows the 216 "web-safe" colors
 * arranged in 6 squares of 36 colors each.
 */
public class ColorPickerNode extends CustomNode {

  /**
   * Sequence of RGB values that are in the 216 "Web safe" colors
   */
  def rgbNums: Number[] = [0x00, 0x33, 0x66, 0x99, 0xCC, 0xFF];
```

```
/**
 * Create the Node
 */
override public function create():Node {
  Group {
    content: bind for (rNum in rgbNums) {
      Group {
        def SQUARE_WIDTH: Number = 15
        layoutY: indexof rNum * (SQUARE_WIDTH * sizeof rgbNums +
                                 SQUARE_WIDTH)
        content: for (gNum in rgbNums) {
          for (bNum in rgbNums) {
            Group {
              var rectRef: Rectangle
              content: [
                rectRef = Rectangle {
                  x: indexof gNum * SQUARE_WIDTH
                  y: indexof bNum * SQUARE_WIDTH
                  width: SQUARE_WIDTH
                  height: SQUARE_WIDTH
                  fill: Color.rgb(rNum, gNum, bNum)
                },
                Text {
                  textOrigin: TextOrigin.BOTTOM
                  visible: bind rectRef.hover
                  font: Font.font("Sans serif", FontWeight.BOLD, 14)
                  content: "rNum:{%1.0f rNum}, "
                            "gNum: {%1.0f gNum}, "
                            "bNum: {%1.0f bNum}"

                }
              ]
            }
          }
        }
      }
    }
  }
}
```

Overriding the CustomNode create() Function

As shown in Listing 5-1, to define a custom node you create a class that extends the CustomNode class and override the create() function. The create() function returns a subclass of Node, in this case a Group. By virtue of the for expression, this Group contains six Group instances (one for each element in the rgbNums sequence). Each of these Group instances contains 36 Group instances, each of which contains a Rectangle and a Text node.

The fill instance variable of each Rectangle is one of the 216 combinations of six red, green, and blue values.

The Text node contains the red, green, and blue values, formatted to have zero decimal places. Look at Chapter 4 to see the options for string formatting.

Using the Node hover Variable

Notice that the visible variable of the Text instance is bound to the hover variable of the Rectangle instance, which is why the string containing red, green, and blue values is only visible while the mouse is hovering over a Rectangle.

Now that you've examined the code for the ColorPickerNode custom node, check out the ColorPickerMain.fx script in Listing 5-2, which creates an instance of this custom node.

Listing 5-2. *ColorPickerMain.fx*

```
package projavafx.colorpicker.ui;

import javafx.stage.Stage;
import javafx.scene.Scene;

Stage {
  title: "ColorPickerMain"
  scene: Scene {
    width: 300
    height: 650
    content: ColorPickerNode {
      layoutX: 20
      layoutY: 20
    }
  }
}
```

As you can see, creating an instance of a custom node is just like creating an instance of any other class in JavaFX.

Let's move on to the ColorPickerSnowFlakeNode class, which is the actual custom node that you could use from the drawing program exercise to enable the user to select a color.

The ColorPickerSnowFlakeNode Example

The ColorPickerSnowFlakeNode custom node, shown in Figure 5-2, builds on the previous example by providing some additional capabilities. These capabilities include reporting which color was picked by the user, functioning similar to a dialog, and arranging the colors in a snowflake pattern.

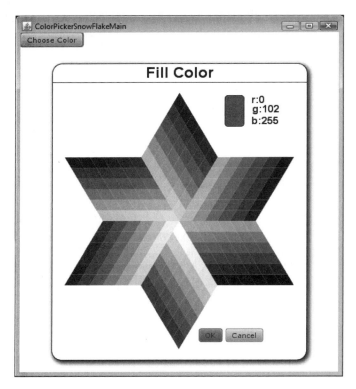

Figure 5-2. *The ColorPickerSnowFlakeNode example*

In the following exercise, you'll run the ColorPickerSnowFlakeNode project; the main program file is ColorPickerSnowFlakeMain.fx.

EXAMINING THE BEHAVIOR OF THE COLORPICKERSNOWFLAKENODE EXAMPLE

When the program starts, a window should appear that has a button labeled Choose Color in the upper-left corner.
To fully examine its behavior, perform these steps:

1. Click the Choose Color button. You'll see a rounded rectangle containing 216 colors in a snowflake pattern,
   along with two buttons.

2. Notice that the snowflake pattern consists of six diamonds, each containing 36 diamonds with unique colors.
   Also notice that there is an empty rounded rectangle located to the upper right of the snowflake.

3. Click and drag on any white area in the large rounded rectangle. Observe that you're able to drag the rectangle within the containing window.

4. Move the mouse over various color swatches, noticing that a diamond-shaped outline appears on the swatch in a color that provides contrast to the color of the swatch.

5. Click on one of the swatches; you'll see that the color appears in the small rounded rectangle and that its RGB values appear to the right of the rectangle.

6. Click the Cancel button. The large rounded rectangle with the colorful snowflake disappears and the background of the window remains white.

7. Click the Choose Color button again, select a color from the snowflake, and click the OK button. The large rounded rectangle with the colorful snowflake disappears, and the background of the window assumes the color that you selected.

Now that you've checked out the appearance and behavior of the `ColorPickerSnowFlakeNode`, let's walk through the code together.

Understanding ColorPickerSnowFlakeNode

Listing 5-3 contains the code for the `ColorPickerSnowFlakeMain` script, which creates the window with the Choose Color button in the upper-left corner. Afterward, we'll highlight concepts in the listing.

Listing 5-3. *ColorPickerSnowFlakeMain.fx*

```
package projavafx.colorpicker.ui;

import javafx.scene.Scene;
import javafx.scene.control.Button;
import javafx.scene.paint.Color;
import javafx.stage.Stage;

Stage {
  var sceneColor: Color = Color.WHITE
  var colorPicker: ColorPickerSnowFlakeNode
  title: "ColorPickerSnowFlakeMain"
  scene: Scene {
    width: 500
    height: 550
    fill: bind sceneColor
    content: [
      Button {
        text: "Choose Color"
        action: function():Void {
          colorPicker.visible = true;
        }
      },
```

```
        colorPicker = ColorPickerSnowFlakeNode {
          layoutX: 50
          layoutY: 50
          title: "Fill Color"
          visible: false
          originalColor: bind sceneColor
          onClose: function(color:Color) {
            sceneColor = color;
          }
        }
      ]
    }
}
```

Making a Node Act Like a Dialog

The easiest way to create a custom dialog in JavaFX that opens in a separate window is to use the JFXtras project described in Chapter 3. But what about the cases in which you want your custom node to act like a dialog while still living in the Scene? This makes one less window for the user to manage, and is also a more natural approach when your JavaFX program is running as an applet in a browser. This example uses the latter approach.

As shown in Listing 5-3 earlier, the Scene contains a Button and a ColorPickerSnowFlakeNode. Notice that the visible instance variable that the latter class inherits from Node is assigned a value of false, which is why it didn't appear when you first invoked the program. In the action event handler of the Button, the visible instance variable of the colorPicker reference is assigned the value of true, and our ColorPickerSnowFlakeNode "dialog" appears.

As you'll see in a moment, when one of the buttons in the "dialog" is clicked, it causes the onClose event handler that we created especially for our custom node to be invoked. Notice that the anonymous function assigned to the onClose variable in Listing 5-3 takes a Color instance as its argument and assigns it to the sceneColor model variable. Because the fill paint of the Scene is bound to the sceneColor model variable, the Scene's background assumes the color that the ColorPickerSnowFlakeNode "dialog" passed to the onClose handler.

Let's continue examining this dialog-like behavior by looking at the code for the ColorPickerSnowFlakeNode class in Listing 5-4.

Listing 5-4. *ColorPickerSnowFlakeNode.fx*

```
package projavafx.colorpicker.ui;

import javafx.scene.CustomNode;
import javafx.scene.Group;
import javafx.scene.Node;
import javafx.scene.control.Button;
import javafx.scene.effect.DropShadow;
import javafx.scene.input.MouseEvent;
import javafx.scene.layout.HBox;
```

```
import javafx.scene.layout.VBox;
import javafx.scene.paint.Color;
import javafx.scene.shape.Line;
import javafx.scene.shape.Polygon;
import javafx.scene.shape.Rectangle;
import javafx.scene.text.*;
import javafx.scene.transform.Rotate;
import javafx.scene.transform.Translate;
import javafx.util.Math;

/**
 * A graphical node that shows the 216 "web-safe" colors arranged in a
 * snowflake pattern consisting of 6 diamonds containing 36 colors each.
 */
public class ColorPickerSnowFlakeNode extends CustomNode {

  /**
   * Width of the diamonds shapes in the color picker
   */
  def DIAMOND_WIDTH: Double = 20;

  /**
   * Sequence of RGB values that are in the 216 "Web safe" colors
   */
  def rgbNums: Number[] = [0xFF, 0xCC, 0x99, 0x66, 0x33, 0x00];

  /**
   * The OK button.
   */
  var okButtonRef:Button;

  /**
   * The title of the color picker
   */
  public var title: String;

  /**
   * The chosen red value
   */
  public var chosenRedNum: Number;

  /**
   * The chosen green value
   */
  public var chosenGreenNum: Number;
```

```
/**
 * The chosen blue value
 */
public var chosenBlueNum: Number;

/**
 * The chosen color
 */
public var chosenColor: Color;

/**
 * The original color
 */
public var originalColor: Color;

/**
 * Override the visible instance variable so it can put itself
 * on top when it becomes visible
 */
public override var visible on replace {
  if (visible) {
    toFront();
    okButtonRef.requestFocus();
  }
}

/**
 * The onClose function attribute is executed when the
 * the OK or Cancel button is pressed, passing the chosen color
 * or original color, depending upon which button was pressed
 */
public var onClose: function(color:Color):Void;

/**
 * Create the Node
 */
override public function create():Node {
  Group {
    def TITLE_BAR_HEIGHT: Number = 30;
    def colorValFont = Font.font("Sans serif", FontWeight.BOLD, 16)
    var outerRectRef: Rectangle
    var buttonsHBoxRef: HBox
    var titleTextRef: Text
    content: [
      outerRectRef = Rectangle {
        var startDragX: Number = 0;
        var startDragY: Number = 0;
```

```
      blocksMouse: true
      width: 400
      height: 480
      fill: Color.WHITE
      stroke: Color.BLACK
      arcHeight: 30
      arcWidth: 30
      effect: DropShadow {
        offsetX: 3
        offsetY: 3
      }
      onMousePressed: function(me:MouseEvent) {
        toFront();
        startDragX = layoutX;
        startDragY = layoutY;
      }
      onMouseDragged: function(me:MouseEvent) {
        layoutX = me.dragX + startDragX;
        layoutY = me.dragY + startDragY;
      }
    },
    Line {
      startX: 0
      startY: TITLE_BAR_HEIGHT
      endX: 399
      endY: TITLE_BAR_HEIGHT
      stroke: Color.BLACK
      strokeWidth: 1
    },
    titleTextRef = Text {
      layoutX: bind (outerRectRef.layoutBounds.width -
                    titleTextRef.layoutBounds.width) / 2
      layoutY: bind (TITLE_BAR_HEIGHT -
                    titleTextRef.layoutBounds.height) / 2
      textOrigin: TextOrigin.TOP
      content: bind title
      fill: Color.BLACK
      font: Font.font("Sans serif", FontWeight.BOLD, 24)
    },
    Group {
      blocksMouse: true
      content: bind for (rNum in rgbNums) {
        Group {
          def diamondHalfHeight: Double =
                Math.sqrt(Math.pow(DIAMOND_WIDTH, 2) -
                Math.pow(DIAMOND_WIDTH / 2, 2))
          def diamondHalfWidth: Double = DIAMOND_WIDTH / 2
```

```
          transforms: [
            Translate.translate(200, 255),
            Rotate.rotate(indexof rNum * 60, 0, 0)
          ]
          content: for (gNum in rgbNums) {
            for (bNum in rgbNums) {
              Group {
                var polyRef: Polygon
                layoutX: indexof bNum * diamondHalfWidth -
                           indexof gNum * diamondHalfWidth
                layoutY: indexof bNum * diamondHalfHeight +
                           indexof gNum * diamondHalfHeight
                content: [
                  polyRef = Polygon {
                    points: [
                      0, 0,
                      diamondHalfWidth, diamondHalfHeight,
                      0, diamondHalfHeight * 2,
                      diamondHalfWidth * - 1, diamondHalfHeight
                    ]
                    fill: Color.rgb(rNum, gNum, bNum)
                    stroke: bind if (polyRef.hover)
                                    Color.rgb((rNum + 128) mod 256,
                                              (gNum + 128) mod 256,
                                              (bNum + 128) mod 256)
                                 else null
                    strokeWidth: 2
                    onMouseClicked: function(me:MouseEvent) {
                      chosenRedNum = rNum;
                      chosenGreenNum = gNum;
                      chosenBlueNum = bNum;
                      chosenColor = Color.rgb(rNum, gNum, bNum);
                    }
                  },
                ]
              }
            }
          }
        },
        HBox {
          layoutX: 270
          layoutY: 50
          spacing: 10
```

```
    content: [
      Rectangle {
        width: 30
        height: 50
        arcWidth: 10
        arcHeight: 10
        stroke: Color.BLACK
        fill: bind if (chosenColor != null) chosenColor
                    else originalColor
      },
      VBox {
        opacity: bind if (chosenColor == null) 0.0 else 1.0
        content: [
          Text {
            font: colorValFont
            textOrigin: TextOrigin.TOP
            content: bind "r:{%1.0f chosenRedNum}"
          },
          Text {
            font: colorValFont
            textOrigin: TextOrigin.TOP
            content: bind "g:{%1.0f chosenGreenNum}"
          },
          Text {
            font: colorValFont
            textOrigin: TextOrigin.TOP
            content: bind "b:{%1.0f chosenBlueNum}"
          }
        ]
      }
    ]
  },
  buttonsHBoxRef = HBox {
    blocksMouse: true
    layoutX: bind outerRectRef.layoutBounds.width -
                    buttonsHBoxRef.layoutBounds.width - 70
    layoutY: bind outerRectRef.layoutBounds.height -
                    buttonsHBoxRef.layoutBounds.height - 30
    spacing: 5
    content: [
      okButtonRef = Button {
        text: "OK"
        strong: true
        action: function():Void {
          visible = false;
          onClose(chosenColor);
        }
      },
```

```
          Button {
            text: "Cancel"
            action: function():Void {
              // Revert to the original color
              visible = false;
              chosenColor = originalColor;
              onClose(chosenColor);
            }
          }
        ]
      }
    ]
  }
}
```

Defining and Invoking an Event Handler

The following snippet from Listing 5-4 continues to demonstrate how we gave our custom node a dialog-like behavior. Notice that an onClose instance variable is defined whose type is a function that takes a Color and returns Void. Moving down to the action event handlers in the Button objects, notice that after making the custom node invisible, the appropriate Color is passed to the onClose function. Its implementation, as we saw earlier, is the anonymous function assigned to the onClose variable in the ColorPickerSnowFlakeMain script.

```
public class ColorPickerSnowFlakeNode extends CustomNode {
  ...code omitted...
  public var chosenColor: Color;
  public var originalColor: Color;
  public override var visible on replace {
    if (visible) toFront();
  }
  public var onClose: function(color:Color):Void;
  override public function create():Node {
    Group {
      ...code omitted...
          Button {
            text: "OK"
            strong: true
            action: function():Void {
              visible = false;
              onClose(chosenColor);
            }
          },
```

```
        Button {
          text: "Cancel"
          action: function():Void {
            // Revert to the original color
            visible = false;
            chosenColor = originalColor;
            onClose(chosenColor);
          }
        }
      }
    ...code omitted...
    }
  }
}
```

Overriding Instance Variables

In the previous snippet, the `visible` variable inherited from `Node` is overridden in the custom node. We did this so that an `on replace` trigger could be introduced to cause our custom node to be brought to the front when it is made visible.

Tip Nodes have a *z-order* within their container (such as a `Scene` or `Group`). The default z-order is the order in which the nodes were defined in the container (with the latest ones on top). You can influence this order by using the `toFront()` and `toBack()` functions of the node.

The DropShadow Effect

As shown in Figure 5-2 earlier, the outline of the large rounded rectangle appears to be casting a shadow on its right and bottom sides. The following snippet, taken from Listing 5-4, shows how this is accomplished:

```
        effect: DropShadow {
          offsetX: 3
          offsetY: 3
        }
```

Peruse the `javafx.scene.effect` package in the JavaFX API docs to see an impressive list of effects that you can use to alter the appearance of your nodes. These include `Blend`, `Bloom`, `BoxBlur`, `ColorAdjust`, `DisplacementMap`, `DropShadow`, `Flood`, `GaussianBlur`, `Glow`, `InnerShadow`, `InvertMask`, `Lighting`, `MotionBlur`, `PerspectiveTransform`, `Reflection`, and `SepiaTone`. Looking at the `DropShadow` effect, you'll see that the two variables used in the previous snippet control the offsets of the shadow in pixels. For example, if you changed the `offsetX` value to -3, then the shadow would appear to the left (and bottom) of the rectangle.

See this chapter's Resources section for a reference to the *Effects Playground* program written by Chris Campbell of the JavaFX team for the purpose of experimenting with effects.

■**Tip** A very nice feature of the JavaFX API documentation is that many of the classes contain example code that is rendered into an image when the Javafxdoc tool is run. This enables you to see an image of the example in the documentation.

Obtaining the Width and Height of a Node

As mentioned in Chapter 3, a common practice for obtaining the width and height of a node is to use its `layoutBounds` variable. We use this approach in the following snippet to center the Text node that contains the title of our "dialog" in Figure 5-2:

```
titleTextRef = Text {
    layoutX: bind (outerRectRef.layoutBounds.width -
                    titleTextRef.layoutBounds.width) / 2
    layoutY: bind (TITLE_BAR_HEIGHT -
                    titleTextRef.layoutBounds.height) / 2
    textOrigin: TextOrigin.TOP
    content: bind title
    fill: Color.BLACK
    font: Font.font("Sans serif", FontWeight.BOLD, 24)
},
```

Now it's time to point out concepts related to creating the colorful snowflake. This is where you'll see some similarities to the `ColorPickerNode` example.

Creating a Polygon Shape

The color swatches in the `ColorPickerNode` example are squares, but they are diamonds in this `ColorPickerSnowFlakeNode` example. To draw each diamond, we're using a `Polygon`, as shown in Listing 5-5, taken from Listing 5-4.

Listing 5-5. *Drawing 36 Diamonds Arranged in One Large Diamond*

```
content: for (gNum in rgbNums) {
    for (bNum in rgbNums) {
        Group {
            var polyRef: Polygon
            layoutX: indexof bNum * diamondHalfWidth -
                        indexof gNum * diamondHalfWidth
            layoutY: indexof bNum * diamondHalfHeight +
                        indexof gNum * diamondHalfHeight
```

```
content: [
  polyRef = Polygon {
    points: [
      0, 0,
      diamondHalfWidth, diamondHalfHeight,
      0, diamondHalfHeight * 2,
      diamondHalfWidth * - 1, diamondHalfHeight
    ]
    fill: Color.rgb(rNum, gNum, bNum)
    stroke: bind if (polyRef.hover)
                    Color.rgb((rNum + 128) mod 256,
                              (gNum + 128) mod 256,
                              (bNum + 128) mod 256)
                 else null
    strokeWidth: 2
    onMouseClicked: function(me:MouseEvent) {
      chosenRedNum = rNum;
      chosenGreenNum = gNum;
      chosenBlueNum = bNum;
      chosenColor = Color.rgb(rNum, gNum, bNum);
    }
  },
  ]
 }
 }
}
```

Each small Polygon, as shown in Listing 5-5, is created from a sequence of numeric values in its points variable. This sequence contains the x and y values of each unique point in the diamond shape. As with the preceding example, the fill variable of this Polygon represents the current rNum, gNum, and bNum values for the Polygon that's created inside the nested for expressions. The values assigned to layoutX and layoutY place the 36 diamond-shaped color swatches into positions that form a larger diamond. We'll show you in the "Transforming Nodes" section later in this chapter how this program creates the six large diamonds and arranges them in the shape of a snowflake.

Using the stroke and strokeWidth Variables

Two of the instance variables that all shapes (descendants of the javafx.scene.shape.Shape class) have are stroke and strokeWidth. The former is the color (actually Paint) of the shape's outline, and the latter is the width in pixels of the shape's outline, assigned a value of 2 in the previous snippet. The color is set to an rgb value that is designed to be distinguishable from the rgb values of the shape's fill color.

Transforming Nodes

To transform nodes, use the instance variables of the Node class listed in Table 5-1.

Table 5-1. *The Transform-Related Instance Variables in the Node Class*

Transform Variables	Description
layoutX	Moves the node horizontally by the assigned number of pixels. Used for *app-managed layout*.
layoutY	Moves the node vertically by the assigned number of pixels. Used for *app-managed layout*.
translateY	Moves the node horizontally by the assigned number of pixels. Used for *container-managed layout*.
translateY	Moves the node vertically by the assigned number of pixels. Used for *container-managed layout*.
scaleX	Transforms the width of the node by the assigned factor. A factor of 1.0 would result in no change of scale. The scaling is performed about the center of the node.
scaleY	Transforms the height of the node by the assigned factor. A factor of 1.0 would result in no change of scale. The scaling is performed about the center of the node.
rotate	Rotates the node by the assigned number of degrees about the center of the node.
transforms	Contains a sequence of Transform functions.

■**Note** The layoutX/Y and translateX/Y variables have similar functionality. As noted in the descriptions in Table 5-1, layoutX/Y is used when the application is managing the position of the nodes, and translateX/Y is used when the container (such as the Flow container discussed in Chapter 3) is managing the position of the nodes. See Chapter 7 for a thorough discussion of these concepts.

You've already seen the layoutX and layoutY variables used in examples in this book. There is one transform-related variable in the Node class, named transforms, listed in Table 5-1 that deserves more explanation here. It enables all of the transformations shown in Table 5-1, and it also provides for transformations such as *shear* (skewing) and *affine*. An affine transformation is one in which both the straightness and parallelism of lines is maintained. Rotate, scale, translate, and shear are all affine transformations.

To understand how to use the transforms variable, take a look at the following snippet from Listing 5-4. This snippet places the diamond-shaped nodes, each consisting of 36 color swatches (created by the code that we just walked through), into a snowflake pattern:

```
Group {
  blocksMouse: true
  content: bind for (rNum in rgbNums) {
    Group {
      def diamondHalfHeight:Double =
              Math.sqrt(Math.pow(DIAMOND_WIDTH, 2) -
              Math.pow(DIAMOND_WIDTH / 2, 2))
      def diamondHalfWidth: Double = DIAMOND_WIDTH / 2
      transforms: [
        Transform.translate(200, 255)
        Transform.rotate(indexof rNum * 60, 0, 0)
      ]
      ...code from Listing 5-5 that draws a large diamond...
    }
  }
},
```

The transforms variable holds a sequence of objects that extend the javafx.scene.
transform.Transform class. In the previous snippet, the Transform.translate() function
returns a Translate instance that expresses the translate, and the Transform.rotate()
function returns a Rotate instance that expresses the rotate. In a transforms sequence, the
transforms contained in its elements are applied sequentially.

Therefore:

1. The translate() invocation in the snippet is applied first, positioning the Group node
    200 pixels horizontally and 255 pixels vertically from the top-left corner of our custom
    node. This Group contains the large diamond with 36 small, colored diamonds.

2. Then, the rotate() invocation is applied, rotating the Group node by a number of
    degrees equal to the product of 60 and a number ranging from 0 to 5 (the value of the
    rNum iteration variable in the for expression just above the Group).

The order of the transforms in the sequence typically matters. For example, try reversing
the order in this example and note that you don't see a star pattern. For information on the
remaining transform functions (scale(), shear(), and affine()), check out the javafx.scene.
transform.Transform class in the JavaFX API docs.

Blocking Mouse Events from Underlying Nodes

Remember when you tried out this example using the steps provided earlier, and one of
the steps was dragging the custom node around the scene? You know from Chapter 3 that
this ability exists by supplying an onMouseDragged event handler. Looking at Listing 5-4
confirms that there is such an event handler defined in the rounded Rectangle that outlines
the custom node.

It probably wouldn't be good, however, for the custom node to move when the user clicks on a color swatch and accidentally drags the mouse a bit. To prevent this, we set the `blocksMouse` instance variable of the `Group` that contains the snowflake pattern to `true`. The `blocksMouse` variable is located in the `Node` class, and it blocks mouse events from occurring on underlying nodes in the z-order. A quick look at Listing 5-4 again will reveal that we're using this capability in the `HBox` node that contains the buttons to prevent accidental dragging when the OK or Cancel button is clicked.

Recall that at the beginning of this chapter we said that there are two ways to create a custom UI component. Now that we've explored how to create a custom UI component by extending the `CustomNode` class, we'll show you how to create skinnable UI controls.

Creating Skinnable UI Controls

Perhaps you want to create a custom UI component that is highly interactive, and whose look and behavior (skin) can be changed at runtime. In that case, defining a skinnable UI control (*UI control* for short) is a good decision.

The classes that you need for creating a UI control are in the `javafx.scene.control` package:

- You'll extend the `Control` class to define the model for your UI control. This model consists of the data as well as some logic for the UI control.

- You'll extend the `Skin` class to define the user interface portion "skin" of the UI control. You can create additional skins by defining additional subclasses of the `Skin` class.

- You'll extend the `Behavior` class to define much of the behavior interaction logic for the UI control.

To demonstrate how to create a UI control, we've created a simple example program, named `StoplightSkinning`, which displays a UI control that looks like a stoplight.

The StoplightSkinning Example

The stoplight UI control in this program has one model and two skins. Each of the radio buttons in Figure 5-3 corresponds to a skin.

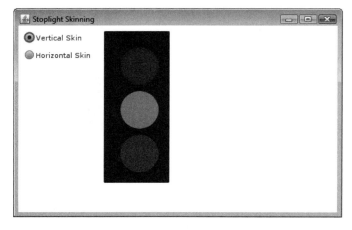

Figure 5-3. *The StoplightSkinning example when first invoked*

In the following exercise, you'll run the StoplightSkinning project; the main program file is StoplightSkinningMain.fx.

EXAMINING THE BEHAVIOR OF THE STOPLIGHTSKINNING EXAMPLE

When the program starts, you'll see the window shown in Figure 5-3 earlier. To fully examine its behavior, perform the following steps:

1. Hover the mouse over the stoplight and notice that its appearance changes slightly; it now has a shadow around the edges of the rectangle.

2. Click once on the stoplight. The outline of the rectangle turns into a dashed line, as shown here, indicating that it has focus:

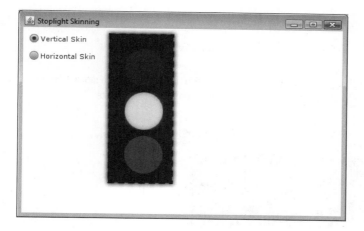

3. Click several times on the stoplight. A different light has a glow effect each time, and the index of the glowing light prints out in the console.

4. Press the Tab key repeatedly. The radio buttons assume a focused appearance, until focus lands on the stoplight UI control. Notice that the outline of the stoplight has a dashed line again.

5. Click on a different window, or on the desktop. The outline turns solid. Click on the window that contains the stoplight and the dashed outline returns, showing that it again has focus.

6. Press the Up Arrow key repeatedly. Different lights glow in an upward sequence. Pressing the Left Arrow key repeatedly has the same effect.

7. Press the Down Arrow key repeatedly. Different lights glow in a downward sequence, just as they did in Step 3 earlier. Pressing the Right Arrow key repeatedly has the same effect.

8. Click the radio button labeled Horizontal Skin. The stoplight assumes a very different appearance (horizontal orientation, size and spacing of buttons), as shown here:

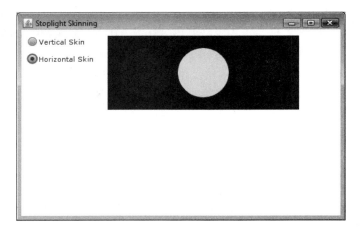

9. Go ahead and try the same things that you did with the other skin. Hovering over the stoplight results in a blurry appearance, and the focused indication is a solid yellow border, as shown here:

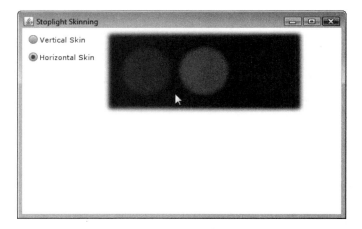

Now that you've seen the appearance and behavior of the StoplightSkinning example, let's examine the code behind it.

Understanding the StoplightSkinning Program

There are five JavaFX source files in this program. The first JavaFX program, in Listing 5-6, is the main script.

Listing 5-6. *StoplightSkinningMain.fx*

```
package projavafx.stoplightskinning.ui;

import javafx.scene.Group;
import javafx.scene.Scene;
import javafx.scene.layout.HBox;
import javafx.scene.layout.VBox;
import javafx.stage.Stage;
import javafx.scene.control.RadioButton;
import javafx.scene.control.ToggleGroup;

var sceneRef: Scene;

var stoplightControl = Stoplight{};
var verticalSelected:Boolean = true on replace {
  if (verticalSelected) {
    stoplightControl.skin = StoplightVerticalSkin{};
  }
};
var horizontalSelected:Boolean = false on replace {
  if (horizontalSelected) {
    stoplightControl.skin = StoplightHorizontalSkin{};
  }
};

Stage {
  title: "Stoplight Skinning"
  scene: sceneRef = Scene {
    width: 500
    height: 300
    content: Group {
      content: [
        HBox {
          layoutX: 10
          layoutY: 10
          spacing: 20
          content: [
            VBox {
              var toggleGrp = ToggleGroup{}
              spacing: 10
              content: [
                RadioButton {
                  text: "Vertical Skin"
                  toggleGroup: toggleGrp
                  selected: bind verticalSelected with inverse
                },
```

```
            RadioButton {
              text: "Horizontal Skin"
              toggleGroup: toggleGrp
              selected: bind horizontalSelected with inverse
            }
          ]
        },
        stoplightControl
      ]
    }
  ]
}
}
}
}
```

Each of the radio buttons causes a different skin to be associated with the control. Notice the use of the toggle group to keep the radio buttons mutually exclusive.

Placing a UI control on the scene is the same as placing any other node. Note that the class that we're making an instance of is Stoplight, which is the one that extends Control. The Stoplight class is shown in Listing 5-7 in the next section.

Creating the Control's Model

The model for a UI control contains primarily *state* (variables) that all of the skins for the UI control can share. Here's a question for you: Thinking back to when you examined the behavior of the StoplightSkinning example, what *state* can you infer that the model contains? Check out Listing 5-7 to see how close you are.

Listing 5-7. *Stoplight.fx*

```
package projavafx.stoplightskinning.ui;

import javafx.scene.Node;
import javafx.scene.control.Control;

public def STOP: Integer = 0;
public def CAUTION: Integer = 1;
public def GO: Integer = 2;

/**
 * The model for the StopLight control
 */
public class Stoplight extends Control {
  /**
   * The index of the selected light in the stoplight
   */
  public var selectedIndex: Integer = 0;
```

```
/**
 * Make the next light bright
 */
protected function nextLight() {
  selectedIndex = ++selectedIndex mod 3;
}

/**
 * Make the previous light bright
 */
protected function prevLight() {
  selectedIndex = (--selectedIndex + 3) mod 3;
}

/**
 * Identify a default skin
 */
override public function create():Node {
  skin = StoplightVerticalSkin {};
  super.create();
}
}
```

As you'll recall, a different light was brighter each time you clicked on the stoplight. There is a variable in the model for the purpose of keeping track of the selected light, arbitrarily named selectedIndex.

Also, notice the three module-level constants (STOP, CAUTION, and GO) at the top of the program that correspond to the states of selectedIndex. They are used by the skins as a self-documenting way to associate a particular light with a selectedIndex state in the model.

In addition to state being held in the Stoplight control class, there are a couple of functions that manipulate this state while ensuring that the integrity of the state is maintained. These functions are shown in the following snippet from Listing 5-7, and cause the selectedIndex variable to be incremented or decremented:

```
protected function nextLight() {
  selectedIndex = ++selectedIndex mod 3;
}

protected function prevLight() {
  selectedIndex = (--selectedIndex + 3) mod 3;
}
```

You'll see where these functions are called when we cover the StoplightBehavior class in the upcoming "Defining Behavior for the Stoplight Control" section.

Associating a Skin with the Model

When you were examining the behavior of the StoplightSkinning example, the first stoplight UI control that appeared was vertical, as shown earlier in Figure 5-3. This is because of the following snippet from the Stoplight class in Listing 5-7:

```
override public function create():Node {
  skin = StoplightVerticalSkin {};
  super.create();
}
```

Note that this snippet contains a create function, which we discussed earlier in this chapter. This assignment to the skin instance variable (inherited from the Control class) causes the Skin subclass named StoplightVerticalSkin to be employed as the user interface for this UI control. It is necessary to call super.create() here so that the Control class can do some internal housekeeping with the skin that was just created.

Creating a Skin for the Control

Listing 5-8 shows the code for creating a skin. Notice that the UI for the skin is defined and then assigned to the node instance variable (which is inherited from the Skin class). This occurs in the init block.

Listing 5-8. *StoplightVerticalSkin.fx*

```
package projavafx.stoplightskinning.ui;

import javafx.scene.Group;
import javafx.scene.control.Skin;
import javafx.scene.effect.Glow;
import javafx.scene.effect.DropShadow;
import javafx.scene.input.MouseEvent;
import javafx.scene.paint.*;
import javafx.scene.layout.VBox;
import javafx.scene.shape.Circle;
import javafx.scene.shape.Rectangle;

/**
 * The skin for a vertical StopLight
 */
public class StoplightVerticalSkin extends Skin {

  /**
   * Reference to the Stoplight control
   */
  public var stoplightControl:Stoplight = bind control as Stoplight;

  /**
   * Reference to the Stoplight behavior
   */
  override var behavior = StoplightBehavior {};
```

```
override public function intersects(localX:Number, localY:Number,
    localWidth:Number, localHeight:Number):Boolean {
  return node.intersects(localX, localY, localWidth, localHeight);
}

override public function contains(localX: Number, localY:Number):Boolean {
  return node.contains(localX, localY);
}

init {
  node = Group {
    focusTraversable: true
    content: [
      Rectangle {
        width: 100
        height: 240
        fill: Color.BLUE
        stroke: Color.BLACK
        strokeWidth: 2
        // Make the stroke a dashed line if the control has focus
        strokeDashArray: bind if (stoplightControl.focused)
                              [8, 8]
                            else [1]
      },
      VBox {
        layoutX: 25
        layoutY: 25
        spacing: 10
        content: [
          Circle {
            radius: 30
            fill: Color.DARKRED
            effect: bind
              if (stoplightControl.selectedIndex == Stoplight.STOP)
                Glow {
                  level: 0.8
                }
              else null
          },
          Circle {
            radius: 30
            fill: Color.DARKORANGE
            effect: bind
              if (stoplightControl.selectedIndex == Stoplight.CAUTION)
                Glow {
                  level: 0.8
                }
              else null
          },
```

```
            Circle {
              radius: 30
              fill: Color.DARKGREEN
              effect: bind
                if (stoplightControl.selectedIndex == Stoplight.GO)
                  Glow {
                    level: 0.8
                  }
                else null
            }
          ]
        }
      ]
    effect: bind if (stoplightControl.hover)
                    DropShadow {}
                 else null
    onMousePressed: function(me:MouseEvent):Void {
      (behavior as StoplightBehavior).facePressed();
    }
  };
  }
}
```

We're assigning an instance of our StoplightBehavior class, which we'll look at in the "Defining Behavior for the Stoplight Control" section, to the behavior variable inherited from the Skin class. Also note that we're overriding a couple of functions (intersects and contains) that are abstract in the Skin class.

Tip When you pressed the Tab key repeatedly while trying this example, this UI control received keyboard focus. This is due to the fact that the focusTraversable variable of a node in this control is assigned a value of true.

Binding the Skin to the Model

The following snippet from Listing 5-8 shows how the skin gets a reference to its model:

```
public var stoplightControl:Stoplight = bind control as Stoplight;
```

The instance variable named control is inherited from the Skin class. It holds a reference to the model, provided one is associated with the skin at the time. We use this reference to bind instance variables in the skin to the state of the model, as in the following snippet from Listing 5-8:

```
            Circle {
              radius: 30
              fill: Color.DARKRED
              effect: bind
                if (stoplightControl.selectedIndex == Stoplight.STOP)
                  Glow {
                    level: 0.8
                  }
                else null
            },
```

This snippet causes the selected light in the stoplight to glow.

Defining Behavior for the Stoplight Control

When designing a UI control, it is a good practice for all of the user interactions to be handled in a Behavior subclass so that if the control has multiple skins, they can all share the Behavior's mouse and keyboard event handling code. To see this demonstrated, check out the code for the StoplightBehavior class in Listing 5-9.

Listing 5-9. *StoplightBehavior.fx*

```
package projavafx.stoplightskinning.ui;

import javafx.scene.control.Behavior;
import javafx.scene.input.KeyCode;
import javafx.scene.input.KeyEvent;
import javafx.scene.input.KeyEventID;

public class StoplightBehavior extends Behavior {

  /**
   * User has clicked the face of the stoplight.
   */
  public function facePressed():Void {
    def stoplightControl:Stoplight = (skin.control as Stoplight);
    if (stoplightControl.focused) {
      stoplightControl.nextLight();
    }
    else {
      stoplightControl.requestFocus();
    }
  }

  /**
   * This function is automatically called by the Control class when
   * a key event occurs.  When the user presses the up and down arrows,
   * it make the lights cycle around in the direction of the arrow
   */
```

```
override public function callActionForEvent(ke:KeyEvent):Void {
  if (ke.impl_EventID == KeyEventID.PRESSED) {
    def stoplightControl:Stoplight = (skin.control as Stoplight);
    if (ke.code == KeyCode.VK_DOWN or ke.code == KeyCode.VK_RIGHT) {
      stoplightControl.nextLight();
    }
    else if (ke.code == KeyCode.VK_UP or ke.code == KeyCode.VK_LEFT) {
      stoplightControl.prevLight();
    }
  }
}
}
```

To handle keyboard input, the Behavior class has a function named callActionForEvent that we're overriding in Listing 5-9. This function is called whenever key events occur while the control has focus. As shown earlier, we're checking to see if the key event type is PRESSED, and if so, whether any arrow keys were pressed. Based on which arrow key was pressed, the desired function in the Stoplight control class is invoked.

Similarly, when the StoplightVerticalSkin instance receives an onMousePressed event (see the bottom of Listing 5-8), it calls the arbitrarily named facePressed function in our StoplightBehavior instance (see Listing 5-9). The facePressed function checks whether the control has keyboard focus. If it doesn't, then it requests that the control receive focus. If it already has focus, it calls the nextLight function of the Stoplight control.

The Code for the Horizontal Stoplight Skin

When you selected the radio button Horizontal Skin earlier, an instance of the StoplightHorizontalSkin class shown in Listing 5-10 replaced the StoplightVerticalSkin instance. Go ahead and examine this code; note the differences from the vertical skin in Listing 5-8.

Listing 5-10. *StoplightHorizontalSkin.fx*

```
package projavafx.stoplightskinning.ui;

import javafx.scene.control.Skin;
import javafx.scene.*;
import javafx.scene.effect.GaussianBlur;
import javafx.scene.input.MouseEvent;
import javafx.scene.paint.*;
import javafx.scene.layout.HBox;
import javafx.scene.shape.Circle;
import javafx.scene.shape.Rectangle;

/**
 * The skin for a horizontal StopLight
 */
public class StoplightHorizontalSkin extends Skin {
```

```
/**
 * Reference to the Stoplight control
 */
public var stoplightControl:Stoplight = bind control as Stoplight;

/**
 * Reference to the Stoplight behavior
 */
override var behavior = StoplightBehavior {};

override public function intersects(localX:Number, localY:Number,
    localWidth:Number, localHeight:Number):Boolean {
  return node.intersects(localX, localY, localWidth, localHeight);
}

override public function contains(localX: Number, localY:Number):Boolean {
  return node.contains(localX, localY);
}

init {
  node = Group {
    focusTraversable: true
    content: [
      Rectangle {
        width: 300
        height: 120
        fill: Color.BLACK
        stroke: Color.YELLOW
        // Increase the strokeWidth to indicate that this
        // UI control has keyboard focus
        strokeWidth: bind if (stoplightControl.focused) 3
                     else 0
      },
      HBox {
        layoutX: 20
        layoutY: 20
        spacing: 10
        content: [
          Circle {
            radius: 40
            fill: Color.RED
            opacity: bind if (stoplightControl.selectedIndex ==
                Stoplight.STOP) 1.0 else 0.5
          },
```

```
                    Circle {
                      radius: 40
                      fill: Color.YELLOW
                      opacity: bind if (stoplightControl.selectedIndex ==
                          Stoplight.CAUTION) 1.0 else 0.5
                    },
                    Circle {
                      radius: 40
                      fill: Color.GREEN
                      opacity: bind if (stoplightControl.selectedIndex ==
                          Stoplight.GO) 1.0 else 0.5
                    }
                  ]
                }
              ]
          effect: bind if (stoplightControl.hover)
                        GaussianBlur {}
                    else null
          onMousePressed: function(me:MouseEvent):Void {
            (behavior as StoplightBehavior).facePressed();
          }
        };
    }
}
```

There's one difference between the skins. A DropShadow effect is applied when the mouse hovers over the Stoplight control in which the active skin is StoplightVerticalSkin. However, a GaussianBlur effect is applied when the mouse hovers over the Stoplight control with a StoplightHorizontalSkin.

As you have seen, UI controls provide the ability to create a model, associate multiple skins that use the model, and define a behavior class that handles user input in a manner that isn't specific to a particular skin.

Deciding Between Creating a Custom Node and a UI Control

You now know that there two ways to create custom UI components for JavaFX programs. The main difference between the two approaches is that UI controls have the ability to create multiple skins, and they encourage a model-view-controller pattern. When these capabilities are desired, creating a UI control (extending Control, Skin, and Behavior) is a good choice. When they aren't needed, creating a custom node (extending CustomNode) is a good choice.

Now that we've discussed how to create custom UI components, we'll switch gears and take a look at the useful charting components that are provided with JavaFX.

Creating Charts in JavaFX

The chart components included in JavaFX give developers an easy way to let the users of their applications visualize a wide variety of data. Six kinds of charts are supported in JavaFX 1.2:

- An *area chart* displays quantitative data like a line chart but with the area between the line and the horizontal axis shaded. This type of chart is good for comparing the magnitude of two or more series of data.

- The *bar chart* is a good way to show data in a way that makes it easy to see how the data changes over time or under a set of different conditions. The data is represented as rectangular area, or in the case of a 3D chart, a cubic volume whose height corresponds to the value of the data point being displayed.

- *Bubble charts* plot data points on a 2-dimensional grid and have the extra ability to display the relative magnitudes of the data by controlling the diameter of the point (or bubble) displayed at each XY coordinate.

- A *line chart* is a simple way to display 2-dimensional data points where each point is connected to the next point in the data series by a line.

- *Pie charts* typically used to display the relative percentages of a series of values on a circle. The value of each piece of data, as a percentage of the total, dictates how much of the circle's area it takes up. In other words, the chart shows how big a slice of the pie each value represents.

- The *scatter chart* is used to plot the points of one or more series of data. These charts are typically used to show the correlation (or not) of the data by comparing how the data points are clustered (or not).

One of these things is not like the others. Other than the pie chart, all of these charts are meant to handle 2-dimensional data points as pairs of XY coordinates. The class hierarchy of the chart components in the `javafx.scene.chart` package reflects this fact (see Figure 5-4).

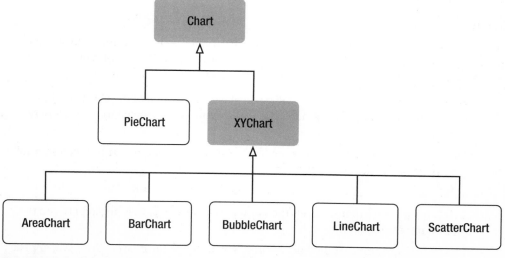

Figure 5-4. *The Chart class hierarchy*

The ChartDemo program, which is included with the Chapter 5 examples and is shown in Figure 5-5, displays an example of each of these types of charts. In the next sections you'll learn how to use each of these different charts and the many ways that they can be customized.

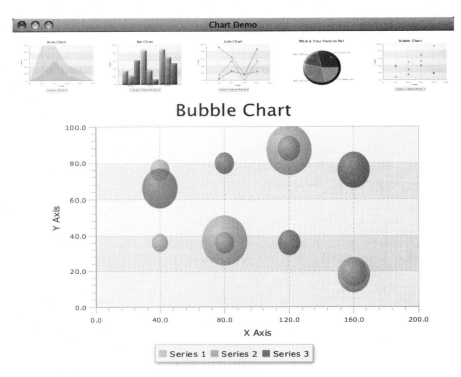

Figure 5-5. *The ChartDemo program*

Common Chart Properties

The Chart abstract base class contains several public variables that are common to all charts. One such property that all charts share is a title. The following public variables in the Chart class control the style, position, and content of the title displayed on a chart.

- title is a String whose contents will be displayed as the title of the chart. Setting this variable to null or an empty string (its default value) causes the chart to be rendered without a title.

- titleFill controls the fill color of the title text. Since it is of type Paint, it can be a solid color as well as a linear or radial gradient.

- titleFont allows you to set the Font to be used to render the title text.

- titleGap is a Number that specifies the number of pixels to leave as a gap between the title and the content of the chart.

- titleSide is an enumeration that specifies which side of the chart the title will appear on. Its type is javafx.scene.chart.part.Side and its possible values are TOP, BOTTOM, LEFT, and RIGHT.

All charts are also capable of displaying a *legend*. The legend is very useful when your charts are displaying more than one data series. It allows the user to easily see which of the plotted data points belongs to each of the data series. The following public variables affect how the legend is presented on a chart:

- `legendGap` is a `Number` that specifies the number of pixels to leave as a gap between the legend and the content of the chart.

- `legendSide` specifies which side of the chart the legend will appear on. Like `titleSide`, the possible values are `TOP`, `BOTTOM`, `LEFT`, and `RIGHT`.

- `legendVisible` is a `Boolean` value that controls whether the legend will be shown on the chart or hidden.

The `Chart` class also has a `public-read` variable named `legend` that provides a reference to the actual `Legend` object used by the chart. This object can be used to customize many aspects of the legend and will be discussed later in the "Customization" section.

Pie Chart

Getting a basic pie chart on the screen is straightforward—all you need is a sequence of `PieChart.Data` objects and a title string. For each value that you want to display in your pie chart, you just create a `PieChart.Data` object and supply the value and a text string to use as the label for the value. The sequence of data objects is then used in the pie chart's declaration. Since every chart *is-a* `Node`, you can just insert the chart into your scene graph in order to display it. Listing 5-11 demonstrates how to create and display a `PieChart`. Notice that we have used the `titleFont` variable to make the chart's title stand out a little more. The source code is from `PieChartIntro.fx`, which can be found in the `ChartIntro` example project.

Listing 5-11. *Displaying a Pie Chart*

```
Stage {
  title: "Pie Chart"
  scene: Scene {
    content: [
      PieChart {
        title: "What Is Your Favorite Pie?"
        titleFont: Font { size: 24 }
        data: [
          PieChart.Data {
            value: 21
            label: "Pumpkin"
          }
          PieChart.Data {
            value: 33
            label: "Apple"
          }
          PieChart.Data {
            value: 17
            label: "Cherry"
          }
```

```
            PieChart.Data {
              value: 29
              label: "3.14159"
            }
          ]
        }
      ]
    }
  }
}
```

This chart is rendered as shown in Figure 5-6. Note that right out of the box, the charts have a modern look with lighting and shading effects baked right in. You can also see that by default the title appears at the top of the chart. If you prefer a more 3-dimensional look to your pie charts, you can use the `PieChart3D` class instead of a `PieChart`, as in Listing 5-11. Everything aside from the class name can remain the same and the result will have the appearance of a 3-dimensional disk instead of a circle.

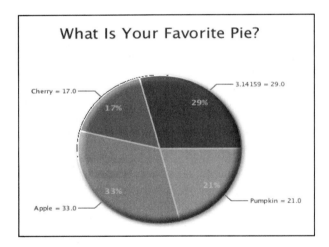

Figure 5-6. *An example pie chart*

XY Charts

The remaining five types of charts are all meant to work with XY data. These charts are all subtypes of the `XYChart` base class. As such, they are rendered against a background grid and include a horizontal and vertical axis.

Bar Chart

A bar chart plots data from a sequence of `BarChart.Series` objects. Each series contains a sequence of `BarChart.Data` objects that each contains the value (the height of the bar) and the category that the bar belongs to. Therefore, a bar chart data object can be declared as shown here:

```
BarChart.Data {
  category: "Category Name"
  value: 42
}
```

The horizontal axis for the bar chart is of type `CategoryAxis`. The public `categories` sequence variable must contain category names that match those given to the `BarChart.Data` objects. The vertical axis of a bar chart is a `ValueAxis`. As of JavaFX 1.2, the only concrete implementation of a `ValueAxis` is the `NumberAxis` class. A `NumberAxis` represents a range of numeric values and has variables that allow for control over the appearance and the number of tick marks and labels that are shown along the axis. A typical axis declaration for a bar chart is shown in Listing 5-12. The code declares a category axis with three categories and a number axis that ranges from 0 to 100 with a labeled tick mark every 20 units for a total of 6 labels (counting the label at 0).

Listing 5-12. *Declaring the Axes of a Bar Chart*

```
BarChart {
  categoryAxis: CategoryAxis {
    categories: [ "Category 1", "Category 2", "Category 3" ]
  }
  alueAxis: NumberAxis {
    label: "Y Axis"
    upperBound: 100
    tickUnit: 20
  }
}
```

Listing 5-13 shows a complete program that displays a bar chart showing the sales report for Acme, Inc. from 2007 to 2009. The data to be displayed in the chart is defined at the top. Each year will be its own category. The data values are generated from the sales figures for each of the three products over the three different years. The vertical axis is a `NumberAxis` that shows the number of units sold and is defined so that it can accommodate the largest sales value. It will have a labeled tick mark every 1,000 units starting at 0 and ending at 3,000. This gives a total of four labels along the vertical axis. The public `data` variable accepts the sequence of `BarChart.Series` objects to plot. Each `BarChart.Series` object also has its own public `data` variable, which accepts a sequence of `BarChart.Data` objects. A `for` expression is used to generate the actual sequence of `BarChart.Data` objects from the sequences defined at the beginning of the listing. Finally, the `categoryGap` variable (highlighted) is used to increase the spacing between the yearly data to provide more differentiation between the categories. The complete source code is in the `BarChartIntro.fx` file from the `ChartIntro` example project.

Listing 5-13. *Displaying a Bar Chart*

```
def years = [ "2007", "2008", "2009" ];

def anvilsSold = [  567, 1292, 2423 ];
def skatesSold = [  956, 1665, 2559 ];
def pillsSold  = [ 1154, 1927, 2774 ];
```

```
Stage {
  title: "Bar Chart Intro"
  scene: Scene {
    content: [
      BarChart {
        title: "Acme, Inc. Sales Report"
        titleFont: Font { size: 24 }
        categoryGap: 25
        categoryAxis: CategoryAxis {
            categories: years
        }
        valueAxis: NumberAxis {
          label: "Units Sold"
          upperBound: 3000
          tickUnit: 1000
        }
        data: [
          BarChart.Series {
            name: "Anvils"
            data: for (j in [0..<sizeof years]) {
              BarChart.Data {
                category: years[j]
                value: anvilsSold[j]
              }
            }
          }
          BarChart.Series {
            name: "Rocket Skates"
            data: for (j in [0..<sizeof years]) {
              BarChart.Data {
                category: years[j]
                value: skatesSold[j]
              }
            }
          }
          BarChart.Series {
            name: "Earthquake Pills"
            data: for (j in [0..<sizeof years]) {
              BarChart.Data {
                category: years[j]
                value: pillsSold[j]
              }
            }
          }
        ]
      }
    ]
  }
}
```

■**Caution** If you forget to declare the axes for a XYChart, then no data will show up on your chart. This is one of the few times you cannot rely on the default values of the chart. In the previous example, if the CategoryAxis or the ValueAxis were left undeclared then no bars would have been drawn on the sales chart.

The resulting chart is shown in Figure 5-7. Much like the pie charts, the default look for bar charts is a clean, modern look with lighting and shading effects built right in. There is also a drop-in replacement for BarChart named BarChart3D, which can be used to give the chart a 3-dimensional appearance.

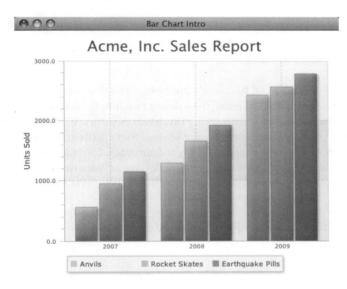

Figure 5-7. *A chart showing sales figures for Acme, Inc.*

Line and Area Charts

A line chart can be constructed using the LineChart class. It can show one or more LineChart. Series, each of which contains a sequence of LineChart.Data objects. This pattern should be familiar now. It is the same for an AreaChart, whose data variable accepts a sequence of AreaChart.Series objects, each of which contains a sequence of AreaChart.Data objects. We will use these charts to plot the mathematical functions sine and cosine, as shown in Figure 5-8. The source code for this program can be found in the LineAreaChartIntro.fx file in the ChartIntro example project.

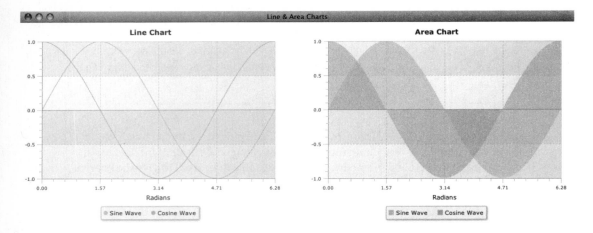

Figure 5-8. *Line and area charts showing sine and cosine waves*

To plot the sine and cosine functions, we need to create a horizontal axis that goes from 0 to 2π and a vertical axis that goes from –1.0 to 1.0. Listing 5-14 shows two functions that generate these NumberAxis objects. You may be wondering why these axis objects are being generated by functions rather than just declaring them as variables and reusing them for both charts. The answer lies in the fact that the Axis base class is derived from Node. Like any Node, an Axis can appear in the scene graph only once. Since we are not allowed to share these axis objects between our two charts, we must write functions that create new axis objects each time they are called.

Listing 5-14. *Generating Axis Objects*

```
/**
 * An x axis that goes from 0 to 2*PI with labels every PI/2 radians.
 * The labels are formatted to display on 2 significant digits.
 */
function createXAxis() {
  NumberAxis {
    label: "Radians"
    upperBound: 2 * Math.PI
    tickUnit: Math.PI / 2
    formatTickLabel: function(value) {
      "{%.2f value}"
    }
  }
}
```

```
/**
 * A y axis that that goes from -1 to 1 with labels every 0.5 units.
 */
function createYAxis() {
  NumberAxis {
    upperBound: 1.0
    lowerBound: -1.0
    tickUnit: 0.5
  }
}
```

The createXAxis function illustrates the use of the formatTickLabel function variable to format the values that will be used as tick labels on the axis. In this case, we format the numbers to keep only two significant digits after the decimal point. In addition, the code to create the y-axis shows how to set a nonzero lower bound for an axis.

Listing 5-15 shows the code that creates the LineChart object and adds it to the scene. This code follows the same pattern we've seen before. LineChart has a public data variable that takes a sequence of LineChart.Series objects. In this case, we have one sequence for the sine wave and one for the cosine wave. Within each series, the data sequence is populated by a range expression that generates the LineChart.Data objects, which correspond to the points along the sine or cosine curves. Since we can't show any data without our axes, we use the createXAxis and createYAxis functions shown earlier. Lastly we have highlighted two lines of code that are used to customize the appearance of this chart. Normally a line chart will plot a symbol at each data point—a circle, triangle, square, or other shape. The lines of the chart then connect these symbols. In this case, we have so many data points that the symbols would obscure the lines. So we tell the chart not to generate the symbols by setting the showSymbols variable to false. Another default setting for line charts is for the data to cast a shadow on the chart's background. Since this makes the lines of this particular chart more difficult to see, we turn off the drop shadow by setting dataEffect to null.

Listing 5-15. *Creating a Line Chart*

```
Stage {
  title: "Line & Area Charts"
  scene: Scene {
    content: [ createLineChart(), createAreaChart() ]
  }
}

function createLineChart() {
  LineChart {
    title: "Line Chart"
    showSymbols: false
    dataEffect: null
    xAxis: createXAxis()
    yAxis: createYAxis()
    data: [
```

```
        LineChart.Series {
          name: "Sine Wave"
          data: for (rads in [0..2*Math.PI step 0.01]) {
            LineChart.Data {
              xValue: rads
              yValue: Math.sin( rads )
            }
          }
        }
        LineChart.Series {
          name: "Cosine Wave"
          data: for (rads in [0..2*Math.PI step 0.01]) {
            LineChart.Data {
              xValue: rads
              yValue: Math.cos( rads )
            }
          }
        }
      ]
    }
}
```

Listing 5-16 shows the function used to generate the AreaChart that plots the sine and cosine waves. This code is almost exactly the same as the line chart code shown previously. The only real change is the lack of the extra customization options since area charts don't use symbols or drop shadow effects by default. This code also sets the translateX variable of the chart's Node in order to position it to the right of the line chart.

Listing 5-16. *Creating an Area Chart*

```
function createAreaChart() {
  AreaChart {
    title: "Area Chart"
    translateX: 550
    xAxis: createXAxis()
    yAxis: createYAxis()
    data: [
      AreaChart.Series {
        name: "Sine Wave"
        data: for (rads in [0..2*Math.PI step 0.01]) {
          AreaChart.Data {
            xValue: rads
            yValue: Math.sin( rads )
          }
        }
      }
```

```
    AreaChart.Series {
      name: "Cosine Wave"
      data: for (rads in [0..2*Math.PI step 0.01]) {
        AreaChart.Data {
          xValue: rads
          yValue: Math.cos( rads )
        }
      }
    }
  ]
  }
}
```

Scatter and Bubble Charts

Scatter and bubble charts are just like the other three XY charts we've looked at. The classes, ScatterChart and BubbleChart respectively, have a public data variable that accepts a sequence of series objects—you guessed it: ScatterChart.Series and BubbleChart.Series. Each of these series has a public data variable that holds a sequence of their respective data objects: ScatterChart.Data and BubbleChart.Data. However, the BubbleChart.Data class also contains a radius variable that is used to set the size of the bubble for each data point. Figure 5-9 shows an example of a scatter chart and a bubble chart. In this program, the charts are just plotting the distribution of points generated by the javafx.util.Math.random function. Using the JavaFX math functions allows our code to remain portable to mobile devices. We will discuss that more in Chapter 10.

The radius of the bubbles in the bubble chart is determined by the order in which the points are generated. The bubbles start small and get bigger as points are generated. You can roughly tell the order in which each point was generated. This is simply an interesting way to view the randomness of the random number generator. You can find the code for this program in ScatterBubbleChartIntro.fx in the ChartIntro example project.

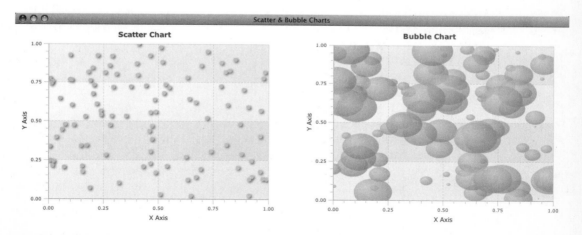

Figure 5-9. *Displaying a scatter chart and a bubble chart of random points*

The code in Listing 5-17 shows how the scatter chart is created. First we define a function that creates a number axis that ranges from 0.00 to 1.00 with labels every 0.25 units. The tick labels are once again formatted to keep only two digits after the decimal points. The createAxis function itself takes a String parameter to use as the label for the number axis. This allows the reuse of the function to create labels for both the x- and y-axes.

The ScatterChart has only one data series, and that series contains a sequence of 100 data objects whose x and y values are generated randomly. The only extra bit of customization done here is to hide the legend since we do have only the one data series.

Listing 5-17. *Creating a Scatter Chart with Random Points*

```
/**
 * An x axis that goes from 0 to 1.0 and displays labels every 0.25 units.
 * The labels are formatted to display on 2 significant digits.
 */
function createAxis( label:String ) {
  NumberAxis {
    label: label
    upperBound: 1.0
    tickUnit: 0.25
    formatTickLabel: function(value) {
      "{%.2f value}"
    }
  }
}

/**
 * Create a scatter chart that displays random points.
 */
function createScatterChart() {
  ScatterChart {
    title: "Scatter Chart"
    legendVisible: false
    xAxis: createAxis( "X Axis" )
    yAxis: createAxis( "Y Axis" )
    data: [
      ScatterChart.Series {
        data: for (i in [1..100]) {
          ScatterChart.Data {
            xValue: Math.random();
            yValue: Math.random()
          }
        }
      }
    ]
  }
}
```

The source code that creates the bubble chart, shown in Listing 5-18, is very similar. The big difference here is the radius variable of the BubbleChart.Data class. This is unique to the bubble chart data and, as previously mentioned, allows us to control the size of the bubble on the plot. The radius values scale based on the axes of the plot. In our case the axes both go from 0.0 to 1.0. Therefore a bubble radius of 0.5 would create a bubble that filled the entire chart (if centered) since its diameter would be 1.0. If our axes went from 0 to 10 instead, then a bubble with a radius of 0.5 would be smaller, taking up only 1/10 of the chart. The code in Listing 5-18 creates bubbles whose radiuses vary from 0.001 to 0.1 as the value of i goes from 1 to 100.

Listing 5-18. *Creating a Bubble Chart*

```
function createBubbleChart() {
  BubbleChart {
    title: "Bubble Chart"
    legendVisible: false
    translateX: 550
    xAxis: createAxis( "X Axis" )
    yAxis: createAxis( "Y Axis" )
    data: [
      BubbleChart.Series {
        data: for (i in [1..100]) {
          BubbleChart.Data {
            xValue: Math.random()
            yValue: Math.random()
            radius: i / 1000.0
          }
        }
      }
    ]
  }
}
```

Adding Interactivity

We will now discuss how to respond to mouse clicks on a chart. The Data base class in the javafx.scene.chart.data package has a public variable named action. This variable can be passed a function to call when a Data object is clicked. Although not all data objects have a visual representation that is clickable, any that do will respond to clicks by calling the action function if it is set. As an example, the BarChartIntro program can be easily modified to add these action functions in order to display details about the bar that is clicked. Listing 5-19 shows the code from the InteractiveBarChartIntro.fx program in the ChartIntro example project.

The highlighted code shows the function that is added to each bar. This anonymous function simply calls the showAlert function with the data that the bar represents. The showAlert function then displays an alert message on the screen. Making similar changes to the series that display the sales figures for rocket skates and earthquake pills will make all of the bars clickable.

Listing 5-19. *Adding Interactivity to a Bar Chart*

```
BarChart.Series {
  def product = "Anvils"
  name: product
  data: for (j in [0..<sizeof years]) {
    BarChart.Data {
      category: years[j]
      value: anvilsSold[j]
      action: function() {
        showAlert( years[j], product, anvilsSold[j] )
      }
    }
  }
}

function showAlert( year:String, product:String, unitsSold:Integer ) {
  Alert.inform( "Acme, Inc sold {unitsSold} {product} in {year}" );
}
```

Figure 5-10 shows the result of clicking on one of the bars in the bar chart. The other side effect of adding an action to a data object is that a highlight will be drawn around the object's visual representation when users move their mouse over the object. The appearance of the highlight is controlled by the public hoverStroke and hoverStrokeWidth variables in the Chart base class. The hoverStroke variable is of type Paint and therefore can be set to a color or a gradient. The hoverStrokeWidth is a Number that allows you to control the size of the highlight being drawn.

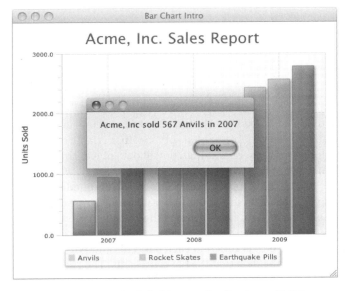

Figure 5-10. *The result of clicking on the first bar of 2007*

Customization

We have already discussed several ways to customize charts. We have seen how to adjust a chart's title font, a bar chart's category gap, the visibility of symbols and effects used in a XYChart, the formatting of axis labels, and the hover effects of data objects with actions attached to them. There are a lot more options available.

We'll start with colors. The background of a chart is controlled by the chartBackgroundFill, chartBackgroundStroke, and chartBackgroundStrokeWidth variables of the Chart class. As usual, the fill and stroke variables are of type Paint, and can therefore be set to a color or a gradient, while the stroke width is a Number. These variables affect the background of the entire chart. These are the colors that appear behind the title, the legend, and the plot. Don't confuse this with the background of the plot itself. XYCharts are rendered on top of a grid whose background is controlled separately. We will come back to this in just a bit.

You probably noticed that the data in the charts are rendered in a nice set of default colors. As you would expect, changing these default data colors is easily done. For pie charts, colors for the individual slices are set in the PieChart.Data class. This class has the usual three public variables: fill, stroke, and strokeWidth. Remember that lighting effects will be applied when the pie chart is rendered. So you can simply set the fill and stroke to solid colors and still achieve a nice result. The colors used to render data in XYCharts are similarly customizable. The Data base class has a fill variable that can be set to a custom color. If it's not set, then the fill variable of the Series base class is checked. If the series fill is not set, then the default chart colors are used. This system allows you to specify a custom color for an entire data series or individually for each data object. As with the pie chart, lighting is applied to the XYChart, so a solid color is usually all you need to specify.

As previously mentioned, the plot of a XYChart is rendered against a background grid that is separate from the background of the chart as a whole. The plot's background grid has a complete set of customization options starting with the usual set of three: plotBackgroundFill, plotBackgroundStroke, and plotBackgroundStrokeWidth. There is another set that controls the grid's horizontal colors and lines. The horizontalAlternateRowFill specifies a Paint to be used to fill the alternating horizontal rows. What is meant by a row? Each tick label along the horizontal or vertical axis starts a new horizontal or vertical row. You can also control the appearance of the horizontal grid lines by using the horizontalGridLineStroke, horizontalGridLineStrokeWidth, and horizontalGridLineStrokeDashArray variables. Or you can just hide the grid lines altogether by using the horizontalGridLineVisible and horizontalZeroLineVisible variables. Each of these horizontal variables has a corresponding vertical variable. For instance, you can set the alternating vertical row fill by setting the verticalAlternateRowFill variable. You can even go so far as to specify custom background content for the plot's grid by passing a Node to the customBackgroundContent variable. The content you provide will be drawn on top of the background grid but underneath the data. Consult the documentation for the javafx.scene.chart. XYChart class for all the details on these options.

There are three charts that use symbols to plot their data: bubble charts, line charts, and scatter charts. These symbols can be customized by setting the bubble variable of BubbleChart. Data or the symbol variable of the LineChart.Data and ScatterChart.Data classes. You can pass any subclass of Node to these variables, but there are several predefined symbols for convenience. The following symbol classes reside in the javafx.scene.chart.part package: PlotSymbol.Circle, PlotSymbol.Cross, PlotSymbol.HollowDiamond, PlotSymbol.HollowTriangle, and PlotSymbol. Square. Consult the JavaFX documentation for details on their use.

You can access the legend of a chart through the `public-read` variable named `legend` in the `Chart` class. The `Legend` class has numerous customization options that include the usual `fill`, `stroke`, and `strokeWidth` variables in addition to those that control the insets of the legend and the font and fill used to render the text of the legend items. There is also nearly full control over how the axes of the charts are rendered. This includes the stroke color and width, the number and size of ticks, and the font and color of the labels as well as their visibility. You can find all of the information in the documentation of the `Axis`, `ValueAxis`, `NumberAxis`, and `CategoryAxis` classes in the `javafx.scene.chart.part` package. We have more or less covered the common set of customizations you may be interested in doing with your chart components. But we strongly encourage you to browse through the documentation of the chart components. There are more customization gems waiting to be discovered.

Now that you know how to create custom UI components and charts, it's almost time to turn to Chapter 6 and learn to use the JavaFX `Media` classes. But first, take some time to congratulate yourself for reaching the halfway point in this book! Also, take some time to do the following exercise.

Putting What You've Learned into Practice

So far in this book you've learned a lot about developing programs in JavaFX. At this point, we'd like to challenge you to an exercise that will help you put what you've learned into practice. Figure 5-11 shows a sample solution to this exercise.

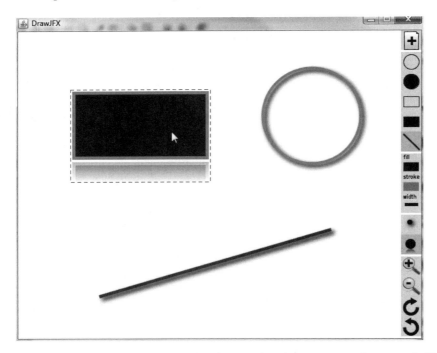

Figure 5-11. *A sample solution to the exercise after drawing some shapes and effects*

REQUIREMENTS FOR THE JAVAFX DRAWING PROGRAM EXERCISE

Your assignment, should you decide to accept it, is to create a program in JavaFX that enables the user to create drawings. The program should contain

- Shape drawing tools, such as the circle, rectangle, and line tools shown on the right side of Figure 5-11.

- Tools that enable the user to choose the fill and outline (stroke) colors of a drawn shape, as well as the width of the stroke. The color-oriented tools should allow the selection of a color (and extra credit for a gradient) by using a custom UI component. You may want to get ideas from the examples in Figures 5-1 and 5-2, or just use the code for the latter example as is.

- Tools that apply effects to a drawn shape, such as the Reflection and DropShadow tools shown in Figure 5-11.

- Tools that perform transforms on drawn shapes, such as the scale and rotate tools shown in Figure 5-11.

- A drawing area in which shapes can be placed and dragged around.

Good luck with this exercise, and we hope that you enjoy it!

Summary

Congratulations; you learned a lot about JavaFX in this chapter. You know that:

- You can create two types of custom UI components in JavaFX: *custom nodes* and *UI controls*.

- Custom nodes extend the `CustomNode` class.

- UI controls have a model that extends the `Control` class, skins that extend the `Skin` class, and behavior that extends the `Behavior` class.

- The `Node` class has a `hover` instance variable that is `true` when the mouse is over the node.

- You can define your own event handlers for your custom UI components.

- The `javafx.scene.effect` package has many effects, such as `Glow` and `DropShadow`, that add to the richness of the nodes in the UI.

- There are two ways to transform nodes. One way is to use the `layoutX/Y`, `scaleX/Y`, and `rotate` variables. The other way is to use the `transforms` variable, which holds a sequence of transforms.

- You can block mouse events from occurring in a node that underlies another node by using the `blocksMouse` instance variable.

- Charting is very flexible and powerful in JavaFX.

Resources

For some additional information using JavaFX effects, consult the following resource:

- The Effects Playground, developed by Chris Campbell of the JavaFX team: `http://javafx.com/samples/EffectsPlayground`

CHAPTER 6

■■■

Using the Media Classes

We keep moving forward, opening new doors, and doing new things, because we're curious and curiosity keeps leading us down new paths.

—Walt Disney

In the previous four chapters, you learned the basics of the JavaFX Script language, how to create user interfaces that look great up on stage, and how to define your own functions and classes. Now we will make good use of all that knowledge while exploring one of the most exciting capabilities of the new JavaFX platform.

The ability to play audio and video files is an important part of many modern Internet-enabled applications. These media files can enrich the user's experience in ways that static images alone cannot. There is a bewildering number of different media formats in use on the Internet. Luckily, JavaFX media classes make it incredibly easy for developers to incorporate playback support for most of the popular formats out there. In this chapter, you will explore the capabilities of these easy-to-use classes. You will see how simple it is to include basic media playback support in your JavaFX applications and then move on to build more sophisticated playback applications.

Unfortunately, for all the ease of use that the engineers at Sun have designed into the media APIs, handling media is not a trivial task. This new library is not without its rough edges. There are pieces here and there that don't quite function as they should. These fragile bits will be described in notes throughout the chapter.

The Foundation

The media classes in JavaFX are based on a new library called the Java Media Components. Support for the playback of audio and video has not been a traditional strength of the Java platform. Now that music and video are ubiquitous on the Internet, it is crucial that JavaFX be able to handle these files with ease. Thus were the Java Media Components born. The primary goal was to be able to play all popular file formats with the minimum amount of hassle on the part of the developer.

The JMC library takes a pragmatic approach, relying on native media players to handle platform-specific file formats but also defining a new cross-platform format, licensed from On2 Technologies, that can be played by any JavaFX runtime—encode once, play anywhere. Table 6-1 lists the more popular file formats that are supported for playback by JavaFX on each of the platforms on which it runs.

Table 6-1. *Popular Media Formats Supported by JavaFX*

Platform	Type	Format	File Extension
Windows	Audio	MP3 (MPEG-1 Audio Layer 3)	`.mp3`
		WAV (Waveform Audio Format)	`.wav`
	Video	Windows Media Video	`.wmv`
		Flash Video	`.flv, .f4v`
Macintosh	Audio	MP3 (MPEG-1 Audio Layer 3)	`.mp3`
		WAV (Waveform Audio Format)	`.wav`
		AAC (Advanced Audio Coding)	`.m4a, .aac`
		AIFF (Audio Interchange File Format)	`.aif, .aiff`
	Video	QuickTime	`.mov`
		MPEG-4	`.mp4`
		Flash Video	`.flv, .f4v`
Cross-platform	Video	FXM (JavaFX Multimedia)	`.fxm`

JavaFX's native video file format, FXM, consists of On2's proprietary VP6 format for video and MP3 for audio. With additional codecs, the native media players on Windows and Macintosh can support other file formats as well. In some cases, these formats will then work in JavaFX also. Sticking with the popular formats listed in Table 6-1 will give you the highest probability of compatibility.

Working with Media

The JavaFX media classes are located in the `javafx.scene.media` package. The class you will use to work with media files is called `Media`. The public `source` variable is used to associate a `Media` object with the `String` representation of the URI of an audio or video file. The `source` URI can start with `http:` when addressing files located on the Internet, `file:` for files located on a local drive, and `jar:` when accessing files located within a `.jar` file. The URI must contain an absolute path to the media file such as `http://some.host.com/media/movie.wmv` or `file:/// Users/jane/Movies/movie.mov`. As of JavaFX version 1.1, only audio files can be played directly from within a `.jar` file and only MP3, AU (Unix audio), and WAV files are supported if played in this manner. There is no support yet for playing video files embedded inside `.jar` files.

The other members of the `Media` class will allow you to obtain information on the media file's duration, width and height (if it's a video file), any metadata associated with the file, and the number of tracks contained in the file. The `duration` field is of type `Duration` and specifies the length of the media file in seconds. The width and height fields are Numbers that tell you the dimensions of the video contained within a video file. These fields may contain a 0 if the file is an audio-only file or if the media is streaming and the dimensions are still unknown. The metadata field is a sequence of Metadata objects, each of which contain a key/value pair. The key is a String and the value is an Object. Note that the Metadata class is located in the same file as the Media class, which makes it a module class that you refer to as Media.Metadata. If a media file supports metadata (such as tags for title, artist, or album in MP3 files), the contents of its metadata fields will be accessible through this sequence. The tracks sequence contains one entry for each track in the media file. Audio files typically have only one track, but video files may have video tracks, audio tracks, and sometimes even special language or commentary tracks. The type of the objects contained in the tracks sequence will be one of the subclasses of the abstract Track class: VideoTrack, AudioTrack, or SubtitleTrack.

The final member of the Media class that we will discuss is the onError function variable. You can pass a function to this variable and it will be called whenever there is an error related to the Media object. These errors involve corrupted, inaccessible, and unsupported media files or other problems of that kind. The JavaFX documentation points out that the onError function should be initialized before the source variable so that you can be notified of errors when the media file is initialized. This will be the case as long as you initialize the onError function in the object declaration.

■**Note** As of version 1.2 of the JavaFX SDK, the track and metadata fields of the Media class are only valid when playing audio files from a .jar file. They will not get set when playing files from disk or from the Internet. When these variables are fully functional, they will add a lot of depth to the media applications that can be built with JavaFX. Unfortunately, playing audio from a .jar file also has its share of problems. The duration field is not always set correctly, and as discussed in the next section, some playback controls don't work correctly.

Playing Audio

The MediaPlayer class presents a convenient interface for playing the various types of media files that can be loaded into Media objects. MediaPlayer has a public variable named media that can be set to an instance of a Media object. Once that is done, a simple call to the play() method is all that is required to begin playback. Listing 6-1 shows a very basic example of a JavaFX program that can play an audio file. If the user gave a command-line argument, it attempts to play the file indicated by that URI string. Otherwise, it defaults to playing a file from within its .jar file. A stage is then created to display the text of the URI string while a MediaPlayer plays the file. Setting the media variable is the only requirement before playback can begin. But it is good practice to install the onError handler so that any errors can be dealt with. In this case, errors are simply printed to standard output.

Listing 6-1. *A Simple Audio Player*

```
/*
 * AudioPlayer1 - A JavaFX Script example program that demonstrates
 * how to play an audio file.
 *
 * Developed 2009 by Dean Iverson as a JavaFX Script SDK 1.1 example
 * for the Pro JavaFX book.
 */

package projavafx.audioplayer1;

import javafx.lang.FX;
import javafx.scene.media.Media;
import javafx.scene.media.MediaError;
import javafx.scene.media.MediaPlayer;
import javafx.scene.Scene;
import javafx.scene.text.Text;
import javafx.stage.Stage;

var uriString = FX.getArguments()[0];
if (uriString == null or uriString.length() == 0) {
  uriString = "{__DIR__}resources/Keeper.mp3";
}

Stage {
  title: "AudioPlayer1"
  scene: Scene {
    content: Text {
      x: 10
      y: 20
      content: uriString
    }
  }
}

MediaPlayer {
  media: Media {
    source: uriString
  }
  onError: function( me:MediaError ) {
    println( "Error Occurred: {me.message}" );
  }
}.play();
```

■Note When playing audio from a `.jar` file, the JMC library will often complain about invalid stop times being specified. Although annoying, this is a nonfatal error and does not typically interfere with the playback. This problem does not affect playback of files from disk or over the Internet.

That's all there is to it if your only requirement is to play an audio file. The developers have stuck to that golden principle of API design: make simple things easy to accomplish. It takes just a few simple lines of code to play an MP3 file or any other supported media file for that matter.

Controlling Playback

There are three main methods in the `MediaPlayer` class that are used to control the playback of `Media` objects: `play`, `pause`, and `stop`. None of these methods takes any parameters. As expected, you use the `play` method to begin the playback of the media. As the media is played, `MediaPlayer`'s `currentTime` variable is continuously updated to indicate the progress of the playback. Since `currentTime` is of type `Duration`, it indicates the position of the playback in milliseconds. The `pause` method will cause the playback to pause and a subsequent call to `play` will restart the playback from where it was paused. Calling the `stop` method stops playback, causes the `onEndOfMedia` callback function to be called (if set), and resets the `currentTime` variable to the start of the `Media`.

When a `MediaPlayer` object is first created, its `status` variable is initialized to `MediaPlayer.PAUSED`. Calling the play method causes the `status` variable to change to `MediaPlayer.PLAYING`. Calling stop or pause will reset the status to `MediaPlayer.PAUSED` again. Other possible values for `status` include `MediaPlayer.BUFFERING` and `MediaPlayer.STALLED`. Buffering means that the player is still loading or streaming the media and is not yet ready to begin playback. The stalled status will occur when a media stream runs out of data during playback and must wait until more data becomes available.

The next example uses these new concepts to start a more traditional implementation of a media player. A play/pause toggle button will be added along with a bar that indicates the current progress of the playback. The progress bar can also be used to adjust the playback position by clicking and dragging the mouse. To start off, the `Media`, `MediaPlayer`, and the playback controls will be encapsulated in a new class called `SimpleMediaPlayer`. Listing 6-2 shows how this new class is declared in the scene.

Listing 6-2. *Switching to SimpleMediaPlayer*

```
Stage {
  var theScene: Scene;
  title: "AudioPlayer2"
  scene: theScene = Scene {
    width: 400
    height: 40
    stylesheets: "{__DIR__}audioPlayer.css"
```

```
    content: SimpleMediaPlayer {
      source: uriString
      width: bind theScene.width
      height: bind theScene.height
    }
  }
}
```

A style sheet was also introduced into the scene to make it easy to adjust the look of the application. The SimpleMediaPlayer class is a subclass of Control so that it is resizable and therefore has a width and height. In our previous declaration, the media player's size is bound to the size of the scene. The SimpleMediaPlayer's only responsibility is to play the source URI it is given. Listing 6-3 shows this first version of the class. You can see that a replace trigger updates the internal media player object when the source string is changed. A bind statement on the media player's source variable could have accomplished the same thing. Since this is a very simple update of one variable by another, there is no reason to incur the overhead of a bind.

You can also see that the MediaPlayer declaration in this class includes the onEndOfMedia callback function now. This callback is a convenient place from which to call the stop function to halt playback and reset currentTime back to the beginning.

Listing 6-3. *The SimpleMediaPlayer*

```
public class SimpleMediaPlayer extends CustomNode, Resizable {
  public var source: String on replace {
    player.media.source = source;
  }

  var player: MediaPlayer = MediaPlayer {
    media: Media {
      source: source
    }
    onError: function( me:MediaError ) {
      println( "Error Occurred: {me.message}" );
    }
    onEndOfMedia: function() {
      player.stop();
    }
  }

  override function create() {
    MediaPlayerControls {
      width: bind width
      isPlaying: bind player.status == MediaPlayer.PLAYING
      mediaDuration: bind player.media.duration
      currentTime: bind player.currentTime with inverse
```

```
    onTogglePlayPause: function( play:Boolean ) {
      if (play) {
        player.play();
      } else {
        player.pause();
      }
    }
  }
}
}
```

The actual controls for the media player are encapsulated into their own
MediaPlayerControls class. Separating the user interface for the controls into another
class gets rid of a lot of clutter and makes SimpleMediaPlayer easier to understand and easier
to extend later on. Everything the controls need to do their job is bound to the CustomNode's
variables in the declaration.

MediaPlayerControls is conceptually similar to other user interfaces you have built in previous chapters. It does not have any direct interaction with the media classes. Therefore, it is
shown in Listing 6-4 for completeness but we won't discuss it in detail. The result of this code
is the very simple media player shown in Figure 6-1. All of the source code for this example can
be found in the AudioPlayer2 project.

Listing 6-4. *The User Interface Code for the Media Playback Controls*

```
public class MediaPlayerControls extends CustomNode {
public var width = 100.0;
  public var isPlaying = false;
  public var mediaDuration: Duration;
  public var currentTime: Duration;
  public var onTogglePlayPause: function( play:Boolean ):Void;

  var percentComplete = bind currentTime.toSeconds() / mediaDuration.toSeconds();
  var height = bind playImg.height;

  def CONTROLS_PADDING = 5;
  def CONTROLS_SPACING = 10;

def playImg = Image {
    url: "{__DIR__}resources/play.png"
  }

  def pauseImg = Image {
    url: "{__DIR__}resources/pause.png"
  }
```

```
def playPauseButton: ImageView = ImageView {
  var hoverEffect = Glow {}
  image: bind if (isPlaying) pauseImg else playImg
  effect: bind if (playPauseButton.hover) hoverEffect else null
  onMousePressed: function( me:MouseEvent ) {
    onTogglePlayPause( isPlaying == false );
  }
}

def progressGroup = Group {
  def progressWidth = bind {
    width - (playImg.width + CONTROLS_SPACING + 2 * CONTROLS_PADDING)
  }
  content: [
    Rectangle {
      id: "progressBackground"
      width: bind progressWidth
      height: bind height
    },
    Rectangle {
      id: "progressForeground"
      width: bind  percentComplete * progressWidth
      height: bind height
    },
    Line {
      id: "progressIndicator"
      startY: 1
      endY: bind height - 1
      startX: bind percentComplete * progressWidth
      endX: bind percentComplete * progressWidth
    }
  ]
  onMouseDragged: function(e) {
    var newTime = if (e.x < 0) 0s else mediaDuration * e.x / progressWidth;
    currentTime = if (newTime < mediaDuration) newTime else mediaDuration - 1ms;
  }
  onMousePressed: function(e) {
    currentTime = mediaDuration * e.x / progressWidth
  }
}
```

```
override function create() {
  Group {
    content: [
      HBox {
        translateX: CONTROLS_PADDING
        translateY: CONTROLS_PADDING
        spacing: CONTROLS_SPACING
        content: [
          playPauseButton,
          progressGroup
        ]
      }
    ]
  }
}
```

Figure 6-1. *A simple media player with a play/pause button and a progress bar*

As a final note on playback, MediaPlayer also contains a variable named autoPlay. This Boolean variable will cause playback to start as soon as possible if it is set to true. Occasionally it is a little too aggressive and I have found that playback will sometimes pause or even restart after a second or two when using this feature with audio files. Therefore I recommend that the play method be used in normal circumstances and that autoPlay only be used in situations where potential glitches in playback are not a serious concern and you just want to "fire and forget" the playback.

Repetition

You can set the playback to repeat itself a certain number of times or to repeat forever. This behavior is controlled by the repeatCount variable. The number of times that playback has been repeated is available in the currentCount variable. When the end of the media is reached, currentCount is incremented and, if it is less than repeatCount, playback will begin again automatically. The onRepeat callback function is called whenever playback is repeated. The usual call to onEndOfMedia will not be made until after the final repetition. Setting repeatCount to the value MediaPlayer.REPEAT_FOREVER will cause the playback to loop indefinitely.

The startTime and stopTime variables in the MediaPlayer class can affect where the media starts and stops playing. As their names indicate, both of these variables are Duration types. The startTime variable is initialized to 0 milliseconds and, even if changed, will not take effect the first time that play is called. On all subsequent repetitions and play calls, however, the startTime variable will control where playback will begin. If a stopTime is set, playback will stop or repeat when that time is reached.

The ability to set the playback to repeat would be a handy feature for the simple media player to have. The MediaPlayerControls class can easily be extended to add a new button to the right of the progress bar. All that is needed is a new image button and a new callback function that can be used to notify the SimpleMediaPlayer when the image button is clicked. Listing 6-5 shows the code that needs to be added to declare the button and the callback function. The button is added to the scene graph by simply adding it to the end of the HBox content sequence.

Listing 6-5. *Adding a Repeat Toggle Button*

```
public var onToggleRepeat: function( repeat:Boolean ):Void;

var repeatButton:ImageView = ImageView {
    var repeat = false;
    var hoverEffect = Glow {}
    var selectedEffect = Glow { level: 0.5 }
    image: Image {
      url: "{__DIR__}resources/repeat.png"
    }
    effect: bind {
      if (repeat) selectedEffect else if (repeatButton.hover) hoverEffect else null
    }
    onMousePressed: function( me:MouseEvent ) {
        repeat = not repeat;
        onToggleRepeat( repeat );
    }
  }
```

The SimpleMediaPlayer needs to handle the onToggleRepeat callback function. This is easily accomplished by defining a function in the MediaPlayerControls declaration of the SimpleMediaPlayer class. The code for the callback function is shown in Listing 6-6. If the callback's repeat parameter is true, the media player's repeatCount is set to repeat forever and the playback will automatically begin again when it reaches the end of the media file. If the repeat parameter is false, the repeatCount is set to REPEAT_NONE, which is equivalent to setting the repeatCount to 1.0. When this happens, the playback will stop the next time it reaches the end of the media file.

Listing 6-6. *Handling the Repeat Function Callback*

```
onToggleRepeat: function( repeat:Boolean ) {
  if (repeat) {
    player.repeatCount = MediaPlayer.REPEAT_FOREVER;
  } else {
    player.repeatCount = MediaPlayer.REPEAT_NONE;
  }
}
```

■**Note** Repetition, duration, start times, and stop times don't always work as expected when playing files from a .jar file. For instance, onRepeat doesn't get called when media repeats and onEndOfMedia gets called instead. The currentCount variable never gets incremented, so any count above 1 effectively loops forever. Also, startTime and stopTime usually have no effect. Hopefully these problems will be fixed in an upcoming version of JavaFX.

Volume and Balance

The MediaPlayer class has two variables that control volume of the audio playback. The volume variable has a range that goes from 0.0 (mute) to 1.0 (maximum volume). This volume setting does not affect the master volume of the computer on which the audio is playing; it only controls the volume of the media player application. The default value for the volume variable is 1.0. There is also a Boolean variable named mute. When this variable is set to true, the volume of the playback will be muted. Although playback continues, no sound will be heard. This is the equivalent of setting the volume variable to 0.0.

The balance variable controls the left-to-right balance of the audio. The range of the variable is from –1.0 (playing from the left speakers only) to 1.0 (playing from the right speakers only). If the audio that is playing has only one track (mono), then that track will be played on both speakers. The balance control will act as a volume control allowing you to adjust how loud the left or right speaker is playing. If the audio has two tracks (stereo), then the left track is played on the left speaker and the right track is played on the right speaker. In this case the balance control will allow you to fade back and forth between the left and right audio tracks. The default value of the balance variable is 0.0.

Two Slider controls can be used to control the volume and balance in the simple media player. The user can drag the slider back and forth horizontally to change its value. By binding the volume or balance variables to a slider's value, the user will be able to change the volume and balance of the audio that is being played. To make room for the two new slider controls, the progress bar will be made half as tall and the sliders will be added underneath. Listing 6-7 shows the new progressGroup declaration that includes the sliders.

Listing 6-7. *Adding Sliders to the Progress Group*

```
public var volume = 1.0;
public var balance = 0.0;

def progressGroup = Group {
  def progressWidth = bind calcProgressWidth() on replace {
    hbox.impl_layout( hbox );
  }
  content: [
    Rectangle {
       id: "progressBackground"
       width: bind progressWidth
       height: bind height / 2
```

```
            onMouseDragged: function(e) {
                var newTime = if (e.x < 0) 0s else mediaDuration * e.x / progressWidth;
                currentTime = if (newTime < mediaDuration) newTime else mediaDuration -
1ms;
            }
            onMousePressed: function(e) {
                currentTime = mediaDuration * e.x / progressWidth
            }
        },
        Rectangle {
            id: "progressForeground"
            width: bind  percentComplete * progressWidth
            height: bind height / 2
        },
        Line {
            id: "progressIndicator"
            startY: 1
            endY: bind height / 2 - 1
            startX: bind percentComplete * (progressWidth - 1)
            endX: bind percentComplete * (progressWidth - 1)
        },
        Slider {
            width: bind (progressWidth - CONTROLS_SPACING) / 2
            translateY: bind (height + CONTROLS_SPACING) / 2
            maxValue: 1.0
            currentValue: bind volume with inverse
            styleClass: "mediaSlider"
        },
        Slider {
            width: bind (progressWidth - CONTROLS_SPACING) / 2
            translateX: bind (progressWidth + CONTROLS_SPACING) / 2
            translateY: bind (height + CONTROLS_SPACING) / 2
            minValue: -1.0
            maxValue: 1.0
            currentValue: bind balance with inverse
            styleClass: "mediaSlider"
        }
    ]
}
```

In Listing 6-7, the mouse callback functions have been moved to the background rectangle of the progress bar now that the group contains more than just the progress bar shapes.
The progress bar shapes are now half of their former height and bind statements have been
used to place the sliders below the progress bar. Two new public variables, volume and balance,
have been created in the class and each of the sliders' currentValue variables have been bound
to the appropriate instance variable using the with inverse modifier. This allows the sliders to
change the value of the variables and also to reflect any changes made in the variables by the
outside world. As usual, the final step is to create the link between the MediaPlayerControls

and the MediaPlayer instances inside the SimpleMediaPlayer class. Listing 6-8 shows the new declaration of the MediaPlayerControls. The lines that have changed to support the volume, balance, and repeat features are emphasized. The source code for this example, including the repeat button and the slider classes, can be found in the AudioPlayer3 project. Figure 6-2 shows what the audio player now looks like.

Listing 6-8. *Adding Support for Volume and Balance Control to the Simple Media Player*

```
override function create() {
    MediaPlayerControls {
      width: bind width
      volume: bind player.volume with inverse
      balance: bind player.balance with inverse
      isPlaying: bind player.status == MediaPlayer.PLAYING
      mediaDuration: bind player.media.duration
      currentTime: bind player.currentTime with inverse
      onTogglePlayPause: function( play:Boolean ) {
        if (play) {
          player.play();
        } else {
          player.pause();
        }
      }
      onToggleRepeat: function( repeat:Boolean ) {
        if (repeat) {
          player.repeatCount = MediaPlayer.REPEAT_FOREVER;
        } else {
          player.repeatCount = MediaPlayer.REPEAT_NONE;
        }
      }
    }
  }
}
```

Figure 6-2. *The media player with repeat, volume, and balance controls*

Streaming Media

Streaming media files over the Internet happens automatically with the JavaFX media API. All you have to do is point a Media object to an HTTP resource and attach it to a MediaPlayer with autoPlay set to true. You can monitor the progress of the stream's buffer using the bufferProgressTime variable in the MediaPlayer class. When data is loaded from a stream or from disk, the amount of time that data will take to play is calculated and this time is regularly updated in the bufferProgressTime variable. By binding to this variable, you can receive these updates and effectively monitor the stream's buffer. The MediaPlayer class also offers onStalled and onBuffering function callbacks. Unfortunately, these callbacks cannot be depended upon on all platforms and for all media types.

Using just the bufferProgressTime variable does allow for the addition of a useful feature to the simple media player. The progress bar can be upgraded to show the progress of the stream download by simply splitting the background rectangle of the progress bar into two rectangles: one that draws its outline and one that draws the fill. If the width of the background fill rectangle is bound to the bufferProgressTime, a nice display of the buffering progress can be achieved. The mouse event handlers in the progress bar also need to be modified to ensure that the user does not click or drag beyond the data that has been buffered. The new code for the progress group is shown in Listing 6-9.

Listing 6-9.The Enhanced Progress Bar

```
public var bufferTime: Duration;
def percentBuffered = bind bufferTime.toSeconds() / mediaDuration.toSeconds();

def progressGroup = Group {
  def progressWidth = bind calcProgressWidth();
  def setCurrentTimeFromMouseX = function( mouseX:Number ) {
    var newTime = if (mouseX < 0) 0s else mediaDuration * mouseX / progressWidth;
    currentTime = if (newTime < bufferTime) newTime else bufferTime - 1ms;
  }
  content: [
    Rectangle {
      id: "progressBackground"
      width: bind progressWidth
      height: bind height / 2
      onMouseDragged: function(e) {
        setCurrentTimeFromMouseX( e.x );
      }
      onMousePressed: function(e) {
        setCurrentTimeFromMouseX( e.x );
      }
    },
    Rectangle {
      id: "progressBuffer"
      width: bind  percentBuffered * progressWidth
      height: bind height / 2
    },

    // … no other changes …
}
```

Notice that a new function named setCurrentTimeFromMouseX has been defined inside the group's declaration. Defining a function in this way is a useful technique when you want to limit a function's scope to a single declaration without having to override a class. In this case, it is a function that is used by our mouse event handlers to ensure that the current time is never set to a value that exceeds the buffer's time. Also note the two rectangles that together make up the modified progress bar's background. They have separate id strings so that they may be styled separately: one with an outline (stroke) only and one with only a fill. Listing 6-10 shows the line that needs to be added to the MediaPlayerControls declaration in SimpleMediaPlayer to bind the MediaPlayer's bufferProgressTime variable to the newly introduced bufferTime variable in MediaPlayerControls. Figure 6-3 shows a screenshot of the new interface while a stream is being buffered.

Listing 6-10. *Binding the Buffer Progress Variables in SimpleMediaPlayer*

```
override function create() {
  MediaPlayerControls {
    width: bind width
    volume: bind player.volume with inverse
    balance: bind player.balance with inverse
    isPlaying: bind player.status == MediaPlayer.PLAYING
    mediaDuration: bind player.media.duration
    bufferTime: bind player.bufferProgressTime
    currentTime: bind player.currentTime with inverse

    // … no other changes …
}
```

Figure 6-3. *The audio player with support for showing the status of the stream's buffer*

Playing Video

From an API standpoint, playing video instead of audio is as simple as wrapping a MediaPlayer with a MediaView and adding the MediaView to the scene graph. Listing 6-11 shows how this is done. You simply point a Media object at a valid source (a Flash movie in this case) and wrap it with an auto-playing MediaPlayer, which, in turn, is wrapped with a MediaView. The final step is to add the MediaView to the scene and set the size of the scene to match the size of the movie. That's all there is to creating an instant movie player.

Listing 6-11. *A Minimalist but Functional Movie Player*

```
import javafx.scene.media.Media;
import javafx.scene.media.MediaPlayer;
import javafx.scene.media.MediaView;
import javafx.scene.Scene;
import javafx.stage.Stage;

Stage {
  var theScene:Scene;

  title: "BasicMoviePlayer"
  scene: theScene = Scene {
    width: 640
    height: 352
    content: MediaView {
      fitWidth: bind theScene.width
      fitHeight: bind theScene.height
      mediaPlayer: MediaPlayer {
        autoPlay: true
        media: Media {
          source: "http://projavafx.com/movies/elephants-dream-640x352.flv"
        }
      }
    }
  }
}
```

Remember that playing movies from `.jar` files is not supported in JavaFX version 1.2. The source variable for the `Media` must be a URI that uses either the `file://` or `http://` protocol specifier and an absolute resource path. You should also be aware that there are issues with playing movies using a `file://` URI on Windows. The `Media` class does not recognize some Windows paths correctly.

Controlling the Size of a MediaView

Since `MediaView` is just another node in the scene graph, it is possible to scale its content using the usual `transforms` or `scaleX` and `scaleY` variables of the `Node` class. There are more convenient ways to get the job done when dealing with `MediaViews`, however. The variables `fitWidth` and `fitHeight` can be used to make the `MediaView` stretch or shrink to the desired size. Using only one of them at a time will make the `MediaView` scale in that dimension only while the size in the other dimension remains unchanged.

If you want to maintain the movie's original aspect ratio as you scale it to fit your application, you can set the `preserveRatio` variable to `true`. If you specify a fit size in one dimension along with setting `preserveRatio` to `true`, then the other dimension will be automatically scaled to match the movie's original aspect ratio as it's being fit along your specified dimension. For example, let's take our example movie: *Elephants Dream*. Its size is originally 640×352 pixels, which gives an aspect ratio of 640 ÷ 352, or approximately 1.82. If you specify a `fitWidth` of 400 and enable `preserveRatio`, then the final height of the movie will be changed from 352 pixels to 400 ÷ 1.82 = 220 pixels. Note that the aspect ratio is preserved since 400 ÷ 220 is also 1.82.

You can also choose to scale in both dimensions by specifying both a fitWidth and a fitHeight value along with enabling preserveRatio. In this case the best fit for the movie will be calculated and the other dimension will be scaled to preserve the original aspect ratio. For example, if the fit area and the movie are both wider than they are tall (the common case), then the movie will be scaled to fit horizontally and the height will be determined by using the aspect ratio to calculate the height needed to match the new width.

There is one problem to look out for when using preserveRatio with streaming media. If the width and height of the media are not known when the fit calculation is originally done, then the aspect ratio of the resulting video will be wrong. This can easily happen in situations where you are dealing with video that has to stream over the Internet since the width and height of such media may not be known originally. Unfortunately, the calculation is not updated when the media size does become available so you have to cause the calculation to be redone manually. Luckily, this is pretty easy to accomplish and we'll show how it can be done in the next example.

One last variable that is worth knowing about in relation to resizing a movie is the smooth variable. This is a Boolean variable that controls the quality of the resulting image after the scale. If smooth is true, the scaling algorithm will produce a higher-quality image at the cost of some extra computation time. If false, the scaling will be done faster but the result will not look as good. This lets the developer make a time versus quality trade-off. When making a movie smaller, there is not a large difference in quality between the smooth and non-smooth options. Although the difference in quality while upscaling is noticeable, it still may be acceptable for some applications. Therefore, if you need to generate and show thumbnails of movies or if you need to play movies on a mobile device where processing power may be limited, this can be a worthwhile option to consider. By default, smooth is set to true.

Listing 6-12 shows a full-screen movie player that uses the fitWidth, fitHeight, and preserveRatio to scale a movie to play using the entire screen. The stage's fullScreen and style variables are used to ensure that only the movie can be seen on the screen. Take special note of the mediaHeight variable that is bound to the Media's height and uses an "on replace" trigger to set preserveRatio to true after the media's height variable has changed. This will cause the scaling calculation to be done and the correct aspect ratio for the movie to be used. In order for this to work properly, the preserveRatio variable must be initialized to false in the MediaView declaration. You will also notice that the MediaView's translateX and translateY variables are used to ensure that the movie is centered on the screen when it is played. The Escape key (Esc) can be used to exit full screen mode and play the movie in a window. Finally, the Q key is used to quit the application by attaching a key event handler to the MediaView node.

Listing 6-12. *A Full-Screen Movie Player That Preserves the Movie's Original Aspect Ratio*

```
var theScene: Scene;
var theView: MediaView;

var mediaHeight = bind theView.mediaPlayer.media.height on replace {
  if (mediaHeight > 0) {
    theView.preserveRatio = true
  }
}
```

```
Stage {
  fullScreen: true
  style: StageStyle.UNDECORATED
  scene:
  theScene = Scene {
    fill: Color.BLACK
    content: [
      theView = MediaView {
        translateX: bind (theScene.width - theView.layoutBounds.width) / 2
        translateY: bind (theScene.height - theView.layoutBounds.height) / 2
        fitWidth: bind theScene.width
        fitHeight: bind theScene.height
        preserveRatio: false
        mediaPlayer: MediaPlayer {
          autoPlay: true
          media: Media {
            source: "http://projavafx.com/movies/elephants-dream-640x352.flv"
          }
        }
        focusable: true
        onKeyPressed: function( ke:KeyEvent ) {
          if (ke.code == KeyCode.VK_Q) {
            FX.exit();
          }
        }
      }
    ]
  }
}
```

Transforming a MediaView

Since MediaView is just a node like any other, you can take advantage of the scene graph's transformation capabilities to produce some interesting effects for your movies. Before applying any transforms, it is good practice to test MediaView's rotatable and transformable variables. If they are set to true, then rotations and transformations are supported.

If rotatable is true, then the Node's rotate variable can be used to rotate your movie while it is playing. The rotate variable is of type Number and specifies a node's rotation in degrees about its center point. If you need more flexibility, you can use the node's transforms variable and specify a Rotate transformation. This allows you to not only set the degrees of rotation, but also the point about which the node will rotate. Using these two options along with an animation would allow for a nice transition where a movie rotates into place on the screen or even spins wildly in or out of frame. As developers, we shouldn't overuse these kind of theatrics (if you will pardon the term), but sometimes they are just what is needed to add some fun to a casual application or a game. With great power comes great responsibility.

When the `transformable` variable is `true`, the `MediaView` can support some additional types of transforms, including scale, shear, and translation. This gives the developer many more options. A small shear in the x or y direction will produce a video viewport that resembles a parallelogram. This could be useful to give the impression of motion as a video is translated off of or on to the screen. In most cases, the `fitWidth` and `fitHeight` variables are more convenient for scaling. However, the `scaleX` and `scaleY` variables can be animated up and down to produce a subtle pulsating effect in order to catch a user's attention. You can also use scaling to create a movie that plays as a mirror image if you set `scaleX` to `-1.0` or upside down if you set `scaleY` to `-1.0`. A `Scale` transform could be set on the `transforms` variable as well. Chapter 7 will cover the differences between these various methods of transforming nodes. Note that the `MediaView` also has x and y variables available that can be used to translate the node within its local coordinate system.

Compositing and Effects

The `MediaView` also has a `compositable` variable that, if set to `true`, means that the movie can be made translucent using the `opacity` variable. This can be a handy way to fade the movie in or out by using a simple animation. With two movies you can accomplish a cross fade between the movies by simply fading one out while fading the other in.

All of the normal effects that can be applied to a node can also be applied to a `MediaView`. Some care must be taken to ensure that the effects are not so expensive as to interfere with the smooth playback of the movie. This is of special concern on operating systems that use the software renderer such as Mac OS X. With that caveat in place, we will go over some of the effects that are commonly in use with media player applications. Reflections (see `javafx.scene.effect.Reflection`) are a popular effect, specifically in demos that are meant to show off a platform's graphical horsepower. A reflection can make the movie look like it is sitting on a shiny surface. The effect is very compelling since the reflection is updated in real time to match the movie. JavaFX's `ColorAdjust` effect can be used to alter the colors in the movie for a fun and visually interesting effect. If you're in a more artsy kind of mood, the `SepiaTone` effect may be just the thing. And of course there is the old reliable `DropShadow` effect to make the movie look like it is floating over the background. We encourage you to use the example programs and experiment with the different effects in the `javafx.scene.effect` package. It is a fun and interesting way to learn about them.

One Player, Multiple Views

There is one variable in the `MediaPlayer` class that we have waited until now to discuss: the `supportsMultiViews` variable. Testing this variable will tell you whether the `MediaPlayer` can support being attached to multiple `MediaViews`. Since they all share the same player, all views will be showing the same frame of video at the same time, but each view can have separate transformations and effects applied.

Each MediaView supports the idea of a viewport. This is a `Rectangle2D` that defines which part of the movie to view. Using the Elephants Dream movie as an example again, the code in Listing 6-13 will create a `MediaView` that shows the upper-left quarter of the video.

Listing 6-13. *Defining a Viewport for a MediaView*

```
MediaView {
  mediaPlayer: MediaPlayer {
    autoPlay: true
    media: Media {
      source: "http://projavafx.com/movies/elephants-dream-640x352.flv"
    }
  }
  viewport: Rectangle2D {
    minX: 0
    minY: 0
    width: 320
    height: 176
  }
}
```

The viewport will become your view of the player's content. If you specify a `fitWidth` or `fitHeight`, any transforms or effects, they will be applied to the viewport just as they would have been applied to the view as a whole.

Playing Movies with SimpleMediaPlayer

Based on what you have learned so far, you may think that extending the `SimpleMediaPlayer` class to play video is a straightforward task, and you would be right. The first thing that needs to be done is to declare the `MediaView` and position it above the `MediaPlayerControls`. This is accomplished using bind statements and the `layoutBounds` of both the `MediaView` and the `MediaPlayerControls`. A gap of 5 pixels is placed around our two nodes to make sure the layout doesn't look too crowded. Note that we have used the `preserveRatio` trick described earlier to make sure that the correct aspect ratio is used even for streaming video. Since the `MediaView` class also defines an `onError` function variable, we now use the same error function callback for both `MediaView` and `MediaPlayer`. Listing 6-14 shows all of these changes.

Listing 6-14. *Adding the MediaView to the SimpleMoviePlayer*

```
public class SimpleMediaPlayer extends Control {
  public var source: String on replace {
    player.media.source = source;
  }

  def player: MediaPlayer = MediaPlayer {
    media: Media {
      source: source
    }
    onError: handleMediaError
    onEndOfMedia: function() {
      player.stop();
    }
  }
```

```
def GAP = 5.0;

def mediaHeight = bind player.media.height on replace {
  view.preserveRatio = true;
}

def view: MediaView = MediaView {
  translateX: bind (width - view.layoutBounds.width) / 2
  translateY: GAP
  mediaPlayer: player
  fitWidth: bind width - (2 * GAP)
  fitHeight: bind height - (2 * GAP + controls.layoutBounds.height)
  preserveRatio: false
  onError: handleMediaError
}

def controls = MediaPlayerControls {
  translateY: bind view.layoutBounds.height + GAP;
  width: bind width
  volume: bind player.volume with inverse
  balance: bind player.balance with inverse
  isPlaying: bind player.status == MediaPlayer.PLAYING
  mediaDuration: bind player.media.duration
  bufferTime: bind player.bufferProgressTime
  currentTime: bind player.currentTime with inverse
  onTogglePlayPause: function( play:Boolean ) {
    if (play) {
      player.play();
    } else {
      player.pause();
    }
  }
  onToggleRepeat: function( repeat:Boolean ) {
    if (repeat) {
      player.repeatCount = MediaPlayer.REPEAT_FOREVER;
    } else {
      player.repeatCount = MediaPlayer.REPEAT_NONE;
    }
  }
}

override function create() {
  Group {
    content: [ view, controls ]
  }
}
```

```
function handleMediaError( me:MediaError ) {
  println( "Error Occurred: {me.message}" );
}
}
```

A few minor changes are also needed to the `Main.fx` file. First, the option to play files from a `.jar` file has been removed since that is not supported for video. If there is no command-line argument, the default is to stream a video from the `projavafx.com` website. Second, the initial size of the scene is increased to make space to show the video. And of course the title of the stage has also been changed. These changes are shown in Listing 6-15, and Figure 6-4 shows the resulting application.

Listing 6-15. *Placing the Movie Player on the Stage*

```
package projavafx.movieplayer;

import javafx.lang.FX;
import javafx.scene.Scene;
import javafx.stage.Stage;

// See if there is an command line argument for the media file
var uriString = FX.getArguments()[0];

if (uriString == null or uriString.length() == 0) {
  uriString = "http://projavafx.com/movies/elephants-dream-640x352.flv";
}

Stage {
  var theScene: Scene;
  title: "MoviePlayer"
  scene: theScene = Scene {
    width: 864
    height: 400
    stylesheets: "{__DIR__}audioPlayer.css"
    content: SimpleMediaPlayer {
      source: uriString
      width: bind theScene.width
      height: bind theScene.height
    }
  }
}
```

Figure 6-4. *The streaming video player in action*

Summary

In this chapter, you learned about a very important aspect of the JavaFX platform: the media classes. We showed you how to accomplish the following:

- Load the various media types supported by JavaFX into a `Media` object.

- Use the `MediaPlayer` class to play audio files from `.jar` files, from disk, and by streaming them over the Internet.

- Build a simple media player that contains a graphical user interface that can be used to control playback of the audio files.

- Play movies in JavaFX, which involves controlling the size of the movie, transforming the movie view, attaching multiple views to a single player, and applying effects such as translucency, reflection, and drop shadows.

- Extend the simple media player to play video.

In the next chapter you will learn about how to layout your nodes dynamically while building a more substantial JavaFX application.

CHAPTER 7

■ ■ ■

Dynamically Laying Out Nodes in the User Interface

When I am working on a problem, I never think about beauty. I think only of how to solve the problem. But when I have finished, if the solution is not beautiful, I know it is wrong.

—Buckminster Fuller

JavaFX has facilities for creating dynamic layouts that allow you to easily create beautiful-looking user interfaces (UIs) that scale to any resolution and are backed by clean code. At your disposal you have the simple, yet elegant, bind statement; powerful custom layouts built on top of the Panel and Container classes; and the built-in layouts, including HBox, VBox, Flow, Tile, and Stack.

In this chapter we will show how you can leverage these dynamic layouts mechanisms to build complicated user interfaces with zero static positioning.

Introducing JavaFX Reversi

To demonstrate the power of dynamic layout in JavaFX, the goal of this chapter will be to build a fully functional version of the popular Reversi game. Reversi is a game of strategy where players take turns on an eight-by-eight game board placing black and white pieces. The objective of the game is to have the most pieces on the board by surrounding your opponent's pieces and flipping them over to your color.

Originally invented in 1880 by Lewis Waterman and James Mollett, Reversi gained considerable popularity in nineteenth-century England, and was one of the first titles published by German game manufacturer Ravensburger. It is more commonly known today as Othello, which is trademarked and sold by Pressman.

The rules of Reversi are extremely simple, which will let us focus on the JavaFX layout. To make things a little more challenging, we are going to bring Reversi into the twenty-first century with a modern RIA style interface, pseudo-3D game board, and fully resizable layout.

Board Layout and Basic Rules

Reversi is a turn-based game where two players choose white and black sides. Each player gets 32 pieces to play; the first player is black.

The initial board setup has four pieces placed in alternating cells in the center of the board (see Figure 7-1).

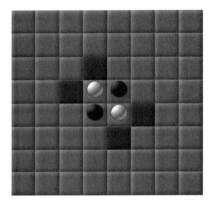

Figure 7-1. *This is the starting board position for Reversi.*

Black gets the first turn and can place a piece anywhere adjacent to one of white's pieces where there is a matching black piece on the same line (vertical, horizontal, or diagonal). From the starting position, there are only four legal moves, which are highlighted in blue. All moves are equal position-wise, so let's assume that black goes in the uppermost position. This allows black to flip the upper white piece, taking that entire column (see Figure 7-2).

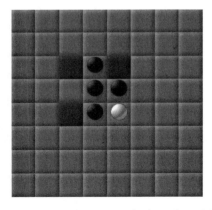

Figure 7-2. *This shows the board position after black's first move.*

White gets the second turn and has three available options highlighted in blue. Let's assume white goes in the lowermost position, flipping one black piece. Now it is black's turn again with five available positions (shown in Figure 7-3).

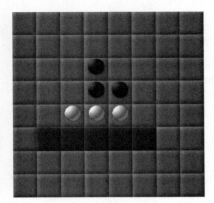

Figure 7-3. *This shows the board position after the next move by white.*

Play continues this way, alternating between black and white unless one player has no moves, in which case they pass on that turn. The game is over when both players have no moves, and the winner is the player with the most pieces on the final board.

Building a JavaFX Model for Reversi

Now that you are armed with knowledge of how Reversi works, it is time to translate that into a simple JavaFX model.

Your `ReversiModel` class needs to contain two primary pieces of information: the current board position and the player whose turn it is. Listing 7-1 shows a simple model class to get you started.

Listing 7-1. *ReversiModel Class for the Reversi Application*

```
public def BOARD_SIZE = 8;

public class Row {
  public var cells = for (i in [1..BOARD_SIZE]) Owner.NONE;
}

public class ReversiModel {
  public var turn = Owner.BLACK;

  public var board = for (i in [1..BOARD_SIZE]) Row {};
}
```

Some things to point out about this model are

- It uses a constant to define the board size, which you can make use of going forward.

- Since sequences cannot be nested, a Row wrapper class is introduced that itself contains a sequence.

- It references an Owner class for both the cell contents and the current turn.

Because there is no concept of enumerations in JavaFX, it is a best practice to use Java enumerations. As shown in the following code, you can use this technique to create an Owner class that contains states for WHITE, BLACK, and (in the case of cells) NONE:

```
public enum Owner {
  NONE,
  WHITE,
  BLACK;

  public Owner opposite() {
    return this == WHITE ? BLACK : this == BLACK ? WHITE : NONE;
  }
}
```

■**Caution** The Owner class must be saved with a .java extension, rather than an .fx extension, because it is a plain Java enumeration.

As an extra bonus, this enumeration class contains a helper function called opposite() to convert from black to white and vice versa, which will be very useful for swapping turns and implementing the game algorithm later.

The final step is to initialize our model to the starting position for a Reversi game. You can accomplish this by adding an initializer to the ReversiModel that places the first four pieces in the center of the board:

```
init {
  def center1 = BOARD_SIZE / 2 - 1;
  def center2 = BOARD_SIZE / 2;
  board[center1].cells[center1] = Owner.WHITE;
  board[center1].cells[center2] = Owner.BLACK;
  board[center2].cells[center1] = Owner.BLACK;
  board[center2].cells[center2] = Owner.WHITE;
}
```

We will come back to the model later, but let's switch over to building out the Reversi user interface by using some of the basic dynamic layout mechanisms in JavaFX.

Dynamic Layout Techniques

JavaFX provides a wide variety of layouts that are suitable for different tasks. They range from the versatile bind, which is the staple of any dynamic layout, to the free-form Panel, which allows you to create an entirely new layout on the fly. There is also a large set of built-in layouts, including HBox, VBox, Stack, Tile, and Flow, that can be composited to accomplish sophisticated layouts.

To demonstrate this, we will show how you can build a UI shell for the Reversi application that has absolutely no static positioned components and that supports dynamic resizing.

Centering Text Using Bind

One of the most powerful facilities in the JavaFX language is the new bind support. Earlier we showed how bind could be used to keep the UI and model in sync with no complicated events or listeners.

Another very powerful use of bind is to keep UI components in alignment by binding to their location and size. This technique can be used to align components to the edges of a window, keep nodes in relative alignment with each other, or center them inside a container, which is what we will show in this example.

To accomplish this, you will need to make use of several new variables of the Node class in combination with bind. The common Node variables that you need to use when doing bind layouts are listed in Table 7-1.

Table 7-1. *Node Variables Commonly Used in Bind Layouts*

Access	Name	Type	Description
public	layoutX	Number	Horizontal offset of the Node for layout positioning
public	layoutY	Number	Vertical offset of the Node for layout positioning
public-init	layoutBounds	Rectangle2D	Boundary of the Node that should be used for layout calculations

To demonstrate, Listing 7-2 is a simple code example that shows how to center the "JavaFX Reversi" title within a Scene.

Listing 7-2. *Example of Centering Text in a Scene*

```
var scene:Scene;
scene = Scene {
  width: 400
  height: 100
  var text:Text;
  content: text = Text {
    layoutX: bind (scene.width - text.layoutBounds.width) / 2
    layoutY: bind (scene.height - text.layoutBounds.height) / 2
    content: "JavaFX Reversi"
    textOrigin: TextOrigin.TOP
    font: Font.font(null, FontWeight.BOLD, 18)
  }
}
```

Some specific points to highlight about Listing 7-2 are

- To access the scene and text within the initialization block, you need to declare them in advance with the correct type. This is a common pattern to use when lining up nodes with `bind`.

- The default value for the `textOrigin` variable of `Text` is `BASELINE`, which aligns to the bottom of the letters, not including descenders. We chose to use `TOP` instead, which makes the origin line up with the top of the letters. This makes `Text` behave similarly to most other `Nodes`, and is much easier to center.

Running this program produces a window where the title stays centered even if you resize the frame (see Figure 7-4).

Figure 7-4. *A Text node centered within a Scene using bind*

Centering Revisited Using a Stack

In the previous section you were able to center text using the `bind` operator. While that is one way to center text, we will show you an alternative approach using the `Stack` class, which has built-in capabilities for declaratively aligning nodes.

The `Stack` class is a layout container that allows you to layer nodes on top of each other to create composite effects. In order for all the nodes in a `Stack` to be visible, the upper nodes must be shaped or transparent so that it is possible to see through them. Table 7-2 lists some of the variables that the `Stack` class uses to layout its contents.

Table 7-2. *Variables Used by the Stack Layout Class*

Name	Type	Default	Defined In	Description
nodeHPos	HPos	HPos.CENTER	Stack	The default horizontal alignment of child nodes
nodeVPos	VPos	VPos.CENTER	Stack	The default vertical alignment of child nodes
content	Node[]	Empty	Group	A sequence of children that will be stacked from back to front

The order of the children in the `content` sequence controls the z-order of the `Stack`, with `content[0]` appearing on the bottom and `content[sizeof content - 1]` on the top. The `nodeHPos` and `nodeVPos` variables can be used to control the default alignment of nodes that do not fill all the available space in the `Stack`; however, the default value of `CENTER` is usually correct.

To build on the previous example, we will invert the text and background by adding a black Ellipse to the scene that covers most of the background and changing the color of the Text node to white. Also, to simplify the alignment and allow layering of nodes, we will use a Stack instead of bind to lay out the nodes as shown in Listing 7-3.

Listing 7-3. *Example of Using Stack to Overlay and Align Nodes*

```
var scene:Scene;
scene = Scene {
  width: 400
  height: 100
  content: Stack {
    width: bind scene.width
    height: bind scene.height
    content: [
      Ellipse {
        radiusX: bind scene.width / 2
        radiusY: bind scene.height / 2
      }     Text {
        content: "JavaFX Reversi"
        font: Font.font(null, FontWeight.BOLD, 18)
        fill: Color.WHITE
      }
    ]
  }
}
```

Notice that there is nothing special that we needed to do to align the Text in the window. The default alignment for nodes in a Stack is to center them, which is exactly what we wanted to happen. Later we will show how you can override this behavior on a per-layout or per-node basis.

Some binds were still required to make the Stack resize with the window, and to keep the Ellipse properly sized. It is common to use bind together with layouts in this fashion.

▪Tip The JFXtras project provides a ResizableScene that automatically resizes its contents, no binding required. You can find out more about this and other JFXtras extensions in Chapter 8.

The completed example is shown running in Figure 7-5.

Figure 7-5. *Inverted JavaFX Reversi logo using a Stack*

Aligning to Edges Using Tiles

Using edge alignment, you can improve the title program to fit in with the Reversi theme. To emphasize the black and white contrast of the Reversi pieces, let's create a design where the words are alternating colors on an alternating background.

To accomplish this visual effect, you need to do the following:

1. Create a Scene, which has a white background (the default).

2. Add a black Rectangle to the scene that covers half the background and is aligned left.

3. Split the words into two Text nodes, aligned to the center.

4. Set the fill of the text on top of the black rectangle to white.

One way of looking at this problem is that you are creating two equal size Tiles that will contain text aligned toward the center of the window. The right side is simply a Text node that is aligned to the left edge, and the left side can be accomplished using a Stack with Text on top of a Rectangle just like we did in the previous section.

To create equal size tiles, we can use a built-in layout called Tile that does exactly what we want. The Tile layout will divide its content into equal-sized areas to fit all of its nodes. The available variables on Tile are shown in Table 7-3.

Table 7-3. *Layout Variables on the Tile Class*

Name	Type	Default	Description
rows	Integer		Number of rows used to lay out the tiles
columns	Integer		Number of columns used to lay out the tiles
hgap	Number	0	Horizontal gap between the columns
vgap	Number	0	Vertical gap between the columns
hpos	HPos	HPos.LEFT	Horizontal position of rows within the container
vpos	VPos	VPos.TOP	Vertical position of columns within the container
nodeHPos	HPos	VPos.CENTER	Default horizontal alignment of nodes within a tile
nodeVPos	VPos	VPos.CENTER	Default vertical alignment of nodes within a tile
tileWidth	Number		Width of the tiles
tileHeight	Number		Height of the tiles
vertical	Boolean	false	true if the Tiles should be laid out from top to bottom

Tile is a very versatile class with lots of options for setting the tile width and height, number of rows and columns, gaps between rows and columns, and the horizontal and vertical position. Most of these have reasonable defaults, such as tileWidth and tileHeight, that will use the largest preferred width/height of all its children. Similarly, rows and columns will be set automatically based on the number of tiles that fit the width and height of the Tile instance.

Just like the `Stack` class, `Tile` also has variables for setting the default `nodeHPos` and `nodeVPos`. Unfortunately, we can't use these, because we want the text aligned to the right on one side and the left on the other.

Fortunately, there is a new addition to the `Node` class called `layoutInfo` that is specifically designed to allow per-node layout defaults. The `layoutInfo` variable can be assigned a `LayoutInfo` object that contains values for any of the variables listed in Table 7-4

Table 7-4. *LayoutInfo per-Node Layout Variables*

Name	Type	Default	Defined In	Description
hpos	HPos		LayoutInfo	The horizontal position of the node in its container
vpos	VPos		LayoutInfo	The vertical position of the node in its container
minWidth	Number		LayoutInfo	The minimum allowed width of this node
minHeight	Number		LayoutInfo	The minimum allowed height of this node
width	Number		LayoutInfo	The preferred width of this node
height	Number		LayoutInfo	The preferred height of this node
maxWidth	Number		LayoutInfo	The maximum allowed width of this node
maxHeight	Number		LayoutInfo	The maximum allowed height of this node
managed	Boolean	true	LayoutInfoBase	Whether this node will be laid out by containers

`LayoutInfo` has variables to set the min, max, and preferred bounds. It also has a horizontal and vertical `position` setting and a `managed` variable that can be used to disable layout altogether. When both the `hpos` in `LayoutInfo` and `nodeHPos` in `Stack` or `Tile` are set, the `LayoutInfo` variable takes precedence. Possible values for `HPos` and `VPos` are shown in Table 7-5 and 7-6, respectively.

Table 7-5. *HPos Constant Values*

Name	Description
LEADING	The leading end of a line based on the language text direction
LEFT	Indicates that the node should be aligned left
CENTER	Indicates that the node should be horizontally centered
RIGHT	Indicates that the node should be aligned right
TRAILING	The trailing edge of the line based on the language text direction

■**Caution** LEADING and TRAILING are unimplemented as of JavaFX 1.2, and will behave identically to LEFT and RIGHT, respectively.

Table 7-6. *VPos Constant Values*

Name	Description
PAGE_START	The top of the page based on the language text direction
TOP	Indicates that the node should be top aligned
CENTER	Indicates that the node should be vertically centered
BASELINE	Indicates that node should be bottom aligned excluding text descenders
BOTTOM	Indicates that the node should be bottom aligned
PAGE_END	The bottom of the page based on the language text direction

■**Caution** PAGE_START, BASELINE, and PAGE_END are unimplemented for the built-in layouts in JavaFX 1.2, and will behave identically to TOP in the case of PAGE_START and BOTTOM for BASELINE and PAGE_END.

■**Tip** The JFXtras ResizableHBox, ResizableVBox, and Grid all support BASELINE alignment. See Chapter 8 for more information about using these layouts.

We will take advantage of the HBox constants of LEFT and RIGHT to align half the text to the right and the other half to the left, as shown in Listing 7-4.

Listing 7-4. *Example Showing How to Use a Tile and Stack to Align Nodes*

```
var scene:Scene;
scene = Scene {
  width: 400
  height: 100
  content: Tile {
    width: bind scene.width
    height: bind scene.height
    content: [
      Stack {
        content: [
          Rectangle {
            width: bind scene.width / 2
            height: bind scene.height
          }
          Text {
            layoutInfo: LayoutInfo {
              hpos: HPos.RIGHT
            }
```

```
            content: "JavaFX"
            font: Font.font(null, FontWeight.BOLD, 18)
            fill: Color.WHITE
          }
        ]
      }
    }
    Text {
      layoutInfo: LayoutInfo {
        hpos: HPos.LEFT
      }
      content: "Reversi"
      font: Font.font(null, FontWeight.BOLD, 18)
    }
  ]
  }
}
```

The completed layout makes use of a Tile for splitting the background, a Stack for layering nodes, LayoutInfo for alignment, and binding to make the contents resize with the Scene. The end result is that the layout resizes correctly when the size of the Scene is changed, including the black rectangle in the background, which always occupies half the area, as shown in Figure 7-6.

Figure 7-6. *Result of running the node alignment example*

Using Flow and Boxes for Directional Alignment

In the previous sections we showed how you can use Stack and Tile to create dynamic nested user interfaces, but what if you simply want to arrange nodes along a vertical or horizontal line? This is where the directional layouts, HBox, VBox, and Flow, come in. They allow you to lay out a string of nodes at their preferred size with or without wrapping.

To demonstrate directional node alignment, we are going to show you how to implement the next piece of the Reversi UI: the player score box. There are two score boxes for the players, each with very similar content:

- *Score*: The number of pieces of the player's color on the board

- *Player Color*: The color of the player's pieces

- *Turns Remaining*: The number of turns remaining

Before starting on the UI, this is a good time to flush out the model with additional methods to capture these requirements. Listing 7-5 shows an example implementation of getScore, getColor, and getTurnsRemaining that will return exactly what we need to populate the player score box UI.

Listing 7-5. *Additional Model Methods to Implement Player Score Backend*

```
public bound function getScore(owner:Owner):Integer {
  def cells = for (row in board, cell in row.cells where cell == owner) {
    cell
  }
  return cells.size();
}

public function getColor(owner:Owner):Color {
  return if (owner == Owner.WHITE) then Color.WHITE else Color.BLACK;
}

public bound function getTurnsRemaining(owner:Owner):Integer {
  def emptyCellCount = getScore(Owner.NONE) as Number;
  return if (turn == owner) {
    Math.ceil(emptyCellCount / 2) as Integer
  } else {
    Math.floor(emptyCellCount / 2) as Integer
  }
}
```

Some points to highlight about Listing 7-5 include

- Both getScore and getTurnsRemaining make use of a for loop with two clauses and a where clause that returns a sequence. Counting the number of elements is then as simple as using the size() function (which is equivalent to sizeof). This is very succinct compared to the equivalent Java code, which would be at least twice as long.

- Both getScore and getTurnsRemaining are defined as bound functions. This is necessary so that the UI can automatically update if there are any changes to the board, but limits the use of expressions with side effects.

- We cast the emptyCellCount to a Number type in getTurnsRemaining to ensure we are using floating point math at the end of the function.

Now that we have the model functions created, you can use them to build a JavaFX UI class that will show each player's score. Because you will need to create the same UI components twice, this is a good time to raise the abstraction level of the UI by creating functions that create portions of the UI. This will let you reuse the same score box for both players.

Listing 7-6 has the first half of the code and shows how to set up a simple two-column Tile layout that will contain the player score boxes.

Listing 7-6. *First Half of Player Score Implementation*

```
def model = ReversiModel {}

Stage {
  title: "Player Score Example"
  var scene:Scene;
  scene: scene = Scene {
    width: 600
    height: 120
    content: Tile {
      width: bind scene.width
      height: bind scene.height
      tileWidth: bind scene.width / 2
      tileHeight: bind scene.height
      content: [
        createScore(Owner.BLACK),
        createScore(Owner.WHITE)
      ]
    }
  }
}
```

Notice that we have explicitly bound the `tileWidth` and `tileHeight`. This will ensure that the tiles resize together with the window.

For the second half, you will need to use the `HBox`, `VBox`, and `Flow` classes. Table 7-7 shows a list of all the variables available, and which layouts they apply to.

Table 7-7. *List of Variables for HBox, VBox, and Flow*

Name	Type	Default	Found In	Description
hpos	HPos	HPos.LEFT	HBox, VBox, Flow	Horizontal position of the entire layout
vpos	VPos	VPos.TOP	HBox, VBox, Flow	Vertical position of the entire layout
nodeHPos	HPos	HPos.LEFT, HPos.CENTER	VBox, Flow	Default horizontal alignment of nodes
nodeVPos	VPos	HPos.TOP, HPos.CENTER	HBox, Flow	Default vertical alignment of nodes
spacing	Number	0	HBox, VBox	Space between nodes in the direction of layout
hgap	Number	0	Flow	Horizontal gap between the rows
vgap	Number	0	Flow	Vertical gap between the columns
vertical	Boolean	false	Flow	True if this Flow runs top-to-bottom, false for left-to-right

The main difference between HBox/VBox and Flow is that Flow layout will wrap when it reaches the container width for horizontal layouts and container height for vertical layouts, while HBox and VBox always retain their orientation.

Listing 7-7 shows the implementation of the createScore method, which takes the model functions you wrote earlier and turns them into a visual representation.

Listing 7-7. *Implementation of createScore Method Using Directional Alignment*

```
function createScore(owner:Owner) {
  var stack:Stack;
  stack = Stack {
    content: [
      Rectangle {
        def shadow = InnerShadow {color: bind Color.DODGERBLUE, choke: 0.5};
        effect: bind if (model.turn == owner) shadow else null
        width: bind stack.width
        height: bind stack.height
        fill: model.getColor(owner.opposite())
      }
      Flow {
        hpos: HPos.CENTER
        vpos: VPos.CENTER
        nodeVPos: VPos.BASELINE
        hgap: 20
        vgap: 10
        content: [
          Text {
            content: bind "{model.getScore(owner)}"
            font: Font.font(null, FontWeight.BOLD, 100)
            fill: model.getColor(owner)
          }
          VBox {
            nodeHPos: HPos.CENTER
            spacing: 10
            content: [
              Ellipse {
                def shadow = DropShadow {color: bind Color.DODGERBLUE, spread: 0.2};
                effect: bind if (model.turn == owner) shadow else null
                radiusX: 32
                radiusY: 20
                fill: model.getColor(owner)
              }
```

```
        Text {
          content: bind "{model.getTurnsRemaining(owner)} turns remaining"
          font: Font.font(null, FontWeight.BOLD, 12)
          fill: model.getColor(owner)
        }
      ]
    }
  ]
}
  ]
}
}
```

Notice that we used a `Flow` as the outer layout and a `VBox` inside to keep the `Ellipse` and `Text` vertically aligned. This ensures that the `Ellipse` will always stay on top of the `Text` but still allows the display to wrap into a vertical layout if horizontal screen real-estate is limited. The result of running the program for a horizontal layout is shown in Figure 7-7, and the resized vertical layout is shown in Figure 7-8.

Figure 7-7. *Output of running the Player Score Example in a horizontally sized window*

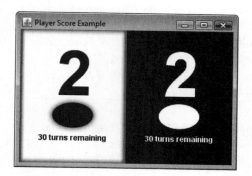

Figure 7-8. *Output of running the Player Score Example in a vertically sized window*

While it may be surprising that the starting score is not zero, if you remember the Reversi starting position, there are four pieces in the center of the board, which gives each player two points. Also, the sum of all the scores and turns remaining should always add up to 64, which is true in this case.

The next step is to combine the logo and score using a `Panel` to build the minimal shell for the Reversi application.

Customizing Layout Behavior Using a Panel

Up to now we have been able to compose the built-in layouts to handle dynamic resizing, but what about custom layouts that are not a good match? Later on we will demonstrate how to use the `Container` class to create reusable layouts, but there is a convenient subclass of `Container` called `Panel` that is perfect for declaring new layouts on the fly.

In this section we will demonstrate how you can use the `Panel` class to create a custom layout that will form the basis of the Reversi application. The `Panel` class exposes variables that allow you to customize its behavior, as shown in Table 7-8.

Table 7-8. *Public Variables That Can Be Set on the Panel Class*

Name	Type	Description
minWidth	function():float	Function that calculates the minimum width of this `Panel`
minHeight	function():float	Function that calculates the minimum height of this `Panel`
prefWidth	function(:float):float	Function that calculates the preferred width of this `Panel`
prefHeight	function(:float):float	Function that calculates the preferred height of this `Panel`
maxWidth	function():float	Function that calculates the maximum width of this `Panel`
maxHeight	function():float	Function that calculates the maximum height of this `Panel`
onLayout	function():Void	Function called to perform layout of this `Panel`'s contents

All of the variables are meant to be set in the object literal declaration. The `min`, `max`, and `pref` functions come into play with nested layouts, but since this `Panel` is going to be the root node of the Reversi application we don't have to worry about setting them. Instead, we will focus on the `onLayout` variable, which will form the basis of the root layout.

The default `onLayout` behavior of the `Panel` class is that it calls `Panel.resizeContent()`, which simply sets the size of every `managed`, `Resizable` child node to its preferred width and height. We are going to replace this with a custom layout handler that will resize the title, grid, and score to fill the window, as shown in Listing 7-8.

Listing 7-8. *Reversi Root Stage Declaration Using a Panel for Layout*

```
def model = ReversiModel {}

Stage {
  title: "JavaFX Reversi"
  var scene:Scene;
  scene: scene = Scene {
    width: 600
    height: 400
    def titleHeight = 30;
    def scoreHeight = 120;
    def title = createTitle();
    def grid = createBackground();
    def score = createScoreBoxes();
    content: bind [
      Panel {
        width: bind scene.width
        height: bind scene.height
        content: [
          title,
          score,
          grid
        ]
        onLayout: function() {
          def boardHeight = scene.height - titleHeight - scoreHeight;
          Container.layoutNode(title, 0, 0, scene.width, titleHeight);
          Container.layoutNode(grid, 0, titleHeight, scene.width, boardHeight);
          Container.layoutNode(score, 0, scene.height - scoreHeight,
                               scene.width, scoreHeight);
        }
      }
    ]
  }
}
```

Notice that in the `Panel.onLayout` function we are using a static function from the `Container` class called `layoutNode`. This function takes a node, and a bounding box specified by its x, y, width, and height as parameters, and will resize the node to fit the bounding box size. We will go over the rest of the available layout functions in "The Grid Layout Algorithm" section.

We are using this to create a dock-like behavior where the title is aligned to the top with a fixed height and the score boxes are aligned to the bottom, also with a fixed height. All remaining space in the center is occupied by the grid. This could also have been done using `bind` expressions, but using a `Panel` guarantees that the layout function will be called once per layout cycle, yielding higher performance.

Listing 7-9 shows a simple abstraction of a createScoreBoxes() function from "Using Flow and Boxes for Directional Alignment," earlier in this chapter. Notice that the tileWidth and tileHeight are bound to the tile itself, which breaks the dependency on the scene.

Listing 7-9. *Create Score Boxes Function*

```
function createScoreBoxes() {
  var tile:Tile;
  tile = Tile {
    tileWidth: bind tile.width / 2
    tileHeight: bind tile.height
    content: [
      createScore(Owner.BLACK),
      createScore(Owner.WHITE)
    ]
  }
}
```

Implementing createTitle is a similar modification of the Scene definition from the earlier section "Aligning to Edges Using Tiles." The additional changes required are highlighted in bold in Listing 7-10.

Listing 7-10. *Changes Required to the Title Creation Code to Turn It into a Bound Function*

```
function createTitle() {
  var tile:Tile;
  tile = Tile {
    content: [
      Stack {
        content: [
          Rectangle {
            width: bind tile.width / 2
            height: bind tile.height
          }
          Text {
            layoutInfo: LayoutInfo {
              hpos: HPos.RIGHT
            }
            content: "JavaFX"
            font: Font.font(null, FontWeight.BOLD, 18)
            fill: Color.WHITE
          }
        ]
      }
    ]
  }
```

```
      Text {
        layoutInfo: LayoutInfo {
          hpos: HPos.LEFT
        }
        content: "Reversi"
        font: Font.font(null, FontWeight.BOLD, 18)
      }
    ]
  }
}
```

Your last task is to create the board background by implementing `createBackground()`. In "The Grid Layout Algorithm" section, later in this chapter, we will show you how to create a container layout to implement the Reversi board, but for now you can simply fill it with a `RadialGradient`. `RadialGradients` are very similar to the `LinearGradients` you have created in past exercises, but will render the colors in an ellipse from the center outward. The parameters include `centerX` and `centerX`, which define the center of the gradient and default to the origin (0, 0); `radius`, which defines the extent of the color pattern and defaults to the size of the shape; and a sequence of `Stops`, as shown in Listing 7-11.

Listing 7-11. *Bound Function to Create the Reversi Board Background*

```
bound function createBackground(width:Number, height:Number):Node {
  Rectangle {
    width: bind width
    height: bind height
    fill: RadialGradient {
      stops: [
        Stop {
          color: Color.WHITE
        }
        Stop {
          offset: 1
          color: Color.color(0.2, 0.2, 0.2)
        }
      ]
    }
  }
}
```

When you run the complete program, you should see a window that looks like Figure 7-9.

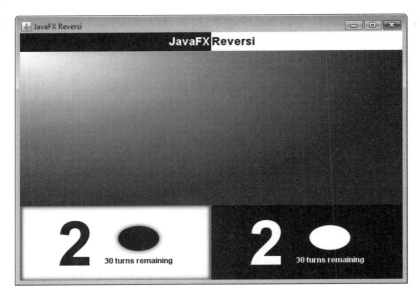

Figure 7-9. *Reversi user interface with title, background, and scores*

Try resizing the window and notice that the Panel keeps the components in stack order and automatically resizes them to fill all available space. This combined example demonstrates how bind, built-in layouts, and Panels can be used to easily compose dynamic layouts in JavaFX.

When to Use Bind vs. Layouts

bind is very powerful, and with enough constraints can be used to construct virtually any dynamic UI you can imagine. However, bind has two primary drawbacks:

- *Complexity*: The more nodes in the user interface, the more edges and constraints each one must adhere to in order to show up in the right location.

- *Performance*: While JavaFX is very efficient about how it evaluates bind statements, too many bound variables will result in reduced performance, and also display artifacts on resizing.

That is where the built-in layouts, such as HBox, VBox, Flow, Stack, and Tile, come in. For the common case where a series of Nodes are stacked horizontally or vertically, using a box layout will result in less complex code than the equivalent bind. Also, unlike bind, layout containers are evaluated only once per display cycle, so you are guaranteed consistent performance regardless of the complexity of your user interface.

In practice, you will usually need to use both layouts and bind together to create a dynamic layout. Table 7-9 explains what situations each type of layout is most suitable for.

Table 7-9. *When to Use Bind vs. Layouts*

Technique	Applicability
bind	Use for resizing fixed Shapes, such as Rectangles, Ellipses, and Lines.
	Easy to create layouts where Nodes overlap.
	Overuse can reduce performance or cause rendering artifacts.
HBox/VBox	Use for vertical or horizontal alignment of nodes.
	High performance; can be used for large number of Nodes.
	Commonly used together with bind for alignment of Nodes.
Flow	Similar to HBox/VBox in usage.
	Useful in situations where the layout should wrap lines to fit.
Stack	Only built-in layout that allows overlapping of Nodes.
	Very useful to create layered effects such as placing text over a background.
Tile	Creates a tiled effect where all nodes are equally sized.
	Is not a replacement for a general purpose Grid (see the JFXtras Grid in Chapter 8).
Panel	Allows complete customizability of the layout behavior.
	Can often be used to replace complicated bind logic with more efficient direct layout.

Creating Resizable Nodes

In the previous section we showed you how you can use bind and the built-in layouts to create homogeneous dynamic layouts. This approach works well for a single class, but does not allow the construction of a modular user interface. Fortunately, JavaFX provides a facility for creating resizable nodes that can be composited into larger user interfaces.

In this section we will show you how to create nodes in JavaFX that are fully resizable to build the Reversi playing pieces and squares that make up the game board. In the following section we will show you how to build dynamic containers from scratch to take these resizable nodes and composite a dynamic playing board that resizes both the squares and the playing pieces.

Building a Resizable Reversi Square

The foundation of the JavaFX container layout is the Resizable class. It has standard functions on it to get bounds preferences for layout and also variables to set the width and height of the Node. In this section we will show you how you can build a Reversi board square that dynamically responds to height and width changes by extending Resizable.

The Resizable class has two variables and six methods, as shown in Tables 7-10 and 7-11, respectively.

Table 7-10. *Variables of the Resizable Class*

Access	Name	Type	Description
public	width	Number	The width of the Node, typically set by the Container
public	height	Number	The height of the Node, typically set by the Container

The width and height of a Resizable node specify the amount of available space the Container allocated to the node for its display.

Table 7-11. *Functions of the Resizable Class*

Access	Abstract?	Signature	Description
public	No	getMinWidth():Number	Function that returns the minimum width of the Node
public	No	getMinHeight():Number	Function that returns the minimum height of the Node
public	Yes	getPrefWidth(height):Number	Function that returns the preferred width of the Node
public	Yes	getPrefHeight(width):Number	Function that returns the preferred height of the Node
public	No	getMaxWidth():Number	Function that returns the maximum width of the Node
public	No	getMaxHeight():Number	Function that returns the maximum height of the Node

The min, max, and pref width and height returned by the Resizable functions are hints to the Container about how it should allocate space to this Node. The only required functions are getPrefWidth and getPrefHeight, which are declared abstract and must be initialized. The height and width passed in to these functions are designed to be used by layouts, such as Flow, where there is a fixed width or height (most other layouts will pass in -1). If your preferred width and height are independent, it is safe to ignore these parameters.

Since Resizable is a mixin, the typical usage is to extend both Node and Resizable. For the ReversiSquare class, we chose to extend CustomNode, which extends Node and exposes a create() function:

```
public class ReversiSquare extends CustomNode, Resizable {
  override function getPrefWidth(height) {30.0}
  override function getPrefHeight(width) {30.0}

  override var layoutBounds = bind lazy BoundingBox {
      minX: 0
      minY: 0
      width: width
      height: height
  }
```

■Tip It is always a good idea to override `layoutBounds` for `CustomNodes` so that it gets updated immediately whenever the `width` and `height` change. Using `bind lazy` ensures that it will only be run when `layoutBounds` is accessed.

You can implement the `create()` function by simply returning a `Rectangle` with some visual effects. The following code shows an example of lighting effects to create a slightly raised edge on the square:

```
override function create() {
  Rectangle {
    effect: Lighting {
      light: DistantLight {
        azimuth: -135
        elevation: 30
      }
    }
    width: bind width
    height: bind height
    fill: Color.BURLYWOOD
  }
}
```

■Caution On platforms without hardware acceleration of effects, the `Lighting` effect may significantly affect performance.

In order to exercise this class, we can use the same `bind` techniques that you learned earlier to create a single `ReversiSquare` that resizes with the scene (shown in Listing 7-12).

Listing 7-12. *Wrapper Script to Show a ReversiSquare That Resizes with the Scene*

```
var scene:Scene;
scene = Scene {
    width: 200
    height: 200
    content: [
        ReversiSquare {
            width: bind scene.width
            height: bind scene.height
        }
    ]
}
```

Running the completed class produces a distinctive board square that dynamically resizes with the window (shown in Figure 7-10).

Figure 7-10. *Single Reversi square that resizes with the window*

Building a Resizable Reversi Piece

Creating a Reversi playing piece is done very similarly to how you created a square in the previous section. Your class should extend CustomNode and Resizable, return reasonable defaults for the preferred width and height, and override layoutBounds to immediately update when the width or height changes:

```
public class ReversiPiece extends CustomNode, Resizable {
  override function getPrefWidth(height) {30.0}
  override function getPrefHeight(width) {30.0}

  override var layoutBounds = bind lazy BoundingBox {
      minX: 0
      minY: 0
      width: width
      height: height
  }
}
```

However, you also need to be able to handle black and white playing pieces, as well as provide some scaling capabilities so the playing piece does not touch the edges of the square:

```
  public var owner:Owner;
  public var scale = 1.0;
```

Also, the create function is a little more complicated due to the RadialGradients and Reflection:

```
  override function create() {
    Ellipse {
      transforms: bind Transform.scale(scale, scale)
      layoutX: bind width / 2
      layoutY: bind height / 2
```

```
      radiusX: bind width / 2
      radiusY: bind height / 2
      fill: bind if (owner == Owner.WHITE) {
        RadialGradient {
          stops: [
            Stop {offset: 0.4, color: Color.WHITE}
            Stop {offset: 0.9, color: Color.GRAY}
            Stop {offset: 1.0, color: Color.DARKGRAY}
          ]
        }
      } else {
        RadialGradient {
          stops: [
            Stop {offset: 0.0, color: Color.WHITE}
            Stop {offset: 0.6, color: Color.BLACK}
          ]
        }
      }
      stroke: Color.color(0.3, 0.3, 0.3)
    }
  }
```

To demonstrate the finished product, you need to make a few additions to the previous sample application to overlay the Reversi piece. The easiest way to accomplish this is to refactor the Scene to use a Stack layout to place the Reversi piece on top of the square, as shown in Listing 7-13.

Listing 7-13. *Wrapper Application That Displays a Reversi Square with a Playing Piece on Top*

```
var scene:Scene;
scene = Scene {
  width: 200
  height: 200
  content: Stack {
    width: bind scene.width
    height: bind scene.height
    content: [
      ReversiSquare {}
      ReversiPiece {
        owner: Owner.WHITE
        scale: 0.7
      }
    ]
  }
}
```

Figure 7-11 shows the completed application with both white and black pieces displayed side by side.

Figure 7-11. *One Reversi square with a white playing piece on it, and another with a black piece*

Creating a Grid Layout Container

Container layouts are a very powerful feature in the JavaFX language and are the foundation for building a modular user interface. The goal of this section is to build a simple grid layout that will serve as the first version of the Reversi playing grid and take advantage of the resizable nodes that you built in the previous chapter.

Understanding the Geometry API

Before building your first layout container, it will be helpful to learn a bit more about the order in which JavaFX applies transforms and effects.

Earlier in the chapter we introduced you to the layoutBounds variable on the Node class to determine the position and size of a given node for layout purposes. There are three different bounds variables on the Node class, each with a very distinct usage (shown in Table 7-12).

Table 7-12. *Node Variables That Represent Different Logical Boundaries*

Access	Name	Type	Description
public-read protected	layoutBounds	Rectangle2D	Raw boundary in the local coordinate system
public-read	boundsInLocal	Rectangle2D	Boundary that should be used for layout calculations, which includes effect and clip
public-read	boundsInParent	Rectangle2D	Boundary in the parent coordinate system, which includes effect, clip, and all transforms

All of the nodes in an application are held in a hierarchical tree within the JavaFX scene graph. To know which boundary is the correct one to use in different situations, it helps to understand the order of scene graph operations in JavaFX.

The first scene graph operation starts with the current Node, which is rendered at a specific position and size according to its variables. The second step is that any effects set on the Node are applied, and may affect the size and position of the Node. The third step is to apply the clip region if set. The fourth step is to apply any transforms set on the Node. In the fifth, sixth, and seventh steps, the scale, rotate, and translate variables from Node are applied (in that order). These steps are illustrated graphically in Figure 7-12.

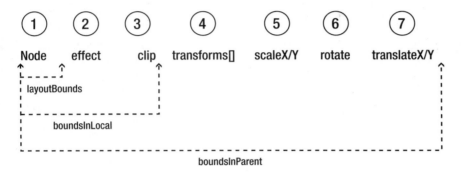

Figure 7-12. *Order of Node operations*

As shown in the illustration, layoutBounds is simply the untransformed bounds of the contained node, boundsInLocal includes the effect and clip, and boundsInParent includes scale, rotation, and translation.

In addition to these bounds, it is often necessary to get the boundary with respect to the scene. While there is no variable available to bind to for this dimension, it is possible to calculate the screen bounds by using the localToScene method to transform the boundsInLocal variable as shown here:

```
def boundsInScene = node.localToScene(node.boundsInLocal)
```

One of the differences between layoutBounds and all the other bounds variables is that it can be updated by subclasses. Doing this is useful to set layout bounds that are larger than the Node bounds, and also to update the layoutBounds in a CustomNode whenever the width and height change as demonstrated in "Building a Resizable Reversi Square."

Another interesting point is that all of the effect and transformation operations are excluded from layoutBounds. This allows interesting visual effects, such as animations that scale or pulse nodes without disrupting the node layout. If you want the effects and transformations to be included in the layout, simply wrap the Node in a CustomNode or Group and they will be treated as part of the layoutBounds of the outer container.

Throughout the rest of this chapter we will continue to use layoutBounds for all layout operations. This is the recommended practice, and part of the contract for Container implementations.

Extending the Container Class

In JavaFX you create a layout container by extending the abstract javafx.scene.layout. Container class, which in turn extends both Group and Resizable. However, unlike a Group, which aggregates the collective bounds of its children, a Container has its own width and height and constrains its children to fit within its bounds.

The `Container` class has no variables itself but inherits key functionality from `Group`, its superclass `Parent`, and `Resizable`. The minimal variables you will need to use to create a new Container are listed in Table 7-13.

Table 7-13. *Superclass Variables and Functions Required to Implement a Container*

Access	Name	Type	Inherited From	Description
public	width	Number	Resizable	Defines the width of the Container
public	height	Number	Resizable	Defines the height of the Container
public	content	Node[]	Group	Children that need to be constrained
protected	doLayout()	returns Void	Parent	Function called to perform layout

To create a new layout, you need to perform the following steps:

1. Create a new class that extends `Container`.

2. Override the `doLayout` function by iterating over the `Nodes` in the `content` sequence and setting their position and size

3. Optionally implement the `getPrefWidth`, `getPrefHeight`, and other `Resizable` functions to return the proper values for the `Container` (`Container` provides a default implementation of `getPrefWidth` and `getPrefHeight` that returns the maximum preferred bounds of all the children).

The following code shows a minimal class stub that is the start of any layout container:

```
public class GridLayout extends Container {
  override function doLayout():Void {
  }
}
```

This class has all the necessary elements by extending `Container` and overriding the `doLayout` method; however, it does nothing to its contents, so it will behave exactly the same as a `Group`. The next step is to implement the `doLayout` function, which will constrain the children.

The Grid Layout Algorithm

Before you can implement this method, you need a couple of additional pieces of information that will help you determine where to place each of the pieces.

- The number of rows and the number of columns in the `Grid`

- The row and column index of each `Node` in the `Grid`

To get the number of rows and columns, add two new public variables to the GridLayout class that will be set on initialization:

```
public-init var numColumns:Integer;

public-init var numRows:Integer;
```

Determining the row and column index requires creating a new Cell class that your ReversiPiece can inherit from to include the row and column coordinates:

```
public mixin class Cell {
  public var x:Integer;
  public var y:Integer;
}
```

■**Note** We have chosen to make Cell a mixin so that it can be added as an attribute to existing Node classes.

Finally, to position the cells you need to make use of the static helper functions on Container. While there are dozens of different functions available to facilitate writing layouts, the more commonly used ones are described in Table 7-14.

Table 7-14. *Static Functions on Container That Help with Content Layout*

Access	Signature	Description
public	getManaged(content:Node[]):Object[]	Returns all the Nodes that have managed set to true
public	positionNode(node:Node, x:Number, y:Number):Void	Moves the node to the given x and y layout coordinates
public	positionNode(node:Node, areaX:Number, areaY:Number, areaW:Number, areaH:Number, hpos:HPos, vpos:VPos):Void	Positions the Node within the given area, using the given hpos and vpos if the Node's layoutInfo does not specify
public	setNodeHeight(node:Node, height:Number):Boolean	Resizes the Node's height if it is Resizable and not bound
public	setNodeWidth(node:Node, width:Number):Boolean	Resizes the Node's width if it is Resizable and not bound
public	resizeNode(node:Node, width:Number, height:Number):Boolean	Resizes the Node's height and width if it is Resizable and not bound
public	layoutNode(node:Node, x:Number, y:Number, width:Number, height:Number):Boolean	Positions and resizes the Node and returns true if any resizing occurred
public	layoutNode(node:Node, areaX:Number, areaY:Number, areaW:Number, areaH:Number, hpos:HPos, vpos:VPos):Boolean	Positions and resizes the Node to fit the given area, using the provided default hpos and vpos, and returning true if any resizing occurred

All nodes now have a managed Boolean flag that defaults to true but can be set to false to indicate that this Node does not participate in layout. To make this easier to work with, Container provides a getManaged function that will only return nodes that have managed equal to true. The remaining methods all provide different ways of setting the position and bounds of the children from the doLayout function.

Now you have everything you need to finish the implementation of doLayout in the GridLayout class. That basic algorithm is to

- Iterate over all the managed Nodes in the content

- Cast each Node to a Cell

- Position each Node in the center of the corresponding grid cell using layoutNode

which can be implemented as follows:

```
public var nodeHPos = HPos.CENTER;
public var nodeVPos = VPos.CENTER;
override function doLayout():Void {
  def cellWidth = width / numColumns;
  def cellHeight = height / numRows;
  for (node in getManaged(content)) {
    def cell = node as Cell;
    layoutNode(node, cell.x * cellWidth, cell.y * cellHeight,
            cellWidth, cellHeight, nodeHPos, nodeVPos);
  }
}
```

To parallel the public variables of the built-in layouts, we have created a nodeHPos and nodeVPos variable that are used as the defaults for the layoutNode function and default to CENTER.

Binding the Layout to the Model

The final step is to add the GridLayout to your ReversiBoard UI to place each of the ReversiPieces on screen. To accomplish this, you first have to update the main UI function to call a new function that builds the grid layout you created in the previous section:

```
def title = createTitle();
def grid = createReversiGrid();
def score = createScoreBoxes();
```

Next you have to create the createReversiGrid() method that builds the Reversi grid. This method will use the GridLayout class twice, once to lay out the board and another time to place the pieces.

To create the 8×8 grid, you can use a simple nested for loop that iterates over the BOARD_ SIZE for both the x and y coordinates:

```
GridLayout {
  numColumns: ReversiModel.BOARD_SIZE
  numRows: ReversiModel.BOARD_SIZE
  content: for (x in [0..ReversiModel.BOARD_SIZE - 1],
                y in [0..ReversiModel.BOARD_SIZE - 1]) {
    ReversiSquare {
      x: x
      y: y
    }
  }
}
```

Laying out the Reversi pieces requires querying the model to check which cells are occupied by which player, but is otherwise very similar:

```
GridLayout {
  numColumns: ReversiModel.BOARD_SIZE
  numRows: ReversiModel.BOARD_SIZE
  content: bind for (row in model.board,
                     cell in row.cells where cell != Owner.NONE) {
    ReversiPiece {
      scale: 0.7
      owner: cell
      x: indexof cell
      y: indexof row
    }
  }
}
```

Finally, you can wrap the preceding two blocks in a Stack and return them from the bound createReversiGrid method:

```
bound function createReversiGrid() {
  Stack {
    content: [
      GridLayout {
        // insert ReversiSquare creation here
      }
      GridLayout {
        // insert ReversiPiece creation here
      }
    ]
  }
}
```

Now running the Reversi application shows us our starting position with two black and two white pieces played, as shown in Figure 7-13.

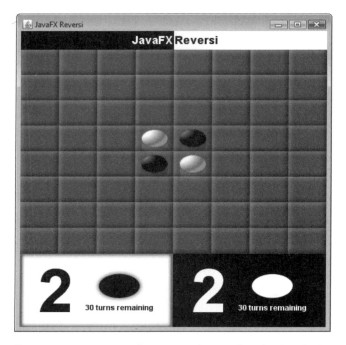

Figure 7-13. *Reversi application with a Grid to display the board and pieces*

A New Perspective on Reversi

The Reversi application is starting to shape up, but is in need of a little perspective to make it more visually appealing. JavaFX ships with a very useful `PerspectiveTransform` effect that lets you create faux three-dimensional effects on any `Node`. However, one of the limitations is that `PerspectiveTransform` does not map mouse events, and thus can't be used for interactive user interfaces.

Instead we will show you how you can create a perspective layout that uses an algorithm similar to the `PerspectiveTransform` effect but treats each node as a separate entity in a grid, thus allowing dynamic placement and mouse interaction.

The Perspective Layout Algorithm

Perspective transformations are a special class of transformations where the straightness of lines is maintained, but unlike affine transformations, the parallelism of lines is not preserved. This is helpful when your aim is to create a sense of depth where objects recede into the background as they get farther away.

The basic technique for perspective transformation is to map the coordinates from the source plane, which in our case is a 2D grid, into the destination plane that is distorted to add perspective. Figure 7-14 shows what is happening visually in this mapping from source to destination coordinates.

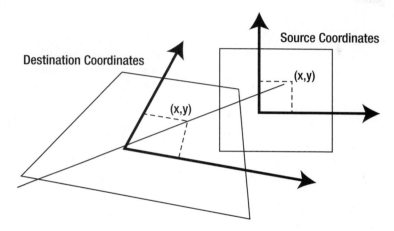

Figure 7-14. *Mapping from source (unit) to destination (transformed) coordinates*

The core of the perspective layout is a PerspectiveTransformer class that does some simple matrix math to convert from a unit square to an arbitrary quadrilateral. The input parameters to the class consist of the upperLeft, upperRight, lowerLeft, and lowerRight corners, as shown in Listing 7-14.

Listing 7-14. *Public Parameters of the PerspectiveTransformer Class*

```
public class PerspectiveTransformer {
  public-init var upperLeft:Point2D;
  public-init var upperRight:Point2D;
  public-init var lowerLeft:Point2D;
  public-init var lowerRight:Point2D;
  ...
}
```

To store the matrix that will be used to do the transformation, nine variables are used that are named by their row and column in the transformation matrix:

```
var m00:Number;
var m01:Number;
var m02:Number;
var m10:Number;
var m11:Number;
var m12:Number;
var m20:Number;
var m21:Number;
var m22:Number;
```

These parameters would be represented in matrix form as

$$
\begin{bmatrix}
m00 & m01 & m02 \\
m10 & m11 & m12 \\
m20 & m21 & m22
\end{bmatrix}
$$

The matrix values needed to convert from a unit square to the given quadrilateral are calculated upon initialization. It is beyond the scope of this book to derive the perspective transform algorithm, but if you are interested there are references at the end of this chapter that describe the mathematics behind this. The code that performs this algorithm is shown in Listing 7-15.

Listing 7-15. *Algorithm for Building a Matrix to Convert from a Unit Square to a Quadrilateral*

```
function buildUnitToQuadMatrix() {
    def dx1 = upperRight.x - lowerRight.x;
    def dx2 = lowerLeft.x - lowerRight.x;
    def dx3 = upperLeft.x - upperRight.x + lowerRight.x - lowerLeft.x;
    def dy1 = upperRight.y - lowerRight.y;
    def dy2 = lowerLeft.y - lowerRight.y;
    def dy3 = upperLeft.y - upperRight.y + lowerRight.y - lowerLeft.y;

    def inverseDeterminant = 1.0/(dx1*dy2 - dx2*dy1);
    m20 = (dx3*dy2 - dx2*dy3)*inverseDeterminant;
    m21 = (dx1*dy3 - dx3*dy1)*inverseDeterminant;
    m22 = 1.0;
    m00 = upperRight.x - upperLeft.x + m20*upperRight.x;
    m01 = lowerLeft.x - upperLeft.x + m21*lowerLeft.x;
    m02 = upperLeft.x;
    m10 = upperRight.y - upperLeft.y + m20*upperRight.y;
    m11 = lowerLeft.y - upperLeft.y + m21*lowerLeft.y;
    m12 = upperLeft.y;
}
```

Finally, to calculate the transformed value of a given input point on the unit square, there is a transform method. This is what you will need to call for each of the corners of the components of the PerspectiveLayout class in order to calculate bounds in the transformed coordinate space. Now that the matrix has already been populated, executing the transform is simply a matter of multiplying your source coordinates (x, y, 1) by the matrix, as shown in the following equation:

$$
\begin{bmatrix}
x^1 \\
y^1 \\
w
\end{bmatrix}
=
\begin{bmatrix}
m_{00} & m_{01} & m_{02} \\
m_{10} & m_{11} & m_{12} \\
m_{20} & m_{21} & m_{22}
\end{bmatrix}
\times
\begin{bmatrix}
x \\
y \\
1
\end{bmatrix}
=
\begin{bmatrix}
m_{00}x & m_{01}y & m_{02} \\
m_{10}x & m_{11}y & m_{12} \\
m_{20}x & m_{21}y & m_{22}
\end{bmatrix}
$$

and then converting the resulting destination coordinates back into nonhomogeneous coordinates by dividing x^1 and y^1 by w:

$$X = x^1 / w$$

$$Y = y^1 / w$$

The code that executes this logic is shown in Listing 7-16.

Listing 7-16. *Transformation of Source Coordinates to Destination Coordinates Using Matrix Math*

```
public function transform(point:Point2D):Point2D {
  def w = m20 * point.x + m21 * point.y + m22;
  return Point2D {
      x: (m00 * point.x + m01 * point.y + m02) / w
      y: (m10 * point.x + m11 * point.y + m12) / w
  }
}
```

As a convenience, this code uses a javafx.geometry.Point2D object to wrap the x and y coordinates in a single value. This class is used throughout the JavaFX API as a declarative replacement for the java.awt.geom.Point2D class, and has a very simple API as shown in Table 7-15.

Table 7-15. *Instance Variables of the java.awt.geom.Point2D Class*

Access	Name	Type	Default	Description
public-init	x	Number	0.0	The x coordinate of the point
public-init	y	Number	0.0	The y coordinate of the point

Now that you have a basic transformation library for doing perspective transformations, it is time to apply this library to the perspective layout algorithm to build the Reversi board.

Creating the Perspective Layout Class

Now that you have done the heavy lifting of creating a PerspectiveTransformer infrastructure class, you'll find that the perspective layout implementation is similar to the earlier grid layout you worked on. To reiterate the basic steps:

1. Create a new class that extends Container.

2. Implement the doLayout function by iterating over the Nodes in the content sequence and setting their position and dimensions.

3. Call requestLayout() when the layout inputs change to force an update.

Listing 7-17 shows a bare-bones skeleton for the PerspectiveLayout class that sets up a basic layout Container and creates an empty layout function.

Listing 7-17. *PerspectiveLayout Container Skeleton*

```
public class PerspectiveLayout extends Container {
  public var upperLeft:Point2D on replace {
    requestLayout();
  }
  public var upperRight:Point2D on replace {
    requestLayout();
  }
  public var lowerLeft:Point2D on replace {
    requestLayout();
  }
  public var lowerRight:Point2D on replace {
    requestLayout();
  }

  public-init var numColumns:Integer on replace {
    requestLayout();
  }

  public-init var numRows:Integer on replace {
    requestLayout();
  }

  public var cells:Cell[];

  override var content = bind cells as Node[];

  public var perspectiveScale = false on replace {
    requestLayout();
  }

  function doLayout():Void {
  }
}
```

The public variables that users of this class will access are listed in Table 7-16 along with their descriptions. This table will serve as requirements for your implementation of the PerspectiveLayout class.

Table 7-16. *Public Variables of the PerspectiveLayout Class*

Access	Name	Type	Description
public	upperLeft	Point2D	The upper-left corner of the perspective layout bounds
public	upperRight	Point2D	The upper-right corner of the perspective layout bounds
public	lowerLeft	Point2D	The lower-left corner of the perspective layout bounds
public	lowerRight	Point2D	The lower-right corner of the perspective layout bounds
public-init	numColumns	Integer	The total number of columns for the grid of children
public-init	numRows	Integer	The total number of rows for the grid of children
public-init	cells	Cell[]	List of child cells that will be processed by this layout
public	perspectiveScale	Boolean	True if the children should have a PerspectiveTransform effect applied that fills their transformed bounding box

The four Point2D parameters are fairly explanatory and mimic the same functionality of the PerspectiveTransform effect class. Also, numColumns and numRows should be familiar from the earlier GridLayout implementation. All of these input variables have an on replace trigger that calls requestLayout() to force an update when they change.

The cells variable is simply a proxy for the content array that enforces all added nodes be of type Cell. It is bound to content and will later be used as an extension point.

The heart of the PerspectiveLayout is the perspectiveScale variable. If left as false, nodes that are laid out by this class will simply be moved to the approximate location of their transformed cell and resized appropriately, but their appearance will not be changed. This variable is what you will use to position the ReversiPieces in the grid so they look like they are floating on top of the game board.

If perspectiveScale is set to true, nodes that are laid out by this class will have a PerspectiveTransform effect applied to them that matches up their corners precisely with the bounding box of their cell. This transformation is what you will use to build a Reversi board from individual squares so that it appears as a single, level playing surface similar to the untransformed version.

Now that we have a basic approach, it is time to write the doLayout algorithm that brings all of this together. First you need to create a PerspectiveTransformer instance that passes in the bounding corners (there's no need to bind the parameters since it is cheap to create a new instance each time this method is called):

```
override function doLayout():Void {
  def transform = PerspectiveTransformer {
    upperLeft: upperLeft
    upperRight: upperRight
    lowerLeft: lowerLeft
    lowerRight: lowerRight
  }
```

Next you need to iterate through all the nodes in the content sequence, casting them to a `Cell`:

```
for (node in getManaged(cells as Node[])) {
  def cell = node as Cell;
```

Now you can call the transform class with the x and y coordinates of the `Cell` to get the transformed corners of the `Cell`'s bounding box:

```
// initialize as Number to avoid conversion for math later
def x:Number = cell.x;
def y:Number = cell.y;
def upperLeftCorner = transform.transform(Point2D {
  x: x / numColumns
  y: y / numRows
});
def upperRightCorner = transform.transform(Point2D {
  x: (x + 1) / numColumns
  y: y / numRows
});
def lowerLeftCorner = transform.transform(Point2D {
  x: x / numColumns
  y: (y + 1) / numRows
});
def lowerRightCorner = transform.transform(Point2D {
  x: (x + 1) / numColumns
  y: (y + 1) / numRows
});
```

■**Note** Because we are dealing with a unit square, all the values are fractional, so it simplifies the math to assign x and y to Number types. If you didn't do this, each time you use x or y in the numerator you would have to cast it to a Number to avoid integer truncation.

This code takes us to the core of the algorithm. When the user wants to apply a `PerspectiveTransform` to each `Node` in the grid, you can let the `PerspectiveTransform` effect take care of all the heavy lifting by simply giving it these four corners:

```
if (perspectiveScale) {
  def resizable = cell as Resizable;
  cell.effect = PerspectiveTransform {
    ulx: upperLeftCorner.x
    uly: upperLeftCorner.y
    urx: upperRightCorner.x
    ury: upperRightCorner.y
```

```
      llx: lowerLeftCorner.x
      lly: lowerLeftCorner.y
      lrx: lowerRightCorner.x
      lry: lowerRightCorner.y
    }
    resizable.width = resizable.getPrefWidth(-1);
    resizable.height = resizable.getPrefHeight(-1);
```

If no PerspectiveTransform is applied, you can simply center the node in the grid cell. This code makes use of the layoutNode function to handle the alignment by providing an area and default position of CENTER:

```
  } else {
    def resizable = cell as Resizable;
    def centerPoint = transform.transform(Point2D {
      x: (x + 0.5) / numColumns
      y: (y + 0.5) / numRows
    });
    def transformedWidth = (lowerRightCorner.x - lowerLeftCorner.x) / 2 +
                           (upperRightCorner.x - upperLeftCorner.x) / 2;
    def transformedHeight = (lowerLeftCorner.y - upperLeftCorner.y) / 2 +
                            (lowerRightCorner.y - upperRightCorner.y) / 2;
    def transformedX = centerPoint.x - transformedWidth / 2;
    def transformedY = centerPoint.y - transformedHeight / 2;
    layoutNode(node, transformedX, transformedY, transformedWidth,
               transformedHeight, HPos.CENTER, VPos.CENTER);
  }
 }
}
```

Some points to highlight about this algorithm are

- The width and height are approximated based on the transformed size of the square.

- The transform algorithm is used to calculate the precise center of the square.

- The built-in layoutNode() function automatically centers the Nodes for us, simplifying the math.

And that completes the PerspectiveLayout class. In the next section we will show you how to integrate this layout with the Reversi application to display a transformed playing board.

Integrating the Perspective Layout

It is time to put your new PerspectiveLayout class to use on the Reversi application. Following the patterns introduced during the integration of the grid layout, you can build a bound function that cleanly abstracts the PerspectiveLayout from the rest of the UI.

Doing so requires a small addition to the Scene contents. To make the board appear to float over the background, we will add it to the end of the content array and set its size to overlap with the title and score box. The changes required are in bold:

```
def title = createTitle();
def background = createBackground();
def board = createReversiBoard();
def score = createScoreBoxes();
...
    content: [
      title,
      background,
      score,
      board
    ]
    onLayout: function() {
      def boardHeight = scene.height - titleHeight - scoreHeight;
      Container.layoutNode(title, 0, 0, scene.width, titleHeight);
      Container.layoutNode(background, 0, titleHeight, scene.width, boardHeight);
      Container.layoutNode(board, 0, titleHeight-5, scene.width, boardHeight+25);
      Container.layoutNode(score, 0, scene.height - scoreHeight,
                               scene.width, scoreHeight);
    }
```

The next step is to implement the `createReversiBoard` method. This starts with a stack declaration:

```
bound function createReversiBoard(x:Number, y:Number, width:Number, height:Number) {
  var stack:Stack;
  stack = Stack {
```

You will need to implement two perspective layouts, one for the playing board built out of `ReversiSquares` and one for the `ReversiPieces`. Since both of these need the same layout bounds, you can setup the corners as a `Point2D` object first:

```
    def upperLeft = bind Point2D {
      x: width / 8
      y: height / 12
    }
    def upperRight = bind Point2D {
      x: width * 7/12
      y: 0
    }
    def lowerLeft = bind Point2D {
      x: 0
      y: height
    }
    def lowerRight = bind Point2D {
      x: width
      y: height * 2/3
    }
```

■**Note** Because the `Point2D` class is immutable, you can't bind the x and y values and instead have to bind the entire class so a new instance gets created.

■**Tip** The choices for the corner points are completely up to you. Feel free to experiment once you get the UI to successfully display.

Since you want the board to display below the pieces, that has be to be added to the content sequence first:

```
content: [
  PerspectiveLayout {
    cache: true
    width: bind stack.width
    height: bind stack.height
    upperLeft: bind upperLeft
    upperRight: bind upperRight
    lowerLeft: bind lowerLeft
    lowerRight: bind lowerRight
    numColumns: ReversiModel.BOARD_SIZE
    numRows: ReversiModel.BOARD_SIZE
    perspectiveScale: true
    cells: for (x in [0..ReversiModel.BOARD_SIZE - 1],
                y in [0..ReversiModel.BOARD_SIZE - 1]) {
      ReversiSquare {
        x: x
        y: y
      }
    }
  },
```

The creation of the `PerspectiveLayout` for the pieces is almost identical, except for the additional logic to filter out cells without an owner via a where clause and some extra variables to initialize the size and position of the pieces:

```
PerspectiveLayout {
  width: bind stack.width
  height: bind stack.height
  upperLeft: bind upperLeft
  upperRight: bind upperRight
  lowerLeft: bind lowerLeft
  lowerRight: bind lowerRight
  numColumns: ReversiModel.BOARD_SIZE
  numRows: ReversiModel.BOARD_SIZE
```

```
        content: bind for (row in model.board,
                           cell in row.cells where cell != Owner.NONE) {
            ReversiPiece {
                owner: cell
                translateY: -3
                scaleX: .8
                scaleY: .8
                x: indexof cell
                y: indexof row
            }
          }
        }
      ]
    }
}
```

When run, the new Reversi application will display a very slick-looking perspective transformed board, as shown in Figure 7-15.

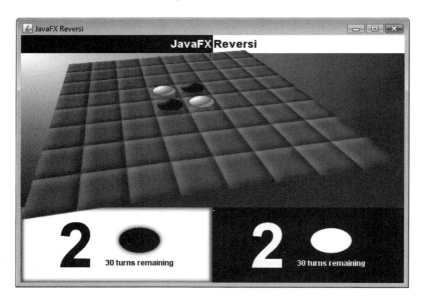

Figure 7-15. *The Reversi application using a perspective transform layout*

Notice that the application remains fully resizable even though you have significantly changed the layout and design of the grid. This is the advantage of using Containers to lay out complex user interfaces that need to be very dynamic.

Bringing Reversi to Life

Up to this point we have been singularly focused on layouts, which is important but doesn't make for a very interesting game. However, the beauty of using dynamic layout is that with a few enhancements to the game algorithm, we can turn this static application into a dynamic, playable game.

Highlighting Legal Moves

The first step of a playable game algorithm is to make sure that pieces can only be placed on legal squares. Rather than simply implement an algorithm in the backend, we will take this as an opportunity to add a feature to the application where it shows you all of the next available moves.

Going back to the Reversi game rules, a move is only valid in the following circumstances:

- There is not already another piece at the same location.

- The piece is placed adjacent to a piece of the opposite color, and on that same line, there is another piece of the same color on the opposite end that would allow a flip of one or more of the opposing player's pieces.

To start with, you need to add a `legalMove` function to the model class that checks if the cell is empty and then verifies all eight directions around a given `Cell`:

```
public bound function legalMove(cell:Cell):Boolean {
  board[cell.y].cells[cell.x] == Owner.NONE and (
    canFlip(cell, 0, -1, turn) or
    canFlip(cell, -1, -1, turn) or
    canFlip(cell, -1, 0, turn) or
    canFlip(cell, -1, 1, turn) or
    canFlip(cell, 0, 1, turn) or
    canFlip(cell, 1, 1, turn) or
    canFlip(cell, 1, 0, turn) or
    canFlip(cell, 1, -1, turn)
  )
}
```

Note We have chosen to implement all the public model functions as bound functions to simplify updates from the UI. This allows the JavaFX compiler to efficiently defer updates until the playing board changes, but restricts the use of any code that would introduce side effects, such as variable definitions or the increment operator.

The canFlip method will validate the second condition for the given direction indicated by the xDir/yDir arguments and the player whose turn is indicated. The first if condition in the method checks to see if the cell in that direction is of the opposite color. If the next cell is of the opposite color, it enters a while loop to handle the case where there may be multiple pieces of the same color that can be flipped together. Finally, the algorithm checks the last piece to see if it is of the current player's color:

```
function canFlip(cell:Cell, xDir:Integer, yDir:Integer, turn:Owner) {
  def opposite = turn.opposite();
  var x = cell.x + xDir;
  var y = cell.y + yDir;
  if (board[y] != null and board[y].cells[x] == opposite) {
    while (board[y] != null and board[y].cells[x] == opposite) {
      x += xDir;
      y += yDir;
    }
    return board[y] != null and board[y].cells[x] == turn;
  }
  return false;
}
```

The last step in highlighting legal moves is to wire the legalMove model function up to the squares. This involves two changes in the ReversiSquare class. First is the introduction of a model variable:

```
public var model:ReversiModel;
```

That's followed by a bind against the legalMove method that changes the fill color:

```
Rectangle {
  effect:  Lighting {
    light: DistantLight {
      azimuth: -135
      elevation: 30
    }
  }
  width: bind width
  height: bind height
  def legalMoveColor = Color.DODGERBLUE.ofTheWay(Color.BLACK, .3) as Color;
  fill: bind if (model.legalMove(this)) legalMoveColor
              else Color.BURLYWOOD
}
```

Also, don't forget to update the Main class to pass the model to the ReversiSquare instances upon creation:

```
ReversiSquare {
  model: model
  x: x
  y: y
}
```

Now upon running the application, it correctly highlights the same four moves for black that were described in the "Board Layout and Basic Rules" section, as shown in Figure 7-16.

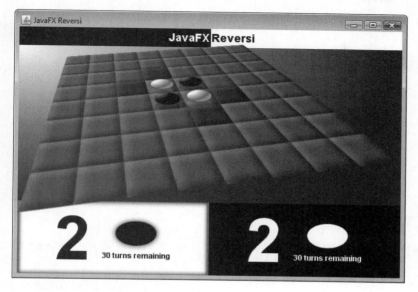

Figure 7-16. *Reversi application highlighting the available moves for black's first turn*

Perspective Mouse Interaction

The next level of interactivity for the application is to allow the user to highlight or click on cells in order to make their move. Normally this would just be a matter of adding event handlers to each of the squares, but we are using the `PerspectiveTransform` effect to align the squares, which has undefined behavior for mouse interaction.

Note If you are using any other transformations such as scale, rotate, or shear, the mouse events would be automatically transformed by JavaFX. This event interception logic is only needed due to the limitations of the `PerspectiveTransform` class.

To provide mouse interaction for the squares, we are going to enhance the perspective layout to trap and forward all mouse events to the cell that is at the given coordinates.

The first change that is required is to make sure that the `PerspectiveLayout` class traps all the mouse events that occur within its bounds. Because the transformed squares are not detected by the JavaFX event system, you need to create an invisible node that traps all events. The easiest way to do this is by adding an invisible `Rectangle` to the back of the layout's content:

```
override var content = bind [
  Rectangle {
    width: bind width
    height: bind height
    fill: Color.TRANSPARENT
  },
  cells as Node[]
];
```

■Tip It is a very useful pattern in `Container` layouts to create a pseudo-content that the user assigns to (in this case, cells) so that the real content can be utilized by the layout container to add additional `Nodes`. Make sure to document this in your API so that users do not change the value of content, thus breaking the layout algorithm.

The next step is to add the mouse event forwarding in. The four mouse events that we will support are shown in Table 7-17.

Table 7-17. *Node Mouse Events Forwarded by Perspective Layout*

Access	Name	Type	Description
public	onMouseClicked	function(:MouseEvent):Void	Function that gets called on mouse clicks (press and release)
public	onMouseEntered	function(:MouseEvent):Void	Function that gets called when the mouse enters the Node
public	onMouseExited	function(:MouseEvent):Void	Function that gets called when the mouse exits the Node
public	onMouseMoved	function(:MouseEvent):Void	Function that gets called when the mouse moves within the Node

Before you can implement any of these functions, you need a mechanism for caching the bounds of all the cells. The `javafx.scene.shape.Polygon` class provides a convenient data structure and also the necessary point containment functions:

```
var boundingPolygons:Polygon[];
```

Populating this sequence can easily be done within the `doLayout()` function, which conveniently gets called any time the bounds change. To build a new `boundingPolygons` sequence each time `perspectiveLayout` is called, you can take advantage of the `for` loop by using the return value:

```
boundingPolygons = for (cell in cells) {
```

which will be a sequence of the last value contained in the loop (newly added code is in bold):

```
      layoutNode(node, transformedX, transformedY, transformedWidth,
               transformedHeight, HPos.CENTER, VPos.CENTER);
    }
    Polygon {
      points: [
        upperLeftCorner.x, upperLeftCorner.y,
        upperRightCorner.x, upperRightCorner.y,
        lowerRightCorner.x, lowerRightCorner.y,
        lowerLeftCorner.x, lowerLeftCorner.y,
      ]
    }
  }
```

The next step is to use the cached bounds to figure out what node is at a given location. This is easily calculated by iterating over the list of bounds and using the contains operator on Polygon:

```
function nodeAt(x:Number, y:Number):Node {
  for (b in boundingPolygons) {
    if (b.contains(x, y)) {
      return cells[indexof b];
    }
  }
  return null;
}
```

Tip The preceding code uses a very common pattern of lock-step sequence traversal. Even though there is no strict relationship between cells and boundingPolygons, because we created the Polygons by iterating over cells, it is easy to pick out the cell that corresponds to a given Polygon by using the JavaFX indexof operator.

The final step is to implement the actual event listeners that will delegate to the nodes. The onMouseClicked handler is the easiest to implement, because it simply passes the event through:

```
override var onMouseClicked = function(e) {
  nodeAt(e.x, e.y).onMouseClicked(e);
}
```

The remaining functions need to keep track of the last node that the cursor was in so that they can create synthetic enter and exit events as the user moves the mouse:

```
var nodeIn:Node;
override var onMouseEntered = function(e) {
  nodeIn = nodeAt(e.x, e.y);
  nodeIn.onMouseEntered(e);
}
override var onMouseExited = function(e) {
  nodeIn.onMouseExited(e);
  nodeIn = null;
}
override var onMouseMoved = function(e) {
  def nodeOver = nodeAt(e.x, e.y);
  if (nodeIn != nodeOver) {
    nodeIn.onMouseExited(e);
    nodeOver.onMouseEntered(e);
    nodeIn = nodeOver;
  }
  nodeOver.onMouseMoved(e);
}
```

Now all of the mouse events that you have captured will automatically forward to the appropriate Node, thus enabling interaction with the Grid.

Highlighting the Active Cell

The simplest example of board interaction is to highlight the current cell that the user has moused over. Rather than highlighting cells that are not playable, you can take advantage of the legalMove() function you defined earlier to only highlight cells that are active.

For the highlight we are going to use a simple Rectangle with a blue stroke to outline the cell the cursor is over. Listing 7-18 shows the additions to the CustomNode create() function in bold.

Listing 7-18. *Additions to the ReversiSquare create() Method to Enable Highlighting*

```
var highlightRectangle:Rectangle;
override function create():Node {
  Group {
    content: [
      Rectangle {
        cache: true
        effect: Lighting {
          light: DistantLight {
            azimuth: -135
            elevation: 30
          }
        }
```

```
        width: bind width
        height: bind height
        def legalMoveColor = Color.DODGERBLUE.ofTheWay(Color.BLACK, .3) as Color;
        fill: bind if (model.legalMove(this)) Color.DODGERBLUE
                    else Color.BURLYWOOD
    }
    highlightRectangle = Rectangle {
        x: 2
        y: 2
        width: bind width - 4
        height: bind height - 4
        stroke: Color.DODGERBLUE
        fill: null
        strokeWidth: 2
        opacity: 0
    }
    ]
  }
}
```

Notice that we also enabled caching on the background rectangle. Doing so will improve performance of the animation, which only affects the foreground rectangle. In addition, adding caching to the entire ReversiSquare class will further improve performance by caching the perspective transform set by the layout:

```
override var cache = true;
```

■**Note** The Node cache variable is an effective mechanism for improving the performance of JavaFX graphics operations at the expense of additional memory.

The opacity of the highlightRectangle referenced in Listing 7-18 will be animated from 0.0 to 1.0 to produce a fade-in effect when the user mouses over the Node. The following code shows the FadeTransition to accomplish this:

```
def highlightTransition = FadeTransition {
    duration: 200ms
    fromValue: 0
    toValue: 1
    node: bind highlightRectangle
}
```

Finally, you need to add in the event listeners that will fire when the user mouses over the Node:

```
public var highlight:Boolean on replace {
  highlightTransition.rate = if (highlight) 1 else -1;
  highlightTransition.play();
}
init {
  onMouseEntered = function(e) {
    if (model.legalMove(this)) {
      highlight = true;
    }
  }
  onMouseExited = function(e) {
    highlight = false;
  }
}
```

When run, the Reversi application now animates a subtle blue outline over the highlighted Node, as shown in Figure 7-17.

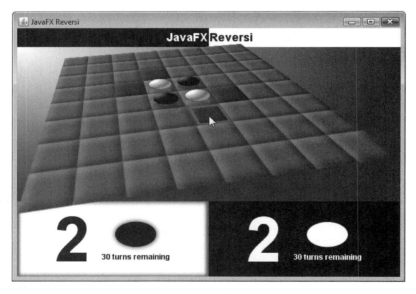

Figure 7-17. *The Reversi application with a highlighted animation over the active cell*

Taking Turns

The last bit of missing functionality in the Reversi application is the ability for players to take turns placing pieces on the board. We already have all the infrastructure needed to accept mouse input and display pieces. All that is needed is a little glue code, plus some model enhancements to finish the game play.

Picking up where we left off in the previous section, the first step is to add an onMouseClicked event handler to the ReversiSquare init method:

```
onMouseClicked = function(e) {
  model.play(this);
  highlight = false;
}
```

This method both calls the model function to play the current turn, and also removes the highlight from the current cell, similar to the onMouseExited event.

The play() function in the model class needs to do several activities for each legal move:

- Set the clicked cell to be owned by the current player

- Flip over captured pieces in any of eight possible directions

- Change the turn to be the opposite player's

An example implementation of the play() method is shown in Listing 7-19.

Listing 7-19. *Example play() Method That Flips Cells in Eight Directions*

```
public function play(cell:Cell):Boolean {
  if (legalMove(cell)) {
    board[cell.y].cells[cell.x] = turn;
    flip(cell, 0, -1, turn);
    flip(cell, -1, -1, turn);
    flip(cell, -1, 0, turn);
    flip(cell, -1, 1, turn);
    flip(cell, 0, 1, turn);
    flip(cell, 1, 1, turn);
    flip(cell, 1, 0, turn);
    flip(cell, 1, -1, turn);
    turn = turn.opposite();
    return true;
  }
  return false;
}
```

Notice that it follows the same pattern as the legalMove() function we defined earlier to determine if any pieces can be flipped. The implementation of the flip method also shares many similarities to the canFlip() method:

```
function flip(cell:Cell, xDir:Integer, yDir:Integer, turn:Owner) {
  if (canFlip(cell, xDir, yDir, turn)) {
    def opposite = turn.opposite();
    var x = cell.x + xDir;
    var y = cell.y + yDir;
    while (board[y] != null and board[y].cells[x] == opposite) {
      board[y].cells[x] = turn;
      x += xDir;
      y += yDir;
    }
  }
}
```

With a completed game algorithm, you can now play a full game with two players at the same computer, as shown in Figure 7-18. Notice that even the turn indicator that you set up at the beginning of the chapter is now properly flipping and indicating the current player.

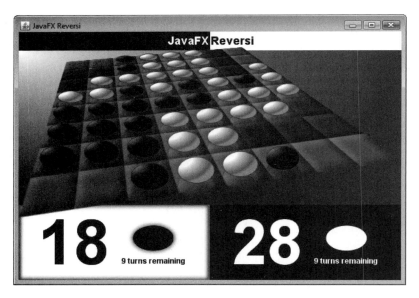

Figure 7-18. *Black's turn in the Final 2006 World Othello Championship*

Besides being a great example of the game in action, Figure 7-18 is also a replay of the famous 2006 World Othello Championship between Caroline Sandberg Odsell (black) and Hideshi Tamenori (white). What should black's next move be to win 37-27? See the Resources section for the answer.

Additional Game Enhancements

The Reversi application that was developed in this chapter is completely dynamic and flexible both in layout and structure, so it is time to take advantage of this and push the limits of your coding skills.

Here are some coding challenges that you can use to take the Reversi application from a well-designed tutorial into a full-fledged application:

- There is one rule that we neglected to implement, which is skipping turns. If, and only if, a player has no available options to play, then the next player can go. Try implementing a facility that automatically detects if there are no legal moves and skips a turn.

- While the PerspectiveLayout algorithm is very dynamic, other than resizing the window we do not take advantage of this characteristic. Try implementing a start-up animation that tilts the board as the application opens.

- Playing against another player on the same computer is not nearly as interesting as playing against a remote opponent. After reading some of the later chapters on backend integration with JavaFX, try implementing a network-capable version of the Reversi application.

- Wouldn't it be great to have a JavaFX AI for playing Reversi? Since JavaFX is compiled down to Java bytecodes, this can be almost as efficient as code written directly in Java. Give it a try, and see if you can create an unbeatable opponent!

Summary

In this chapter you were able to fully leverage the JavaFX layout capabilities to do dynamic layout of a complex application. Along the way, you learned how to

- Align Nodes using bind
- Use Stack to layer Nodes and create composite layouts
- Use Tile to do fixed-size layouts
- Use Flow, HBox, and VBox to do directional layouts with and without wrapping
- Create custom layouts declaratively using Panel
- Build Resizable controls that work within layout containers
- Use the JavaFX Geometry API
- Use PerspectiveTransform to create pseudo 3D effects
- Develop a complex Container layout from scratch
- Build a rich user interface backed by a game model
- Apply JavaFX effects, animation, and caching

After experiencing the advantages of dynamic layout, you will be hard-pressed to go back to static positioning of components with fixed sizes. In the next chapter we will introduce you to third-party libraries that, among other features, include prebuilt layouts that you can take advantage of today to build dynamic layouts faster and easier than ever.

Resources

For more information about dynamic layouts, consult the following resources:

- Amy Fowler's blog on layouts and JavaFX: `http://weblogs.java.net/blog/aim/`

- JavaFX 1.2 Layout Primer: `http://java.sun.com/developer/technicalArticles/javafx/v1_2_newlayouts/`

The following resources will help you learn more about the mathematics behind the Perspective Transform algorithm:

- "A Plane Measuring Device," by A. Criminisi, I. Reid, and A. Zisserman at the University of Oxford. URL: `http://www.robots.ox.ac.uk/~vgg/presentations/bmvc97/criminispaper/`

- "Perspective Transform Estimation," by Christopher R. Wren at the Massachusetts Institute of Technology. URL: `http://xenia.media.mit.edu/~cwren/interpolator/`

Finally, to learn more about the game of Reversi, please refer to the following resources:

- Wikipedia, "Reversi." URL: `http://en.wikipedia.org/wiki/Reversi`

- The Othello Wiki Book Project. URL: `http://www.othello.dk/book/index.php/Main_Page`

- The solution for the Reversi challenge shown in Figure 7-12 can be found at the following URL: `http://www.othello.dk/book/index.php/Solution_solitaire`

■ ■ ■

CHAPTER 8

Extending JavaFX with Third-Party Libraries

Civilization advances by extending the number of operations which we can perform without thinking about them.

— Alfred North Whitehead

While JavaFX provides a lot of capabilities out of the box, a number of third-party extensions are available that will simplify the development of any application. We'll introduce several of these libraries in this chapter, and we'll take advantage of them throughout the rest of this book.

All of the third-party extensions introduced in this chapter are available as free or open source libraries. This ensures that anyone can make use of these libraries, and also guarantees that you will not be locked into a specific vendor.

Creating Desktop Widgets with WidgetFX

JavaFX applications are typically deployed using applets in a browser or Java Web Start. This works great for web applications and large desktop applications, but for small, informational applications the overhead of running in a browser or installing a separate application is prohibitive.

WidgetFX, as shown in Figure 8-1, fills the gap between applets and Web Start applications by providing a desktop dock that dynamically runs widgets written in JavaFX.

Figure 8-1. *WidgetFX docking framework*

Some of the advantages WidgetFX provides over other Java deployment models include

- *Has a low memory footprint*: WidgetFX runs all the widgets in a single Java Virtual Machine (JVM), reducing the memory footprint required to run a large number of widgets simultaneously.

- *Opens on startup*: The WidgetFX dock starts up automatically on login, and will remember the position of the dock and restart any widgets that were running previously. This helps maintain a constant desktop presence for your application.

- *Follows the widget trend*: Desktop widgets are becoming a mainstream application deployment model, as shown by the large number of frameworks available or included with operating systems. WidgetFX makes JavaFX applications a first-class citizen with desktop integration across different platforms.

WidgetFX is not the only desktop framework out there. Quite a few other desktop widget containers are available for free or come bundled with an operating system. Some of the most popular ones include the Apple Dashboard, Microsoft Gadgets, and Google Desktop Gadgets, so why choose WidgetFX?

The most obvious reason for Java or JavaFX developers is the low barrier of entry. You can convert any JavaFX application into a widget by simply wrapping it in a `Widget` class. Deployment across different mediums such as applets, Web Start, and desktop widgets is also possible from the same codebase, because the `Widget` base class extends `javafx.scene.layout.Panel` and operates seamlessly outside of the WidgetFX container.

Table 8-1 compares WidgetFX to the other main widget containers that are available today.

Table 8-1. *Comparison of the Major Desktop Widget Containers*

Name	Creator	License	OS Support	Primary Languages
Dashboard	Apple Computer	Commercial	Mac OS X	XML, JavaScript, HTML, CSS
Google Desktop	Google	Free for non-commercial use	Mac OS X, Windows, Linux	XML, JavaScript, HTML, CSS
Microsoft Gadgets	Microsoft	Commercial	Windows Vista only	XML, JavaScript, HTML, CSS
Plasma	Aaron Seigo	Open source (GPL)	Mac OS X, Windows,[a] Linux	
Yahoo! Widgets	Yahoo!	Free for non-commercial use	Mac OS X, Windows	XML, JavaScript, HTML, CSS
WidgetFX	Stephen Chin	Open source (BSD)	Mac OS X, Windows, Linux[b]	JavaFX, Java, CSS

[a] *Plasma is part of the KDE desktop, which has been ported to Mac OS X and Windows, with some known stability issues.*

[b] *WidgetFX runs on any platform JavaFX can be deployed to, including Linux, but has limitations related to transparent and shaped (nonrectangular) windows.*

Some of the other reasons for choosing WidgetFX when compared against the other widget containers are

- *Cross-platform*: WidgetFX deploys on all major operating systems with a single click. Many of the other widget frameworks are tied to a specific operating system, or encumbered with a large up-front installation (Plasma, for instance, requires installation of the KDE desktop environment).

- *Commercial-friendly open source license*: WidgetFX is released under the New Berkeley Software Distribution License (BSD) and is the only fully open source widget framework that is safe for use by individuals as well as companies. Many of the commercial widget frameworks, such as Google Desktop and Yahoo! Widgets, have explicit clauses in their end-user license agreements (EULAs) that prohibit commercial use. GPL-licensed widget frameworks require that widgets also be licensed as GPL, which prevents development of commercial applications.

- *Robust security model*: WidgetFX inherits the sandboxed security model from Java, allowing it to support distribution of unsigned widgets without concern about malware or viruses. All the other widget frameworks require that you trust the widget originator to have verified the security of the widget, leaving an opportunity for computer hijacking or harvesting of personal information.

- *Rich Internet application capabilities*: WidgetFX is built on top of JavaFX, exposing all the rich media and graphics capabilities of the platform to widget developers. In contrast, most of the other widget containers rely on legacy web technologies, such as JavaScript, HTML, and CSS.

If you are still not convinced that WidgetFX is the best option for deploying your application to the desktop, keep reading and we will take you through a guided tutorial to show how easy it is to create a desktop widget in JavaFX from scratch.

Creating a Movie Widget

In this section we will show you how to create a simple movie widget by wrapping the SimpleMoviePlayer class from Chapter 6 in a Widget main class.

Creating a WidgetFX widget is as simple as extending the Widget class that is provided in the WidgetFX software development kit (SDK). Since the Widget class simply extends from the JavaFX built-in Panel class, you can run simple widgets as stand-alone JavaFX applications. However, to take advantage of advanced features, such as configuration and event callbacks, you will need to run within the WidgetFX dock.

The first step is to download the latest SDK from the WidgetFX site:

http://code.google.com/p/widgetfx/downloads/list

The SDK includes a JavaDoc, samples, and the required JAR files. The only files you need to complete this sample are widgetfx-api.jar and JFXtras.jar, which are located in the lib directory. Be sure to add these to your application classpath when building this sample.

The next step is to create a widget Main.fx file that returns an object of type Widget. Some of the variables available on the Widget class that we will make use of in this section are listed in Table 8-2.

Table 8-2. *Widget Variables*

Name	Type	Inherited From	Description
width	Number	Resizable	Initial width of the widget
height	Number	Resizable	Initial height of the widget
aspectRatio	Number	Widget	If set, defines a fixed aspect ratio for the widget width and height
content	Node[]	Group	The graphical nodes that make up the widget

The following code sample creates a new widget that has an initial width and height of 640 and 352, respectively. It also has a fixed aspect ratio that matches the dimensions of the loaded media clip:

```
var widget: Widget;
...
widget = Widget {
    width: 640
    height: 352
    aspectRatio: bind player.media.width / player.media.height
    content: bind player
}
```

To load the media clip, create a new instance of the `SimpleMoviePlayer` class from Chapter 6. You also have to bind the `width` and `height` of the player instance to the dimensions of the widget so that it resizes when the user changes the size of the widget:

```
// only for use with the projavafx samples
var source = "http://projavafx.com/movies/elephants-dream-640x352.flv";
var player = bind SimpleMoviePlayer {
    media: Media {
        source: source
    }
    width: bind widget.width
    height: bind widget.height
}
```

Now you are ready to run the widget. Since the `Widget` class extends `Panel`, it is a valid JavaFX program and can be run straight from the command line. Executing the program will result in the video window shown in Figure 8-2.

Figure 8-2. *Widget running from the command line*

However, if you run the same code as a Web Start application, it will automatically launch in the Widget Runner and give you a preview of how the widget will behave once deployed, complete with support for resizing, transparency, fixed aspect ratio, and all the other dock features (see Figure 8-3).

Figure 8-3. *Widget running within the Widget Runner*

HOW THE WIDGET RUNNER WORKS

The Widget Runner is a convenient mechanism to test widgets during development without opening and closing the WidgetFX dock. It exists as a parallel execution path for the production WidgetFX instance, so when you invoke the Widget Runner you will get identical behavior to deployed widgets.

There are two ways to launch the Widget Runner:

- *Automatic execution*: Simply running a widget as a Web Start application outside of the dock will cause it to launch the Widget Runner automatically. This is the easiest way to launch the Widget Runner, but it can take a little longer, because the relaunching takes place in a separate JVM.

- *Direct execution*: Similar to how you create a URL to launch a widget in the dock (see the "Deploying Widgets to the Web" section later in this chapter for details), you can also create a URL that will launch the Widget Runner directly. The URL has to be structured as follows: `http://widgetfx.org/dock/runner.jnlp?arg=<widgetUrl>`.

Most users will choose to use the automatic execution, because it requires no manual steps or special tooling, and lets you test widgets just as they will behave when deployed. However, if you are an advanced user or tool designer, the direct execution provides the most efficient way to launch a test container for widgets.

In the next section we will show you how to add simple configuration on the fly so you can change which movie file is playing.

Widget Configuration

WidgetFX provides a simple persistence mechanism that you can use to persist the entire configuration for your widget between sessions. This makes sure that the widget comes up with the same settings even after the users closes and reopens the dock.

To take advantage of the WidgetFX configuration, you need to do two things. First, define a set of properties that will be persisted to disk when the widget is saved and read back in when the widget is loaded. Second, create a configuration dialog box that will be displayed to users when they click the wrench icon in the widget toolbar.

The WidgetFX property persistence mechanism has classes that allow you to save all the JavaFX data types, as well as sequence versions of the same. The full set of classes is listed in Table 8-3.

Table 8-3. *Property Persistence Classes in the WidgetFX API*

Class Name	Type	Description
BooleanProperty	Boolean	Allows you to persist Booleans
BooleanSequenceProperty	Boolean[]	Allows you to persist sequences of Booleans
IntegerProperty	Integer	Allows you to persist Integers
IntegerSequenceProperty	Integer[]	Allows you to persist sequences of Integers
LongProperty	Long	Allows you to persist Longs
LongSequenceProperty	Long[]	Allows you to persist sequences of Longs
NumberProperty	Number	Allows you to persist Numbers
NumberSequenceProperty	Number[]	Allows you to persist sequences of Numbers
StringProperty	String	Allows you to persist Strings
StringSequenceProperty	String[]	Allows you to persist sequences of Strings

Each of the persistence classes has a name that uniquely identifies the property, a value that is persisted and read from disk, and an autoSave setting. AutoSave will associate a trigger with the property so that whenever the value changes it will be automatically written to disk. This is usually not necessary, because changes are saved whenever the configuration dialog box is closed, but it can be useful to update properties that change often, such as the last displayed image in a slide show.

To give a more detailed example of how to use properties, we will show you how to enhance the movie widget example from the previous section to support dynamic configuration of the playing movie.

The first step is to add in a StringProperty that is bound to the source variable in the main widget file:

```
widget = Widget {
    ...
    configuration: Configuration {
        properties: [
            StringProperty {
                name: "source"
                value: bind source with inverse
            }
        ]
        scene: Scene {} // defined in the next code fragment
    }
}
```

By bidirectionally binding the source to the StringProperty value, the WidgetFX configuration framework can save the current value and inject new values with no other changes to your program. For more complicated cases, you also have the option of defining your own onLoad and onSave event handlers that will be triggered on these operations.

To allow configuration of the source setting, you can define a simple dialog box using the JFXtras Grid and pass it in as the configuration Scene:

```
scene: Scene {
    content: Grid {
        rows: row([
            Text {
                content: "Source URL:"
            },
            TextBox {
                columns: 30,
                value: bind source with inverse
            }
        ])
    }
}
```

This is a very simple use of the JFXtras Grid that takes advantage of the automatic baseline alignment and resize behavior. We will go into more detail on how to use the JFXtras Grid later in this chapter.

The final step is to add a replace trigger to the movie player so that when a new source is loaded, the previous movie will stop playing. Without this, the old movie would continue to play in the background, consuming resources and interfering with the sound. The modified lines are highlighted in bold in the following code:

```
var player = bind SimpleMoviePlayer {
    media: Media {
        source: source
    }
    width: bind widget.width
    height: bind widget.height
} on replace = oldPlayer {
    oldPlayer.player.stop();
}
```

Now when you run the widget in the Widget Runner you will see a wrench icon that you can click to open the configuration dialog box and change the movie that is running. Figure 8-4 shows the same widget running the Big Buck Bunny movie.

In the next section we will show you how you can deploy your widget so that you enable your users to run it from within the WidgetFX dock with a single click.

Figure 8-4. *Widget configuration dialog box*

Deploying Widgets to the Web

WidgetFX provides one-click installation of the widget framework and any number of widgets from a single URL. The deployment model for widgets is analogous to applets or Web Start applications with hosted JAR files that are referred to by a standard Java Network Launching Protocol (JNLP) file.

The first step is to create a JNLP file for your widget. WidgetFX understands a subset of the JNLP syntax, but will safely ignore all other tags so that you can reuse the same JNLP file for other deployment formats. Listing 8-1 shows a basic WidgetFX JNLP file for the movie widget sample.

Listing 8-1. *Minimal WidgetFX JNLP Descriptor*

```
<?xml version="1.0" encoding="UTF-8"?>
<jnlp spec="1.0+" codebase="http://projavafx.com/samples/MovieWidget/"
      href="MovieWidget.jnlp">
    <information>
        <title>Movie Widget</title>
        <vendor>Pro JavaFX</vendor>
        <homepage href="http://projavafx.com"/>
        <description>Movie widget for displaying videos on the desktop</description>
    </information>
```

```
    <resources>
        <j2se version="1.6+"/>
        <extension name="JavaFX Runtime"
                    href="http://dl.javafx.com/1.2/javafx-rt.jnlp"/>
        <jar href="MovieWidget.jar" main="true"/>
        <jar href="lib/JFXtras-0.3.jar"/>
        <jar href="lib/WidgetFX-API-1.1.jar"/>
    </resources>
    <application-desc main-class="projavafx.moviewidget.Main"/>
</jnlp>
```

Because widgets run within the same JVM as the framework, some of the provided information will be ignored by WidgetFX:

- The Java version requirement will be ignored. WidgetFX requires a Java 1.6 JVM or higher, so you can safely use Java 1.6 language features and APIs.

- The JavaFX runtime will default to that of the dock. The WidgetFX framework automatically updates each time users start the dock, so you will always have the latest JavaFX runtime to build widgets against.

- The WidgetFX API and JFXtras JAR files are used by the framework and will always be on the latest available version. You can safely omit these dependencies.

To deploy your widget to a web server, simply copy the JNLP and JAR files to the location specified in the codebase. The same rules about Web Start MIME types apply, so make sure your web server is configured to serve up JNLP and JAR files via the following rules:

- JNLP: `application/x-java-jnlp-file`

- JAR: `application/java-archive jar`

You can now construct a URL that will enable launching of your widget. In the syntax for widget URLs, you first reference the widget framework, and then add URL parameters for each of the widgets you want to have loaded as follows:

`http://widgetfx.org/dock/launch.jnlp?arg=<widgetUrl1>&arg=<widgetUrl2>`

For the movie widget sample, your URL should look similar to the following:

`http://widgetfx.org/dock/launch.jnlp?arg=http://projavafx.com/samples/`➡
`MovieWidget/MovieWidget.jnlp`

To help users distinguish widget links on a page, a standard widget launch link is provided (see Figure 8-5).

Figure 8-5. *Standard widget launch link*

The completed HTML link with the standard image would look like this:

```
<a href="http://widgetfx.org/dock/launch.jnlp?arg=http://projavafx.com/samples/➥
        MovieWidget.jnlp">➥
<img src="http://widgetfx.googlecode.com/svn/site/images/
            WidgetFX-launch-icon.png" />
</a>
```

If you now clicked that link in a web browser, it would do the following:

1. Install the WidgetFX framework if it is not already installed.

2. Launch the WidgetFX framework if it is not already open.

3. Add the movie widget to the dock if it has not already been added.

The completed widget running in the dock is shown in Figure 8-6.

Figure 8-6. *Completed widget running in the WidgetFX dock*

Congratulations on successfully completing a fully configurable desktop widget! Since WidgetFX is built on the JavaFX platform, the sky is the limit in terms of what widgets you can create yourself. In the next section we will show some examples of widgets that other users have created and shared with the world.

Third-Party Widgets

The real value of a framework is in its widespread use and adoption. Even though WidgetFX is a very new product release, it already has a rapidly growing community of users writing desktop widgets.

This section highlights some of widgets that have been publicly released since the WidgetFX launch. If you have a great widget, it could be featured here in the next edition of the book.

DiskSpace Widget

Developed by Pär Dahlberg (`http://pmdit.se/widgets/diskspace/`), the DiskSpace Widget (Figure 8-7) monitors the amount of remaining space on your hard drive and displays it in a progress bar. The widget can be configured to monitor any drive in your system by changing the settings in the configuration dialog box.

Figure 8-7. *The DiskSpace Widget*

This tool is great for monitoring your BitTorrent download folder to make sure it does not bring your computer to a halt by consuming all the available space.

World Clock Widget

Ludovic Hochet (`https://worldclock-application.dev.java.net/#Widget`), author of the Java world clock and screensaver, brings his application to WidgetFX as a desktop widget (see Figure 8-8). The configuration dialog box lets you choose the text color and select a file with cities in it to be listed on the map. This widget is also an excellent example of integrating Java Swing into a JavaFX UI.

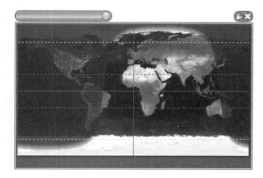

Figure 8-8. *The World Clock Widget*

And for those of you wondering, yes, most of this book was written very, very late in the evening…

World Smiley Widget

Enrique Ceja (`http://tareitas.webs.com/fx/WorldWidget/`) recently released the World Smiley Widget (see Figure 8-9), which allows you to vote on the state of the world. The widget communicates back to a JBoss application server to aggregate the results, which is a great example of JavaFX communication with a back-end server.

Figure 8-9. *The World Smiley Widget*

You know you want your expression to be heard, so download the widget and vote today!

The Future of WidgetFX

WidgetFX is already a powerful framework that can be used to bring your applications to the desktop today, but it is also constantly improving to meet the needs of its user community. This section will give you a glimpse into the future of WidgetFX, showing you what to expect.

Here are some of the items that are already in progress:

- *Additional widget life-cycle hooks*: In addition to the current event handlers, additional hooks will be added for onClose, onShow, and onHide events.

- *Browse drag-and-drop integration*: Imagine dragging a widget right off a web page and onto the WidgetFX dock! This technique has already been prototyped, and is very close to becoming a reality.

- *WidgetFX community site*: The WidgetFX team is working on a community-driven site that will allow you to publish and share your widgets with the world.

- *Mobile widgets*: Since WidgetFX is built on the JavaFX platform, any widgets that use the common profile are already mobile-compatible. This will extend that support to create a first-class widget container on mobile phones.

In addition to these items, you can help shape the future of WidgetFX. Submit your ideas and suggestions to the WidgetFX team via the mailing list and issue tracker, or join the WidgetFX open source team and make your vision a reality.

Building a Media Explorer with JFXtras

JavaFX provides a solid foundation for building dynamic applications, but it is currently missing a lot of features needed to build full-blown commercial applications. To help solve this need, the JFXtras project was created. JFXtras is an open source library for JavaFX that includes additional layout, components, and utilities that can help you build more powerful JavaFX applications.

JFXtras started off as a small collection of utilities that augmented the features available in the core JavaFX API libraries. Since then it has turned into the fastest-growing JavaFX open source project, attracting a large number of users and contributors who have been helping increase the scope and capabilities. It is licensed under the New BSD License, making it suitable for both open source and commercial applications.

In this section we will show you how to leverage JFXtras to build a rich media explorer application that can be used to browse and view images and movies saved on your computer. The emphasis of this example is on keeping the code simple, maintainable, and testable by leveraging JFXtras to reduce complexity.

Laying Out a Resizable Directory Navigator

As a simple example of how to use some of the JFXtras classes, let's begin with a DirectoryNavigator component to browse the file system. This will form the basis for choosing directories to explore and navigate to display media.

To ensure the reusability of this component, we will abstract this component out into a separate node class and make sure it is fully resizable when added to a container.

The driver class will simply wrap the DirectoryNavigator component in a Scene and Stage:

```
Stage {
    title: "Directory Navigator"
    width: 250
    height: 400
    scene: ResizableScene {
        content: DirectoryNavigator {}
    }
}
```

Notice that rather than using a regular JavaFX scene, we used a JFXtras ResizableScene. This is one of many classes that we will use in this section to automatically take care of resizing components. Some of the other components you will need to use are listed in Table 8-4.

Table 8-4. *Equivalent Resizable Classes in JFXtras*

Class Name	Package	Description
ResizableScene	org.jfxtras.scene	Resizes its child content to fit the scene bounds
ResizableCustomNode	org.jfxtras.scene	CustomNode extension that propagates resizable variables to and from its content
ResizableHBox	org.jfxtras.scene.layout	Drop-in replacement for HBox that will constrain its Resizable children to fit the box bounds
ResizableVBox	org.jfxtras.scene.layout	Drop-in replacement for VBox that will constrain its Resizable children to fit the box bounds

All of these classes are drop-in replacements for their JavaFX equivalents, adding additional support for resizing within a container and nesting of Resizable children.

For the `DirectoryNavigator` class itself, we will implement it as a `CustomNode` and display a few different controls arranged using box layouts. At the top will be a `SwingComboBox` to list directories and a `Button` to navigate back up. At the bottom will be a `ListView` that shows all the subdirectories that can be traversed.

The following application skeleton shows the minimal code to create and layout stub components for this user interface:

```
public class DirectoryNavigator extends ResizableCustomNode {
    var parentList = SwingComboBox {}

    var mediaList:ListView = ListView {}

    var upButton = Button {text: "Up"}

    override function create() {
        ResizableVBox {
            spacing: 2
            content: [
                ResizableHBox {
                    spacing: 3
                    content: [
                        parentList,
                        upButton
                    ]
                },
                mediaList
            ]
        }
    }
}
```

Running this application will lay out the components correctly in a window that properly constrains its components when resized (as shown in Figure 8-10).

Figure 8-10. *Automatic layout of the navigator components*

Normally developing a layout like this would require complicated binding to keep the components positioned and negotiate resizing, but all of this is taken care of by the ResizableVBox and ResizableHBox layout containers. In the next section we will go into more detail on the JFXtras Default Layout system, which negotiates the component sizes.

WHEN TO USE REGULAR AND RESIZABLE BOXES

Both the built-in HBox and VBox classes and the JFXtras ResizableHBox and ResizableVBox classes are useful for different purposes, but they can be easily confused because they are similar in name and parameters. Some of the criteria that will help you decide which type of box is better for a particular purpose include:

- Are the components resizable? If you are laying out child nodes that implement the Resizable interface, you can take advantage of the JFXtras resizable boxes to automatically allocate space according to their min, max, and preferred bounds. Nonresizable components will be treated identically in either type of layout, so the choice is yours.

- Do you want to fill the available space? The JFXtras resizable boxes will attempt to fill all available space according to the layoutInfo of the child nodes. If you simply want to stack the components without resizing, the built-in HBox and VBox classes are a better choice.

- Are you nesting layouts? If you have multiple levels of nested layouts, you will probably be better served using the JFXtras layouts, including ResizableHBox and ResizableVBox. All the JFXtras layouts dynamically trickle up layout defaults to make nesting of multiple layouts completely seamless. The next section on defaults goes into this in more detail.

Using the right tool for the job will make your program much simpler to write and easier to maintain.

To complete this example, you need to finish the implementation of the directory components. The parentList is a simple combo box that is bound to a list of files:

```
var parents:File[];
var parentList = SwingComboBox {
    selectedIndex: 0
    items: bind [
        for (parent in parents) FileWrapper {file: parent}
        FileWrapper {}
    ]
}
```

This implementation relies on a FileWrapper helper class that extends SwingComboBoxItem and handles special cases such as the null root:

```
class FileWrapper extends SwingComboBoxItem {
    var file:File on replace {
        value = file;
        text = toString();
    }
```

```
        override function toString() {
            if (file == null) {
                "Root"
            } else if (file.getName().length() == 0) {
                file.toString()
            } else {
                file.getName()
            }
        }
    }
}
```

To get the list of files for the selected directory, you can create some bound variables that trigger off the parentList's selectedItem:

```
var selectedParent = bind (parentList.selectedItem as FileWrapper).file;
var roots:File[] = File.listRoots();
var selectedFiles:File[] = bind selectedParent.listFiles(FileFilter {
    override function accept(file) {
        return file.isDirectory();
    }
});
var files:File[] = bind if (selectedParent == null) roots else selectedFiles;
```

For this example we are using a filter that only accepts files that are directories. There is no need to show files, because the next section will create a visual media grid to display them.

The mediaList binds a set of FileWrappers off the files sequence into a ListView to display the results:

```
public-read var currentDirectory =
    bind (mediaList.selectedItem as FileWrapper).file;
var mediaList:ListView = ListView {
    items: bind for (file in files) FileWrapper {file: file}
    onMouseClicked: function(e) {
        if (e.clickCount == 2) {
            navigateTo((mediaList.selectedItem as FileWrapper).file);
        }
    }
}
```

In addition to populating the list, we have also set up an onMouseClicked event handler that will navigate to the selected directory when the user double-clicks. It is the navigateTo function that populates the parent list, completing the circular dependency between the two controls:

```
public function navigateTo(file:File) {
    parents = [];
    var parent = file;
    while (parent != null) {
        insert parent into parents;
        parent = parent.getParentFile();
    }
    parentList.selectedIndex = 0;
}
```

The final touch is to add in the upButton implementation. Since the lists are circularly bound, the only change needed to update the active directory is to increment the selected index of the parent list:

```
var upButton = Button {
    text: "Up"
    disable: bind parentList.selectedIndex >= parentList.items.size() - 1
    action: function() {
        parentList.selectedIndex++;
    }
}
```

Now when you run the example, the content is a little more interesting. Figure 8-11 shows what the completed DirectoryNavigator looks like, with the size intentionally changed to demonstrate the automatic resizing in action.

Figure 8-11. *The completed DirectoryNavigator*

In the next section we will build on this example to show how to display the files in each directory in a rich media grid.

Building a User Interface with Defaults

In the previous section we showed you how to create a simple DirectoryNavigator using the resizable classes in the JFXtras library. The next step is to add the DirectoryNavigator to a larger user interface composed using a Grid for layout.

JFXtras provides a powerful Grid layout that allows you to declaratively set up the contents of the screen, and then let the layout be taken care of dynamically, taking into account your supplied layout settings and fitting the contents to the available area. This makes it so simple to build dynamic, resizable user interfaces that you may never feel the need to manually position a component again!

The core of the JFXtras Grid is a Grid class that contains a list of Rows. Each row contains a list of Nodes or Cells. To demonstrate the basic use of the Grid class, here is a simple example that takes the DirectoryNavigator and puts it in a 2×2 layout together with a title text, progress bar, and placeholder for the media grid:

```
var title = Text {content: "Media Explorer", font: Font.font("Serif", 48)}
var navigator = DirectoryNavigator {}
var progressBar = ProgressBar {};
var mediaGrid = ResizableRectangle {fill: Color.BLUE, width: 500}
Stage {
    title: "Media Explorer"
    scene: ResizableScene {
        width: 800
        height: 500
        content: [
            Grid {
                rows: [
                    row([title, progressBar]),
                    row([navigator, mediaGrid])
                ]
            }
        ]
    }
}
```

We used a new class called ResizableRectangle as the placeholder. This is another one of the JFXtras Resizable class extensions that behaves very similarly to the JavaFX Rectangle class, and is handy to drop into a Grid or other layout as a quick background.

Also, notice that we used a row function to generate the Row class objects for the Grid. This is one of the convenience methods in the LayoutConstants class, which was statically imported for this example. It is also equally correct to rewrite the Grid portion as follows:

```
Grid {
    rows: [
        Row {
            cells: [title, progressBar]
        },
        Row {
            cells: [navigator, mediaGrid]
        }
    ]
}
```

Which style do you prefer? Throughout this chapter we are going to use the former style for brevity, but feel free to use either in your programs.

Upon running the application, you will see an application window appear with content, as shown in Figure 8-12.

Figure 8-12. *First Grid mockup of the Media Explorer*

Notice that since we defined the DirectoryNavigator component as a ResizableCustom-Node it drops in effortlessly and resizes with the window. Similarly, the Text node, ProgressBar, and ResizableRectangle all fell in place with reasonable defaults.

The reason why all the components knew how to align themselves is due to the JFXtras Default Layout system. All the components picked up default LayoutInfo settings based their class type or explicitly by extending the DefaultLayout mixin. In fact, there are default layouts defined for all the JavaFX and JFXtras classes so that they will show up properly within different layout containers.

Table 8-5 shows the available layout settings. Some of them are on the LayoutInfo base class, which applies for all layout containers, while others are on the ExtendedLayoutInfo and GridLayoutInfo subclasses, which are specific to JFXtras.

Table 8-5. *JFXtras Layout Settings and Their Values*

Variable	Class	Value	Description
managed	LayoutInfoBase	Boolean	True if layout will affect this node
hpos	LayoutInfo	LEFT, CENTER, RIGHT, HFILL	Horizontal orientation within the cell
vpos	LayoutInfo	TOP, MIDDLE, BOTTOM, BASELINE, VFILL	Vertical orientation within the cell
height	LayoutInfo	Number	Overrides the Resizable prefHeight property

Variable	Class	Value	Description
width	LayoutInfo	Number	Overrides the Resizable prefWidth property
maxHeight	LayoutInfo	Number	Overrides the Resizable maxHeight property
maxWidth	LayoutInfo	Number	Overrides the Resizable maxWidth property
minHeight	LayoutInfo	Number	Overrides the Resizable minHeight property
minWidth	LayoutInfo	Number	Overrides the Resizable minWidth property
fill	ExtendedLayoutInfo	VERTICAL, HORIZONTAL, BOTH, NONE	Fills all allocated space
layoutBounds	ExtendedLayoutInfo	Rectangle2D	Overrides the node layoutBounds variable
hspan	GridLayoutInfo	Integer	The number of columns that this node will span
vspan	GridLayoutInfo	Integer	The number of rows that this node will span
hgrow	GridLayoutInfo	ALWAYS, SOMETIMES, NEVER	Priority for allocating unused horizontal space in the Grid
vgrow	GridLayoutInfo	ALWAYS, SOMETIMES, NEVER	Priority for allocating unused vertical space in the Grid

The constant values in uppercase are available on the LayoutInfo classes and mirrored in the LayoutConstants class for convenient importing via a single static import. They all map to enumeration values in the HPos, VPos, Grow, and Fill classes, but are a convenient shorthand for typing the full enum name.

The horizontal and vertical position settings affect the orientation within the cell. BASELINE is a special alignment that can be used for any node, but is specifically useful when paired with a Text node that has a TextOrigin of BASELINE. This keeps Text nodes lined up with each other on the bottom of the characters, and also properly lines them up with other components, such as TextBoxes.

The fill setting controls how space within the allocated cell is used. If set to VERTICAL or HORIZONTAL, all available space in that orientation will be taken by the component. This setting effectively overrides the position setting for the given orientation.

The grow settings determine how extra space within a Grid is divided among rows and columns. Space is allocated first to nodes with the ALWAYS Grow value, followed by SOMETIMES. Nodes marked with a NEVER Grow setting will never be sized larger than their preferred bounds.

The LayoutInfo class also contains a mirror set of min/max/preferred variables that allow you to override the like-named variables in Resizable. This is important, because the Resizable properties are declared protected, which only allows them to be set from within subclasses.

The default layout settings for some of the JavaFX and JFXtras classes are shown in Table 8-6. Wherever there is an asterisk (*) specified, the global defaults are applied instead.

Table 8-6. *Default Layout Settings for Common JavaFX and JFXtras Classes*

Class	hpos	vpos	fill	hspan	vspan	hgrow	vgrow
Button	LEFT	•	•	•	•	•	•
CheckBox	LEFT	•	•	•	•	SOMETIMES	•
Label	LEFT	BASELINE	•	•	•	•	•
ProgressBar	•	•	HORIZONTAL	•	•	SOMETIMES	•
ScrollBar	RIGHT	BOTTOM	Calculated	•	•	Calculated	Calculated
Slider	•	•	HORIZONTAL	•	•	SOMETIMES	•
TextBox	•	•	HORIZONTAL	•	•	ALWAYS	•
SwingComboBox	•	•	HORIZONTAL	•	•	SOMETIMES	•
SwingList	•	•	BOTH	•	•	ALWAYS	ALWAYS
ResizableImageView	•	•	•	•	•	ALWAYS	ALWAYS
ResizableRectangle	•	•	BOTH	•	•	SOMETIMES	SOMETIMES
ResizableHBox	•	•	BOTH	•	•	Calculated	Calculated
ResizableVBox	•	•	BOTH	•	•	Calculated	Calculated
Grid	•	•	BOTH	•	•	Calculated	Calculated
DEFAULT	CENTER	MIDDLE	NONE	1	1	NEVER	NEVER

The layout classes, such as `ResizableHBox`, `ResizableVBox`, and `Grid` are a special case. Rather than having fixed defaults for `hgrow` and `vgrow`, they pick up their defaults based on the layout defaults of their children. This makes nesting of layout containers seamless, and the reason why the nested boxes in the directory navigator behaved correctly without modifying the settings of the inner box.

The other calculated default is used in the `ScrollBar` class to dynamically change the layout settings based on the orientation of the scroll bar.

Now that you are armed with knowledge on layout settings, it is time to apply this to the Media Explorer layout. Specifically, you need to constrain the `DirectoryNavigator` to meet the following requirement:

> • It should continue to resize vertically, but have a fixed horizontal width of 300 pixels.

Applying layout settings to the `DirectoryNavigator` is straightforward. All that you need to do is to set the `layoutInfo` variable to a new instance of the `GridLayoutInfo` class that has your desired defaults:

```
var navigator = DirectoryNavigator {
    layoutInfo: GridLayoutInfo {
        width: 300
        hgrow: NEVER
    }
}
```

The final step is to plug these back in to the main script. As an added bonus, the code in Listing 8-2 has some additional spacing, a background gradient, and a reflection effect to enhance the application look and feel.

Listing 8-2. *Media Explorer Grid Mockup with Layout Settings Applied*

```
var text = Text {
    content: "Media Explorer"
    font: Font.font("Serif", 48);
}
var navigator = DirectoryNavigator {
    layoutInfo: GridLayoutInfo {
        width: 300
        hgrow: NEVER
    }
}
var mediaGrid = ResizableRectangle {fill: Color.BLUE}
var progressBar = ProgressBar {}

Stage {
    title: "Media Explorer"
    scene: ResizableScene {
        width: 800
        height: 500
        content: [
            ResizableRectangle {
                cache: true
                fill: RadialGradient {
                    radius: 1.4
                    stops: [
                        Stop {offset: 0.0, color: Color.web("#3582ca")},
                        Stop {offset: 0.45, color: Color.WHITE},
                        Stop {offset: 0.452, color: Color.web("#8a9ed9")},
                        Stop {offset: 0.48, color: Color.web("#000f39")},
                        Stop {offset: 0.62, color: Color.web("#6d88c4")},
                        Stop {offset: 1.0, color: Color.WHITE}
                    ]
                }
            },
            Grid {
                effect: Reflection {}
                border: 20
                vgap: 12
                hgap: 12
                rows: bind [
                    row([text, progressBar]),
                    row([navigator, mediaGrid])
                ]
            }
        ]
    }
}
```

The updated application with the new layout settings will appear as shown in Figure 8-13. Notice that when the window is resized, the media grid placeholder and progress bar fill to take all the available space.

Figure 8-13. *The completed Media Explorer grid layout*

In the next section we will show you a more advanced use of the JFXtras Grid in which we'll display a dynamic Grid of media for the current directory.

Displaying Media in a Dynamic Grid

TIn the previous section we demonstrated how you can take a wide variety of components, toss them into a Grid, add some custom layout settings, and turn that into a full user interface. In this section we will explore how to turn this application into a true Media Explorer by dynamically building the contents of the Grid to display a variable list of media.

Similar to how you built the DirectoryNavigator, you will start with a ResizableCustomNode that has a public variable for the mediaFiles it is viewing:

```
public class MediaGrid extends ResizableCustomNode {

    public var mediaFiles:File[];
```

The mediaFiles sequence can then be used to construct a dynamic list of rows with the media arranged in a square formation:

```
    var rows:Row[];

    var thumbnailsPerSide:Integer;
```

```
def thumbnails = bind for (mediaFile in mediaFiles) createThumbnail(mediaFile)
               on replace oldThumbnails {
    thumbnailsPerSide = Math.ceil(Math.sqrt(thumbnails.size())).intValue();
    rows = for (i in [0..thumbnailsPerSide - 1]) Row {
        cells: for (j in [0..thumbnailsPerSide - 1]) {
            thumbnails[i * thumbnailsPerSide + j]
        }
    }
}
```

The stubbed implementation of createThumbnail can simply return a ResizableRectangle for now as a placeholder:

```
function createThumbnail(mediaFile:File):Thumbnail {
    ResizableRectangle {fill: Color.color(0, 0, Math.random())}
}
```

Note We are using a random function from the javafx.util.Math library to vary the darkness of the placeholder image purely for visual impact.

To complete the MediaGrid class, you can populate the Rows into a Grid. For some added polish, the Grid border and gaps can also be calculated based on the number of items:

```
override function create() {
    Grid {
        var gap = bind if (thumbnailsPerSide == 0) 0
                      else height / thumbnailsPerSide * 0.15;
        border: bind gap
        vgap: bind gap
        hgap: bind gap
        rows: bind rows
    }
}
}
```

Now that the MediaGrid class is complete, you need to load the list of media files in the DirectoryNavigator class. There is a convenience helper in JFXtras called ImageUtil that can list all the supported image formats, but for the media types you will have to create your own list:

```
public var MEDIA_EXTENSIONS = ["flv", "fxm", "avi", "wmv", "mov"];

public function isMediaType(name:String) {
    sizeof MEDIA_EXTENSIONS[ext | name.toLowerCase().endsWith(ext)] >= 1
}
```

These can then be used in the DirectoryNavigator to create a publicly accessible list of media files:

```
public-read var mediaFiles:File[] = bind currentDirectory.listFiles(
    FilenameFilter {
        override function accept(dir, name) {
            return ImageUtil.imageTypeSupported(name) or isMediaType(name);
        }
    }
);
```

The final step is to replace the placeholder mediaGrid in the Main.fx class with a new instance of MediaGrid that has its mediaDirectory bound to the DirectoryNavigator's current directory:

```
var mediaGrid = MediaGrid {
    mediaFiles: bind navigator.mediaFiles
}
```

Running the Media Explorer will now show a set of placeholder Rectangles equal in number to the Images and Media in the directories you navigate to, as shown in Figure 8-14.

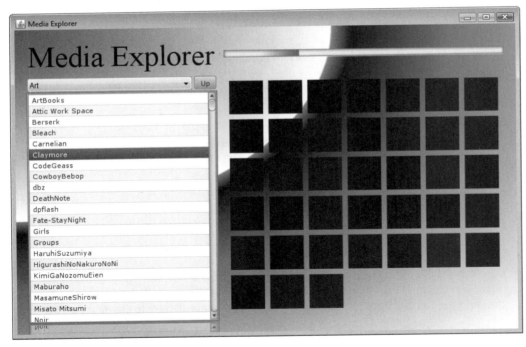

Figure 8-14. *Media Explorer with a full Grid of placeholder Rectangles*

The Grid is now displaying and positioning the correct number of media files for each directory you navigate to, all calculated using bind and replace triggers in JavaFX.

To complete the example, we need to create a few wrapper classes to display thumbnails for the media types we want to support. To make sure that the thumbnails resize correctly in the Grid, they need to extend Resizable and DefaultLayout, which is most easily accomplished by starting with a ResizableCustomNode.

Listing 8-3 shows an abstract Thumbnail base class that provides variables to inject a mediaFile and function to stop loading. It also provides some transitions to fade the nodes in as they are loaded and do a subtle scale on hover.

Listing 8-3. *Abstract Thumbnail Class for Media*

```
public abstract class Thumbnail extends ResizableCustomNode {

    public-init var mediaFile:File;

    public abstract function stop():Void;

    public-read protected var progress:Number on replace {
        if (progress == 100) {
            FadeTransition {
                duration: 1s
                node: this
                toValue: 1.0
            }.play();
        }
    }

    override var opacity = 0;

    var scaleTransition = ScaleTransition {
        node: this
        duration: 200ms
        fromX: 1.0
        fromY: 1.0
        toX: 1.3
        toY: 1.3
    }

    override var hover on replace {
        scaleTransition.rate = if (hover) 1 else -1;
        scaleTransition.play();
    }
}
```

The Thumbnail base class can be implemented for various types of Media; however, for this example we will restrict it to Images and Movies. The ImageThumbnail class shown in Listing 8-4 returns a ResizableImageView that is populated with an Image loaded off the mediaFile.

Listing 8-4. *Image Implementation of the Thumbnail Class*

```
public class ImageThumbnail extends Thumbnail {

    var image:Image;

    override function stop() {
        image.cancel();
    }

    override var progress = bind image.progress;

    override function create() {
        ResizableImageView {
            preserveRatio: true
            smooth: true
            image: image = ImageFix {
                width: 250
                height: 250
                preserveRatio: true
                backgroundLoading: true
                url: ImageUtil.getURL(mediaFile)
            }
        }
    }
}
```

■**Note** In Listing 8-4 we used the ImageFix JFXtras class to work around Image backgroundLoading
defect RT-3590 in JavaFX 1.2. The JFXtras project often provides an early work-around for bugs as XXXFix
classes to unblock the development community on critical issues.

ResizableImageView is a class defined in JFXtras as a drop-in replacement for ImageView
that also supports resizing within containers. By using it you don't need to worry about
layoutInfo or binding, because all of the layout magic is taken care of by the underlying component.

Another JFXtras feature used in the previous code is ImageUtil.getURL. Besides converting
a file into a string URL, which is required by the JavaFX Image class, it also takes care of URL
encoding special characters, which normally will cause image loads to fail. By using a well-
tested utility library, you don't have to worry about catching all the corner cases in your own
application code.

The code for the equivalent media implementation of Thumbnail is shown in Listing 8-5.

Listing 8-5. *MediaThumbnail Implementation*

```
public class MediaThumbnail extends Thumbnail {

    var mediaPlayer: MediaPlayer;

    override function stop() {
        mediaPlayer.stop();
    }

    init {
        mediaPlayer = MediaPlayer {
            mute: bind not hover
            media: Media {
                source: ImageUtil.getURL(mediaFile)
            }
        }
        FX.deferAction(function():Void {
            mediaPlayer.play();
        });
        progress = 100;
    }

    override function create() {
        ResizableMediaView {
            mediaPlayer: mediaPlayer
        }
    }

    override var defaultLayoutInfo = bind GridLayoutInfo {
        width: 250
        height: 250 * mediaPlayer.media.height / mediaPlayer.media.width
    }
}
```

This class makes use of ResizableMediaView, which is also a wrapper class provided by JFXtras. This implementation will actually play the media right in the Grid, but will only enable the volume for the media clip your mouse is hovering over.

The MediaThumbnail class also demonstrates the use of default layout information to override the Resizable preferred values. It sets the preferred width to 250 and the preferred height to a proportional value in order to keep the media thumbnails equally sized to the images in the Grid.

To complete this example, you have to wire up the thumbnails to the MediaGrid by implementing the createThumbnail function:

```
function createThumbnail(mediaFile:File) {
    if (ImageUtil.imageTypeSupported(mediaFile.getName())) {
        ImageThumbnail {mediaFile: mediaFile}
    } else {
        MediaThumbnail {mediaFile: mediaFile}
    }
}
```

Also remember to stop the thumbnails from playing when a new file is uploaded:

```
function stop(thumbnails:Thumbnail[]) {
    for (thumbnail in thumbnails) {
        thumbnail.stop();
    }
}

def thumbnails = bind for (mediaFile in mediaFiles) createThumbnail(mediaFile)
                 on replace oldThumbnails[a..b]=newThumbnails {
    stop(oldThumbnails[a..b]);
    ...
```

and update the progress by averaging the progress of all the active thumbnails:

```
public-read var progress =
    bind SequenceUtil.avg(for (thumbnail in thumbnails)  thumbnail.progress);
```

Tip This example uses the JFXtras SequenceUtil, which is one of many utility classes that can reduce the amount of code you have to write.

The mediaGrid is already bound to the Main class, but the progress isn't, so the final step is to bind the progress variable to the mediaGrid.progress in ProgressBar. Since the Image class supplies progress on a scale of 0 to 100 and the ProgressBar expects a decimal from 0 to 1, we often have to adjust the scale. Fortunately, ProgressBar has a handy computeProgress method that takes the range and does the conversion for you:

```
var progressBar = ProgressBar {
    progress: bind ProgressBar.computeProgress(100, mediaGrid.progress)
}
```

The Media Explorer running with the examples of both Image and Media thumbnails displayed in the same grid is shown in Figure 8-15.

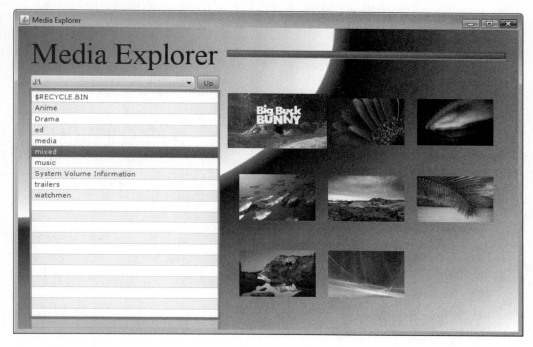

Figure 8-15. *Media Explorer with a fully populated grid of image thumbnails*

Try rolling your mouse over the images to see the scale transition in action. Also, if you rollover a video in the Grid it will play the sound while the mouse is hovering.

In the next section we will show you how to add full-sized versions of media complete with animation and borders.

Wrapping Media with Borders in a Deck

In the previous section we demonstrated how to build a Grid that shows all the media in the current directory, including showing thumbnails of pictures and playing movies. In this section we will show you how to use the JFXtras border support and Deck layout to build a reusable MediaViewer that can be shown when a thumbnail is clicked.

The JFXtras Deck layout is analogous to a stack of cards. It has a single content element just like the Group class, but unlike a Group, the JFXtras Deck will size all of its children to fit the available space. This forces all of the children to stack on top of each other like a deck of cards, where the children on the bottom are only visible where the overlapping nodes are transparent or don't fill the container.

WHEN TO USE A DECK VS. A STACK

The JFXtras Deck is a drop-in enhancement for the JavaFX Stack class. It does everything that a Stack does, with the addition of the following functionality:

- *Oversizing prevention:* The JFXtras Deck respects the fill property of ExtendedLayoutInfo. This means that if you have a control that just wants to be sized as large as its preferred size, but no larger (fill = NONE), it will respect this. You can take advantage of this without writing a line of code, because all the built-in controls have reasonable defaults for the fill property already set.

- *Seamless nesting:* The layout settings of nodes nested in a Deck will be aggregated and passed up to the parent layout. This means that you will get identical behavior from nesting a node within a Deck as you would if you directly inserted the node into the outer layout. One use for this is to aggregate nodes inside a Grid cell without affecting the layout of surrounding nodes.

Since the variables and API are identical between the Stack and Deck classes, it is easy to start with a Stack and upgrade to a Deck later as your program becomes more complicated.

The Deck layout is a useful container for creating different visual effects. For this example, we are going to use a Deck to implement the following behavior:

- When a thumbnail is clicked, it will expand in a full-sized view.
- Clicking on an image view will close it.
- Clicking anywhere surrounding an image or media view will close it.
- Clicking on another thumbnail will close the current view and open a new one.

Listing 8-6 shows a basic implementation of the MediaViewer class that makes use of a Deck to stack a transparent rectangle for catching input events below the active FileViews.

Listing 8-6. *MediaViewer Basic Implementation Using a Deck*

```
public class MediaViewer extends ResizableCustomNode {

    var mediaViews:FileView[];

    var backgroundRectangle = ResizableRectangle {
        fill: Color.TRANSPARENT
        onMouseClicked: function(e) {
            if (sizeof mediaViews > 0) {
                var view = mediaViews[sizeof mediaViews - 1];
                closeView(view);
            }
        }
    }
}
```

```
    override function create() {
        Deck {
            content: bind [
                backgroundRectangle,
                mediaViews
            ]
        }
    }
}
```

Notice that the contents of the Deck are ordered from back to front, so the backgroundRectangle is place in first, followed by the mediaViews. A bind is used on the content sequence to make sure that when the mediaViews variable changes, the UI updates.

The backgroundRectangle is implemented as a simple ResizableRectangle with a TRANSPARENT fill and a mouse event handler. Since the ResizableRectangle class has a default fill of BOTH, it will expand to cover the entire Deck background, allowing it to trap any events that miss the mediaViews. This will let us bind a close event handler that calls closeView, which is shown here:

```
    public function closeView(view:FileView) {
        var bounds = view.fromNode. localToScene(view.fromNode.boundsInLocal);
        TranslateTransition {
            duration: 500ms
            node: view
            toX: (bounds.minX + bounds.maxX - scene.width) / 2
            toY: (bounds.minY + bounds.maxY - scene.height) / 2
        }.play();
        ScaleTransition {
            def scale = Math.max(bounds.width / scene.width,
                                 bounds.height / scene.height);
            duration: 500ms
            node: view
            toX: scale
            toY: scale
            action: function() {
                view.stop();
                delete view from mediaViews;
            }
        }.play();
    }
```

Other than the action at the end of the ScaleTransition, most of the code is just to line up the closing view with the thumbnail. The implementation of showView looks very similar:

```
public function showView(view:FileView) {
    view.blocksMouse = true;
    insert view into mediaViews;
    var bounds = view.fromNode. localToScene(view.fromNode.boundsInLocal);
    TranslateTransition {
        duration: 1s
        node: view
        fromX: (bounds.minX + bounds.maxX - scene.width) / 2
        fromY: (bounds.minY + bounds.maxY - scene.height) / 2
        toX: 0
        toY: 0
    }.play();
    ScaleTransition {
        def scale = Math.max(bounds.width / scene.width,
                             bounds.height / scene.height);
        duration: 1s
        node: view
        fromX: scale
        fromY: scale
        toX: 1
        toY: 1
    }.play();
}
```

To bind everything together, there is a bit of plumbing that we are missing. To add the MediaView into the scene graph, you can modify the Main.fx file to instantiate a new instance:

```
var mediaViewer = MediaViewer {}
```

and add it in to the scene content:

```
        content: [
            ....
            mediaViewer
        ]
```

In order for it to be used when thumbnails get clicked, it will need to be passed down through the mediaGrid:

```
var mediaGrid:MediaGrid = MediaGrid {
    mediaFiles: bind navigator.mediaFiles
    mediaViewer: mediaViewer;
}
```

to a new variable:

```
    public-init var mediaViewer:MediaViewer;
```

that gets set on the thumbnails when they are created:

```
function createThumbnail(mediaFile:File) {
    if (ImageUtil.imageTypeSupported(mediaFile.getName())) {
        ImageThumbnail {mediaFile: mediaFile, mediaViewer: mediaViewer}
    } else {
        MediaThumbnail {mediaFile: mediaFile, mediaViewer: mediaViewer}
    }
}
```

That completes the implementation of the MediaView. The next step will be to create the view classes that the deck shows and hides when the thumbnails are clicked. To make the views more visually appealing, we will use the JFXtras border framework to wrap the images and media and set them apart from the background.

The full list of available JFXtras borders is shown in Figure 8-16.

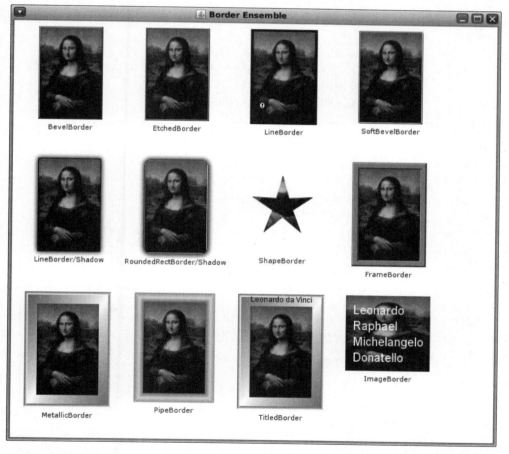

Figure 8-16. *JFXtras border samples from Jim Clarke's blog*

The borders can be used individually, and can also be composited into a large border via declaration nesting. In addition, they all provide full configurability via CSS and can be used together with shapes and images for even more dramatic effects.

Table 8-7 summarizes the configuration options of each of the border classes. In addition to the individual CSS properties, all borders inherit the base properties from the Border class.

Table 8-7. *CSS Properties for the JFXtras Borders*

Border Class	CSS Properties
Border	border-top-width, border-left-width, border-bottom-width, border-right-width
BevelBorder	background-fill, raised, highlight-outer, highlight-inner, shadow-inner, shadow-outer
CenteredBorder	background-fill
EllipseBorder	background-fill, raised, highlight-outer, highlight-inner, shadow-inner, shadow-outer
EmptyBorder	No additional
EtchedBorder	background-fill, raised, highlight, shadow
FrameBorder	background-fill, raised, highlight-outer, highlight-inner, shadow-inner, shadow-outer
ImageBorder	background-fill, background-image
LineBorder	line-color, thickness
MetallicBorder	raised, outer, inner
PipeBorder	raised, highlight-inner, highlight-outer, highlight
RoundedRectBorder	background-fill, raised, highlight, shadow, arc
ShapeBorder	horizontal-alignment, vertical-alignment, horizontal-offset, vertical-offset
SoftBevelBorder	background-fill, raised, highlight-outer, highlight-inner, shadow-inner, shadow-outer
TitledBorder	font, text-color, background-fill, title-vertical-offset, title-horizontal-offset

For the view implementations, we will start with a base FileView class that can be used to abstract out common functions between Images and Media as shown here:

```
public abstract class FileView extends ResizableCustomNode {

    public-init var file:File;

    public-init var fromNode:Node;

    public var onClose:function();
}
```

The variables will be used for the following purposes:

- file: The image or media file that will be loaded by the view.

- fromNode: The thumbnail node that this view originated from. This will be used for bounds animations calculations, and needs to be dynamic, because the layout may change between when the view is opened and when it is closed.

- onClose: An event handler that will be called by the MediaView when the view is closed.

The ImageFileView implementation will extend the FileView class, but also accept a thumbnail Image as a public-init variable. This will allows the ImageFileView to immediately show a low-resolution version of the Image while a higher-resolution version is loaded in the background as shown here:

```
public-init var thumbnail:Image;
var image = Image {
    width: fromNode.scene.width
    height: fromNode.scene.height
    preserveRatio: true
    backgroundLoading: true
    placeholder: thumbnail
    url: ImageUtil.getURL(file)
}
```

The second parameter is a reference to the mediaViewer that can be used to close this view when the mouse is clicked:

```
public-init var mediaViewer:MediaViewer;
override var onMouseClicked = function(e) {
    mediaViewer.closeView(this);
}
```

The create function of ImageFileView will add that image to the scene graph wrapped by a couple of nested borders. We have chosen to use a FrameBorder wrapped with a TitleBorder, but you can use whatever borders you like from the available set:

```
override function create() {
    TitledBorder {
        id: "imageTitle"
        title: file.getName()
        content: FrameBorder {
            id: "imageFrame"
            content: ResizableImageView {
                layoutInfo: GridLayoutInfo {
                    hgrow: NEVER
                    vgrow: NEVER
                }
                preserveRatio: true
                smooth: true
                image: bind image
            }
        }
    }
}
```

Notice that we have set ids on each of the border nodes. This will allow us to modify the border appearance by adding in a CSS file with additional configuration properties. Here is a basic CSS file that sets the frame width, frame fill, title font, and title color:

```
#imageFrame {
    border-left-width: 12;
    border-top-width: 12;
    border-bottom-width: 20;
    border-right-width: 12;
    background-fill: #00007020;
}

#imageTitle {
    position: "bottom";
    justification: "center";
    font: bold 12pt Serif;
    text-color: #000060;
}
```

To include this in the application, simply add a stylesheets variable to the main Stage like this:

```
scene: ResizableScene {
    stylesheets: "{__DIR__}Border.css"
```

Finally, you need to instantiate the ImageView class whenever the user clicks on an ImageThumbnail by adding the following event handler:

```
override var onMouseClicked = function(e) {
    mediaViewer.showView(
        ImageFileView {
            file: mediaFile
            thumbnail: image
            fromNode: this
            mediaViewer: mediaViewer
        }
    );
}
```

Now when you run the Media Explorer and click an image thumbnail, it will zoom open into a full window view, as shown in Figure 8-17.

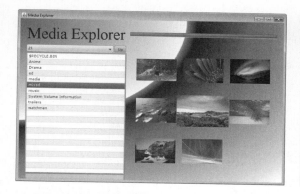
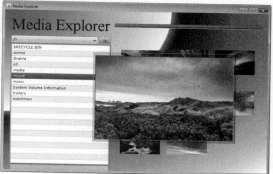

Figure 8-17. *Completed ImageFileView shown as it is expanding to fill the window*

The MediaFileView class that displays movie clips is similar to ImageFileView but ends up being quite a bit simpler. Rather than creating a new mediaPlayer, you can reuse the same mediaPlayer instance as a parameter that gets passed in. This has the added advantage that the video clip will pick up at the same point where it was playing in the thumbnail view, creating a seamless transition. The full code of MediaFileView is shown in Listing 8-7.

Listing 8-7. *MediaFileView Implementation*

```
public class MediaFileView extends FileView {

    public-init var player:MediaPlayer;

    override function create() {
        TitledBorder {
            id: "mediaTitle"
            text: file.getName()
            content: FrameBorder {
                id: "mediaFrame"
                content: SimpleMediaPlayer {
                    player: player
                }
            }
        }
    }
}
```

While the choice of borders is the same, by making use of CSS properties, you can style the media frame to be completely different. When added to Border.css, the following CSS snippet will use a darker frame, with the title on top rather than at the bottom:

```
#mediaFrame {
    border-left-width: 10;
    border-top-width: 16;
    border-bottom-width: 10;
    border-right-width: 10;
    highlight-outer: black;
    highlight-inner: gray;
    background-fill: #000020B0
}

#mediaTitle {
    position: "top";
    justification: "center";
    font: bold 11pt Serif;
    text-color: lightgray;
}
```

The final step is to instantiate the MediaFileView when a MediaThumbnail is clicked. This can be accomplished by adding an onMouseClicked event handler:

```
override var onMouseClicked = function(e) {
    viewerOpen = true;
    mediaViewer.showView(
        MediaFileView {
            file: mediaFile
            fromNode: this
            player: mediaPlayer
            onClose: function() {viewerOpen = false}
        }
    );
}
```

and also a `viewerOpen` variable that is needed to ensure the volume remains turned on while the view is open:

```
var viewerOpen = false;
init {
    mediaPlayer = MediaPlayer {
        mute: bind not (hover or viewerOpen)
```

Now the Media Viewer implementation is complete. If you run the Media Explorer application again, you will be able to click individual media thumbnails to get an enlarged view, as shown in Figure 8-18.

 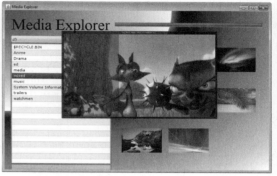

Figure 8-18. *The movie expands to fill the Media Explorer window.*

Since the view is backed by the same `SimpleMediaPlayer` used in the `MovieWidget` example earlier, you can also see the progress and change the play position by clicking anywhere on the movie.

In the next section we will show you how to add in more advanced search capabilities by using `JFXWorker` and `MigLayout`.

Creating an Asynchronous Search Form with MigLayout

In addition to the layout capabilities already discussed, JFXtras brings the power of `MigLayout` to the JavaFX platform. `MigLayout` was created by Mikael Grev to make writing Swing applications easy. It is an extremely powerful layout manager that ranks eighth of the most requested components for Sun to include in the core Java distribution.

Through the cooperation of Mikael Grev and Dean Iverson, the JFXtras `MigLayout` port was born. It provides all the power and flexibility of the Swing version of `MigLayout` applied to JavaFX nodes.

In this section you will learn how to use the JFXtras version of `MigLayout` to add a search form to the Media Explorer. In addition, we will show you how to use `JFXWorker`, the JFXtras asynchronous worker class, to run the search on a background thread so the user interface is still responsive.

Laying Out the Search Form with MigLayout

The JFXtras `MigLayout` implementation retains all the power of `MigLayout` with a simple declarative syntax. The main class is `MigLayout`, which has the properties listed in Table 8-8.

Table 8-8. *MigLayout Public Variables*

Name	Type	Description
constraints	String	The constraints for the entire layout
columns	String	The per-column constraints in String format
rows	String	The per-row constraints in String format
content	Node[]	Sequence of nodes to be laid out by the grid

The `constraints`, `columns`, and `rows` variables follow the `String` format defined by the `MigLayout` documentation. We will show some examples that demonstrate the basic use and some common arguments later. The `content` sequence is inherited from `Parent` and takes nodes with constraints specified via a special `LayoutInfo` subclass called `MigNodeLayoutInfo`, as described in Table 8-9.

Table 8-9. *MigNodeLayoutInfo Layout Settings*

Name	Type	Description
managed	Boolean	Whether `MigLayout` will perform layout on this node
constraints	String	The per-cell constraints in `MigLayout`'s String format

While the API is fairly simple, the `String` constraints supported by `MigLayout` are rich and complex. The best way to see how this comes together in a JavaFX layout is to see an example.

Before you can get started with `MigLayout`, you will need to include an extra JAR file in your classpath. JFXtras ships with a compatible version of `MigLayout`, with a file name of `miglayout-x.x.jar`. Be sure to include this in the libraries for your project.

Listing 8-8 demonstrates a basic `MediaSearch` UI that is laid out by `MigLayout`. While all the UI components are stubbed out for now, the layout populates all the necessary components needed for the `MediaSearch` class.

Listing 8-8. *Basic MigLayout for the Media Explorer Search Form*

```
public class MediaSearch extends ResizableCustomNode {
    package var name:String;
    package var date:String;
    package var dateOptions = SwingComboBox {}
    package var size:String;
    package var sizeOptions = SwingComboBox {}
    package var mediaTypes = SwingComboBox {}
    var resultText:String;
    var searchButton = Button {text: "Search"}
    var cancelButton = Button {text: "Cancel"}

    override function create() {
        MigLayout {
            constraints: "fill, wrap, insets 10"
            rows: "[][][][]4mm[][]push[]"
            columns: "[][][]"
            content: [
                migNode(Text {content: "Name"}, "alignx right"),
                migNode(TextBox {text: bind name with inverse}, "span, growx"),
                migNode(Text {content: "Date modified"}, "alignx right"),
                migNode(dateOptions, "growx"),
                migNode(TextBox {text: bind date with inverse}, "growx"),
                migNode(Text {content: "Size (KB)"}, "alignx right"),
                migNode(sizeOptions, "growx"),
                migNode(TextBox {text: bind size with inverse}, "growx"),
                migNode(Text {content: "Media type"}, "alignx right"),
                migNode(mediaTypes, "growx, wrap"),
                migNode(cancelButton, "span 2, tag cancel"),
                migNode(searchButton, "tag ok"),
                migNode(Text {content: bind resultText}, "span"),
                migNode(Line {endX: bind width - 20}, "span")
            ]
        }
    }
}
```

Some things we'd like to point out about this layout include

- The constraints variable has the parameters of fill, wrap, and insets 10. The fill parameter tells the layout to take all available space even if the individual cells are not defined to grow. wrap turns on automatic wrapping mode, and insets 10 will leave a 10 pixel border around the whole layout.

- The rows have a parameter string of [ ][ ][ ][ ]4mm[ ][ ]push[ ]. Each of the bracket pairs signifies an individual row, seven in total. Between the brackets you can put explicit spacing, which can be of several different unit types, but in this case mm refers to millimeters. The push argument is a special operation that will fill all available space and push the remaining components to the bottom of the layout.

- The columns have a parameter string of [ ][ ][ ]. Similar to rows this indicates three columns total, and since wrap is turned on, after the third component is added it will automatically go to the next row.

- The children are added in the content sequence, which is constructed of nodes with String constraints. In this case, we have statically imported the MigLayout class to take advantage of the migNode helper function, which has the node as the first argument and the constraints as the second argument.

In order to see the MediaSearch class displayed, you need to add a button to toggle between the file list and search screen:

```
var searchMode = false;
var modeButton = Button {
    text: bind if (searchMode) then "Browse" else "Search"
    action: function() {
        searchMode = not searchMode;
    }
}
```

and also create an instance of MediaSearch that is bound into the ResizableVBox layout:

```
var mediaSearch = MediaSearch {
    directory: bind selectedParent
}
override function create() {
    ResizableVBox {
        content: bind [
            ResizableHBox {
                content: [
                    parentList,
                    upButton,
                    modeButton
                ]
            },
```

```
            if (searchMode) {
                mediaSearch
            } else {
                mediaList
            }
        ]
    }
}
```

Running the updated Media Explorer will now reveal a Search button that when clicked displays the `MediaSearch`, as shown in Figure 8-19.

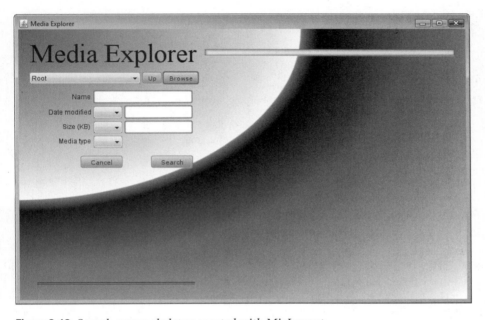

Figure 8-19. *Search screen skeleton created with MigLayout*

JFXTRAS GRID VS. MIGLAYOUT

One of the beliefs of the JFXtras project team is that developers deserve choices in technology. That is why the project fully supports and endorses the use of both the JFXtras `Grid` and `MigLayout`. Let's discuss some of the advantages of each of the technologies to make it less confusing for end users to decide which one is the right choice for their project or task.

The JFXtras `Grid` has the following strengths:

- It is written 100 percent in JavaFX, so it can be used on mobile and embedded devices.

- It takes full advantage of the JFXtras Default Layout system, making composing complicated layouts simple.

- It is declarative, and fully type-safe, so any errors will be caught at compile time.

`MigLayout` has the following strengths:

- It is an established, robust layout framework that has a large existing user base.

- It provides an exhaustive set of options that can handle even the most complicated layouts.

- It has many extended features that go beyond a basic grid, including flow layouts and docking.

Depending on your experience and what type of task you are working on, here is some guidance on which layout grid to start with:

- For arranging graphical elements, compositing nodes, or doing a dynamic layout, the JFXtras `Grid` is an ideal choice.

- For building complicated forms, doing precise alignment, or matching a template, the power of `MigLayout` will be advantageous.

- For creating reusable components or controls that need to interact seamlessly in JavaFX, the JFXtras `Grid` works well.

- For porting over existing layouts from Swing or SWT, `MigLayout` provides a seamless transition.

The best way to learn about both of these excellent grid options is to give them a try. With both of these tools at your disposal, there is no layout in JavaFX that is too hard to create.

Adding Asynchronous Search with the JFXWorker

All of the JavaFX code that you write gets invoked from the event dispatch thread (EDT). This single thread is responsible for doing all of the user interface display and rendering, so whenever your script is executing no UI refreshes can take place.

This is fine for simple examples, but most real-world applications need to invoke time-consuming tasks during which it would be unacceptable to block the user interface. This is where the JFXtras `org.jfxtras.async.JFXWorker` comes in. It is a lightweight wrapper around the `SwingWorker` class that allows you to invoke JavaFX code on a background thread without blocking the EDT.

■**Caution** The `JFXWorker` is powerful, but can be dangerous if not used properly. JavaFX code executed on the background thread must not change anything in the GUI or modify shared state accessed by the main thread. This also applies to reads or writes of bound variables which may trigger such an action. In the future, JavaFX will provide a built-in facility that makes it easier to write thread-safe code.

To use the `JFXWorker`, all you have to do is instantiate a new instance, and pass your JavaFX code in to special function handlers. The `JFXWorker` public variables are listed in Table 8-10, and the public methods are listed in Table 8-11.

Table 8-10. *JFXWorker Public Variables*

Name	Type	Description
inBackground	function():Object	The code to be executed on a background thread, which must not change the GUI or modify shared state
onDone	function(result:Object):Void	Invoked on the EDT after inBackground completes
onFailure	function(e:ExecutionException):Void	Invoked on failure or exception
result	Object	Return value of invoking inBackground, also passed to onDone
cancelled	Boolean	True if the cancel method has been called to stop the task
process	function(data:Object[]):Void	Callback to process data from the publish function

Table 8-11. *JFXWorker Public Methods*

Name	Signature	Description
cancel	function():Void	Stops execution of the background thread and sets cancelled to true
publish	function(data:Object[]):Void	Publishes data for later processing by the process function

Once a JFXWorker instance is created, it immediately kicks off the following life cycle:

1. The inBackground function is fired off on a background thread.

2. The main EDT continues processing subsequent commands in parallel.

3. Any calls from inBackground to publish are scheduled for delivery.

4. When the EDT thread is idle, process is called with the accumulated data.

5. When the inBackground thread is completed, it returns a result object.

6. At the next opportunity, onDone is called on the EDT with the result passed in.

At any time during this life cycle, cancel can be called to terminate execution. It will attempt to stop the running background thread by throwing an InterruptedException, but it is often more reliable to check the cancelled state of JFXWorker and manually break out of the inBackground thread.

Before getting started with JFXWorker, you will need to include an additional JAR file in your project. The JFXtras distribution comes with a back-ported version of the SwingWorker in swing-worker-1.2.jar. This is required for maximum portability since JavaFX is supported on Java 1.5 for Mac OS X.

Listing 8-9 shows a basic implementation of a background search worker for the MediaSearch class. It makes use of JFXWorker to execute a search method on a background thread, and while the inBackground method returns null, the search method makes use of the publish method to push partial results to be processed on the EDT.

Listing 8-9. *JFXWorker Search Implementation for the MediaSearch Class*

```
public var searchResults:File[];
var worker:JFXWorker;
var count:Integer;
var resultText:String;
var searchButton = Button {
    text: "Search"
    action: function() {
        worker.cancel();
        searchResults = [];
        count = 0;
        resultText = "Searching...";
        worker = JFXWorker {
            inBackground: function() {
                search(directory);
                return null;
            }
            process: function(data) {
                var files = data as File[];
                insert files[0..(24-count)] into searchResults;
                count += sizeof data;
                resultText = "Found {count} files";
            }
            onDone: function(results) {
                if (count == 0) {
                    resultText = "No results found";
                }
            }
        }
    }
}

function search(directory:File):Void {
    var files = directory.listFiles();
    for (file in files) {
        if (worker.cancelled) {
            return;
        }
        if (file.isDirectory()) {
            search(file);
        } else if (matches(file)) {
            worker.publish([file]);
        }
    }
}
```

```
package function matches(file:File):Boolean {
    return (ImageUtil.imageTypeSupported(file.getName()) or
            DirectoryNavigator.isMediaType(file.getName())) and
            file.getName().contains(name);
}

var cancelButton = Button {
    text: "Cancel"
    action: function() {
        worker.cancel();
    }
}
```

Some things to highlight in this implementation include:

- At the beginning of the search, cancel is called to stop any previous searches from overlapping in execution.

- The search method checks to see if the search has been cancelled in the inner loop, providing a very responsive search termination.

- The process method limits the result size to [0..24], or 25 records total, so that the application does not run out of memory. This may make a good additional configuration parameter.

- Even though the onDone method does not process the results, it is used as a callback to update the search status.

To complete the implementation, you need to hook up the search results in the DirectoryNavigator by modifying the mediaFiles variable as shown here:

```
public-read var mediaFiles = bind if (searchMode) mediaSearch.searchResults
                                   else directoryMedia;

var directoryMedia = bind currentDirectory.listFiles(
    FilenameFilter {
        override function accept(dir, name) {
            return ImageUtil.imageTypeSupported(name) or isMediaType(name);
        }
    }
);
```

Now when you run the Media Explorer, you will be able to choose a directory and search for any files that match a given name, as shown in Figure 8-20.

Although this is very powerful, it is also limiting in that many of the results returned may not be the sort of files you were expecting. For instance, several of the images returned by the query in Figure 8-20 were very low-fidelity pieces of a clock flower theme. In the next section, we will show you how to refine the search to yield more relevant results.

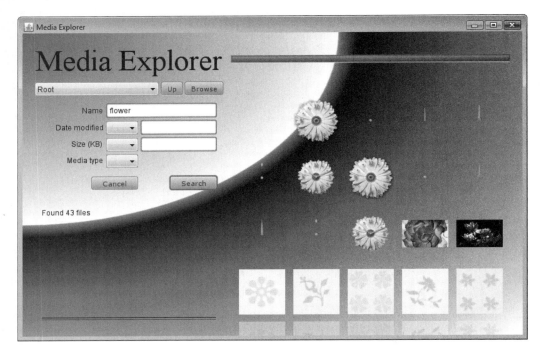

Figure 8-20. *Media Explorer basic search results*

Refining the Search with Filters

Now that the form and search infrastructure are in place, it is possible to add filters to refine the search. The various searches that you will add support for include

- *Date modified filter:* Restricts the results to files that were last modified on, before, or after the date specified by the user with day granularity

- *File size filter:* Restricts the results to files that have a size equal to, greater, or less than the specified size with kilobyte (KB) granularity

- *Media type filter:* Restricts the results to files that are images, videos, or of either type

As a simple, reusable pattern for filtering, you can make use of JavaFX closures. All filters will be defined as functions with the following signature:

```
function(:File):Boolean
```

And these functions will be set as the value of the corresponding SwingComboBoxItems so they can be easily retrieved.

Listing 8-10 shows the completed date filter implementation as a new version of the dateOptions variable that has several SwingComboBoxItems defined for each of the cases.

Listing 8-10. *Date Filter Implementation*

```
package var dateFormat = new SimpleDateFormat("MM/dd/yy");

function getUserCalendar() {
    var calendar = Calendar.getInstance();
    calendar.setTime(dateFormat.parse(date));
    return calendar;
}

function getDayGranularityCalendar(date:Date) {
    var calendar = Calendar.getInstance();
    calendar.setTime(date);
    calendar.clear(Calendar.HOUR);
    calendar.clear(Calendar.HOUR_OF_DAY);
    calendar.clear(Calendar.MINUTE);
    calendar.clear(Calendar.SECOND);
    calendar.clear(Calendar.MILLISECOND);
    return calendar;
}

package var dateOptions = SwingComboBox {
    items: [
        SwingComboBoxItem {
            text: "any"
            value: function(file:File):Boolean {true}
            selected: true
        }
        SwingComboBoxItem {
            text: "is"
            value: function(file:File):Boolean {
                getDayGranularityCalendar(new Date(file.lastModified())).
                  equals(getUserCalendar());
            }
        }
        SwingComboBoxItem {
            text: "is before"
            value: function(file:File):Boolean {
                getDayGranularityCalendar(new Date(file.lastModified())).
                  <<before>>(getUserCalendar());
            }
        }
```

```
                SwingComboBoxItem {
                    text: "is after"
                    value: function(file:File):Boolean {
                        getDayGranularityCalendar(new Date(file.lastModified())).
                          <<after>>(getUserCalendar());
                    }
                }
            }
        ]
    }
```

Some points to highlight in the date filter implementation include

- The any item has a simple function that always returns true, which will be a common strategy across all the filters.

- Two helper functions were introduced to handle Calendar manipulation, one to convert the user String into a Calendar object, and another to reduce the file date from a millisecond granularity down to day granularity to aid in comparisons.

- The Calendar functions before and after had to be escaped by double angle brackets (French quotes) because they are JavaFX keywords.

The size search can be implemented very similarly, as shown in Listing 8-11.

Listing 8-11. *Size Filter Implementation*

```
package var size:String;

function getSize():Integer {
    if (size.length() == 0) 0 else Integer.parseInt(size)
}

package var sizeOptions = SwingComboBox {
    items: [
        SwingComboBoxItem {
            text: "any"
            value: function(file:File):Boolean {true}
            selected: true
        }
        SwingComboBoxItem {
            text: "equals"
            value: function(file:File):Boolean {
                file.length() / 1024 == getSize();
            }
        }
        SwingComboBoxItem {
            text: "is less than"
            value: function(file:File):Boolean {
                file.length() / 1024 < getSize();
            }
        }
```

```
            SwingComboBoxItem {
                text: "is greater than"
                value: function(file:File):Boolean {
                    file.length() / 1024 > getSize();
                }
            }
        ]
    }
```

The only complexity with implementing the size filter is you have to be sure to divide through by 1,024 to convert bytes to kilobytes. Since the type returned by file.length() is an Integer, it will be automatically truncated.

The final filter to implement is media types. This is the simplest filter to implement, because it relies on existing functions in the ImageUtil and DirectoryNavigator classes, as shown in Listing 8-12.

Listing 8-12. *Media Type Filter Implementation*

```
package var mediaTypes = SwingComboBox {
    items: [
        SwingComboBoxItem {
            text: "any"
            selected: true
            value: function(file:File):Boolean {
                ImageUtil.imageTypeSupported(file.getName()) or
                DirectoryNavigator.isMediaType(file.getName())
            }
        }
        SwingComboBoxItem {
            text: "images"
            value: function(file:File):Boolean {
                ImageUtil.imageTypeSupported(file.getName())
            }
        }
        SwingComboBoxItem {
            text: "videos"
            value: function(file:File):Boolean {
                DirectoryNavigator.isMediaType(file.getName())
            }
        }
    ]
}
```

To complete the implementation, you need to update the matches function to extract the filter functions from the selected item for each SwingComboBox and use them in a Boolean expression to check the file, as shown in Listing 8-13.

Listing 8-13. *Updated matches Implementation That Uses Filters*

```
package function matches(file:File):Boolean {
    var dateFilter = dateOptions.selectedItem.value as
                     function(:File):Boolean;
    var sizeFilter = sizeOptions.selectedItem.value as
                     function(:File):Boolean;
    var mediaFilter = mediaTypes.selectedItem.value as
                     function(:File):Boolean;
    return file.getName().contains(name) and dateFilter(file) and
           sizeFilter(file) and mediaFilter(file);
}
```

Now that all the filters have been updated, when you run the Media Explorer the drop-downs will filter the returned search results. By restricting the filter to a specific date, size, or type range, you can greatly increase the relevance of the results. Figure 8-21 shows the same query executed earlier with the addition of a size and type filter that cut the result size by 95 percent.

Figure 8-21. *Media Explorer search page with completed filters*

Congratulations on successfully completing the Media Explorer example! If you look back on the total amount of code written for this example, you will find that the entire application was completed in less than a thousand lines of code. This is relatively small considering the complexity and feature set of the application, and is a testament to the power of JavaFX and JFXtras.

The Rest of JFXtras

In the previous section you made use of components from JFXtras including the Grid, Borders, MigLayout, and other utilities to create a rich, compelling application. However, there are even more capabilities in JFXtras that we have not yet touched on.

In this section we will describe some of the other key capabilities of JFXtras, including the unit-testing capabilities and the extended shapes library. Both of these capabilities are powerful all by themselves, and can be utilized in your application development to reduce cycle time and build richer interfaces.

JFXtras Test

The JFXtras project team values both quality and frequent releases. While these two values may seem to be at odds, it is possible to achieve both if you have a good suite of automated unit tests that can catch defects with little manual verification. This is why the JFXtras team put together a JavaFX test library that makes it easy to write JavaFX tests in JavaFX.

The cornerstone of the JFXtras test library is the Test class, which wraps one or more test cases in a declarative syntax. Table 8-12 shows the public variables on the Test class.

Table 8-12. *JFXtras Test Public Variables*

Name	Type	Description
say	String	Verbal requirement for what the test should accomplish
assume	Assumption[]	Conditions that must be met for this test to run
do	function():Object	Main execution block of the unit test
expect	Expectation[]	List of expectations that can fail the test
expectException	FXClassType	Optionally defines an exception that is expected to be thrown
test	Test[]	A list of nested test cases
cleanup	function():Void	Cleanup function called after test execution has completed

The fundamentals of any Test are say, do, and expect. In a declarative form, this describes the test, executes the test, and validates the results, respectively. Listing 8-14 shows a simple test example that demonstrates this pattern.

Listing 8-14. *Basic Test Case*

```
import org.jfxtras.test.Test;
import org.jfxtras.test.Expect.*;

Test {
    say: "A sequence should initially be empty"
    do: function() {
        var sequence:String[];
        return sequence.size();
    }
    expect: equalTo(0)
}.perform();
```

Notice that this test includes Expect as a static import. This automatically includes all the built-in expectations such as equalTo, which is used in this example. Running this test case on the command line produces the output shown here:

```
test: A sequence should initially be empty.
Test Results: 1 passed, 0 failed, 0 skipped.
Test run was successful!
```

JFXtras Test takes advantage of the fact that any script with top-level declarations can be run straight from the command line to provide a simple way to kick off individual test cases.

Nesting Test Cases

Having a single test case per file is not very practical, and you often have groups of related tests that need to be associated, which is why JFXtras allows arbitrary nesting of test cases.

Some of the advantages of allowing nesting of tests include

- Descriptions in say can be stacked to facilitate behavior-driven development (BDD).
- The surrounding do clauses can be used for test case setup.
- Test suites can be created on the fly to set up parameterized tests.

The code in Listing 8-15 shows how to set up a simple nested test case. The outer do block will be run once before each individual nested test case to make sure there are no side effects that cross over between test cases.

Listing 8-15. *Nested Test Case Example*

```
Test {
    say: "Every sequence"
    var sequence:Integer[];
    do: function() {
        sequence = [1, 2, 3, 4];
        null;
    }
    test: [
        Test {
            say: "should have a max"
            do: function() {Sequences.max(sequence)}
            expect: equalTo(4)
        }
        Test {
            say: "should have a min"
            do: function() {Sequences.min(sequence)}
            expect: equalTo(1)
        }
    ]
}.perform();
```

The results of running this example are as follows:

```
test: Every sequence should have a max.
test: Every sequence should have a min.
Test Results: 2 passed, 0 failed, 0 skipped.
Test run was successful!
```

Notice that the say clauses are concatenated to form a single sentence. This models the BDD practice that all test cases should describe a behavior, which is a single sentence describing what the object should do.

■**Note** BDD is a testing practice supported by JFXtras Test, but is neither a requirement nor outcome of using it. Plenty of resources on BDD are available, including a very informative Wikipedia article: http://en.wikipedia.org/wiki/Behavior_Driven_Development#Tools.

Fluent Expectations

So far, the test case examples have only used equalTo, which is one of the simplest expectations. However, JFXtras Test supports a full library of Expectations that can be chained in a fluent manner to read like a sentence. Table 8-13 lists all the expectations that are available as part of the 0.3 JFXtras release.

Table 8-13. *List of Expectations in JFXtras*

Expectation	Type Supported	Description
anything	N/A	Expectation that will always pass
equalTo	Object	Checks that the expected and actual values are equal
closeTo	Number	Will pass if numbers are equal within a tolerance of 0.0001
typeIs	FXType or String	Checks that the object type matches the given class type
instanceOf	FXType or String	Checks that the object is an instance of the given type
is	Expectation or Object	Syntactic sugar when passed an Expectation
isNot	Expectation or Object	Negates the Expectation passed in

We have already shown several examples of the equalTo expectation, which behaves exactly as it appears. The closeTo expectation is similar to equalTo, except it accommodates for a tolerance in floating-point arithmetic, which is very useful when comparing Numbers. The following test demonstrates an example where closeTo passes successfully:

```
Test {
    say: "should add numbers"
    do: function() {
        SequenceUtil.sum([10.4, 20.3]);
    }
    expect: closeTo(30.7)
}.perform();
```

Yet if you use equalTo instead of closeTo, you will get the following failure:

```
test: should add numbers.
TEST FAILURE:
Expected: equal to "30.7"
  Actual: 30.699999
Test Results: 0 passed, 1 failed, 0 skipped.
```

The typeIs and instanceOf expectations are similar, yet slightly different. The typeIs expectation compares an exact match between two types, while the instanceOf expectation behaves exactly the same as the instanceof method, also considering whether the types are assignable. They both accept either String or FXType arguments for maximum flexibility. If a String is used, it must be the fully qualified class name, while supplying an FXType has the benefit of compile-time type safety.

■**Tip** While using the JavaFX reflection APIs to get an FXType can be cumbersome, all of the JFXtras Exceptions extend JFXObject, which provides a getJFXClass() convenience method for retrieving the class type.

Listing 8-16 shows some examples of typeIs and instanceOf tests, all of which pass or expect an exception to be thrown. For context, it is helpful to know that ExpectException extends JFXException.

Listing 8-16. *Sample Test Demonstrating typeIs and instanceOf Expectations*

```
Test {
    say: "Check type is"
    test: [
        Test {
            say: "equal with FXType"
            do: function() {ExpectationException {}}
            expect: typeIs(ExpectationException {}.getJFXClass())
        },
        Test {
            say: "equal with String"
            do: function() {ExpectationException {}}
            expect: typeIs("org.jfxtras.test.ExpectationException")
        },
        Test {
            say: "not equal"
            do: function() {ExpectationException {}}
            expect: typeIs(JFXException {}.getJFXClass())
            expectException: ExpectationException {}.getJFXClass()
        },
        Test {
            say: "instance of"
            do: function() {ExpectationException {}}
            expect: instanceOf(JFXException {}.getJFXClass())
        }
    ]
}.perform();
```

The anything, is, and isNot expectations are most useful when chained together with other expectations. The is expectation is mostly used for syntactic sugar to make more readable expressions, while the isNot expectation is used for negation. Both of these expectations accept either another Expectation or an Object as the argument. If an Object is passed in, they behave like equalTo or not equalTo, respectively.

Listing 8-17 demonstrates some uses of is, isNot, and chained expectations.

Listing 8-17. *Example of is, isNot, and Chained Expectations*

```
Test {
    say: "Expect"
    test: [
        Test {
            say: "is equal to"
            do: function() {"boat"}
            expect: is(equalTo("boat"))
        },
```

```
            Test {
                say: "is"
                do: function() {5}
                expect: is(5)
            },
            Test {
                say: "is (fail)"
                do: function() {1}
                expect: is(2)
                expectException: ExpectationException {}.getJFXClass()
            },
            Test {
                say: "is not equal to"
                do: function() {"boats"}
                expect: isNot(equalTo("boat"))
            },
            Test {
                say: "is not"
                do: function() {1}
                expect: isNot(2)
            },
        ]
}
```

Parameterized Testing

One of the techniques for reducing the amount of duplicated code in complex tests is to use parameterized testing. Rather than writing a separate test case for each case, parameterized testing lets you iterate over a set of values as inputs to the test.

Most test frameworks need special infrastructure to implement parameterized testing; however, due to the declarative nature of JFXtras Test, parameterized testing comes naturally. Listing 8-18 shows an example of parameterized testing where a simple for loop is used to iterate over three separate tests.

Listing 8-18. *Simple Parameterized Testing Example*

```
Test {
    say: "A list of fruit"
    var fruits = ["apple", "orange", "pear"]
    test: for (fruit in fruits) Test {
        say: "should have a {fruit}"
        do: function() {
            fruits[Sequences.indexOf(fruits, fruit)];
        }
        expect: equalTo(fruit)
    }
}.perform();
```

The output of running this test is shown here. Notice that each iteration of the loop is treated like a separate test case and run individually:

```
test: A list of fruit should have a apple.
test: A list of fruit should have a orange.
test: A list of fruit should have a pear.
Test Results: 3 passed, 0 failed, 0 skipped.
Test run was successful!
```

This example demonstrates the basic pattern of parameterized testing in JFXtras Test; the pattern follows these steps:

1. Define a sequence of values to iterate over.

2. Create a list of Test instances in a loop.

3. Use a nested test to run the sequence of tests generated by the loop.

Using Assume to Calculate Output

A more realistic application of parameterized testing that also shows the use of assume was inspired from a Calculator example that Dean Iverson wrote as a tutorial on Jim Weaver's blog: http://learnjavafx.typepad.com/weblog/2009/01/javafx-calculator.html.

As shown in Figure 8-22, the calculator application is fairly simple, with the numbers 0 through 9 and basic math operators. Testing all the possible combinations of numbers and operators would normally be daunting, but can be greatly simplified by using parameterized testing.

Figure 8-22. *Dean Iverson's calculator example*

For example, Listing 8-19 shows a simple addition test that will check all the combinations of single-digit sums.

Listing 8-19. *Parameterized Testing of Addition*

```
Test {
    say: "A Calculator should"
    var calculator = Calculator {}
    test: [
        for (a in [0..9], b in [0..9]) {
            Test {
                say: "add {a} + {b}"
                do: function() {calculator.add(a, b)}
                expect: equalTo("{a + b}")
            }
        }
    ]
}.perform();
```

While the test itself is only 13 lines, it generates 100 unique test cases, as shown here:

```
test: A Calculator should add 0 + 0.
test: A Calculator should add 0 + 1.
test: A Calculator should add 0 + 2.
test: A Calculator should add 0 + 3.
test: A Calculator should add 0 + 4.
test: A Calculator should add 0 + 5.
test: A Calculator should add 0 + 6.
test: A Calculator should add 0 + 7.
test: A Calculator should add 0 + 8.
test: A Calculator should add 0 + 9.
test: A Calculator should add 1 + 0.
test: A Calculator should add 1 + 1.
...
Test Results: 100 passed, 0 failed, 0 skipped.
Test run was successful!
```

One of the unique requirements of this JavaFX calculator was that it display numbers without the decimal point if they were integral. The same test if applied to division would fail on all integral results. However, by making use of assume to limit the tests that are counted only to those that are nonintegral return values, you can still apply parameterized testing, as shown in Listing 8-20.

Listing 8-20. *Example of assume to Skip Invalid Tests*

```
Test {
    say: "A Calculator should"
    var calculator = Calculator {}
    test: [
        for (aInt in [0..9], bInt in [1..9]) {
            var a = aInt as Number;
            var b = bInt as Number;
            [
```

```
            Test {
                assume: that(a / b, closeTo(floor(a / b)))
                say: "divide {a} / {b} without a decimal"
                do: function() {calculator.divide(a, b)}
                expect: equalTo("{(a / b) as Integer}")
            },
            Test {
                assume: that(a / b, isNot(closeTo(floor(a / b))))
                say: "divide {a} / {b} with a decimal"
                do: function() {calculator.divide(a, b)}
                expect: equalTo("{a / b}")
            }
        ]
    }
  ]
}.perform();
```

When this test is run, only the tests that pass the assume clause will be counted in the results, so even though there are a total of 180 tests created, only 90 will execute, as shown here:

```
...
test: A Calculator should divide 0.0 / 1.0 without a decimal.
test: A Calculator should divide 0.0 / 2.0 without a decimal.
test: A Calculator should divide 0.0 / 3.0 without a decimal.
test: A Calculator should divide 0.0 / 4.0 without a decimal.
test: A Calculator should divide 0.0 / 5.0 without a decimal.
test: A Calculator should divide 0.0 / 6.0 without a decimal.
test: A Calculator should divide 0.0 / 7.0 without a decimal.
test: A Calculator should divide 0.0 / 8.0 without a decimal.
test: A Calculator should divide 0.0 / 9.0 without a decimal.
test: A Calculator should divide 1.0 / 1.0 without a decimal.
test: A Calculator should divide 1.0 / 2.0 with a decimal.
test: A Calculator should divide 1.0 / 3.0 with a decimal.
test: A Calculator should divide 1.0 / 4.0 with a decimal.
test: A Calculator should divide 1.0 / 5.0 with a decimal.
test: A Calculator should divide 1.0 / 6.0 with a decimal.
test: A Calculator should divide 1.0 / 7.0 with a decimal.
test: A Calculator should divide 1.0 / 8.0 with a decimal.
test: A Calculator should divide 1.0 / 9.0 with a decimal.
...
Test Results: 90 passed, 0 failed, 90 skipped.
Test run was successful!
```

Unit-Testing the Media Search with Custom Expectations

While JFXtras Test provides a lot of testing capabilities out of the box, it is also extensible, which means you can create your own custom Expectations. This section will demonstrate how to create a simple custom Expectation in the context of a real unit-testing example used in the development of the MediaSearch class for this book.

The Expectation class is the core of the JFXtras Test system. The check method on Expectation gets called with the object returned by the do method. This invokes apply or applyNumber as appropriate to see if the Expectation passed. If apply throws an ExpectationException, that is counted as a test failure; otherwise the Expectation passes. The public methods you need to implement to create a new Expectation are listed in Table 8-14.

Table 8-14. *Public Variables of the Expectation Class*

Name	Type	Description
describeAs	String	Description of the expectation, which will be output on failure
apply	function(actual:Number):Void	Function to run on expectation check
applyNumber	function(actual:Number):Void	Alternate version of apply typed for Number

The MediaSearchTest creates a couple of custom Expectations to check if a given File is valid according to the matches function. This is easily accomplished by instantiating a new Expectation and setting the describeAs and apply variables as shown in Listing 8-21.

Listing 8-21. *Expectations for Checking Media Search Matches*

```
var mediaSearch: MediaSearch;

var mediaMatch = Expectation {
    describeAs: "media should match"
    apply: function(actual) {
        if (not mediaSearch.matches(actual as File)) {
            throw ExpectationException {
                actual: "media didn't match"
            }
        }
    }
}

var mediaFailMatch = Expectation {
    describeAs: "media should not match"
    apply: function(actual) {
        if (mediaSearch.matches(actual as File)) {
            throw ExpectationException {
                actual: "media matched"
            }
        }
    }
}
```

These expectations can then be used to test all of the different filters in the MediaSearch class by checking if matches returns the correct value. Listing 8-22 shows a subset of the test suite that checks the name filter.

Listing 8-22. *MediaSearch Name Filter Unit Tests*

```
Test {
    say: "Media"
    var imageTempFile: File;
    var mediaTempFile: File;
    var otherTempFile: File;
    do: function() {
        mediaSearch = MediaSearch {};
        imageTempFile = File.createTempFile("image", ".jpg");
        mediaTempFile = File.createTempFile("media", ".flv");
        otherTempFile = File.createTempFile("other", ".foo");
    }
    test: [
        Test {
            say: "name search should"
            test: [
                Test {
                    say: "match"
                    do: function() {
                        mediaSearch.name = "image";
                        imageTempFile;
                    }
                    expect: mediaMatch
                }
                Test {
                    say: "fail"
                    do: function() {
                        mediaSearch.name = "something-else";
                        imageTempFile;
                    }
                    expect: mediaFailMatch
                }
            ]
        }
    ]
}.perform();
```

Running the MediaSearchTest results in the following output:

```
test: Media name search should match.
test: Media name search should fail.
Test Results: 2 passed, 0 failed, 0 skipped.
Test run was successful!
```

To view the full test suite with all 23 tests for the different combinations of positive and negative tests per filter, see the source code in the MediaExplorer4 project.

Extended Shapes

JFXtras provides a large library of extended shapes that you can use to build rich user interfaces. This includes everything from standard shapes like triangles and polygons to specialized shapes like balloons, crosses, and astroids. These shapes complement the built-in shapes that come with JavaFX, which makes it possible to construct intricate, scalable user interfaces purely with vector graphics.

A shapes demo comes with JFXtras that shows all of the available shapes and is an excellent example of how to use the shapes library. In Figure 8-23 you can see the JFXtras shapes demo showing some Lauburu variations.

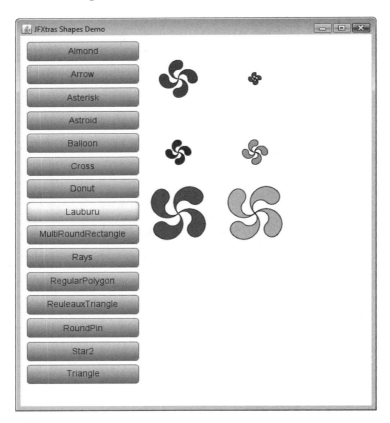

Figure 8-23. *The JFXtras shapes demo showing Lauburu variations*

All of the JFXtras shapes are rendered as vector graphics and are fully configurable; you can modify the line style, line weight, line color, fill color, and size. In addition, many of the shapes have additional configuration options that let you further customize their appearance. Table 8-15 lists all the available shapes in the JFXtras library, including their configuration capabilities.

Table 8-15. *JFXtras Shapes and Variables That Can Be Configured*

Shape	Name	Description	Variable That Can Be Configured
	Almond	Intersection of two circles (Vesica Piscis)	centerX, centerY, width
	Arrow	Arrow shape	x, y, width, height, depth, rise
	Asterisk	Asterisk with rounded corners	centerX, centerY, width, radius, beams, roundness
	Astroid	Hypocloid with four cusps	centerX, centerY, radius
	Balloon	Rectangular shape with a tab	x, y, width, height, arc, anglePosition, tabWidth, tabHeight, tabLocation, tabDisplacement
	Cross	Symmetrical cross shape	centerX, centerY, width, radius, roundness
	Donut	Regular polygon with a hole	centerX, centerY, innerRadius, outerRadius, sides
	Lauburu	Four comma-shaped heads	centerX, centerY, radius
	MultiRoundRectangle	Rectangle with configurable corners	x, y, width, height, topLeftWidth/Height, topRightWidth/Height, bottomLeftWidth/Height, bottomRightWidth/Height
	Rays	Multiple rays extend from center	centerX, centerY, rays, radius, extent, rounded
	RegularPolygon	Polygon with equal sides	centerX, centerY, sides, radius
	ReuleauxTriangle	Curved triangle shape	centerX, centerY, radius

Continued

Table 8-15. *Continued*

Shape	Name	Description	Variable That Can Be Configured
	RoundPin	Cone with rounded top	centerX, centerY, height, radius
	Star2	Multipoint star	centerX, centerY, innerRadius, outerRadius, count
	ETriangle	Equilateral triangle	x, y, width
	ITriangle	Isosceles triangle	x, y, width, height
	RTriangle	Right triangle	x, y, width, height, anglePosition

There is also a wealth of additional information and examples in the JFXtras Javadoc documentation, which is included in the source distribution and can also be accessed from the main web site.

As an additional example of how to use the JFXtras shapes, we will show you how to extend the drawing program from Chapter 3 to include these additional shapes.

DRAWJFXTRAS: EXTENDING DRAWJFX WITH SHAPES

In this exercise you will take the DrawJFX program defined in Chapter 3 and extend it to include the ability to draw all of the JFXtras shapes.

The first step is to add the JFXtras JAR file to the classpath of your application. You can download the latest source distribution from the JFXtras project web site:

http://code.google.com/p/jfxtras/downloads/list

Next you will need to add additional DrawingToolNodes for each of the JFXtras shapes. The procedure is similar for all the shapes, so we will show a few representative samples and let you define the rest of the shapes yourself.

The AbstractFillableDrawingToolNode implementation for the Almond shape is shown here:

```
public class AlmondDrawingToolNode extends AbstractFillableDrawingToolNode {

    override var shapeProducer = ShapeProducer {
        produceShape: function() {
            Almond {width: 0}
        }
        sizeShape: function(shape, x, y) {
            var almond = shape as Almond;
            almond.width = Math.sqrt(Math.pow(Math.abs(x), 2)
                        + Math.pow(Math.abs(y), 2));
```

```
            almond.transforms =
                Transform.rotate(Math.toDegrees(Math.atan(y / x))
                + (if (x > 0) 270 else 90), 0, 0);
        }
    }

    init {
        toolFaceNode = Almond {
            centerX: 16
            centerY: 16
            width: 8
            fill: bind if (filled) Color.BLACK else Color.TRANSPARENT
            stroke: Color.BLACK
        }
    }
}
```

It uses a similar algorithm to the CircleDrawingToolNode to calculate the width of the Almond based on the distance from the center of the shape. However, in addition to setting the width to the distance from the center, it also calculates the angle of the cursor and uses that to rotate the shape.

The Arrow shape is a little different in that it has both a width and height that can be set independently. The code to create an ArrowDrawingToolNode is next:

```
public class ArrowDrawingToolNode extends AbstractFillableDrawingToolNode {

    override var shapeProducer = ShapeProducer {
        produceShape: function() {
            Arrow {width: 0, height: 0}
        }
        sizeShape: function(shape, x, y) {
            var arrow = shape as Arrow;
            arrow.width = x;
            arrow.height = y;
        }
    }

    init {
        toolFaceNode = Arrow {
            x: 3
            y: 5
            width: 26
            height: 22
            fill: bind if (filled) Color.BLACK else Color.TRANSPARENT
            stroke: Color.BLACK
        }
    }
}
```

All the other shapes end up being variations of one or the other algorithm. However, you can get creative about how to map the x and y coordinates to shape variables. As an example, here is a RoundPin sizeShape implementation that sets the radius to the x coordinate and the height to the y coordinate:

```
sizeShape: function(shape, x, y) {
    var distance = Math.sqrt(Math.pow(Math.abs(x), 2)
                    + Math.pow(Math.abs(y), 2));
    var roundPin = shape as RoundPin;
    roundPin.radius = x;
    roundPin.height = y;
}
```

After creating all of the DrawingToolNodes for the different shapes, the last step is to wire them up to the main tool palette. All of the code changes are in the DrawJFXMain file starting with the Stage title:

```
Stage {
    title: "DrawJFXtras"
```

And then we add the shape title to the scene content:

```
// Shape text
Text {
    content: "Extra Shapes:"
    textOrigin: TextOrigin.TOP
    layoutX: 635
    layoutY: 2
    font: Font.font(null, 9)
}
```

And finally we add in two VBoxes that refer to all 15 of the JFXtras shapes:

```
// Second row of tools
VBox {
    spacing: 0
    layoutX: 635
    layoutY: 12
    content: [
        AlmondDrawingToolNode {filled: false}
        ArrowDrawingToolNode {filled: false}
        AsteriskDrawingToolNode {filled: false}
        AstroidDrawingToolNode {filled: false}
        BalloonDrawingToolNode {filled: false}
        CrossDrawingToolNode {filled: false}
        DonutDrawingToolNode {filled: false}
        LauburuDrawingToolNode {filled: false}
        MultiRoundRectangleDrawingToolNode {filled: false}
        RaysDrawingToolNode {filled: false}
        RegularPolygonDrawingToolNode {filled: false}
        ReuleauxTriangleDrawingToolNode {filled: false}
        RoundPinDrawingToolNode {filled: false}
```

```
            Star2DrawingToolNode {filled: false}
            TriangleDrawingToolNode {filled: false}
        ]
    }
}
// Third row of tools
VBox {
    spacing: 0
    layoutX: 667
    layoutY: 12
    content: [
        (above repeated with filled: true)
    ]
}
```

Upon running the completed program, the DrawJFX program will now have three times as many tools, with access to all the different types of shapes available from JFXtras, as shown here:

Try drawing a scene with the new shapes to see what you can come up with!

The Future of JFXtras

Since its inception, the JFXtras project has taken off with lots of additional functionality contributed by top-notch open source developers. There are already several new initiatives in the works for future releases, as well as some great ideas on where to take the project.

While nothing is set in stone, some of things to anticipate in future JFXtras releases include

- Custom components written in pure JavaFX

- Graphing and charting components

- More native JavaFX layouts

- UI test automation from JavaFX

- Mobile distribution (common profile only)

Also, the JFXtras project is always looking for additional contributors to help expand and improve the library. If you are interested, feel free to sign up on the developers mailing list and contribute whatever you can!

Other Libraries

Java has one of the most active and thriving open source communities of any technology in the world. This has greatly contributed to its success as a platform, which has led the way in innovation.

JavaFX has the same potential to become a mecca of open source projects. Many Java open source teams are branching out to include JavaFX components in their distribution, and there is a crop of new JavaFX-based projects that is appearing at a rapid pace.

In this section we will highlight some of the new free and open source JavaFX projects that have appeared since its launch, with a focus on libraries and frameworks that you can build on.

Atomic Tile: 2D Tile-Based Game Authoring

Atomic Tile (Figure 8-24) is the brainchild of Joshua Marinacci. It currently consists of a visual tile editor program to author new maps and a JavaFX runtime for rendering the maps as an online game. The sample game featured on the project web site, Block Mover, is a throwback to classic tile games where level design made the game.

The goal of Block Mover is to help your little pig-tailed horn girl escape from the maze by making it to the exit. You can lift stack blocks by lifting them up and dropping them on top of each other. But be careful, because you can only jump one block high, so it is easy to get trapped!

Atomic Tile's level editor (Figure 8-25) allows you to take collections of pictures and drop them into a grid of 64×64 squares. The level editor also automatically grows the game area to fit all the tiles, and has a convenient brush mode to replicate the same tile by dragging.

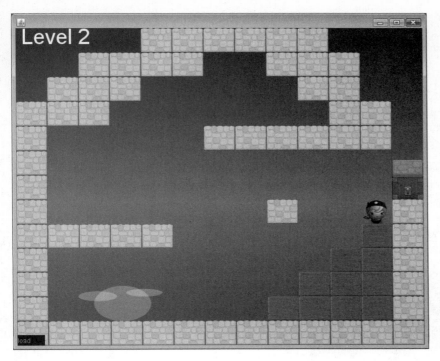

Figure 8-24. *Escaping from the maze in Block Mover*

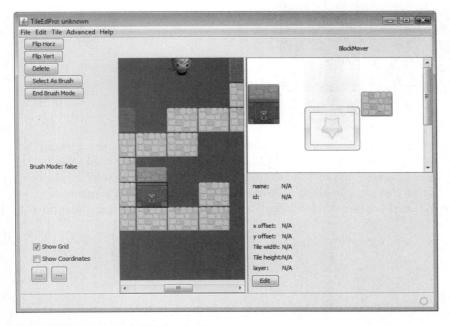

Figure 8-25. *The Atomic Tile level editor*

If you have ever dreamed of creating the next great puzzle game craze to sweep the nation, then Atomic Tile is the project for you. You can run the projects and download the code from the open source repository at

```
http://kenai.com/projects/atomictile/
```

I am sure Josh would appreciate the extra contributions. Also, the technology is licensed under a liberal BSD license, so there is nothing stopping you from leveraging this as part of a larger undertaking.

FXUtil: Inverse Kinetics Library

FXUtil is an inverse kinetics library developed by Michael Heinrichs of Sun. He published it publicly as a free JavaFX library, which has already been getting quite a bit of attention.

Figure 8-26 shows a simple kinetic snake demo that is featured on the web site. Anywhere you click the snake will follow, bending and curving according to the skeleton and bone structure set up in the code.

Figure 8-26. *The FXUtil kinetic snake demo*

The public APIs for FXUtil are simple but powerful. You define a set of Bones to be animated that can be organized in any arbitrary tree hierarchy. These Bones are then added to a Skeleton, which extends Node and can be added to the scene graph. You can then use the custom FXUtil animation classes to modify the whole structure by only moving a single point.

A more complicated sample, which will also form the basis of the official FXUtil tutorial, is shown in Figure 8-27.

Figure 8-27. *The FXUtil stick man from the tutorial*

You can grab any part of the stick man's body and drag to animate the whole figure. Some things to expect in the future versions of FXUtil include

- Different target shapes
- More types of animations
- Ability to fix positions and angles
- Soft constraints like springs or masses

If you are interested in doing more with FXUtil, be sure to check out the public web site at

`http://www.fxutil.com/`

FEST-JavaFX: Automated UI Testing of JavaFX

Alex Ruiz, the author of FEST-Swing, has embarked on a mission to bring JavaFX UI test automation to the masses. FEST is designed for functional UI testing, which complements the unit-testing capabilities of JFXtras Test.

While the FEST-JavaFX project is still in its infancy, Alex has already shown some impressive demos of what it is capable of. Most recently he demonstrated a test of drag-and-drop capabilities on his blog, as shown in Figure 8-28.

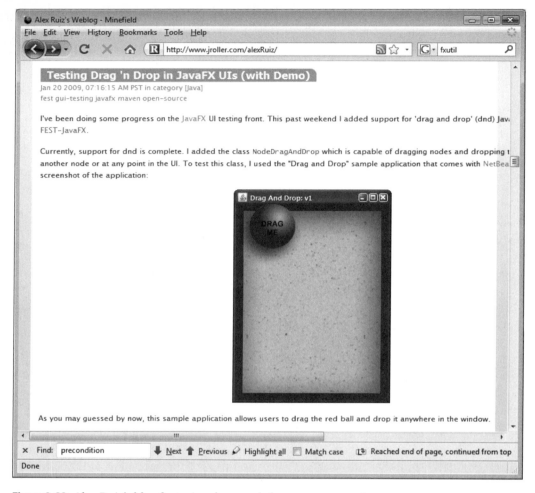

Figure 8-28. *Alex Ruiz's blog featuring drag-and-drop test automation*

FEST-JavaFX tests are written in Java and run via a standard JUnit or TestNG test runner. They are written using a fluent syntax that is similar to FEST-Swing. Listing 8-23 shows a sample calculator test that was published by Alex on his blog at: http://www.jroller.com/alexRuiz/

Listing 8-23. *Sample FEST-JavaFX Test from Alex Ruiz's Blog*

```
@Test public class CalculatorTest {

  private JavaFxRobot robot;
  private FrameFixture calculator;
```

```
@BeforeMethod public void setUp() {
  robot = BasicJavaFxRobot.robotWithNewAwtHierarchy();
  JFrame calculatorFrame = launch(Calculator.class);
  calculator = new FrameFixture(robot, calculatorFrame);
}

@AfterMethod public void tearDown() {
  robot.cleanUp();
}

public void shouldUpdateTextBoxWithPressedNumber() {
  calculator.swingButton(withText("8")).click();
  calculator.textBox().requireText("8");
  calculator.swingButton(withText("6")).click();
  calculator.textBox().requireText("86");
}
}
```

FEST-JavaFX has not yet been released, but is available in source from the Google Code repository. For more information about FEST-JavaFX, be sure to check out the project site:

```
http://code.google.com/p/fest-javafx/
```

MemeFX: Rich JavaFX Components

MemeFX is a new set of JavaFX components developed by Mauricio Aguilar. He has done an excellent job of documenting the library from Web Start demos and documentation to full YouTube videos of the components in action. Figure 8-29 shows the Images Accordion demo from the project web site.

Figure 8-29. *MemeFX Images Accordion Demo*

Here's the full range of components that MemeFX offers:

- *Images Accordion*: An image-based accordion control that can be oriented vertically or horizontally, and supports a slick spring-based animation transition.

- *Stage Controller*: A JavaFX Stage utility class that can position the Stage at the edge of the screen, receive callbacks on resize or move, animate Stage movement, and persist the Stage's coordinates.

- *TextHTML*: A new control that allows you to render a subset of HTML in JavaFX. Supports hyperlinks that can be bound to application actions.

- *Gauges and Knobs*: Includes a set of basic gauges in different sizes and orientations, as well as a knob dial that is similar to a slider. Some of the options include basic skinning, configurable rotation speed, and vibration of the needle. (See Figure 8-30.)

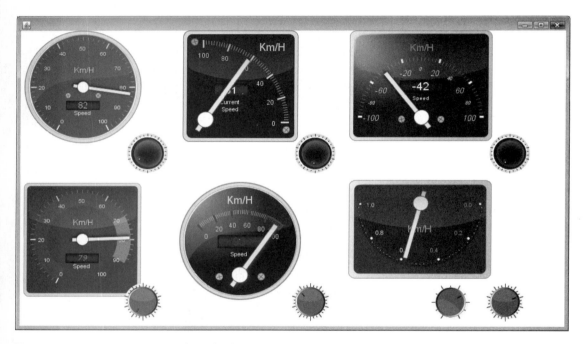

Figure 8-30. *MemeFX Gauges and Knobs demo*

Licensed under the New BSD License, MemeFX is suitable for use both in open source and commercial applications. The latest release is available in source and binary format on the Google Code project web site:

http://code.google.com/p/memefx/

MemeFX is sure to be a valuable addition to your tool chest of JavaFX components and libraries.

Predicting the Future of JavaFX

There are a lot of good indications about what future versions of JavaFX will provide based on public information on Sun blogs, forums, and in the issue-tracking system.

Some things that are likely to be in JavaFX's future are

- *Scene graph and effects performance*: Like any new technology, JavaFX has some performance warts, especially related to complicated scene graphs and rendering of effects. Addressing the performance issues is the number one focus of the JavaFX team, which was proven by some of the foundational support they did on more efficient data types and refactoring of the scene graph.

- *Browser integration*: Sun hinted at integration with WebKit to provide a cross-platform embedded browser solution, and while it did not make the early JavaFX releases, expect this to come out soon.

- *3D*: Many of the early JavaFX demos featured 3D integration, and again, while it did not make the early JavaFX releases, this is on the list of features that we'll see later.

- *Visual designer*: Sun is planning to deliver a JavaFX visual designer to reduce the barrier of entry for graphics designers to build complicated JavaFX user interfaces. This will augment the existing Production Suite support to bridge the gap between developers and designers.

One of the best places to find out more about the upcoming releases, as well as to contribute defects and enhancements, is the public issue-tracking system at

```
http://javafx-jira.kenai.com/secure/Dashboard.jspa
```

Figure 8-31 shows a snapshot of SoMa, the next release after JavaFX 1.2, which already has 299 runtime defects lined up.

Perhaps the most important driver for future innovation in JavaFX is you, the developer. Take the opportunity to give feedback back to the JavaFX team on what features you need via the community forums, blogs, and issue tracker. Better yet, take matters into your own hands and built your own free or open source project to extend JavaFX in new and innovative ways.

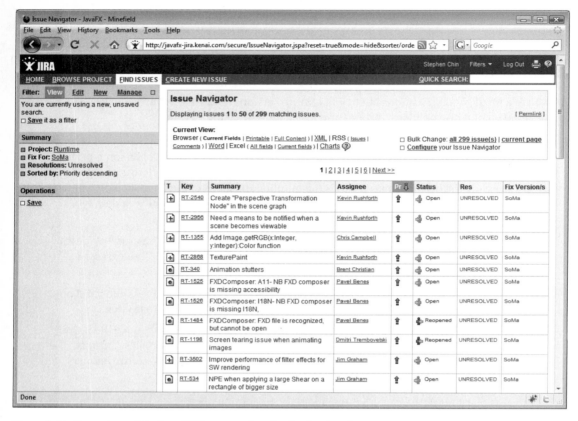

Figure 8-31. *Snapshot of the JavaFX issue tracker for the SoMa release*

Summary

This chapter has introduced you to some of the third-party tools and technologies available for JavaFX. In this chapter you learned how to:

- Deploy your JavaFX application as a desktop widget using WidgetFX
- Easily create resizable user interfaces using the JFXtras layouts
- Build complex, dynamic grids and forms using JFXtras `Grid` and `MigLayout`
- Improve the performance and responsiveness of your application using the `JFXWorker`
- Apply borders and shapes from the JFXtras project to enhance your application
- Unit test your JavaFX application using JFXtras Test and FEST-JavaFX
- Take advantage of other third-party free and open source libraries

Most important, by leveraging projects such as JFXtras and WidgetFX together with the JavaFX platform, you were able to build a full Media Browser application with a rich, interactive user interface today, without reinventing the wheel.

References

- The WidgetFX home page, where you can download the WidgetFX dock and the developer SDK: http://widgetfx.org/

- The JFXtras project page, where you can download the latest release: http://code.google.com/p/jfxtras/

- WidgetFX and JFXtras project leader Stephen Chin's blog: http://steveonjava.com/

- Jim Clarke's blog on JavaFX and JFXtras: http://code.google.com/p/jfxtras/

- MigLayout home page, which includes additional documentation: http://www.miglayout.com/

- Behavior-driven development Wikipedia article: http://en.wikipedia.org/wiki/Behavior_Driven_Development#Tools

- Atomic Tile project home page: http://kenai.com/projects/atomictile/

- FXUtil project home page: http://www.fxutil.com/

- FEST-JavaFX project home page: http://code.google.com/p/fest-javafx/

- MemeFX project home page: http://code.google.com/p/memefx/

- JavaFX Issue Tracker: http://javafx-jira.kenai.com/secure/Dashboard.jspa

CHAPTER 9

■ ■ ■

Building a Professional JavaFX Application

The only way to learn a new programming language is by writing programs in it.

—Brian Kernighan and Dennis Ritchie

The purpose of this chapter is to show you some of the professional techniques we use to write real-world JavaFX applications. These techniques are useful when you need to go beyond the flashy demos and fun applets that are all the rage on the Web. You will need them when you have to work with a graphic designer. You will find them useful when you are confronted with the memory usage and performance trade-offs that developers need to consider for real applications. And of course, you'll see tips and techniques for taking care of the number one thing you have to worry about for real applications that you don't for demos: enhancing the user's experience.

You do have to take into account one other thing when developing a professional application: the schedule. Real-world business considerations mean that you do not have unlimited time to develop your applications. This chapter will show you how to get the most out of the JavaFX SDK classes and some time-saving third-party libraries, and how to leverage the power of the Java platform.

The applications that are shown in this chapter are of a particular type. They are Rich Internet Applications (RIAs if you enjoy trendy acronyms). These applications all rely on the ability to communicate with RESTful web services over the Internet. This chapter is heavy on code examples; lots of show and not as much tell. We firmly believe that not only is this the best way to demonstrate programming techniques, but also, and even more importantly, reading other people's code is the best, and fastest, way to become a better developer yourself. So get ready for a fast-paced tour of the wonderful world of Rich Internet Applications!

Writing RESTful Web Service Clients

Before you go forth and populate desktops, websites, and mobile devices everywhere with beautiful JavaFX Internet applications, one little detail needs to be covered. How do you connect to and exchange information with a server on the Internet using the JavaFX platform? We're so glad you asked. Read on!

Rise of the RESTful Web

The past few years have seen a rise in so-called RESTful web services. REST, an acronym for representational state transfer, is an architectural style that is used to describe the way in which the World Wide Web was implemented. In a nutshell, a RESTful web service is one in which you use HTTP, the underlying protocol of the Web, to interact with resources that exist on a server. It is perhaps more accurate to say that you are interacting with the representation of a resource on the server. The resource may represent a conceptual resource, such as a user account, or a physical resource, such as an image or a particular web page. Instead of humans, another piece of software will typically read the data returned by a RESTful web service. So rather than HTML, the web service will usually return XML or JavaScript Object Notation (JSON) data. Some web services are capable of returning either.

Normally when you ask for a web page, you are performing a request using HTTP's GET method. In REST terms, you are getting the HTML representation of a web page resource. Three other HTTP methods are commonly used in addition to GET. The POST method is used to create a new instance of a resource, the PUT method is used to update the data associated with a resource, and finally, the DELETE method is used to delete a resource. Using these four methods (also sometimes called *verbs* or *actions*), you can accomplish a remarkably wide variety of tasks.

Using the HttpRequest Class

JavaFX supports communicating with RESTful web services using the HttpRequest class located in the javafx.io.http package. The requests made using this class are inherently asynchronous; they always take place in a background thread. The HttpRequest class defines a plethora of instance variables that are callback functions. These are used to notify your code when a significant event takes place in the life cycle of your request. The interface for this class is exceedingly elegant and powerful, providing you with everything you will need to implement the communication portion of a web service client.

The most common usages of HttpRequest are covered in this section. The documentation for the HttpRequest class is excellent and can be used to fill in the remaining details. Each request can be broken down into a series of steps. At each step there is both an instance variable and a callback function that you can use to track the progress of the request as it executes in the background thread. For example, when a new request starts, a Boolean instance variable named started will be set to true. Also, a callback function instance variable named onStarted will be called if it is non-null.

We will start by examining the GET request. This is the most common type of request you will deal with. It is used to retrieve information from a web server. To begin with, a connection is made to the server. The request is then sent, and the client waits for the server's response. The response, when it arrives, consists of the status line, one or more headers, and the message body. The life cycle of a GET request made using the HttpRequest class is detailed in the following steps:

1. The request is started. The started variable will be set to true and onStarted called.

2. A connection attempt is made to the server. The connecting variable is set to true, and onConnecting is called. If the connection is successful, the doneConnect variable is set to true, and onDoneConnect is called.

3. The HTTP GET request is sent to the server, and a response is received.

4. The reading of the response begins. The readingHeaders variable is set to true, and the onReadingHeaders function is called.

5. The response code is read. The responseCode variable is set to the integer value of the server's response code, and onResponseCode is called with the responseCode passed as a parameter. A response code in the 200s indicates success, a code in the 300s indicates a redirection, a code in the 400s indicates an error with the request, and a code in the 500s indicates a server error.

6. The response message is read. Each response code has a corresponding human-readable message. For example, the success code 200 has the message "OK," while the message "Not Found" corresponds to error code 404. The responseMessage string variable is set when the response message is read. The onResponseMessage function is called, and the responseMessage is passed as its parameter.

7. If the response code and message indicate an error, the server may also send additional error information as part of the message body. If so, the error variable will be set to the input stream containing the message body, and onError will be called and the error input stream passed as a parameter.

8. The response headers are read. The onResponseHeaders function is called, and a sequence containing the header names is passed as a parameter. Calling the request's getResponseHeaderValue() function and passing a header name as the parameter can obtain the values of the headers. After the headers have been read, the doneHeaders variable is set to true, and onDoneHeaders is called.

9. The reading of the response body begins. The reading variable is set to true, and onReading is called.

10. If the server has sent a Content-Length header that indicates the size of the response body, the toread variable will be set to the content length, and the onToRead function will be called and toread passed as the parameter.

11. The response body is read. As the body is read, the read variable will be updated to indicate the number of bytes that have been read so far. Whenever the read variable is updated, onRead is also called, and the read variable is passed as the parameter.

12. Once the response has been read, the input stream will be made available. A reference to the input stream is placed in the `input` variable, and the `onInput` function will be called with the `input` variable as the parameter. It is the application's responsibility to close the input stream after it has been read.

13. When the input stream has been closed, the `doneRead` variable will be set to `true`, and the `onDoneRead` function will be called to indicate that the reading of the response body is now complete.

14. The request is now complete, and the `done` variable is set to `true` and `onDone` called. This is step is always executed, regardless of whether the request completed successfully, the server returned an error, or an exception occurs during one of the previous steps.

If an exception occurs during one of the preceding steps, a reference to the exception will be placed in the `exception` variable, the `onException` function will be called, and the `exception` will be passed as a parameter. In practice, you will rarely need to monitor every step in the life cycle of your requests. Typically, only a few of them are of interest to an application. Two other variables are frequently used when declaring an `HttpRequest`:

- `location`: The URL string that is the target for this request.

- `method`: A string, which can be `HttpRequest.GET`, `HttpRequest.POST`, `HttpRequest.PUT`, or `HttpRequest.DELETE`. The default value is `HttpRequest.GET`.

Listing 9-1 shows an example of an `HttpRequest`. In the example, a `GET` request is made to this book's website, which is located at `http://www.projavafx.com`. The example demonstrates how to read headers, track the progress of the reading of the response body, and actually read the resulting input stream (always remember to close the stream when finished!).

Listing 9-1. *An `HttpRequest` to http://www.projavafx.com*

```
var getRequest:HttpRequest = HttpRequest {
  location: "http://www.projavafx.com"

  onResponseHeaders: function( headerNames:String[] ) {
    println( "Headers:" );
    for (name in headerNames) {
      println( "  {name}: {getRequest.getResponseHeaderValue( name )}" );
    }
    println( "" );
  }

  onRead: function( bytes:Long ) {
    if (getRequest.toread > 0) {
      var progress = (bytes as Number) / (getRequest.toread as Number) * 100.0;
      println( "Read progress: {bytes} bytes read ({progress} %)");
    }
  }
  onInput: function( inputStream:java.io.InputStream ) {
    var br:BufferedReader;
    println( "\nHTML Response:" );
```

```
      try {
        br = new BufferedReader( new InputStreamReader( inputStream ) );
        var line = br.readLine();
        while (line != null) {
          println( line );
          line = br.readLine();
        }
      } finally {
        if (br != null) {
          br.close();
        } else {
          inputStream.close();
        }
      }
    }

    onException: function(ex: java.lang.Exception) {
      println("onException - exception: {ex.getClass()} {ex.getMessage()}");
    }

    onDone: function() {
      if (getRequest.responseCode >= 400) {
        println( "Error during request: {getRequest.responseMessage}" );
      }
    }
  }
}
getRequest.start();
```

■Caution The HttpRequest will not execute in a normal command-line script. If you want to experiment with the HttpRequest class, you are advised to create a simple stage in order to run a foreground window while the request executes.

A heavily abridged version of the output produced by this request is shown here:

```
Headers
  :
  date: Thu, 05 Mar 2009 22:15:07 GMT
  server: Apache/2.2.3 (CentOS)
  last-modified: Mon, 12 Jan 2009 10:13:58 GMT
  etag: "28e2274-1074-460465d694580"
  accept-ranges: bytes
  content-length: 4212
  connection: close
```

```
    content-type: text/html
    x-pad: avoid browser bug

Read progress: 168 bytes read (3.9886038 %)
Read progress: 336 bytes read (7.9772077 %)

... some progress omitted ...

Read progress: 4200 bytes read (99.7151 %)
Read progress: 4212 bytes read (100.0 %)

HTML Response:
<html xmlns="http://www.w3.org/1999/xhtml">
<head>
<meta http-equiv="Content-Type" content="text/html; charset=utf-8" />
<title>Pro JavaFX Platform</title>
<style type="text/css">

... many lines of HTML omitted ...

</body>
</html>
```

A DELETE request is similar to a GET request except that the method variable of the request is set to HttpRequest.DELETE. During a DELETE request, there is no response body to read. Therefore, the following life-cycle steps are not present: onReading, onToRead, onRead, onInput, and onDoneRead. When making a PUT or a POST request, the method variable of the request is set to HttpRequest.PUT or HttpRequest.POST, respectively. The PUT and POST requests share a similar life cycle that has additional steps due to the fact that they involve sending a message body to the server as part of the request. Referring back to the life-cycle list for a GET request, the PUT and POST requests add the following steps after step 2 of the previous list (the onConnecting/onDoneConnect step).

2a. The writing of the message body begins. The writing variable will be set to true, and onWriting is called.

2b. The output stream is made available so the application can write data into the request. A reference to the output stream is placed in the output variable, the onOutput function is called, and output is passed as a parameter. The application must close the output stream after it has finished writing its data.

2c. The output stream is closed, and the message body is about to be sent to the server. The towrite variable will hold the number of bytes to be written, and onToWrite is called with towrite as the parameter.

2d. Progress is updated as the data is written to the server. The written variable will be updated with the latest count of bytes transmitted. Whenever the written variable is updated, the onWritten function is also called, and written is passed as a parameter.

2e. The sending of data to the server is complete. The doneWrite variable is set to true, and onDoneWrite is called.

After these steps, the life cycle continues exactly the same as for the GET request. As you can see, a lot of functionality is packed into this one class. But retrieving data from the server is only half the battle when writing a web service client. You also need to make sense of the returned data by parsing it into your own data structures so you can present it to your user. The next sections will show you how to parse both JSON and XML data in JavaFX.

Writing JSON Clients

JSON is a simple format for data interchange over the Web. JSON is becoming a popular choice for web services due to its compact and efficient format. Its data is plain text and is easily readable by both humans and computers. Best of all, because it is so simple, you can learn pretty much all there is to know about the syntax in about 5 minutes of casual reading. Start your timer.

JSON supports two types of data: an object and an array. An *object* is simply a list of comma-separated name/value pairs enclosed by curly brackets. Each name/value pair is separated by a colon as shown here:

```
{ name1 : value1, name2 : value2, ... nameN : valueN }
```

An *array* is simply a list of comma-separated values enclosed by square brackets:

```
[ value1, value2, value3, ... valueN ]
```

A name is a string, and a value can be an object, a number, a string, another array, or any of the following special values: true, false, null. A string is enclosed by double quotes and can be any valid Java string (including support for Unicode characters). The following code snippet is an example of JSON syntax:

```
{ "elements" : [
  { "symbol" : "H", "name" : "Hydrogen",  "atomicNumber" : 1 },
  { "symbol" : "He", "name" : "Helium",   "atomicNumber" : 2 },
  { "symbol" : "C", "name" : "Carbon",    "atomicNumber" : 6 },
  { "symbol" : "O", "name" : "Oxygen",    "atomicNumber" : 8 }
]}
```

If you have extra time left on your 5-minute timer, you can check the resources at the end of the chapter for more information on JSON syntax.

Parsing JSON in JavaFX

The class used to parse both JSON and XML documents in JavaFX is the PullParser class located in the javafx.data.pull package. The PullParser is built around the concept of events. The parser issues an event whenever it encounters a new token that has structural significance in the document being parsed. In JSON, this includes things like the start and end of the document, the start and end of a value, and the start and end of an array. All of these things will cause an event to be created by the parser. Parsing a document, then, is simply an exercise in handling the events you care about. If you look at the documentation for PullParser, you will see a plethora of variables in the class. Most of these are defined constants used in event notification. Only a few variables really need to be considered when instantiating a parser:

- documentType should be set to either `PullParser.XML` or `PullParser.JSON` depending on which type of document you are parsing.

- input is the `java.io.InputStream` that will be parsed. Always remember to close the input stream when the parser is finished.

- event will always be set to the current parser event.

- onEvent is a callback function that allows you to handle events as the parser generates them.

Listing 9-2 illustrates how to write a JSON pull parser that simply prints every event to the console.

Listing 9-2. *An Example of a JSON Pull Parser*

```
try {
   var parser = PullParser {
     input: inputStream
     documentType: PullParser.JSON;
     onEvent: function( e:Event ) {
       print( "{%-20s e.typeName} {%-20s e.name}" );
       if (e.name == "atomicNumber" ) {
         println( "{%-20d e.integerValue}" );
       } else {
         println( "{%-20s e.text}" );
       }
     }
   }
   println( "{%-20s "Event Type"} {%-20s "Event Name"} {%-20s "Data"}" );
   println( "{%-20s "=========="} {%-20s "=========="} {%-20s "===="}" );
   parser.parse();
} finally {
   inputStream.close();
}
```

This is an example of using a pull parser in callback mode. In this mode, you assign a callback function to `PullParser`'s onEvent variable and then just call the parse() method. The parser then reads the inputStream and automatically sends you each event it generates.

If inputStream in the code in Listing 9-2 contained the periodic table elements from the example in the previous section, the output would look something like this:

```
Event Type            Event Name           Data
==========            ==========           ====
START_DOCUMENT
START_ELEMENT
START_VALUE           elements
START_ARRAY           elements
START_ARRAY_ELEMENT   elements
START_ELEMENT
```

```
START_VALUE          symbol
TEXT                 symbol              H
END_VALUE            symbol              H
START_VALUE          name
TEXT                 name                Hydrogen
END_VALUE            name                Hydrogen
START_VALUE          atomicNumber        0
INTEGER              atomicNumber        1
END_VALUE            atomicNumber        1
END_ELEMENT
END_ARRAY_ELEMENT

  ... the rest of the periodic elements omitted ...

END_ARRAY
END_VALUE            elements
END_ELEMENT
END_DOCUMENT
```

In this format, you can easily see the sequence of events generated by the parser. Note that not all event types have valid names, and not all event types with valid names have valid data. In fact, the only events that have valid data associated with them are END_VALUE, TEXT, INTEGER, and NUMBER. The data is available on both the actual data event and on its associated END_VALUE event. As you would expect, the value of the data is not yet available with START_VALUE events.

Values that are one of the predefined types of null, true, or false are slightly different. They don't have explicit data values but are instead their own type of event. To illustrate this, take a look at the following piece of JSON:

```
{
  "stringValue": "Hello",
  "intValue": 42,
  "numValue": 3.14,
  "nullValue": null,
  "trueValue": true,
  "falseValue":false
}
```

If a parser similar to that in Listing 9-2 parses this data, you would see the output that follows. You can see from this output that the predefined data types must be handled by checking their event type and not the event data.

```
Event Type           Event Name          Data
==========           ==========          ====
START_DOCUMENT
START_ELEMENT
START_VALUE          stringValue
TEXT                 stringValue         Hello
```

```
END_VALUE              stringValue        Hello
START_VALUE            intValue           0
INTEGER                intValue           42
END_VALUE              intValue           42
START_VALUE            numValue           0.000000
NUMBER                 numValue           3.140000
END_VALUE              numValue           3.140000
START_VALUE            nullValue
NULL                   nullValue
END_VALUE              nullValue
START_VALUE            trueValue
TRUE                   trueValue
END_VALUE              trueValue
START_VALUE            falseValue
FALSE                  falseValue
END_VALUE              falseValue
END_ELEMENT
END_DOCUMENT
```

Who Is My Representative?

Now that you know how to make HTTP requests and parse the JSON responses, you are ready to write your first JavaFX web service client. Ben Pilkerton wrote a handy web service, available at http://whoismyrepresentative.com, that lets you look up the contact information for United States senators and representatives. If you are a U.S. citizen, you can use this service whenever you want to, you know, tell them what a great job they are doing. Even if you are not a U.S. citizen, this is still an easy example to follow along with, and it's better than yet another Twitter client, right? The request for the contact information is very simple:

```
http://whoismyrepresentative.com/getall_mems.php?zip=90210&output=json
```

All you need to do is call the PHP script and pass the zip and output parameters. The output parameter is needed because the default output format of the service is XML. The response from the web service (slightly reformatted for clarity) is also pretty straightforward:

```
{ "results": [
  { "type": "rep", "name": "Henry A. Waxman", "party": "D", "state": "CA",
    "district": "30", "phone": "(202) 225-3976", "office": "2204 Rayburn",
    "link": "http://www.henrywaxman.house.gov/" },
  { "type": "rep", "name": "Howard L. Berman", "party": "D", "state": "CA",
    "district": "28", "phone": "(202) 225-4695", "office": "2221 Rayburn",
    "link": "http://www.house.gov/berman/" },
  { "type": "sen", "name": "Barbara Boxer", "web": "http://boxer.senate.gov",
    "party": "D", "state": "CA",
    "office": "112 HART SENATE OFFICE BUILDING WASHINGTON DC 20510",
    "phone": "(202)224-3553", "contact": "http://boxer.senate.gov/contact" },
```

```
{ "type": "sen", "name": "Dianne Feinstein",
  "web": "http://feinstein.senate.gov", "party": "D", "state": "CA",
  "office": "331 HART SENATE OFFICE BUILDING WASHINGTON DC 20510",
  "phone": "(202)224-3841", "contact": "http://feinstein.senate.gov/email.html" }
]}
```

The senators and representatives differ in their type fields; this makes them easy to tell apart. Other than that, only minor differences exist in the JSON for each type of congressional member. Representatives have a link, whereas senators have a field called web, and the contact field appears to be optional.

The first thing that needs to be done is to define a simple model class for the application. The data that will be needed in the model is mainly the ZIP code to look up and the sequences of senators and representatives to display. Some ZIP codes cover multiple congressional districts, so we need to allow for the possibility of multiple representatives in addition to the two senators each ZIP code should have. A new ZIP code should trigger the application to send a new HTTP request to the server, and the response should be parsed into the sequences. Listing 9-3 shows the model class. A replace trigger on the zipcode variable clears the existing data and initiates a new HTTP request to the web service every time a new ZIP code is entered. The request's onDone callback checks the result of the request, and if there has been an error or if no data was returned (perhaps a bad ZIP code is entered), an error message is placed in the model's message variable. The user interface can check the contents of this variable and display an error message if needed. Note that because onDone needs a reference to its own object instance inside the instance declaration, a req variable must be defined and given a type before the actual declaration of the HttpRequest instance.

Listing 9-3. *The Model for the WhoIsMyRepJson Application*

```
public class ApplicationModel {
  public-read var senators: Senator[];
  public-read var representatives: Representative[];
  public-read var message: String;

  public var zipcode: String on replace {
    message = "";
    delete senators;
    delete representatives;

    if (zipcode.length() > 0) {
      var url = "http://whoismyrepresentative.com/getall_mems.php?"
                "zip={zipcode}&output=json";
      var req: HttpRequest;

      req = HttpRequest {
        method: HttpRequest.GET
        location: url
        onInput: parseResponse
        onDone: function() {
```

```
          if (req.responseCode != 200) {
            message = req.responseMessage;
          } else if (sizeof senators == 0 and sizeof representatives == 0) {
            message = "No members found for {zipcode}";
          }
        }
        onException: function(ex: java.lang.Exception) {
          println("Exception: {ex.getClass()} {ex.getMessage()}");
        }
      }
      req.start();
    }
  }

  function setMemberProperty( member:Senator, name:String, value:String ) {
    if( name == "name" ) {
      member.name = value;
    } else if( name == "party" ) {
      member.party = value;
    } else if( name == "state" ) {
      member.state = value;
    } else if( name == "phone" ) {
      member.phone = value;
    } else if( name == "office" ) {
      member.office = value;
    } else if( name == "web" or name == "link") {
      member.website = value;
    } else if( name == "contact" ) {
      member.contact = value;
    } else if( name == "district" ) {
      if (member instanceof Representative) {
        (member as Representative).district = value;
      }
    }
  }

  function parseMemberOfCongress( member:Senator, parser:PullParser ) {
    while (parser.event.type != PullParser.END_DOCUMENT) {
      parser.forward();
      if (parser.event.type == PullParser.END_ARRAY_ELEMENT) {
        break;
      } else if (parser.event.type == PullParser. TEXT) {
        setMemberProperty( member, parser.event.name, parser.event.text );
      }
    }
  }
```

```
function parseResponse( is:InputStream ) {
  try {
    var parser = PullParser {
      input: is
      documentType: PullParser.JSON;
    }

    while (parser.event.type != PullParser.END_DOCUMENT) {
      parser.seek( "type" );
      if (parser.event.type == PullParser.START_VALUE) {
        parser.forward();
        if (parser.event.text == "rep") {
          var rep = Representative{}
          parseMemberOfCongress( rep, parser );
          insert rep into representatives;
        } else if (parser.event.text == "sen" ) {
          var sen = Senator{}
          parseMemberOfCongress( sen, parser );
          insert sen into senators;
        }
      }
    }
  } finally {
    is.close();
  }
}
}
```

The parser in Listing 9-3 is being used in pull mode where, instead of using the parse() method and responding to events, the application is using the PullParser's forward() and seek() methods to control the parsing of the data. Because the application is in control, using the parser in this mode is a little more straightforward if you need to maintain a lot of state data between events. All of the data in the response are strings, so this parser just looks at all the TEXT events and reads each event's name and text value. The JSON response is being parsed into two kinds of JavaFX objects: Senator and Representative. Listing 9-4 shows the definitions of these two classes. The variables of these two classes are all publicly readable, but package writable. This allows the parser code in the model to set their values because the classes are all in the same package, while at the same time allowing read-only access by classes outside of the package (i.e., the user interface).

Listing 9-4. *The Senator and Representative Classes*

```
public class Senator {
  public-read package var honorific = "Sen.";
  public-read package var name:String;
  public-read package var party:String;
  public-read package var state:String;
```

```
  public-read package var phone:String;
  public-read package var office:String;
  public-read package var website:String;
  public-read package var contact:String;
}

public class Representative extends Senator {
  override var honorific = "Rep.";
  public-read package var district:String;
}
```

The user interface for the application is pictured in Figure 9-1. The interface makes use of the arrow shapes, resizable layout containers, and MigLayout classes in the JFXtras library. The interface code will not be discussed in detail here. It is available in the WhoIsMyRepJson example project located in the Chapter09 examples directory.

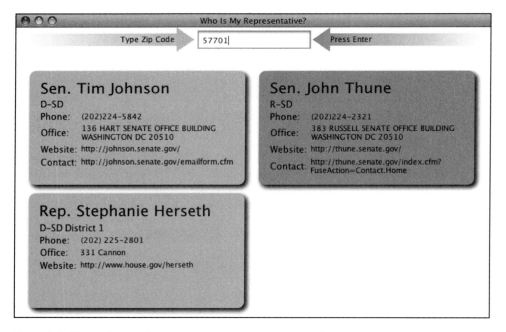

Figure 9-1. *Using the whoismyrepresentative.com web service*

Writing XML Clients

At its core, XML is deceptively simple. The basic idea, a structured way to describe arbitrary data, is a powerful concept. From these humble beginnings, it has evolved into a gigantic hammer meant for a world in which every data storage or interchange problem looks like a nail. Whether this is a good thing or a bad thing depends on how adept you are at swinging this particular hammer, with its multitude of weird and wonderful attachments and add-ons.

In this section, we will briefly examine the basic structure of an XML document and then show you how to parse it using the JavaFX `PullParser` class. The data in an XML document is represented by elements, attributes, and character data.[1] Elements define the structure of the document. They consist of strings enclosed in angle brackets. An opening element has the form `<element_name>`. In XML, every opening element must be matched by a closing element of the form `</element_name>`. Here the forward slash indicates that this is a closing element. The element name of the opening and closing elements must match. Between the opening and closing elements, you can place other opening/closing element pairs, character data, or some combination of these two. Let's see what our list of elements (of the periodic table variety) would look like as a list of elements (of the XML variety).

```
<?xml version="1.0" ?>
<elements>
  <element>
    <symbol>H</symbol>
    <name>Hydrogen</name>
    <atomicNumber>1</atomicNumber>
  </element>
  <element>
    <symbol>He</symbol>
    <name>Helium</name>
    <atomicNumber>2</atomicNumber>
  </element>
  <element>
    <symbol>C</symbol>
    <name>Carbon</name>
    <atomicNumber>6</atomicNumber>
  </element>
  <element>
    <symbol>O</symbol>
    <name>Oxygen</name>
    <atomicNumber>8</atomicNumber>
  </element>
</elements>
```

The first line in the document is known as the *XML declaration*. It declares that what follows is an XML document. The version number currently is always 1.0. The XML elements are `elements`, `element`, `symbol`, `name`, and `atomicNumber`. Some of these, like `symbol`, enclose character data only. Others, like `element` and `elements`, enclose other elements (of the XML variety). Notice that every element pair opens and closes at the same level of the document. In the example, the levels are nicely indented so you can see them easily. It would invalidate the document if you were to close the `atomicNumber` element after its closing `element` tag. An XML parser would be completely within its rights to complain about your careless human ways and refuse to continue parsing the document.

---

1   XML documents can also contain things such as processing instructions, schema definitions, and references to external entities. We will not use these features in this chapter, but you can consult the resources at the end of the chapter for more information.

Parsing XML in JavaFX

Let's take a look at how you would parse the document from the preceding section using the PullParser in JavaFX. Listing 9-5 shows the analog of the JSON parser that was used previously. A few differences have been highlighted in the listing. First, PullParser.XML is specified as the document type. As you would expect, this will tell the PullParser to invoke its underlying XML parser for this input stream. You will also notice a difference in how the event name is handled. In XML, names can be more complicated than the simple text strings in JSON. Therefore, a special class called QName (located in the javafx.data.xml package) is required to represent an XML qualified name. A qualified name includes things like prefixes and namespaces, none of which we use in our example XML. We are using simple text strings for our element names, and therefore we only need to access the QName's name variable. This is done in the example parser via the event's qname variable: e.qname.name.

Listing 9-5. *Using the PullParser to Read XML Data*

```
try {
   var parser = PullParser {
      input: inputStream
      documentType: PullParser.XML;
      onEvent: function( e:Event ) {
         println( "{%-20s e.typeName} {%-20s e.qname.name} {%-20s e.text}" );
      }
   }
   println( "{%-20s "Event Type"} {%-20s "Event Name"} {%-20s "Data"}" );
   println( "{%-20s "=========="} {%-20s "=========="} {%-20s "===="}" );
   parser.parse();
} finally {
   inputStream.close();
}
```

If the parser is put to work on our example XML document, you can once again see a full accounting of the events emitted by the parser, shown in the output that follows. It looks similar to the event list generated by the JSON document. This is a very good thing. The JavaFX team has done an excellent job of abstracting away the significant differences that exist between parsing XML and JSON. Instead of getting value events, now element events are received. Just like JSON, though, data is valid for TEXT events and for END_ELEMENT events (the equivalent of JSON END_VALUE events).

Event Type	Event Name	Data
==============	===========	====
START_DOCUMENT	null	
START_ELEMENT	elements	
START_ELEMENT	element	
START_ELEMENT	symbol	
TEXT	symbol	H
END_ELEMENT	symbol	H
START_ELEMENT	name	

```
TEXT                name                Hydrogen
END_ELEMENT         name                Hydrogen
START_ELEMENT       atomicNumber
TEXT                atomicNumber        1
END_ELEMENT         atomicNumber        1
END_ELEMENT         element             1

    ... the rest of the periodic elements omitted ...

END_ELEMENT         elements            1
END_DOCUMENT        elements
```

■Note The output just presented was obtained by using the example XML document with all of the whitespace between the elements removed in order to eliminate superfluous TEXT events in the parser.

So far we have covered two of the three major pieces of an XML document: elements and character data. Attributes are the third piece. An opening element can optionally include any number of attributes. Attributes are used to provide additional information about their opening element. The format of an attribute is simply a name/value pair that is separated by an equal sign. The value half of the attribute must be quoted; either single or double quotes are acceptable.

The XML document that follows shows the same list of elements as before, but rewritten to be attributes instead of enclosed elements. You can see that this makes the XML document significantly more compact. The choice to use elements versus attributes is the subject of some debate in XML circles. The general rule of thumb is that if the data describes the element, it could be an attribute. If you have a lot of attributes or if you would like to impose more structure on your document, you should consider using enclosed elements. The bottom line is that attributes are a nice option for reducing the verbosity of an XML document, but they should not be abused.

```
<elements>
  <element symbol='H' name='Hydrogen' atomicNumber='1'/>
  <element symbol='He' name='Helium' atomicNumber='2'/>
  <element symbol='C' name='Carbon' atomicNumber='6'/>
  <element symbol='O' name='Oxygen' atomicNumber='8'/>
</elements>
```

One further thing to discuss is the lack of closing elements. Instead, the opening element includes a forward slash before its closing angle bracket. This is called an *empty element*. Empty elements are useful when you represent all of an element's data as attributes, as we have done here. They can also be used when all you need is a simple marker in your document rather than a data container.

This leads to the question of how attributes are parsed. The Event class has two functions for this purpose. The first, called getAttributeNames(), returns a list of QName objects that represent the names of the element's attributes. The second function, getAttributeValue(), is used to get the value of the attribute given its name. If you know the name of the element's attribute beforehand, you can use getAttributeValue() directly without querying the list of QNames. The parameter of getAttributeValue() can be a QName object as shown in Listing 9-6, or it can simply be a string containing the attribute's name.

Listing 9-6. *Using the PullParser to Parse XML with Attributes*

```
try {
  var parser = PullParser {
    input: inputStream
    documentType: PullParser.XML;
    onEvent: function( e:Event ) {
      println( "{%-20s e.typeName} {%-20s e.qname.name} {%-20s e.text}" );
      for (qname in e.getAttributeNames()) {
        var value = e.getAttributeValue(qname);
        println( "{%-20s "  ATTRIBUTE"} {%-20s qname.name} {%-20s value}");
      }
    }
  }
  println( "{%-20s "Event Type"} {%-20s "Event Name"} {%-20s "Data"}" );
  println( "{%-20s "=========="} {%-20s "=========="} {%-20s "===="}" );
  parser.parse();
} finally {
  inputStream.close();
}
```

The parser in Listing 9-6 will print out any attribute values it can find. It uses the string ATTRIBUTE in the Event Type column to denote that an attribute is being printed. For clarity, this string is indented two spaces to show that it belongs to an event. The output of this parser is as follows. The attributes are available with the START_ELEMENT event and the END_ELEMENT event.

```
Event Type            Event Name            Data
==========            ==========            ====
START_DOCUMENT        null
START_ELEMENT         elements
START_ELEMENT         element
  ATTRIBUTE           symbol                H
  ATTRIBUTE           name                  Hydrogen
  ATTRIBUTE           atomicNumber          1
END_ELEMENT           element
  ATTRIBUTE           symbol                H
  ATTRIBUTE           name                  Hydrogen
  ATTRIBUTE           atomicNumber          1
```

```
... the rest of the periodic elements omitted ...

END_ELEMENT          elements
END_DOCUMENT         elements
```

Who Is My Representative? in XML

Returning to the whoismyrepresentative.com web service, we will now examine the changes needed to parse the response in XML rather than JSON. The output parameter can be omitted from the request because XML is the default format for this service. Without that parameter, the request now looks something like this:

```
http://whoismyrepresentative.com/getall_mems.php?zip=77001
```

The XML-based response follows. The result element encloses the list of congress members. Two other types of elements are shown: rep and sen. These two elements each contain a number of attributes that list the contact information of each member. These attributes exactly correspond to the name/value pairs of the JSON version.

```
<result>
  <rep name='Sheila Jackson-Lee' party='D' state='TX' district='18'
    phone='(202) 225-3816' office='2435 Rayburn'
    link='http://jacksonlee.house.gov/' />
  <sen name='John Cornyn' web='http://cornyn.senate.gov/' party='R' state='TX'
    office='517 HART SENATE OFFICE BUILDING WASHINGTON DC 20510'
    phone='(202)224-2934' contact='http://cornyn.senate.gov/contact/index.html' />
  <sen name='Kay Bailey Hutchison' web='http://hutchison.senate.gov/' party='R'
    state='TX' office='284 RUSSELL SENATE OFFICE BUILDING WASHINGTON DC 20510'
    phone='(202)224-5922' contact='http://hutchison.senate.gov/contact.cfm' />
</result>
```

The parser for the XML version shown in Listing 9-7 actually consists of fewer lines than its JSON counterpart. Here, the parser is used in event-driven mode. Whenever a start element is encountered, the element's name is checked, and either a new Representative or a new Senator object is declared. This new object and the event are passed to the parseMemberOfCongress() function, where the event's attributes are used to populate the instance variables of the member object.

Listing 9-7. *Parsing the XML Response from whoismyrepresentative.com*

```
function parseMemberOfCongress( member:Senator, event:Event ) {
    for (qname in event.getAttributeNames()) {
      var value = event.getAttributeValue( qname );
      setMemberProperty( member, qname.name, value );
    }
  }
```

```
function parseResponse( is:InputStream ) {
  try {
    PullParser {
      input: is
      documentType: PullParser.XML;
      onEvent: function( e:Event ) {
        if (e.type == PullParser.START_ELEMENT) {
          if (e.qname.name == "rep") {
            var rep = Representative{}
            parseMemberOfCongress( rep, e );
            insert rep into representatives;
          } else if (e.qname.name == "sen" ) {
            var sen = Senator{}
            parseMemberOfCongress( sen, e );
            insert sen into senators;
          }
        }
      }
    }.parse();
  } finally {
    is.close();
  }
}
```

The rest of this application is identical to the JSON version. The complete source code for the XML version can be found in the WhoIsMyRepXml project. The project is located in the Chapter09 code examples directory.

Developing a Rich Internet Application

It is now time to move on to a larger project. Throughout the rest of this chapter, we will be developing an application that uses the Amazon Associates Web Service API to power a client application for an imaginary bookstore named Browning's Books. A graphic designer has come up with the concept shown in Figure 9-2 for the application's main page. The main idea is to show the current top-ten titles in the books, music, and video categories when the application starts. The images and the data for each title will be populated dynamically using the web service, but the header, the logo, the tabs, and the background images are all static. The ability to take advantage of the artist's work would give us a nice jumpstart in our development work. A free suite of tools available from Sun called the JavaFX Production Suite will allow us to do just that.

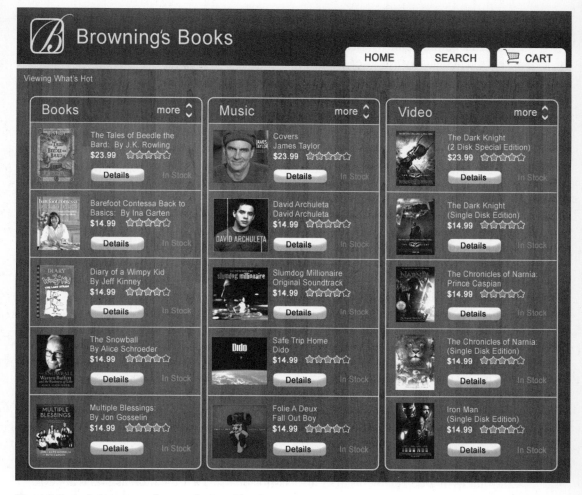

Figure 9-2. *Artist's concept for our fictional bookstore*

Making Use of Assets with the JavaFX Production Suite

If you work with graphic designers, they probably use Adobe Illustrator and Adobe Photoshop. The JavaFX Production Suite includes plug-ins for both of these tools to make it easy for artists to export their work in a format that can be used directly by JavaFX. The plug-ins produce FXZ files, otherwise known as JavaFX Content Files. An FXZ file is a ZIP file containing at least an FXD file and possibly image and font files as well. The FXD file contains the JavaFX source code description of the graphic that was exported. If this graphic includes images or fonts, they will be included in the FXZ file as well.

Exporting graphics for use in JavaFX is easy. The artist only needs to prepend the string "jfx:" to the layer name of any graphic that needs to be used in JavaFX. When the plug-in exports the graphics, the jfx: string will be stripped off, and the developer will be able to access the node using this layer name. As an example, a layer named jfx:background would be accessed by the developer as the background node. NetBeans 6.5 provides developers with the ability to view the contents of FXZ files and to generate UI stub classes, which provide easy access to the contents of the file. We'll cover the exact classes and functions that are used to obtain access to exported graphics in the "Inside the NodeFactory" section later in this chapter.

If you don't use the Adobe tools, you can still produce artwork to be used by JavaFX. As long as you have a tool that can produce SVG files, you can use the SVG Converter application included with the JavaFX Production Suite to translate them to FXZ files. A good choice for a free and open source SVG editor is Inkscape (see the resources at the end of this chapter for a link to the Inkscape project home page). Another option for developers is to obtain SVG files from the Internet. Artwork is available from projects such as the Tango Desktop Project and the Open Clip Art Library. Links to these projects appear in the "Resources" section at the end of this chapter. When using artwork you've downloaded, you need to pay attention to the licenses attached to the files you are using. Make sure you have the right to use them, and always give credit where it is due.

■**Note** In Inkscape, the layer name that you can edit from within the application is not the layer ID used in the SVG conversion process. You will still need to do some text editing to give your resultant SVG files meaningful id attributes. Inkscape is an X11 application on Mac OS X. Therefore, you will need to make sure X11 is running before you start Inkscape. X11 is located in /Applications/Utilities on Mac OS X 10.5.

Instead of layer names, the SVG Converter uses the id attribute of SVG's group element, the g element, as a means of accessing the graphics. If your SVG file doesn't have any id attributes or group elements, they are easy to add using a text editor, as SVG is an XML-based format. The SVG Converter has the option to only convert groups whose id attributes start with the jfx: string. If you enable this option in the SVG Converter user interface, make sure your id attribute values begin with jfx:, or they will not be converted. If you don't use this option, all graphics in the SVG file will be converted, and you can use their id values to access them.

The JavaFX Production Suite can be freely downloaded at http://www.javafx.com. The installation includes a Help directory that contains detailed information on using the suite.

■**Note** If you will only be handling the development side of things, you no longer need to download the JavaFX Production Suite. As of JavaFX 1.1, all of the classes you need make use of the data exported by the Adobe tools is included in the SDK.

Using the Amazon Associates Web Service API

We will be using the Amazon Associates Web Service. This service lets us make REST requests to Amazon's servers and receive information about their products. All Amazon web services require an access key ID. The Amazon Associates Web Service is free, but you will still need to obtain this ID. If you don't already have one, you can set one up at http://aws.amazon.com. You will need to insert your access key into the example application in order to get it to run correctly.

Making a REST request to Amazon uses the following URL format:

```
http://ecs.amazonaws.com/onca/xml?Service=AWSECommerceService&
AWSAccessKeyId=[Your Access Key]&Operation=[Operation Type]
```

You can see that all requests go to the onca/xml resource located on the ecs.amazonaws.com server. Everything else is determined by the parameters of the request. The three parameters in the example URL are all required. The Service parameter specifies which of Amazon's services this request is for. This application always uses the AWS e-commerce service as shown in the example URL. The AWSAccessKeyId parameter is where you enter the access key you obtained from Amazon. The Operation parameter is also required and specifies the type of operation to be performed by the e-commerce service. Several different types of operations can be specified, which range from finding item information to managing the shopping cart. Our application will use three of these operations:

- ItemSearch: This operation allows you to do a keyword search on Amazon. You can limit your search to certain categories of items, certain price ranges, specific merchants, and the condition of the item (new, used, etc.).

- BrowseNodeLookup: You can use this operation to get information about specific categories of products at Amazon. Browse nodes define a tree-like hierarchy of categories and subcategories into which Amazon's entire inventory is placed. Some browse node hierarchies are static, for instance, mystery books, science fiction movies, or classical music. Others are dynamic, such as the top-ten sellers in the books category. Items can be in multiple browse nodes; a mystery book can also be a top seller.

- ItemLookup: If you have an Amazon Standard Identification Number (ASIN), perhaps returned from a BrowseNodeLookup operation, you can use it to obtain detailed information about an item with the ItemLookup operation.

For convenience, we will wrap up all of this knowledge about how to make a generic Amazon e-commerce REST request into a specialized class called AmazonHttpRequest. It will itself be a wrapper around a plain JavaFX HttpRequest. The code for this class is shown in Listing 9-8. Creating this class gives us not only an easy way to call an Amazon web service, but also a convenient place to keep track of how many requests are currently in progress. Please note the defined constant ACCESS_KEY in this class. This is where you need to insert your own Amazon access key if you want to build and run this example yourself.

Listing 9-8. *A Class Used to Send Requests to the Amazon Associates Web Service*

```
public-read var requestsInProgress = 0;

package class AmazonHttpRequest {
  def ACCESS_KEY = "Your Access Key Goes Here";
  def BASE_URL = "http://ecs.amazonaws.com/onca/xml?Service=AWSECommerceService"
                 "&AWSAccessKeyId={ACCESS_KEY}&Version=2009-01-06";

  public-init var operation: String;
  public-init var extraParams: String;
  public-init var onInput: function( :java.io.InputStream ):Void;
  public-init var onError: function( message:String ):Void;
  public-init var onDone: function():Void;

  var request: HttpRequest;

  postinit {
    request = HttpRequest {
      method: HttpRequest.GET
      location: composeUrl()
      onInput: onInput
      onDone: function() {
        requestsInProgress--;
        if (request.responseCode != 200) {
          onError( request.responseMessage );
        }

        onDone();
      }

      onException: function(ex: java.lang.Exception) {
        onError("onException - exception: {ex.getClass()} {ex.getMessage()}");
      }
    }
  }

  public function start():Integer {
    requestsInProgress++;
    request.start();
  }

  function composeUrl():String {
    "{BASE_URL}&Operation={operation}&{extraParams}";
  }
}
```

The main purpose of these web service operations is to return lists of *items* in XML format. Listing 9-9 shows an Item class that is used to represent these items in our application. This class holds all of the basic information about a book, movie, or music album. Details vary depending on the type of item, so a sequence of strings is used to store name/value pairs that can be displayed when the item's details are shown.

Listing 9-9. *The Item Class*

```
public class Item {
    public var title: String;
    public var creator: String;
    public var price: String;
    public var imageURL: String;
    public var detailedImageURL: String;
    public var details: String[];
    public var rating = -1;
}
```

User Interface Considerations

We are off to a good start on our big fictional BookStoreFX application. We are sure the imaginary customer is impressed and pleased. The graphical theme of the application has been established, and the necessary research into our back-end web service has been done. A few reasonable abstractions have even been created for the web service we will be using. It is now time to focus some attention on where it matters most: the user. We know the home page will contain three top-ten lists for books, movies, and music. These lists will display five items at a time and give a summary of each item. The artist's concept also shows a search page and a shopping cart page. The search page will be kept nice and simple. Taking a cue from Google, the page will at first show just a basic text input box that will allow users to type in their keyword search terms. The search results will be displayed in a nice list of item summaries with the option to display more details by clicking an item. The shopping cart page will be the easiest of all because it will consist only of a placeholder graphic. This is, after all, only an example in a book; we don't really want to collect any money nor ship any books!

The next question to answer might be how we are planning to move between the pages. The tabs on the page header present a common navigation metaphor. By clicking a tab, the user goes to that page. Rather than simply switching the pages instantaneously, we can do something a little smoother and a little less jarring. JavaFX has first-class animation capabilities, so we should take advantage of that. Caution is required, though, because page transitions will happen quite often while the application is in use. If the animation that is used is too flashy or just takes too long, the user will become irritated with it as soon as the novelty wears off. A quick, visually interesting, but somewhat subtle animation is what is required here. It should be something that gives users a little flash of delight the first time they see it, but that doesn't get in the way or call undue attention to itself once it gets old.

We now have enough information to create the main structure of the application. Listing 9-10 shows the main script used to create our application. The scene will consist of a wood texture background, a header with the tabs, the Browning's Books logo, and whichever page is currently being displayed. A class named NodeFactory is created to serve as the interface between the application's code and the assets that were exported by the artist from Photo-shop. The listing shows that this allows us to deal with the assets at a slightly higher level. For instance, rather than retrieving the individual tabs and the header graphics from the FXZ file and composing them on the fly, we can ask the NodeFactory to do that work for us by calling its getHeader method. Another advantage of the NodeFactory is that it encapsulates all of the access to the FXZ files in one place. If those files ever change, only the internals of NodeFactory need to change with them. This isolates the rest of the code, and therefore developers avoid having to hunt through the code base for references to FXZ files (or the names of resources in those files) that need to be updated.

Listing 9-10. *The Main Script for the BookStoreFX Application*

```
var model = BookStoreModel { }
var slideDeck: SlideDeck;
var logo = NodeFactory.getLogo();

Stage {
  title: "BookStoreFX"
  resizable: false
  scene: Scene {
    width: 1024
    height: 900
    stylesheets: "{__DIR__}bookStoreStyles.css"
    content: [
      NodeFactory.getBackground(),
      logo,
      NodeFactory.getHeader(showPage(0), showPage(1), showPage(2)),
      slideDeck = SlideDeck {
        def homePage = HomePage { model: model }
        def searchPage = SearchPage { model: model }
        def cartPage = CartPage { }

        content: [ homePage, searchPage, cartPage ]
        inTransitions: [
          homePage.pageInTransition(),
          searchPage.pageInTransition()
          cartPage.pageInTransition()
        ]
        outTransitions: [
          homePage.pageOutTransition(),
          searchPage.pageOutTransition()
          cartPage.pageOutTransition()
        ]
      }
    ]
  }
}
```

```
function showPage( index:Integer ): function() {
  function() {
    slideDeck.slideIndex = index;
  }
}
```

Another new class can be created to manage the display of and transitions between the pages. This class will be called SlideDeck, and its job will be to hold references to a sequence of pages, taking care to attach only one at a time to the scene graph. Because each page could potentially hold a large number of nodes, it is good practice to only attach one page to the scene graph rather than adding them all in and simply toggling their visible variables. You can see in the listing that the SlideDeck class contains a variable called slideIndex, which is used to tell the deck which slide to display. The NodeFactory's getHeader function has three parameters that are the functions to call when the user clicks the Home, Search, and Cart tabs. The slideIndex variable needs to be set to 0 when the user clicks the Home tab. Similarly, slideIndex should become 1 when the Search tab is clicked and 2 for the Cart tab. Rather than duplicate these callback function definitions three times, a function called showPage was created instead. This function takes the desired slide index as a parameter and creates a function that will set slideIndex to the value of that parameter when called. This function is then returned to the caller, where it is passed into the getHeader method as the function to call when the corresponding tab is clicked. Being able to pass functions around is a very powerful technique that is used heavily in GUI applications.

You may also have noticed that a style sheet was defined for the scene. This is another highly recommended practice that yields two important advantages. First, this collects all of the presentation details of your application in one place, the style sheet, that is easy to edit and therefore to change. The flip side of this is that all of those presentation details are now out of your classes, out of your way, and out of your mind. Your code becomes cleaner, and you can focus on what the code does rather than what the UI looks like. Another important detail is that the artist designed this interface for a specific scene size: 1024 pixels wide by 900 pixels tall. While fixed-sized windows are not optimal from a user's perspective, we'll just go with it for now. The interface can always be made resizable later.

Inside the NodeFactory

As promised earlier, we will now take you inside the NodeFactory to take a look at how resources that have been exported from Adobe Photoshop or Illustrator can be used in JavaFX. Recall that when a graphic is exported from one of the Adobe tools or converted from an SVG file, the result is a FXZ content file. Your program can access the FXZ file once it is copied into one of your source packages. You have two ways to accomplish this. If you use NetBeans, you can have it generate a UI stub class for you. The UI stub class will contain public variables that contain a reference to each of the named nodes that were exported or converted by the JavaFX Production Suite. These variables can then be used in your program just like any other variable that contains a reference to a node. An example of a UI stub class will be shown later in the "The Cart Page" section.

If you aren't using NetBeans, using your exported resources requires just a few lines of code. The first step is to use the FXDLoader class to load the content of the FXD file from the FXZ archive in which it is stored. FXDLoader is located in the javafx.fxd package. The class contains a static function named loadContent that returns an instance of the FXDContent class.

Once you have a reference to the FXDContent object, you can use its getNode, getGroup, or getShape functions to obtain references to the nodes contained in the file. Recall that the FXD file is just a text file whose content consists of JavaFX source code. Therefore, what you are really doing is loading and dynamically compiling a source code description of the exported graphic. The dynamic load-and-compile step does take a little bit of time. This time can start to add up if you have to load a large number of FXD files. If this is the case, you may need to load your resources on demand rather than at startup as is done by NodeFactory.

Listing 9-11 illustrates the loading process using some of the code from the NodeFactory. In this case, the FXZ file is located in the res package, a subpackage of the one in which NodeFactory is located. The __DIR__ pseudo-variable is used to specify the path to the file when its contents are loaded. Once the FXD contents are loaded, it is simply a matter of using the getNode function to obtain references to the nodes. One special consideration is whether the nodes loaded from the FXD file will be used just once or multiple times within the application. Because nodes can only be attached to the scene graph once, you will need to duplicate any nodes that are required to be shown in multiple places at the same time. One example of this that can be seen in Listing 9-11 is the details button. This button is replicated in multiple places on a single page, so the Duplicator class is used to create a copy of the nodes that comprise the button each time the createDetailsButton method is called.

Listing 9-11. *Usage of Exported Resource Files in the* NodeFactory

```
var assets = FXDLoader.loadContent("{__DIR__}res/bookStoreAssets.fxz");
var headerBg = getAndUnparent(assets, "headerBg");
var mainBg = getAndUnparent(assets, "mainBg");
var logo = getAndUnparent(assets, "logo");
var homeTab = getAndUnparent(assets, "homeTab");

// ... some lines omitted ...

public function getBackground():Node {
    Group {
        content: [mainBg, headerBg]
    }
}

public function createDetailsButton( onAction: function() ):Node {
    var button = Duplicator.duplicate( detailsButton );
    makeButton( button, onAction );
    Group {
        content: [
            button,
            Duplicator.duplicate( detailsText ),
        ]
    }
}

// ... the rest of the source code omitted ...
```

The Home Page

It is time to look at the specifics of the individual pages, beginning with the home page; this will become the focus of the remainder of this chapter. The home page is shown by default when the application starts. It contains the top-ten sellers in each of three categories: books, music, and video. The top sellers are displayed in three-item stacks that show the data for the top-selling items in the store, five at a time. The background of the item stacks will be comprised of graphics that the artist drew in Photoshop. NodeFactory has three methods that return each of these backgrounds as a Group node: getBookStackFrame, getMusicStackFrame, and getMovieStackFrame.

The next step is putting something on top of those backgrounds. The summary data for each item returned by Amazon is displayed in an ItemSummary node. This custom node displays an item's thumbnail image, title, rating, price, and a details button. These different elements are arranged using a MigLayout container. Listing 9-12 shows the ItemSummary class. There are a few interesting techniques used in this class. First, note the use of style classes throughout the various node definitions. This clears away all of the presentation details, allowing you to focus only on what the class does. One example of this is the stars used to display the item's rating. The star shape itself comes from the JFXtras shapes. So the only thing that requires the attention of the programmer is how the stars are arranged (in an HBox). How they look when they are filled or empty is determined solely on their style class. The programmer's job is to simply determine which style each star needs based on one small if statement.

Listing 9-12. *The ItemSummary Class*

```
package def WIDTH = 300;
package def HEIGHT = 130;

public class ItemSummary extends CustomNode {
  def TITLE_WIDTH: Number = 200;
  def TITLE_HEIGHT: Number = 30;

  public-init var imageCache: ImageCache;
  public var item: Item;
  public var onShowDetails: function( item:Item );

  var title = Text {
    content: bind item.title
    wrappingWidth: TITLE_WIDTH
    styleClass: "summaryTitle"
    textOrigin: TextOrigin.TOP
    clip: Rectangle {
      width: TITLE_WIDTH
      height: TITLE_HEIGHT
    }
  }
}
```

```
    var price = Text {
      content: bind item.price
      styleClass: "summaryPrice"
    }

    var thumbnail = ImageView {
      image: bind imageCache.getImage( item.imageURL );
    }

    var rating = HBox {
      content: bind for (i in [1..5]) {
        Star2 {
          outerRadius: 8;
          innerRadius: 5;
          styleClass: if( i <= item.rating ) "filledStar" else "emptyStar"
        }
      }
    }

    function detailsAction() {
      onShowDetails( item );
    }

    override function create():Node {
      NodeFactory.makeButton( thumbnail, detailsAction );
      Group {
        content: [
          MigLayout {
            width: WIDTH
            height: HEIGHT
            constraints: "fill, wrap"
            columns: "[80!]5mm[]"
            rows: "[30!][][][]"
            content: [
              migNode( thumbnail,  "spany, center"),
              migNode( title,      "w 200"),
              migNode( price,      ""),
              migNode( rating,     ""),
              migNode( NodeFactory.createDetailsButton(detailsAction), "" )
            ]
          }
        ]
      }
    }
}
```

A bind statement is used everywhere that ImageSummary references fields from the Item object. By doing so, the item being shown by the summary can be changed from outside the class, and all of the nodes that display the item's data inside the class will get updated automatically. The use of JFXtras' MigLayout support removes a lot of the binding and positional calculations that would normally clutter up a class with this kind of layout requirement. The JFXtras Grid class would also be a good choice for this type of layout. This class also makes use of the NodeFactory to create the details button and to turn the image thumbnail into a button. And finally, you may have noticed the use of an image cache to obtain the thumbnail for the item currently being shown by the summary. Caching frequently used data is a common technique in Internet applications, because access to data on a remote server can be time consuming. Images tend to be larger than text files, so significant performance gains can be realized by caching them. We will take a peek at the implementation of the image cache later in this section as the application's model class is being discussed.

Now that we have background graphics and nodes that can display the top-selling items, all that remains is to stack the items over the backgrounds in the proper places. The ItemStack class was created to manage the details of displaying these vertical stacks of items. ItemStack is a CustomNode that adjusts its contents based on which items need to be displayed at any given time. These content adjustments are made in response to calls to the up and down functions defined in the class. A custom node was used rather than a layout container due to the precise pixel positioning that was required to match the stack's contents with the background graphics. It was easier just to position the nodes manually. There is nothing new or particularly novel about the code behind the ItemStack class, so it will not be shown here. Consult the source code of the example project if you are curious.

In terms of the classes that have just been described, the home page is made up of three ItemStacks that show the top-ten ItemSummary objects in each category. Listing 9-13 shows the source code of the home page. One thing that has not been covered yet is the subject of page transitions. You can see from the source code that two sequences of keyframe values are created to describe the start and end points of the transitions. The home page transition is defined as a translation of the stacks off the screen. The book stack moves offscreen to the left, the music stack moves down, and the movie stack moves right. Two separate timelines are defined: one for moving the stacks offscreen, pageOutTransition, and another for moving them back onscreen, pageInTransition. You may be wondering why we don't define just one page-out transition that is played in reverse for the page in transition. The Timeline class in JavaFX 1.1 has a small glitch when playing timelines in reverse. The interpolated value jumps back to the beginning for one frame before the timeline starts to play in reverse. This can sometimes cause a visual artifact in the animation.

Listing 9-13. *The Home Page*

```
public class HomePage extends CustomNode {
  public-init var model: BookStoreModel;

  def STACK_ITEM_START_Y = 82;
  def STACK_ITEM_HEIGHT = 130;
  def STACK_ITEM_COUNT = 5;
```

```
var bookStack: Group = Group {
  var bframe: Node;
  var bstack = ItemStack {
    x: bind bframe.layoutBounds.minX
    y: STACK_ITEM_START_Y
    stackItemCount: STACK_ITEM_COUNT
    stackItemHeight: STACK_ITEM_HEIGHT
    imageCache: model.imageCache
    items: bind model.topBooks
  }

// ... initialization code for the musicStack and movieStack omitted ...

var keyFrameValuesStart = [
  bookStack.translateX => 0 tween LINEAR,
  musicStack.translateY => 0 tween LINEAR,
  movieStack.translateX => 0 tween LINEAR,
];

var keyFrameValuesEnd = [
  bookStack.translateX => -bookStack.layoutBounds.width tween LINEAR,
  musicStack.translateY => musicStack.scene.height tween LINEAR,
  movieStack.translateX => movieStack.layoutBounds.width tween LINEAR,
];

public function pageOutTransition():Timeline {
  Timeline {
    keyFrames: [
        at(0s) { keyFrameValuesStart }
        at(0.25s) { keyFrameValuesEnd }
    ]
  }
}

public function pageInTransition():Timeline {
  Timeline {
    keyFrames: [
      at(0s) { keyFrameValuesEnd }
      at(0.25s) { keyFrameValuesStart }
    ]
  }
}
```

```
  override function create() {
    Group {
      content: [
        NodeFactory.getViewingWhatsHot(),
        bookStack,
        musicStack,
        movieStack,
      ]
    }
  }
}
```

A Java-Based Image Cache

The home page gets a reference to the application's model when it is created. This gives the page references to the sequences of top-selling items as well as the application's image cache. The image cache provides quick access to images that have already been downloaded from Amazon. The actual implementation of the cache is based on Java's LinkedHashMap class. The code is shown in Listing 9-14. This simple class illustrates one of JavaFX's advantages—the ability to leverage the power of the Java platform. You get the power of Java underneath combined with the simplicity and ease of GUI development of JavaFX on top.

Listing 9-14. *The Java Implementation of the Image Cache*

```
class ImageCacheImpl extends LinkedHashMap<String, Object> {
    private int cacheSize;

    public ImageCacheImpl( int cacheSize, int capacity, float loadFactor ) {
        super( capacity, loadFactor, true );
        this.cacheSize = cacheSize;
    }

    @Override
    public boolean removeEldestEntry( Map.Entry<String, Object> eldest ) {
        return size() > cacheSize;
    }
}
```

Listing 9-15 shows the JavaFX side of the image cache implementation. This top layer of the cache is responsible for creating the image objects when new images are requested and storing their references in the Java LinkedHashMap. When the image is requested again, the cache is checked to see whether the image is still present. If so, the cached image is returned. This is a least recently used (LRU) cache, which means that if the cache gets filled, the image that has gone unused for the longest amount of time will be kicked out of the cache and replaced by a new image. This lets us achieve a nice balance between performance and memory usage. Overriding the removeEldestEntry method in the Java LinkedHashMap enforces the LRU policy.

Listing 9-15. *The JavaFX Side of the Image Cache Implementation*

```
public class ImageCache {
  public-init var cacheSize = 50;
  public-init var defaultWidth = 100;
  public-init var defaultHeight = 100;
  public-init var preserveAspectRatio = true;

  var map: ImageCacheImpl;

  postinit {
    map = new ImageCacheImpl( cacheSize, calculateCapacity(cacheSize), 0.75 );
  }

  public function getImage( url:String ):Image {
    getImage( url, defaultWidth, defaultHeight );
  }

  public function getImage( url:String, width:Integer, height:Integer ):Image {
    var image = map.get( url );
    if (image == null) {
      image = Image {
        url: url
        width: width
        height: height
        preserveRatio: preserveAspectRatio
        backgroundLoading: true
        placeholder: Image {
          url: "{__DIR__}images/loading{if (width > 100) "150" else "80"}.png"
        }
      }
      map.put( url, image );
    }
    return image as Image;
  }

  public function clear() {
    map.clear();
  }

  public function size() {
    map.size();
  }

  function calculateCapacity( cacheSize:Integer ):Integer {
    Math.ceil( cacheSize / 0.75 ) + 1 as Integer;
  }
}
```

The image cache always loads images in the background by setting the image's `backgroundLoading` variable to `true`. This is always a good idea if there is a possibility that the loading of the image will take a while. You never want to block the user interface thread for an extended amount of time. While the image is loading, it is possible to display a place-holder image. This is only a good idea if the placeholder can be loaded quickly, of course. Therefore, placeholder images are included inside the application's JAR file. This way an image will appear in the UI instead of a blank space. Lastly, when the image is declared, both the width and height are specified in order to make the image fit within a defined area. Setting `preserveRatio` ensures that the rescaled image will not be distorted.

Getting the Top Sellers from Amazon

Submitting a `BrowseNodeLookup` request and asking for the `Response Group` named `TopSellers` will retrieve the top-selling items for a particular category on Amazon. `BrowseNodeId` specifies whether you want the top-selling books, movies, music, or some other predefined Amazon category. The top-sellers query will return an XML document containing a list of ASINs. It is a simple matter to write a pull parser to parse this one XML element into a sequence. From there, the sequence is used to create a new `ItemLookup` query that returns information about the item associated with each ASIN. The items in the `ItemLookup` response can then be parsed into `Item` objects for display on the home page. This entire process takes place in a class named `AmazonTopSellers`. The class is a thin wrapper around the two `AmazonHttpRequests` just described.

One of the variables that need to be initialized when an `AmazonTopSellers` instance is declared is specification of the category to query. The predefined categories supported by the bookstore application are defined in a Java enum. Because JavaFX doesn't support enum types yet, it is good practice to declare them in Java rather than take the old pre–Java 1.5 route of defining static integer values. Java enums are easily used in JavaFX and are type-safe. Listing 9-16 shows the `Category` enum, one of the Java enums used by the bookstore application.

Listing 9-16. *The Enumeration of Predefined Categories Used by the Bookstore Application*

```
public enum Category {
  BOOKS("Books", "283155"),
  MOVIES("DVD", "130"),
  MUSIC("Music", "5174");

  private String searchIndex;
  private String browseNodeId;

  private Category(String searchIndex, String browseNodeId) {
    this.searchIndex = searchIndex;
    this.browseNodeId = browseNodeId;
  }

  public String getBrowseNodeId() {
    return browseNodeId;
  }
```

```
  @Override
  public String toString() {
    return searchIndex;
  }
}
```

The usage of these classes by the bookstore application's model class is shown in Listing 9-17. You can see the declaration of the image cache and the sequences that hold the top-selling books, movies, and music. Those sequences are actually populated in the postinit function of the class. You will recall that this method is called after all variable initializations in both the model class and any super classes have completed. Therefore, the last thing that happens as the model class is instantiated is that three AmazonTopSeller requests are created and kicked off in the background. The Category enum is used in the creation of the query for each category. When each query completes, its onDone function is called. This function is passed the item sequence that is the result of the query.

Listing 9-17. *The Bookstore Application's Model Class*

```
public class BookStoreModel {
  def MAX_THUMBNAIL_WIDTH = 80;
  def MAX_THUMBNAIL_HEIGHT = MAX_THUMBNAIL_WIDTH * 1.33 as Integer;

  public-read var imageCache = ImageCache {
    cacheSize: 100
    defaultWidth: MAX_THUMBNAIL_WIDTH
    defaultHeight: MAX_THUMBNAIL_HEIGHT
    preserveAspectRatio: true;
  }

  public-read var topBooks: Item[];
  public-read var topMovies: Item[];
  public-read var topMusic: Item[];
  public-read var busy = bind AmazonHttpRequest.requestsInProgress > 0;

  postinit {
    AmazonTopSellers {
      category: Category.BOOKS
      onDone: function( items:Item[] ) {
        topBooks = items;
      }
    }.start();

    AmazonTopSellers {
      category: Category.MUSIC
      onDone: function( items:Item[] ) {
        topMusic = items;
      }
    }.start();
```

```
    AmazonTopSellers {
      category: Category.MOVIES
      onDone: function( items:Item[] ) {
        topMovies = items;
      }
    }.start();
  }
}
```

A busy variable is also declared as part of this class. This is a Boolean variable that is bound to the expression `AmazonHttpRequest.requestsInProgress > 0`. This is a simple way for the model to tell the application that a web service request is in progress. What is needed is a way for the application to communicate this information to the user. The solution chosen for the bookstore application is to make the bookstore's logo flash. This is a handy choice, as the logo appears on every page. If it is desirable to indicate the progress of the requests, the item parsers could also expose the number of items parsed. If this is made available to the model class, it could then expose a progress complete percentage to the application. For now, we will stick to an indeterminate progress indicator just to let the user know that something is happening in the background. The code to flash the logo appears in the application's main script and is shown in the following code snippet:

```
var logo = NodeFactory.getLogo();

var busyAnimation = FadeTransition {
  node: logo
  duration: 0.5s
  fromValue: 1.0
  toValue: 0.3
  autoReverse: true
  repeatCount: Timeline.INDEFINITE
}

var busy = bind model.busy on replace {
  if (busy) {
    busyAnimation.playFromStart();
  } else {
    busyAnimation.stop();
    logo.opacity = 1.0;
  }
}
```

And finally, Figure 9-3 shows the result of all of this hard work. The reward for the developer and the user alike is a pretty but functional interface. By comparing Figures 9-2 and 9-3, you can see the benefit of being able to use the graphics directly from the artist. The artist's vision for the interface was matched very closely. As developers, we were able to get something up and running quickly by concentrating on the functionality of the application rather than its look.

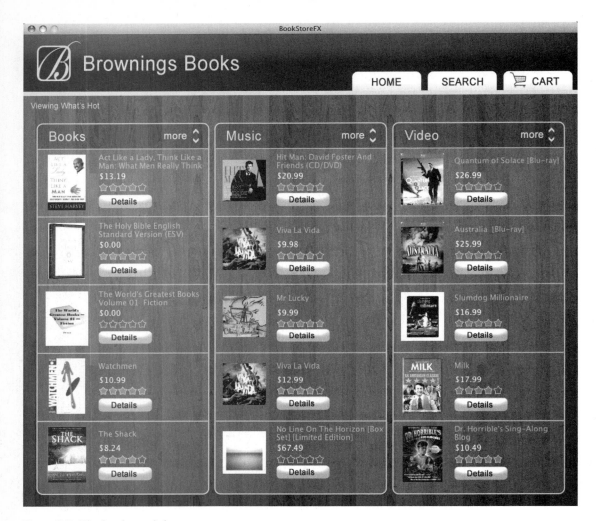

Figure 9-3. *The bookstore's home page*

The Search Page

The search page is shown in Figure 9-4. It is a fairly simple interface that includes a search box, a horizontal list of search results, and a details display for the currently selected item from the results list. The tricky part is that the search results list displays an unknown number of ItemSummary nodes. This raises performance and memory usage concerns. A method is needed to display a large list of items with the smallest possible number of ItemSummary nodes.

Figure 9-4. *The search page interface*

The implementation used by the bookstore application uses seven ItemSummary nodes to display an arbitrarily large sequence of items. The seven nodes rotate their positions rapidly as the list scrolls. When an ItemSummary goes off one end of the screen, it is repositioned at the other end and given a new Item to display. The new Item triggers the binding expressions inside the ItemSummary, and all of the data is automatically updated. This includes fetching a new image from the image cache as well. If the user starts to scroll in the opposite direction, the ItemSummary nodes will be placed back at the other side of the list. You can see in Figure 9-4 that at any given time there are four ItemSummary nodes visible on the screen. The two nodes positioned immediately to the left and right of the visible nodes are called *guard* nodes. The remaining node in our seven-node scheme is called the *floater*. The floater node stays on the side of the screen that the user is scrolling toward. When the current guard node on that side becomes visible, the floater becomes the new guard node, and the guard node from the opposite side is moved over to become the new floater. Figure 9-5 shows a diagram of this process.

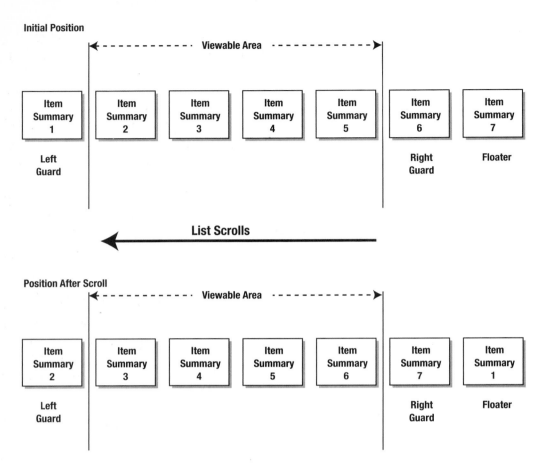

Figure 9-5. *Movement of guard nodes and floater nodes during a scroll*

The `ItemCarousel` class contains the implementation of this dynamic scrolling capability. The `ItemSummary` nodes are repositioned on the fly using their `translateX` variables. When the position of the list is updated, the x translations of the nodes are checked. The process of rearranging the nodes is triggered whenever a guard node becomes visible on the screen. Another nice feature of `ItemCarousel` is that rather than being tied directly to the list's slider, its movement is governed by calculation that accelerates and then decelerates the `ItemSummary` nodes to provide a nice animated scrolling effect. The portion of the code from `ItemCarousel` that implements the animated scrolling is shown in Listing 9-18.

Listing 9-18. *Implementation of the List Scrolling Animation*

```
/**
 * The x variable is the translation of the list contents
 * in the x direction.
 */
```

```
var x = 0.0 on replace {
    if (guardsEnabled) {
        // Is left guard onscreen?
        if (itemSummaries[leftGuardIndex].boundsInParent.maxX > x and
                leftGuardItemIndex > 0) {
            moveFloaterToLeftGuard();

        // Is right guard onscreen?
        } else if (itemSummaries[rightGuardIndex].boundsInParent.minX <
                    x + scene.width and rightGuardItemIndex < (sizeof items) - 1) {
            moveFloaterToRightGuard();
        }
    }
}

var speed: Number on replace {
    if (Math.abs( speed ) < MIN_SPEED) {
        speed = 0;
        t.pause();
    }
}

var t: Timeline = Timeline {
    keyFrames: KeyFrame {
        time: FRAME_TIME
        action: function() {
            // Calculate acceleration needed to reach the target in 1 second
            // This is derived from the basic motion formula: dist = v*t + 0.5*a*t*t
            var accel = ((itemSlider.currentValue - x) / FRAMES_PER_SEC - speed) /
                        (FRAMES_PER_SEC / 2);
            speed = speed + accel;
            x = x + speed;
        }
    }
    repeatCount: Timeline.INDEFINITE;
}
```

Adding Item Search to the Application Model

Searching for items on Amazon requires the use of the ItemSearch operation of the Amazon Associates Web Service call. You give this operation the keywords to search for and optionally the category of the search (books, movies, music). You can also specify the way in which you would like the results sorted. The code that implements the item search in the application's model class is shown in Listing 9-19. A new read-only sequence of items named searchResults is declared to hold the results of the search. A new public string named keywords is used by the application to hold the search terms typed by the user. A replace trigger on this variable kicks off a new search whenever the keywords change. The user may trigger a new search at any time, so care must be taken to cancel any existing search and ensure that the search results from the existing search do not get confused with the results from the new search. The fact that the callback methods from the `HttpRequest` class are executed only on the UI thread make this somewhat simpler than it otherwise would be.

Listing 9-19. *The Source Code Added to the Application's Model Class to Implement Item Searching*

```
/**
 * The sequence of items returned by the search.
 */
public-read var searchResults: Item[];

var currentSearch: AmazonItemSearch;

/**
 * This variable is set by the application when the user
 * types one or more search terms into the search box.  A
 * change in the contents of this variable triggers a new
 * search to begin.
 */
public var keywords = "" on replace {
  // Cancel the current search when a new one begins
  if (currentSearch != null) {
    currentSearch.cancel();
  }

  // Clear the search results
  delete searchResults;

  // If there are keywords, then start a new search
  if (keywords.length() > 0) {
    var search: AmazonItemSearch = AmazonItemSearch {
      sortBy: SortBy.SALES_RANK
      category: Category.BOOKS
      keywords: keywords
      maxResults: 50
      onResultsAvailable: function( items:Item[] ) {
        if (not search.canceled) {
          insert items into searchResults;
        }
      }
      onDone: function() {
        if (not search.canceled) {
          currentSearch = null;
        }
      }
    }
  }
```

```
    currentSearch = search;
    currentSearch.start();
  }
}
```

You can see a new web service request wrapper in use named AmazonItemSearch. Just like the AmazonTopSellers class that was described previously, this is another thin wrapper around an AmazonHttpRequest. It uses another Java-based enum called SortBy to specify the desired sorting of the results. It also allows the developer to specify the maximum number of search results to return. Amazon will only return ten results at a time. Because a maximum of 50 results is specified, the one request that we declare is actually performing up to five HTTP requests. Each set of 10 results takes about 1 second to process. In order to display the results to the user as quickly as possible, the onResultsAvailable variable holds a callback function that passes results back to the caller as they are returned from each HTTP request.

The Cart Page

The cart page simply contains a placeholder graphic that was converted to a FXZ file from an SVG source file. The SVG graphic is a public domain graphic that came from Open Clip Art Library (http://openclipart.org), which has some great stuff. This particular graphic had one group element at the root of the document, but it did not have an id attribute. In order to make it usable, the file had to be edited, and an id attribute of money was added. SVG Converter then converted the file to the FXZ format, and it was added to the bookstore application's Net-Beans project. A UI stub was created by right-clicking the FXZ file in NetBeans and choosing the Generate UI stub option. This UI stub is shown in Listing 9-20. This FXZ file contains only one graphic, so it is a very simple class. NetBeans generated a public variable named money that corresponds to the group with the money attribute from the SVG file. When the MoneyBagUI class is instantiated, the update method is called, and the money variable obtains a reference to the graphic residing in the FXD file embedded inside the FXZ archive.

Listing 9-20. *The UI Stub for the Money Bag Graphic*

```
public class MoneyBagUI extends FXDNode {
  override public var url = "{__DIR__}res/moneyBag.fxz";

  public-read protected var money: Node;

  override protected function contentLoaded() : Void {
    money=getNode("money");
  }

  protected override function getObject( id:String) : Object {
    var obj = super.getObject(id);
    if ( obj == null) {
      System.err.println("WARNING: Element with id {id} not found in {url}");
    }
    return obj;
  }
}
```

Once a `MoneyBagUI` object is instantiated, any JavaFX class can use the `money` variable just like any other node. In this case, the node is added to the scene graph as part of the cart page's UI. The result is shown in Figure 9-6.

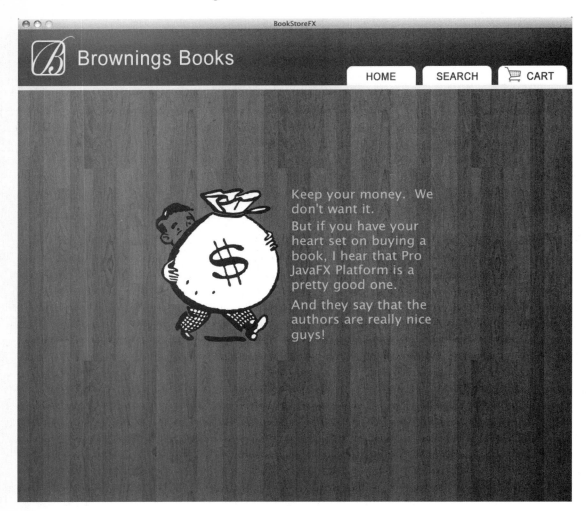

Figure 9-6. *The former SVG graphic as it appears on the cart page*

Summary

Congratulations, you made it! This chapter showed several techniques that can be used to write real JavaFX applications by using the SDK, some useful third-party libraries, and leveraging the power of the underlying Java platform. We have covered

- The HttpRequest class and how to use it to send requests to servers on the Internet

- The PullParser class and how to use it to parse both JSON and XML documents

- The implementation of a simple Internet application to display members of congress for a particular ZIP code

- How to load graphics that have been exported from Adobe Photoshop or Illustrator or have been converted from an SVG file

- The use of the Amazon Associates Web Service to retrieve information about items listed for sale on Amazon's website

- Using animation (but not too much!) to make your application come alive

- The use of third-party layout containers such as MigLayout to make easy work of complex layouts

- How to take advantage of the power of the Java class libraries to implement an image cache for a JavaFX platform

- The use of Java enum classes to get type-safe enumerations in JavaFX

- How to save memory and scene graph load by implementing a scrollable list with a minimal number of nodes

Only one more chapter to go! In the next chapter, we will discuss how to take your JavaFX programming expertise and apply it to a mobile platform. You will see how to take one of the example programs in this book and get it ready to run on a mobile device!

Resources

For additional information on JSON, check out these sites:

- http://www.json.org

- http://en.wikipedia.org/wiki/JSON

Go here for addition information on XML:

- http://www.w3.org/XML

- http://en.wikipedia.org/wiki/XML

- http://www.w3schools.com/XML/xml_whatis.asp

You'll find additional tools and information on the JavaFX Production Suite here:

- http://www.javafx.com (Download the JavaFX Production Suite from this site.)

- http://javafx.com/docs/gettingstarted/production_suite/

- http://www.inkscape.org/screenshots/index.php?lang=en

- http://www.openclipart.org

- http://tango.freedesktop.org/Tango_Desktop_Project

For additional information on the Amazon Associates Web Service, try these sites:

- `http://aws.amazon.com/associates/`
- `http://docs.amazonwebservices.com/AWSECommerceService/2009-01-06/DG/`

■ ■ ■

CHAPTER 10

Developing JavaFX Mobile Applications

Simple things should be simple and complex things should be possible.

—Alan Kay

The Java language was originally developed back in 1991 by a small team called "the Green Project" led by James Gosling. Their mission was to create a device-independent language that could be used in embedded applications such as set-top boxes or other consumer devices. After limited success in an immature market, the Java language was repurposed as a network operating system for the World Wide Web. The rest is history with the explosive growth of Java in the Web, on the desktop, and in enterprise server applications led by the powerful branding of "Write once, run anywhere."

Fast-forward to 2009. Handheld smartphones are the new Internet with faster processors, larger screens, and high-speed network connections. Set-top boxes are pervasive and provide even more advanced capabilities, from high-definition television to digital video recording. Most importantly, over 2.6 billion of these consumer devices are already running Java ME, a lightweight version of Java.

JavaFX Mobile is the technology that will finally bring the original vision of Java full circle. It lets you take full-featured rich Internet applications that use media, graphics, animation, and web services and seamlessly run them on cell phones and set-top boxes. This chapter will show you how you can write applications that run on both the desktop and mobile platform with exactly the same code.

The Vision of JavaFX Mobile

JavaFX Mobile is one the most exciting features of the JavaFX platform, because it allows the same applications you write for the desktop to run on mobile devices as well. Following an initial beta, the first public release of JavaFX Mobile came with JavaFX 1.2 on February 12, 2009, in preparation for the market rollout at Mobile World Congress. Eric Klein, VP of Java Marketing, and Jeet Kaul, VP of Java Engineering, did a video announcement for the release, as shown in Figure 10-1.

Figure 10-1. *Announcement of JavaFX Mobile on the JavaFX launch page*

■**Tip** Both Terrence Barr and Hinkmond Wong's blogs are excellent places to learn about the latest advances in JavaFX Mobile technology. URLs can be found in the Resources section at the end of this chapter.

JavaFX Mobile is built on top of the Java ME platform, so it has a very broad range of devices that it can be run on, while also taking advantage of mobile-specific features such as GPSs, accelerometers, and touch screens. Since JavaFX is a software platform, not an OS, it can be ported to run on almost any type of device, from feature phones to Linux or Windows-based smartphones.

Several handset partners are already lined up to produce JavaFX Mobile–enabled phones. Both Sony Ericsson and LG Electronics have announced partnerships with Sun, and there are expected to be more device manufacturers in the near future.

Sun has announced the availability of handsets that come preinstalled with JavaFX Mobile. These phones will first be made available to developers so they can build mobile-enabled applications, and will later be generally available for end users to purchase.

The JavaFX 1.2 release comes with a Mobile Emulator that can be used to develop and test JavaFX Mobile applications today with no special hardware. We will use the emulator throughout the rest of this chapter to demonstrate some of the capabilities of the JavaFX Mobile platform.

Mobile Hello Earthrise

The first example of JavaFX development presented in this book was a rich user interface with text, graphics, and animation. In this section we will show you how to enhance that application so it is fully mobile compatible, while still retaining its ability to run on the desktop.

There are four primary differences in mobile application development that need to be taken into account:

- *Screen size*: Mobile devices have much smaller screen resolution than their desktop counterparts. This means that your application has to be capable of running within a resolution of 320×240 or possibly even smaller, and needs to adapt to different screen sizes based on the device.

- *Common Profile*: Mobile applications are limited to the JavaFX APIs that are part of the Common Profile, which is a subset of the Desktop Profile. This limits some available functionality, but also provides a solid foundation where components will behave the same on mobile and desktop devices.

- *User input*: Many mobile devices do not support touch screens, so to support a wide range of devices your application needs to be fully navigable by the keypad alone. Even where a touch screen is available, there is no mouse pointer, so hover and the related mouse events will not work.

- *Performance*: Mobile applications run on much less powerful devices, so they have fewer CPU and memory resources available to work with. This means that you have to pay particular attention to the performance and resource usage of your application.

To convert the Hello Earthrise application, we will go through the code to address each of these issues so that it runs equally well on mobile devices as well as the desktop.

Listing 10-1 shows the original code of the Hello Earthrise application, with lines that are dependent on either screen size or features of the Desktop Profile highlighted in bold.

Listing 10-1. *Original Hello Earthrise Application*

```
var textRef:Text;

// Provides the animated scrolling behavior for the text
var transTransition = TranslateTransition {
  duration: 75s
  node: bind textRef
  toY: -820 // dependent on window size
  interpolator: Interpolator.LINEAR
  repeatCount: Timeline.INDEFINITE
}

Stage {
  title: "Hello Earthrise"
  scene: Scene {
    content: [
      ImageView { // image too large for a mobile display (516x387)
        image: Image {
          url: "http://projavafx.com/images/earthrise.jpg"
        }
      },
      Group {
        layoutX: 50  // dependent on window size
        layoutY: 180 // dependent on window size
        content: [
          textRef = Text {
            layoutY: 100
            textOrigin: TextOrigin.TOP
            textAlignment: TextAlignment.JUSTIFY
            wrappingWidth: 380 // dependent on window size
            // Note that this syntax creates one long string of text
            content: "Earthrise at Christmas: "
                     "[Forty] years ago this Christmas, a turbulent world "
                     "looked to the heavens for a unique view of our home "
                     "planet. This photo of Earthrise over the lunar horizon "
                     "was taken by the Apollo 8 crew in December 1968, showing "
                     "Earth for the first time as it appears from deep space. "
                     "Astronauts Frank Borman, Jim Lovell and William Anders "
                     "had become the first humans to leave Earth orbit, "
                     "entering lunar orbit on Christmas Eve. In a historic live "
                     "broadcast that night, the crew took turns reading from "
                     "the Book of Genesis, closing with a holiday wish from "
                     "Commander Borman: \"We close with good night, good luck, "
                     "a Merry Christmas, and God bless all of you -- all of "
                     "you on the good Earth.\""
```

```
          // The approximate color used in the scrolling Star Wars intro
          fill: Color.rgb(187, 195, 107)
          font: Font.font("SansSerif", FontWeight.BOLD, 24); // font won't fit
        }
      ]
      clip:
        Rectangle {
          width: 430 // dependent on window size
          height: 85
        }
    }
  ]
}
}
// Start playing an audio clip
MediaPlayer {
  autoPlay: true
  repeatCount: MediaPlayer.REPEAT_FOREVER
  media: Media {
    source: "http://projavafx.com/audio/zarathustra.mid"
  }
}
// Start the text animation
transTransition.play();
```

Fortunately, there is nothing in this example that is not a part of the Common Profile. We will go over the differences between the Desktop and Common Profiles in more detail in the next section, but with over 80 percent of the JavaFX API covered in the Common Profile, there is only a small set of functions that cannot be used.

On the other hand, there are lots of places where the application will break on a smaller screen, including absolute positioning of components, fixed widths, and an image that is too large for the mobile display.

While any dependencies on the Desktop Profile would prevent the code from compiling on mobile devices, the other changes will not prevent the application from running, so you can try to run it as a mobile application right out of the box.

Running in the Mobile Emulator

The easiest way to run an application in the Mobile Emulator is to use an IDE that supports mobile development. For example, running a mobile application from NetBeans is as simple as changing the Run setting in the Project Properties screen, as shown in Figure 10-2.

Once you have configured your project to run in the Mobile Emulator, all compilations will use the mobile profile and all project runs will fire off the Mobile Emulator.

It is also possible to run mobile applications directly from the command line. The first step is to tell the javafxpackager application to compile your code using the Mobile Profile by passing in the following option:

```
-profile MOBILE
```

This will tell the `javafxpackager` to limit the application compilation to only use functions available in the Mobile and Common profiles, preverify the JAR file, and also package up the application as a MIDlet. The MIDlet consists of a JAR file containing all the class and resource files for your application and a Java Application Descriptor (JAD) file preconfigured to run your JavaFX Mobile application.

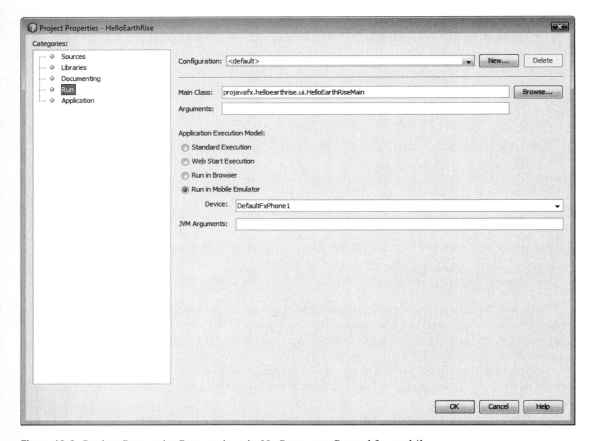

Figure 10-2. *Project Properties Run settings in NetBeans configured for mobile*

To run the application within the Mobile Emulator, you have to run the `emulator` executable under the `emulator/bin` directory of the JavaFX distribution with your application JAD file as the argument:

```
<Path to JavaFX SDK>/emulator/bin/emulator.exe -Xdescriptor:<Path to Project>➥
/dist/HelloEarthRise.jad
```

You can also pass in a device via the `-Xdevice` option; otherwise, the default JavaFX phone will be used.

The unmodified Hello Earthrise application running in the Mobile Emulator is shown in Figure 10-3.

Congratulations, you have successfully run your first JavaFX mobile application!

Figure 10-3. *Hello Earthrise application running in the Mobile Emulator*

Fitting Applications on the Mobile Screen

From the screenshot at the end of the previous section, it is clear that there is a little work to do in order to make the Hello Earthrise application fit the mobile screen size. As we explained earlier, there are various places in the code that either use absolute positioning or fixed widths or depend on the image size.

One of the most important considerations for mobile development is that you really do not know the size of the mobile screen. While a lot of JavaFX samples hard-code the 320×240 screen size of the emulator, here are some reasons why this is a bad practice:

- Different mobile devices have different screen sizes. This is essential if want to target a broad range of mobile devices and protect your application against future innovations, such as the Sony XPERIA with a massive 800×480 resolution.

- The available screen size may be smaller than the physical screen resolution. As an example, Windows CE devices often reserve space at the top and bottom for menus and keyboard controls, so the usable height given to your application is reduced.

- The screen may be vertical or horizontal. Many new phones can detect the orientation of the device and will automatically rotate the display. If your application is hard-coded for a vertically oriented layout, it may break when the phone is rotated.

Fortunately, JavaFX provides an easy facility to check the available size of the screen allocated to the application. The dimensions of the Stage and Scene are both set to the available screen space upon initialization, and can be bound to trigger change dimensions or trigger actions when the display is rotated.

As an example of this, it is possible to dynamically change the amount of border on the left and right of the text in the Hello Earthrise application by using the following:

```
var scene:Scene;
def borderWidth = bind scene.width / 10;
Stage {
  title: "Hello Earthrise"
  scene: scene = Scene {
  ...
    Group {
      layoutX: bind borderWidth
```

Now you can continue to replace the rest of the hard-coded positions and widths so the program is fully size independent. However, in order to have the program continue to work on the desktop there is one other special case that needs to be considered. The primary difference in Scene and Stage size is as follows:

- *Mobile* Scene/Stage: The width and height are fixed according to the screen resolution.

- *Desktop* Scene/Stage: The width and height are calculated to fit the contents.

This dichotomy introduces a problem with our approach of basing the component width and height on the scene. For example, if we center the image in the middle of the scene it will work great on the mobile device; however, since the image is used to calculate the size of the scene on the desktop it will initially center on the origin (0, 0), causing the window to size too small.

A simple fix for this is to check the size of the scene first, and position the image without centering initially:

```
imageView = ImageView {
    x: bind if (scene.width == 0) then 0 else (scene.width - image.width) / 2
    y: bind if (scene.height == 0) then 0 else (scene.height - image.height) / 2
    image: image = Image {
```

Now the image will be initially placed at the origin, but centered after the scene width and height are set.

The same pattern can be used to set the wrappingWidth of the text so that it does not throw off the window width:

```
wrappingWidth: bind (if (scene.width == 0) then image.width
                     else scene.width) - borderWidth * 2
```

Listing 10-2 shows the updated code for the Hello Earthrise application. The new code makes everything from the font size to the animation transition dependent on the screen size. All of the updates from the original listing are highlighted in bold.

Listing 10-2. *Hello Earthrise Application Updated for the Mobile Screen Size*

```
var textRef:Text;

// Provides the animated scrolling behavior for the text
var transTransition = TranslateTransition {
  duration: 75s
  node: bind textRef
  toY: bind -(textRef.layoutBounds.height + 85)
  interpolator: Interpolator.LINEAR
  repeatCount: Timeline.INDEFINITE
}

var scene:Scene;
def borderWidth = bind scene.width * .10;
Stage {
  title: "Hello Earthrise"
  scene: scene = Scene {
    var image:Image;
    var imageView:ImageView;
    content: [
      imageView = ImageView {
        x: bind if (scene.width == 0) then 0 else (scene.width - image.width) / 2
        y: bind if (scene.height == 0) then 0 else (scene.height - image.height) / 2
        image: image = Image {
          url: "http://projavafx.com/images/earthrise.jpg"
        }
      },
```

```
         Group {
           layoutX: bind borderWidth
           layoutY: bind imageView.layoutBounds.minY + 180
           content: [
             textRef = Text {
               layoutY: 100
               textOrigin: TextOrigin.TOP
               textAlignment: TextAlignment.JUSTIFY
               wrappingWidth: bind (if (scene.width == 0) then image.width
                                    else scene.width) - borderWidth * 2
               // Note that this syntax creates one long string of text
               content: "Earthrise at Christmas: "
                        "[Forty] years ago this Christmas, a turbulent world "
                        "looked to the heavens for a unique view of our home "
                        "planet. This photo of Earthrise over the lunar horizon "
                        "was taken by the Apollo 8 crew in December 1968, showing "
                        "Earth for the first time as it appears from deep space. "
                        "Astronauts Frank Borman, Jim Lovell and William Anders "
                        "had become the first humans to leave Earth orbit, "
                        "entering lunar orbit on Christmas Eve. In a historic live "
                        "broadcast that night, the crew took turns reading from "
                        "the Book of Genesis, closing with a holiday wish from "
                        "Commander Borman: \"We close with good night, good luck, "
                        "a Merry Christmas, and God bless all of you -- all of "
                        "you on the good Earth.\""
               // The approximate color used in the scrolling Star Wars intro
               fill: Color.rgb(187, 195, 107)
               font: bind Font.font("SansSerif", FontWeight.BOLD, scene.width * .05);
             }
           ]
           clip:
             Rectangle {
               width: bind scene.width
               height: 85
             }
         }
       ]
     }
   }
}
// Start playing an audio clip
MediaPlayer {
  autoPlay: true
  repeatCount: MediaPlayer.REPEAT_FOREVER
  media: Media {
    source: "http://projavafx.com/audio/zarathustra.mid"
  }
}
// Start the text animation
transTransition.play();
```

■**Caution** A large number of `bind` operations can increase the compiled footprint of your application significantly. If you have a large number of variables to update, consider using an `on replace` trigger instead.

Running the updated application in the emulator will now show a properly sized application for the mobile screen, as shown in Figure 10-4.

Figure 10-4. *Hello Earthrise application sized for the mobile screen*

If you now rotate the display in the emulator by selecting View ➤ Orientation ➤ 90 Degrees, you will see that it properly adjusts for the wider resolution, as shown in Figure 10-5.

Finally, if you run the application in the original desktop profile, you can confirm that the same code is now fully cross-device compatible, as shown in Figure 10-6.

Figure 10-5. *Hello Earthrise application on a horizontally oriented screen*

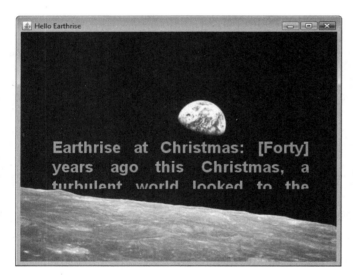

Figure 10-6. *Modified Hello Earthrise code running in original desktop configuration*

Congratulations! You now have experience porting an application to the mobile screen dimensions while also having it still work on the desktop.

Developing for the Common Profile

In the previous section, you learned how to modify an application to run on the mobile platform by dynamically changing the size based on the scene dimensions. However, many desktop applications will not be as easy to port, because they rely on features that are exclusively part of the Desktop Profile. This section will discuss the different profiles available for JavaFX development.

The JavaFX 1.2 release ships with two different profiles. The Common Profile has all of the core functionality needed to do images, video, text, and animation, and to call out to services. It is also supported on all devices where JavaFX runs, including desktop computers, cell phones, and, in the future, set-top boxes.

On top of this is a Desktop Profile that adds functionality exclusive to desktop computers. This includes all of the Swing-based components, graphics effects, style sheets, and other features that are not easy to port to embedded devices.

In the future there will also be a Mobile Profile that may contain APIs specific to mobile devices, such as Bluetooth, motion detectors, GPSs, and other features of portable devices. However, until additional mobile features are included, references to the Mobile Profile are equivalent to the Common Profile.

■Note You can still access mobile specific APIs by calling down to the underlying Java ME code. See the section "Advanced Mobile Features" later in this chapter for more details.

When writing JavaFX mobile applications, it is important to know what features are part of the Common Profile, and what features are only available in the Desktop Profile. If any APIs from the Desktop Profile are used, they will cause compilation failures, preventing you from even building your application.

Table 10-1 lists the most important features that are only part of the Desktop Profile and thus cannot be used in any mobile applications.

Table 10-1. *Desktop Profile APIs Not Available for Mobile Applications*

Package	Class(es)	Affected Variables and Methods
javafx.ext.swing	All	All
javafx.reflect	All	All
javafx.scene	Node	effect, style
javafx.scene	Scene	stylesheets
javafx.scene.effect	All	All
javafx.scene.effect.light	All	All
javafx.scene.shape	ShapeIntersect	All
javafx.scene.shape	ShapeSubstract	All
javafx.scene.text	Font	autoKern, embolden, letterSpacing, ligatures, oblique, position
javafx.stage	AppletStageExtension	All
javafx.util	FXEvaluator	All
javafx.util	StringLocalizer	All

■Note Table 10-1 is accurate for the JavaFX 1.2 release. Expect the gap between the Common and Desktop Profiles to continue to close in subsequent releases.

A lot of the mobile omissions are based on the fact that Java ME, which JavaFX Mobile is based on, has no UI toolkit equivalent to Swing. Therefore, you can't use any of the classes in the `javafx.est.swing` package or methods that work with Swing classes such as `java.awt.Color` or `java.awt.image.BufferedImage`. There are some pure JavaFX components that you can use instead, such as `Text` and `TextBox`, and the next major release of JavaFX is focused on delivering additional components that will be part of the Common Profile.

There is other functionality that has no equivalent, such as reflection, style sheets, effects, and localization. It is best to avoid these features if you know you will want to support a mobile version of your application.

Another example is `FXEvaluator`, which is used to compile and run JavaFX snippets on the fly. This feature requires a JSR 223–compliant scripting engine, which is not available on mobile devices.

Finally, if you use any Java libraries you need to make sure that there is a Java ME version available.

In the next section, you can apply your knowledge of the Common Profile to perform a conversion of a larger application that has more dependencies.

Mobile DrawJFX

In Chapter 5 you had the opportunity to develop DrawJFX, a JavaFX drawing application, as an example of creating custom UI components. In this section we will show you how you can take that application and modify it so that it can be run on mobile devices as well as the desktop.

The Mobile DrawJFX application is composed of a color picker and a drawing canvas. It was introduced as two separate projects, and since both will need some updates we will tackle the color picker first.

Creating a Mobile Color Picker

Figure 10-7 shows a picture of the color picker application developed in Chapter 5. Even without looking at the code, some of the changes that you will need to make are obvious:

- The color picker window has a drop shadow effect that cannot be used from the Mobile Profile.

- The size of the color picker is much too large to fit on a mobile screen. The inner window itself is 400×480 pixels.

Figure 10-7. *Current color picker application*

Removing the drop shadow effect is simple enough. Just delete these lines from `ColorPickerSnowFlakeNode.fx`:

```
effect: DropShadow { // remove
  offsetX: 3
  offsetY: 3
}
```

The next step is to change everything to be relative sized. Since the entire color picker is composed of small diamonds, it makes sense to use that as the basis for sizing the entire window. This involves making the diamond width a `public-init` variable:

```
/**
 * Width of the diamonds shapes in the color picker
 */
public-init var diamondWidth: Double = 20;
```

and changing all the locations with absolute positioning or fixed widths to use this:

- Title Bar: `def TITLE_BAR_HEIGHT: Number = diamondWidth * 1.5;`

- Color Font: `var colorValFont = Font.font("Sans serif", FontWeight.BOLD, diamondWidth * 0.8)`

- Outer Rect Width: `width: 20 * diamondWidth`

- Outer Rect Height: `height: 26 * diamondWidth`

- Line Width: `endX: 20 * diamondWidth - 1`

- Title Font: `Font.font("Sans serif", FontWeight.BOLD, 1.2 * diamondWidth)`

- Chosen Color Box X: `layoutX: 13.5 * diamondWidth`

- Chosen Color Box Y: `layoutY: 2.5 * diamondWidth`

- Chosen Color Rectangle Width: `width: 1.5 * diamondWidth`

- Chosen Color Rectangle Height: `height: 2.5 * diamondWidth`

- Diamond dimensions:

```
def diamondHalfHeight: Double =➥
    Math.sqrt(Math.pow(diamondWidth, 2)➥
    Math.pow(diamondWidth / 2, 2))
```

■**Caution** If you use the `java.lang.Math` library in your application, you may run into mobile compilation issues with certain functions, such as `log`, `exp`, and `pow`. Instead, import the `javafx.util.Math` library, which is a drop-in replacement that includes mobile-safe implementations of these functions.

The positions of the OK and Cancel buttons also need to be corrected so that those buttons do not overlap the color picker. This is a simple matter of adjusting the relative positioning of the `buttonsHBoxRef` to 10 pixels off the right and bottom edge:

```
layoutX: bind outerRectRef.layoutBounds.width -
               buttonsHBoxRef.layoutBounds.width - 10
layoutY: bind outerRectRef.layoutBounds.height -
               buttonsHBoxRef.layoutBounds.height - 10
```

The final update is back in the main class; set the positioning and diamond width to something reasonable for mobile devices:

```
colorPicker = ColorPickerSnowFlakeNode {
    layoutX: 20
    layoutY: 40
    diamondWidth: 10
```

One additional fix is required that will not be obvious until you run the program. Because Java ME does not support string formatters, the formatting syntax used to print out the color values, {%1.0f double}, will not work. Instead, you have to use a cast to an Integer to truncate the decimals, as shown here:

```
Text {
  font: colorValFont
  textOrigin: TextOrigin.TOP
  content: bind "r:{chosenRedNum as Integer}"
},
Text {
  font: colorValFont
  textOrigin: TextOrigin.TOP
  content: bind "g:{chosenGreenNum as Integer}"
},
Text {
  font: colorValFont
  textOrigin: TextOrigin.TOP
  content: bind "b:{chosenBlueNum as Integer}"
}
```

Running the final application will display a smaller version of the color picker that is fully functional, as shown in Figure 10-8.

Figure 10-8. *Completed mobile color picker application*

Refactoring DrawJFX for Mobile Devices

Now that you have successfully gotten the Color Picker working on a mobile device, the next step is to integrate that back in to the main DrawJFX application and complete the conversion of the rest of the application.

Some of the changes that you will have to make in the DrawJFX application follow:

- Remove tools that use effects for drawing, such as the `Reflection` and `DropShadow` tools

- Remove application graphics effects such as the `Glow` effect on tool rollover

- Replace uses of APIs not supported on mobile devices, such as `Math.sqrt` and `Math.pow`

- Modify the canvas size to fit the mobile screen dimensions

- Reduce the number of tools on the palette to fit the screen height

Starting with the tool removal, you can delete the `DropShadowDrawingToolNode.fx` and `ReflectionDrawingToolNode.fx` source files. Also, remember to remove the references to these classes in `DrawJFXMain.fx`:

```
DropShadowDrawingToolNode {}, // remove
ReflectionDrawingToolNode {},
```

and the `currentEffect` in `DrawJFXModel.fx`:

```
public var currentEffect:Effect; // remove
```

The other use of an effect that needs to be removed is the `Glow` effect on rollover in `AbstractDrawingToolNode.fx`. This can be replaced with a simple mouse-released action listener that performs the action with no effect:

```
onMouseReleased: function(me:MouseEvent):Void {
    action();
}
```

The rest of the changes (to make the canvas fit the screen size, integrate the mobile color picker, and reduce the number of tools) are all in the `DrawJFXMain` class. Listing 10-3 shows the completed class with all of the changes highlighted in bold.

Listing 10-3. *Completed DrawJFXMain Class File with Changes for Mobile Deployment*

```
def djfxModel = DrawJFXModel.getInstance();

function createSeparator() {
    Rectangle {
        width: 32
        height: 3
        fill: Color.WHITE
    }
}
```

```
var fillColorPicker = ColorPickerSnowFlakeNode {
    layoutX: 15    // reposition
    layoutY: 35
    diamondWidth: 10 // shrink the color picker
    title: "Fill Color"
    visible: bind djfxModel.fillColorPickerVisible with inverse
    originalColor: bind djfxModel.currentFill
    onClose: function(color:Color) {
        if (djfxModel.currentSelectedNode != null) {
            (djfxModel.currentSelectedNode as Shape).fill = color;
        } else {
            djfxModel.currentFill = color;
        }
    }
}


var strokeColorPicker = ColorPickerSnowFlakeNode {
    layoutX: 25    // reposition
    layoutY: 45
    diamondWidth: 10 // shrink the color picker
    title: "Stroke Color"
    visible: bind djfxModel.strokeColorPickerVisible with inverse
    originalColor: bind djfxModel.currentStroke
    onClose: function(color:Color) {
        if (djfxModel.currentSelectedNode != null) {
            (djfxModel.currentSelectedNode as Shape).stroke = color;
        } else {
            djfxModel.currentStroke = color;
        }
    }
}


var firstTool:AbstractDrawingToolNode;

var scene:Scene;
Stage {
    title: "DrawJFX"
    resizable: false
    scene: scene = Scene { // save off the scene
        var drawingAreaNode:DrawingAreaNode;
        content: [
            drawingAreaNode = DrawingAreaNode {
                width: bind scene.width - 32  // resize with scene
                height: bind scene.height
            },
            fillColorPicker,
            strokeColorPicker,
```

```
        // The drawing tool box
        VBox {
            layoutX: bind scene.width - 32  // stick to screen width
            content: [ // sequence modified to reduce tool count
                firstTool = CircleDrawingToolNode {filled: false},
                CircleDrawingToolNode {filled: true},
                RectangleDrawingToolNode {filled: false},
                RectangleDrawingToolNode {filled: true},
                LineDrawingToolNode {},
                PaintDrawingToolNode {fill: true},
                PaintDrawingToolNode {fill: false},
                StrokeWidthDrawingToolNode {},
                ScaleDrawingToolNode {plusDirection: true},
                RotateDrawingToolNode {plusDirection: true}
            ]
        }
        ]
    }
}

// Click the circle tool so it is highlighted on startup
firstTool.action();
```

Now when you run the DrawJFX application in the Mobile Emulator, it will be fully functional. Figure 10-9 shows an example of what you can draw with the Mobile DrawJFX application, and right beside it is a fully working version deployed to an XPERIA X1 JavaFX Mobile Device.

Congratulations on converting a sizable application to JavaFX Mobile! With your knowledge of the Common Profile and experience converting several applications, you should now be able to size up any application to see if it is a good fit for mobile deployment and determine how much effort is required to work around some of the limitations.

The next section goes into some advanced topics about leveraging the Java ME APIs for additional functionality and performance-tuning your application.

Figure 10-9. *Completed DrawJFX application running in the Mobile Emulator (left) and on the XPERIA X1 (right)*

Advanced Mobile Features

The JavaFX Mobile platform sits on top of the Java ME stack, which means that you can take advantage of any features that are supported in the underlying Java ME APIs just as you can take advantage of Java SE features on the desktop.

Wherever possible it is preferable to use the equivalent JavaFX Mobile functionality from the Common Profile instead. This will ensure that your application remains portable from the desktop to mobile devices with no changes. However, there are certain features of mobile devices, like accelerometers, GPSs, and Bluetooth connectivity, that may not be available on the desktop.

At a minimum, any JavaFX Mobile–enabled device will come with support for Connected Limited Device Configuration (CLDC) 1.1 and Mobile Information Device Profile (MIDP) 2.0. It may also support the Mobile Java Specification Requests (JSRs) listed in Table 10-2.

Table 10-2. *Mobile JSRs That You May Find on JavaFX Mobile Devices*

JSR	Name	Description
JSR 75	PDA Optional Packages	Access to personal information management (PIM) and the mobile file system
JSR 135	Mobile Media API	Audio, video, and other time-based multimedia support
JSR 172	Mobile Web Services	REST and SOAP client services
JSR 177	Security and Trust Services API for J2ME	Security features and smart card access
JSR 184	Mobile 3D Graphics API	3D graphics APIs for mobile phones
JSR 226	Scalable 2D Vector Graphics API	Allows rendering of scalable 2D vector graphics, including SVG
JSR 234	Advanced Multimedia Supplements	Access to the camera, radio, and advanced audio processing

To find out what version of MIDP the device supports, you can inspect the `javafx.me.profiles` property while your application is running. This can be accomplished via the following code:

```
FX.getProperty("javafx.me.profiles")
```

Printing out the value of this in the JavaFX 1.2 Mobile Emulator will result in the following output:

```
MIDP-2.1 JAVAFX-1.2
```

■**Tip** An easy way to check whether you are running on a desktop or mobile platform at runtime is to use the __PROFILE__ variable. This returns either "desktop" or "mobile" based on the profile of the running application.

Some other Mobile JSRs that may be useful to access advanced features of the device you are deploying are shown in Table 10-3.

Table 10-3. *Additional Mobile JSRs Available per Device*

JSR	Name	Description
JSR 83	Bluetooth	Bluetooth API for Java devices
JSR 179	Location Data	Access physical location information from a GPS
JSR 256	Mobile Sensor API	Measure acceleration, temperature, air pressure, wind speed, or other available sensors

If you use any of these Mobile JSRs, you may limit your portability across devices, even if they support JavaFX Mobile. Also, because none of these are supported out of the box with the JavaFX Mobile Emulator, you will need to manually modify the configuration settings to change the JSR support.

■ **Tip** Joshua Marinacci describes the full process of configuring the JavaFX Mobile Emulator to use additional JSRs at the end of his accelerometer example on the JavaFX samples website: `http://javafx.com/samples/AccelerometerTest/index.html`.

In the future, some of these capabilities may be added to the Mobile Profile, making the need to access these JSRs directly unnecessary.

Performance-Tuning JavaFX Mobile Applications

One of the biggest differences between desktop and mobile development that we have not touched on yet is optimizing performance. Mobile devices have slower CPUs and less available memory than their desktop counterparts, making application performance even more crucial.

Michael Heinrichs, one of the JavaFX Mobile team members, did an excellent series on mobile application performance on his blog, followed by a detailed article for the Sun Developer Network:

`http://java.sun.com/developer/technicalArticles/javafx/mobile/index.html`

Some of his findings in profiling JavaFX Mobile applications were

- *Binding is expensive*: Binding is a very convenient and powerful facility that is fully supported on JavaFX Mobile. However, currently for mobile applications it is twice as slow as the same code written with an on `replace` trigger. For an application with a lot of state changes, this could be a significant factor.

- *Large scene graphs are slow*: In desktop applications, it is common to hide nodes that will get displayed at some point in the future. However, for mobile applications the size of the scene graph has a dramatic impact on performance, so removing and adding nodes rather than hiding them will often speed up the rest of the application.

- *Simple shapes are faster than images*: Especially for images that cover large areas of the screen, it is faster to render a simple shape than to draw an image. This also conserves memory.

- *Small images are faster than complex shapes*: If you are drawing a small portion of the screen, like an icon, it will often be faster to draw an image from a file than to render a complicated set of shapes.

- *Scaling views is expensive*: Both in terms of performance and memory, it is more efficient to scale the Image rather than the ImageView. This will guarantee the image saved in memory is optimally sized and that scaling has to only occur once.

- *Image loading slows startup*: If you have a lot of images to load, it can slow down the startup time of your application. Loading images in the background instead can greatly improve the perceive performance.

- *Use integers instead of numbers*: Floating-point operations are much more resource intensive than integer mathematics, which can have a significant difference for mobile applications running on constrained devices.

Note These performance tips are focused on the JavaFX 1.2 release and may not be applicable to future releases. The JavaFX Mobile team is very focused on improving performance.

One other consideration in profiling your application is that while the Mobile Emulator is a great tool to execute a fast develop, build, and test cycle, it often does not give the best indication of deployed performance. When benchmarking your application for both performance and memory usage, there is no substitute for testing on a physical device.

Summary

In this chapter you learned the basics of JavaFX Mobile development. These basics will enable you to write portable applications that will work on both desktop and mobile devices. This chapter covered the following:

- Creating a simple mobile Hello Earthrise application

- Understanding the Common Profile and limitations of mobile development

- Converting the color picker application to run on mobile devices

- Refactoring the DrawJFX application to work on a mobile handset

- Taking advantage of the Java ME capabilities beneath JavaFX Mobile

- Using JavaFX Mobile best practices that will enable you to write high-performance applications

The JavaFX Mobile revolution is just beginning, but you are armed with practical experience and knowledge to begin writing rich, engaging mobile applications today.

References

- Terrence Barr's Blog, an excellent resource for mobile news: `http://weblogs.java.net/blog/terrencebarr/`

- Hinkmond Wong's Blog, JavaFX Mobile and Java ME news from the trenches: `http://blogs.sun.com/hinkmond/`

- Joshua Marinacci's accelerometer example on the JavaFX samples website: `http://javafx.com/samples/AccelerometerTest/index.html`

- Michael Heinrichs' article on mobile performance tuning: `http://java.sun.com/developer/technicalArticles/javafx/mobile/index.html`

- Michael Heinrichs' blog on JavaFX Mobile and other topics: `http://blogs.sun.com/michaelheinrichs/entry/best_practices_for_javafx_mobile3`

■ ■ ■

Keywords and Operators

This appendix presents keywords and the operators of JavaFX Script.

JavaFX Script keywords are divided into *reserved words* and *nonreserved words*. Reserved words cannot be used as names in JavaFX Script without being enclosed in French quotes (<< >>). The following list contains the JavaFX Script reserved words:

abstract	catch	from	override	super
after	class	function	package	then
and	continue	if	private	this
as	def	import	protected	throw
assert	delete	indexof	public	true
at	else	insert	public-init	try
attribute	exclusive	instanceof	public-read	typeof
before	extends	lazy	return	var
bind	false	mixin	reverse	while
bound	finally	mod	sizeof	
break	for	or	static	

The following is the list of JavaFX Script nonreserved words:

first	into	on	step	where
in	inverse	postinit	trigger	with
init	last	replace	tween	

■**Note** The keywords `attribute`, `exclusive`, `first`, `last`, `private`, `static`, `trigger`, and `typeof` are once active keywords of JavaFX Script. They no longer play any syntactic roles in JavaFX Script 1.2. However, the compiler still recognizes them as keywords and issues deprecation warning messages for some of them. The `assert` keyword is not used in JavaFX Script 1.2, but the compiler team wishes to reserve the option of supporting an assertion facility in a future version of the compiler.

JavaFX Script operators follow the precedence and associativity rules outlined in Table A-1.

Table A-1. *Operator Precedences and Associativities*

Operator	Meaning	Precedence	Associativity	Examples
++	Pre/postincrement	1	None	++i, i++
--	Pre/postdecrement	1	None	--i, i--
o.a	Member access	1	None	
foo()	Function invocation	1	None	
seq[]	Member access	1	None	seq[1], seq[2..3]
-	Numeric negation	2	None	-2
not	Boolean negation	2	None	not cond
sizeof	Sequence size	2	None	sizeof seq
indexof	Element index in sequence comprehension	2	None	indexof x
reverse	Reverse a sequence	2	None	reverse seq
*	Multiply	3	Left-to-right	2 * 5, 1h * 4
/	Divide	3	Left-to-right	9 / 3, 1m / 3
mod	Modulo	3	Left-to-right	20 mod 3
+	Add	4	Left-to-right	0 + 2, 1m + 20s
-	Subtract	4	Left-to-right	32 - 3, 1h - 5m
==	Equal	5	Left-to-right	value1 == value2, 4 == 4
!=	Not equal	5	Left-to-right	value1 != value2, 5 != 4

Operator	Meaning	Precedence	Associativity	Examples
<	Less than	5	Left-to-right	`value1 < value2, 4 < 5`
<=	Less than or equal	5	Left-to-right	`value1 <= value2, 5 <= 5`
>	Greater than	5	Left-to-right	`value1 > value2, 6 > 5`
>=	Greater than or equal	5	Left-to-right	`value1 >= value2, 6 >= 6`
`instanceof`	Is instance of class	6	None	`node instanceof Text`
as	Cast	6	None	`node as Text`
and	Logical and	7	Left-to-right	`cond1 and cond2`
or	Logical or	8	Left-to-right	`cond1 or cond2`
+=	Add and assign	9	Right-to-left	`value += 5`
-=	Subtract and assign	9	Right-to-left	`value -= 3`
*=	Multiply and assign	9	Right-to-left	`value *= 2`
/=	Divide and assign	9	Right-to-left	`value /= 4`
=	Assign	9	Right-to-left	`value = 7`

Index

You Need the Companion eBook

Your purchase of this book entitles you to buy the companion PDF-version eBook for only $10. Take the weightless companion with you anywhere.

We believe this Apress title will prove so indispensable that you'll want to carry it with you everywhere, which is why we are offering the companion eBook (in PDF format) for $10 to customers who purchase this book now. Convenient and fully searchable, the PDF version of any content-rich, page-heavy Apress book makes a valuable addition to your programming library. You can easily find and copy code—or perform examples by quickly toggling between instructions and the application. Even simultaneously tackling a donut, diet soda, and complex code becomes simplified with hands-free eBooks!

Once you purchase your book, getting the $10 companion eBook is simple:

❶ Visit **www.apress.com/promo/tendollars/**.

❷ Complete a basic registration form to receive a randomly generated question about this title.

❸ Answer the question correctly in 60 seconds, and you will receive a promotional code to redeem for the $10.00 eBook.

THE EXPERT'S VOICE™

2855 TELEGRAPH AVENUE | SUITE 600 | BERKELEY, CA 94705

Offer valid through 1/10.